The Dictionary of Multimedia
Terms & Acronyms

1998 Edition

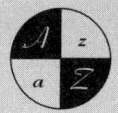

Brad Hansen

Chicago · London

> **Dedication**
> For my son, Graham.

Editor	Jim Leisy
Manuscript Editor	Karen Foley
Technical Editor	Peter Sylwester
Proofreaders	Tom Sumner
	Anna Keesey
Technical Illustrations	Jeff Ong
	Bill DeRouchey
Interior Design & Production	Karen Foley

© 1997 Franklin, Beedle & Associates Incorporated

This *Library Edition* is produced in association with Franklin, Beedle & Associates, Wilsonville, Oregon. All rights are reserved, including the right of reproduction in whole or in part in any form.

For information, write to:

FITZROY DEARBORN PUBLISHERS
70 East Walton Street
Chicago 60611
USA

or

FITZROY DEARBORN PUBLISHERS
11 Rathbone Place
London W1P 1DE
ENGLAND

British Library and Library of Congress Cataloging-in-Publication Data are available.

ISBN 1-57958-017-3

First published in the United States and United Kingdom, 1997

Contents

Foreword	iv
Preface	v
The Dictionary of Multimedia	1
Copyright Issues	237
DOS Commands	248
Standards Organizations	261
The World Wide Web	271
Basic Tutorial on HTML	272
Table of HTML Tags with Attributes	300
HTML 3.2 Elements	308
HTML 3.2 Color Tables	313
HTML Coded Characters	321
Common Gateway Interface (CGI)	325
Recommended Reading	338

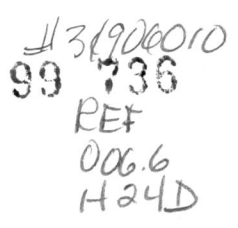

Foreword

New technologies are usually accompanied by new terminology. Today's multimedia industry had its genesis in the late 1970s when the first videodisc players were connected to computers and "interactive video" was born. In its nearly 20-year history, we have witnessed many changes in the industry. What was once driven by the video side of that early configuration is now driven by the computer side and increasingly by the communications side. Multimedia has evolved from a narrowly defined set of technologies in limited market segments to a broad horizontal term that crosses all video, computer, telecommunications, and general media industries. This convergence has caused turmoil in the marketplace as businesses try to sort out the new business models and opportunities, and customers try to keep up with the changes.

As these segments begin to overlap, converge, and in many cases collide, one common problem becomes evident. In addition to differing business models, each industry segment has its own jargon, language, acronyms, and culture. Thus, what is a common form of meaningful shorthand to one group may be Greek to another. Or worse, the same word in one sector may mean something entirely different to a listener from another field. For a banker, and most consumers, an ATM is an Automated Teller Machine. For communications people, however, ATM stands for Asynchronous Transfer Mode. And computer folks might think you are referring to Adobe Type Manager. Such sources of confusion abound.

As the umbrellas of multimedia broaden, it is important that we take time to define our own terms and learn the terms of others. In *The Dictionary of Multimedia*, Brad Hansen has done an admirable job of defining the necessary jargon of the day. The book provides a good stake in the ground, and it will help guide you through the common usage at this point in the still short history of these new technologies. It is also important to recognize that the pace of new technology innovation is always increasing, and with that growth will come no shortage of new terms. Keeping up with the language of multimedia is an ongoing challenge for both users and definers of the terms. I trust Brad is already gathering material for his next edition.

—*Rockley L. Miller*
Publisher & editor, Multimedia Monitor
President, Interactive Multimedia Association

Preface

This book is for programmers, graphic artists, writers, video producers, audio engineers, network managers, hardware technicians, and telecommunications professionals who embrace the complex world of multimedia and realize the need for a common language to communicate with one another. Although many dictionaries and other existing references address individual disciplines, this book is unique in bringing together definitions of critical terms and concepts drawn from the diverse bodies of knowledge incorporated in the production of multimedia.

Multimedia, which may be defined as interactive digital media, is a synthesis of traditional forms of art and communication with the rapidly evolving fields of computing and networking. This dictionary addresses a vocabulary that results from the convergence of diverse disciplines and bodies of knowledge. Multimedia is an art, a science, and a new medium of expression that has engendered a truly interdisciplinary body of information that is growing at an incredible rate.

Terms were included based on their relevance to multimedia production and distribution. A creative team builds graphic, audio, and video products that are digitized by computer hardware and programmed for interactive access. The products are distributed on CD-ROM and other media, or they are delivered from a file server over a network or telecommunications system. For this team to function, its members must have some common definitions for the words they use to communicate. The terms in this dictionary originate from the disciplines represented by members of the multimedia team. The following list includes some of these disciplines and content pertaining to each:

> *Audio*—acoustics, engineering, music, MIDI, recording, signal processing
> *Graphics*—imaging, animation, drawing, color theory, photography, semiology
> *Hardware*—computers, electronics, components, interfaces, media, physics
> *Networking*—transfer of data, protocols, connections, standards, the Internet
> *Human factors*—organizations, committees, individuals, ergonomics
> *Software*—logic, programming, data, file structures, scripting, applications
> *Telecommunications*—telephony, broadcast, radio, television, cable, satellite
> *Video*—lighting, post-production, editing, film, tape formats, compression

Preface

The nature of multimedia requires teamwork and the contribution of many minds and hands. Likewise, scores of individuals who contributed directly and indirectly to this book should be credited. Many members of computer-user groups and professional associations have shared their knowledge unselfishly, including the International Interactive Communications Society (IICS), the Association for Computing Machinery (ACM), the Institute of Electrical and Electronics Engineers (IEEE), the International Multimedia Association and the International MIDI Association (IMA), the Audio Engineering Society (AES), and the International Television Association (ITVA). Kevin Yorke at the National Multimedia Association (NMA) and John Melchi at the National Center for Supercomputing (NCSA) have personally assisted in making information available.

In addition to definitions of terms and acronyms, several relevant appendices have been added that expand on topics related to multimedia. For those who at times find themselves at a prompt on the command line, a complete listing of MS-DOS commands is provided, courtesy of Carolyn Gillay.

Developers for the Web who seek a quick reference on the HTML language will find help in the World Wide Web appendix. The Basic Tutorial on HTML and the description of CGI script conventions both appear courtesy of the NCSA. Additionally, a table of HTML tags and attributes, a list of coded characters, and the HTML 3.2 color designations are included.

Another extensive appendix carefully outlines the issues surrounding copyrights, particularly pertaining to digital media and ownership of assets. For support in developing the copyright appendix, thanks go to Terrence J. Carroll, an attorney with Cooley Godward Castro Huddleson & Tatum in Palo Alto, California. His FAQ is located at http://www.aimnet.com/~carroll/copyright/faq-home.html.

Since the issue of standardization is critical to multimedia production and implementation, an appendix is devoted to standards organizations and sources of information about international standards. Thanks to Markus Kuhn for his research.

The final appendix is a categorical listing of books on multimedia. Books, software manuals, and documentation explaining the installation and operation of multimedia devices and programs served as critical sources of information for the dictionary, along with current periodicals.

Definitions in this dictionary are located beside commonly used acronyms, and the words represented by the acronyms are spelled out where they appear alphabetically.

The reader is referred to the acronyms for the definitions. Words, symbols, and numbers are ordered alphabetically as they would be spelled. For example, "C++" follows "courseware," and "16-bit" follows "site." To avoid confusion in quantifying data, one convention to which we adhere should be pointed out. The abbreviation for kilobits is Kb, while kilobytes is KB. A similar convention applies to megabits (Mb) and megabytes (MB). The need for accuracy, clarity, and precision in writing about this field has remained a high priority in preparing this document.

Jim Leisy and his entire staff at Franklin, Beedle & Associates have been wonderful partners in fulfilling our collective vision (Karen, Tom, Susan, Dan, Vic, Sue, Eric, Laura, Cary, Chris, and Ann). Thanks to Jeff Ong and Bill DeRouchey for their fine illustrations. Astute comments from Harvey Smythe, Mark Farley, and Rockley Miller, who all reviewed early drafts, were greatly appreciated. My wife Jani, son Graham, and daughter Claire deserve heartfelt thanks for their support and for permitting me to make time to write this book.

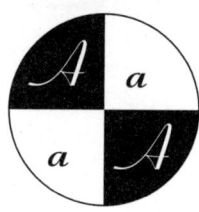

A:B:C notation (n.) The standard way to describe relationships in digital video formats. Three numbers are used to represent ratios as follows:

(A) The basic sample rate compared to the color clock rate.
(B) The color horizontal downsampling rate compared to the basic sampling rate.
(C) The color vertical downsampling rate plus 1.

A standard 4:2:2 format indicates that sampling is done at four times the color clock, which is 3.58 megahertz (MHz); two horizontal chroma samples are taken for every four luminance samples; there is no reduction in vertical color resolution (1+1).

abend (n.) <u>Ab</u>normal <u>end</u>; an error message that indicates unexpected termination of a program or signal, which may be either recoverable or unrecoverable.

ABI (n.) <u>A</u>pplication <u>b</u>inary <u>i</u>nterface; the emulation in software of a hardware/software platform other than the native one, which allows foreign applications to run. An example would be running a Windows application under the UNIX operating system.

ABIOS (n.) <u>A</u>dvanced <u>B</u>asic <u>I</u>nput/<u>O</u>utput <u>S</u>ystem; service routines built into IBM-compatible computers that support multitasking.

ablation (n.) Using a laser beam, the burning of pits into thin metal film for optical data storage.

abort (v.) To cancel a computing procedure while in progress.

A-B roll (n.) An editing process in which videotape is played from two tape machines. The tapes are rolled sequentially, in order to dub portions of each onto a third tape, the composite master. Video editors use this technique to import footage from multiple sources. The resulting product is often enhanced by placing transitions between the cuts and using special effects.

absolute time (n.) The time elapsed from the exact beginning of an audio CD or a digital audio tape (DAT) to any given point in the program material that follows. It is useful to determine the start and stop times of sound segments. The term refers to the time elapsed from the beginning of an entire sequence or group of events rather than a single piece.

abstract class (n.) In object-oriented programming, a class without instances. Instead it has concrete classes as subclasses. For example, mammal is an abstract class, and cow is a concrete class.

AC (n.) Alternating current; in the United States, 120-volt electricity that is delivered by utility companies and changes polarity from positive to negative 60 times per second. In other countries, the rate of alternation is often 50 cycles per second. Direct current, by contrast, is a continuous stream of current in one direction with constant polarity. The regular pulse of AC can be picked up by audio systems that are not well grounded, introducing a 60-cycle hum.

accelerator card (n.) A circuit board inserted into a slot on the motherboard that increases the processing speed and performance of the CPU. Graphics accelerators are used to increase the productivity of artists.

acceptable use policy See *AUP*.

access (v.) To seek and retrieve information from a hard disk, floppy disk, CD-ROM, or any other digital or analog storage medium.

access time (n.) The time required to locate and load data from storage after the seek command. Typically, this measurement includes the time it takes the reading head to move between the most distant segments of the media.

ACD (n.) Automatic call distribution; in telecommunications, a method of routing and tracking telephone signals.

ACID test (n.) A test of the atomicity, consistency, isolation, and durability of transaction processing. Passing the ACID test exhibits a high degree of resilience and recoverability. The term is derived from the process of testing metals with strong acid to determine gold content.

ACK (n.) An acknowledgment character that is returned to a sending device by a receiving device to indicate that the data has been received correctly.

ACM (n.) Association for Computing Machinery; a group dedicated to the advancement of computing knowledge.

acquisition (n.) The process of capturing assets or transferring information from an analog to a digital format.

Acrobat (n.) A program developed by Adobe for cross-platform document exchange in which files are created in Portable Document Format (.pdf) from PostScript files. The full complement of Acrobat tools consists of the Distiller, the Exchange package, the Catalog package, and the Reader. The Reader is freely distributed so that it can be installed and used on any computer along with an Acrobat document.

ActionMedia II (n.) An early video capture card developed by Intel that employs their Digital Video Interactive (DVI) compression technology. It has been replaced by the Intel Smart Video Recorder.

active-matrix display (n.) An LCD panel that has three transistors (R,G,B) for each pixel and yields better color and resolution than a passive-matrix display. Thin film transistor (TFT) technology makes this possible.

active video lines (n.) Lines of video that are scanned on the screen between the horizontal and vertical blanking intervals. About 483 lines are visible or active in the NTSC 525-line system used in the United States.

active window (n.) The portion of the screen that is prepared to accept input from an input device.

adapter (n.) An interface card that connects to peripherals or a network.

Adaptive Data Compression See *ADC*.

adaptive differential pulse code modulation See *ADPCM*.

ADB (n.) Apple Desktop Bus; the standard I/O port and protocol used on a Macintosh to connect the keyboard, mouse, and other devices.

ADC 1. (n.) Adaptive Data Compression (a Hayes modem protocol). 2. (n.) Analog-to-digital converter.

ADCCP (n.) Advanced Data Communications Control Procedures; a standard protocol used by the United States government for communications.

ADCIS (n.) Association for the Development of Computer-Based Instruction Systems.

A/D converter (n.) Analog-to-digital converter; a circuit that converts changes in voltage, pressure, or motion over time into a stream of digits that defines an event with time-based binary data.

additive color mixing (n.) The process of creating hues by mixing colors of light rather than pigments. Mixing the additive primary colors in equal proportions results in white.

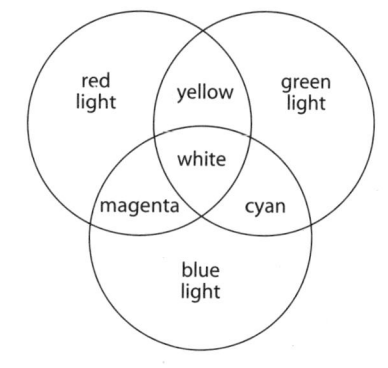

additive color mixing

additive synthesis (n.) The production

of a composite waveform by summing multiple individual waveforms.

address 1. (n.) Any label that identifies the location of data in either static or dynamic memory, such as a frame number on coded videotape. 2. (v.) To send a message to a particular location.

address code 1. (n.) Time code stamped on a tape that identifies each frame of video. The hour, minute, second, and frame numbers are expressed by eight digits in the format hh:mm:ss:ff. 2. (n.) The cue code placed in the vertical blanking interval of a videodisc frame as a point of reference.

addressable converter (n.) A device connected to a cable television receiver to give the program provider the capacity to send or block services to individual subscribers.

Address Resolution Protocol See *ARP*.

Adobe Type Manager See *ATM*.

ADPCM (n.) Adaptive differential pulse code modulation; the IMA version of this standard is used for storing audio information in a digital format in multiple-session CD-ROM XA and CD-i. The procedure reduces the amount of data needed by examining previously encoded data and adaptively predicting future encoding, eliminating some redundancy, and storing the differences between successive digital samples rather than full values. It is an extension of the PCM audio encoding format. Standardized by the CCITT for telecommunications applications, another version of this audio encoding process can transmit a voice over a 32-kilobit per second (Kbps) digital channel. Each sample is defined by three or four bits that represent the difference between adjacent samples.

ADR (n.) Automatic dialog replacement; in audio sweetening, an automated process for substituting a new voice track for the original.

ADSL (n.) Asynchronous Digital Subscriber Line; a communications protocol that allows the transfer of high data rates over twisted-pair telephone wire connections. It is useful for networking compressed video and audio at up to 1.5 megabits per second (Mbps).

ADSR (n.) Attack, decay, sustain, release; refers to a common way of shaping synthesized sounds and the circuit that performs the process. ADSR stands for four stages in the envelope of a sound. In sound synthesis, the ADSR settings define the shape of a note or its amplitude over time, not the pitch.

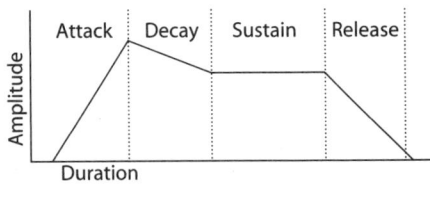

ADSR curve

Advanced Data Communications Control Procedures See *ADCCP*.

Advanced Research Projects Agency See *ARPA*.

Advanced RISC Machine See *ARM*.

Advanced SCSI Programming Interface See *ASPI*.

advanced wave effects See *AWE*.

AECT (n.) Association for Educational Communications and Technology.

AES/EBU (n.) Audio Engineering Society/European Broadcast Union; the two groups that developed similar digital audio transmission standards, specifying transmission of data in a stream with encoded stereo audio signals along with optional information.

AF (n.) Audio frequency; sounds within the normal range of human hearing, approximately 20 hertz (Hz)–20 kilohertz (kHz).

AFC (n.) Automatic frequency control; the process of locking a receiver to a TV or FM station's frequency.

affordance (n.) A tangible aspect of an object that allows action or manipulation. Examples are handles, buttons, and scroll bars.

AFSK (n.) Audio frequency-shift keying. In telecommunications, a method of modulating a carrier wave with audio frequencies (AF) to send digital signals.

AGC (n.) Automatic gain control; a limiting circuit used in audio playback systems to prevent damaging high volume levels.

AI (n.) Artificial intelligence; software that makes decisions based on accumulated experience and information. Functions normally associated with human intelligence, such as learning, adapting, reasoning, and self-correction are features of the software.

AIFF (n.) Audio interchange file format; a sound file format defined by Apple Computer and others that can include both sampled sound and MIDI data. The AIFF-C variation stores the data in compressed form. AIFF files may be imported by most multimedia authoring programs for the Macintosh and by some programs running on IBM-compatible computers.

A-law (n.) A digital audio encoding method for telephony used primarily in Europe. Defined by the CCITT G.711 standard, it is based on the 2048-kilobit (Kb), 30-channel PCM system. It compresses at a 2:1 ratio and is similar to the mu-law encoding scheme used in the United States and Japan.

algorithm (n.) A type of formula that defines a sequence of steps necessary to perform a process.

algorithmic (adj.) Describes a program

structured like a mathematical procedure that solves a problem in a limited number of steps.

alias (n.) In a Macintosh system 7.0 and higher, an icon that represents or points to the original file. Multiple aliases may be created and placed where they may provide convenient access to the original file.

aliasing 1. (n.) The appearance of unwanted visual effects, known as "jaggies," in digitized images. An example is the stair-step effect on raster display systems without high enough resolution to reproduce smooth diagonal lines or circles. 2. (n.) In audio sampling, all frequency components higher than half the sampling frequency are reflected in the lower range. This distortion-producing reflection is referred to as aliasing, and it results in artifacts. It can be avoided by processing the waveform to be sampled with a low-pass filter at half the sample rate before digitizing.

alignment 1. (n.) In a tape recorder, the positioning of the head in relation to the tape path. 2. (n.) In a word-processed or graphic document, the horizontal and vertical relationships of elements.

alpha blending (n.) A technique used to produce atmospheric effects in three-dimensional graphics. Alpha values determine the degree of transparency of a pixel.

alpha channel (n.) In video production, a separate signal used to control visual effects such as overlay and transparency. In a digital graphics environment, the bits that control the percentage of visibility between upper and lower layers, or foreground and background elements.

alphanumeric (adj.) Describes a combination of alphabet letters, numerals, and other symbols used for codes and computational expressions.

alpha test (n.) The initial testing on software that evaluates general functionality. It occurs prior to a beta test, in which it is field-tested by users.

AM (n.) Amplitude modulation; the process of adding information to a constant carrier signal by modulating or changing its amplitude in direct correlation to another signal.

ambient (adj.) Describes a natural state, such as room temperature. Ambient sounds are referred to as "environmental" because they exist in a natural environment.

American Society of Composers, Authors, and Publishers See *ASCAP*.

American Standard Code for Information Interchange See *ASCII*.

America Online See *AOL*.

Amiga (n.) A computer system based on the Motorola 68000 family of processors and similar in design to a Macintosh. It was developed by Commodore International, which is no longer in existence. A popular application for the Amiga is the Video Toaster, a digitizing card that facilitates titling and effects for digital video production. The presence of onboard genlock capabilities made the Amiga system unique among microcomputers.

A-mode (n.) The mode a video editing system is in while it is assembling the segments in the order listed on the edit decision list (EDL). This process usually involves multiple changes of source reels.

ampere (n.) A measurement of electrical current equal to one volt applied to one ohm of resistance.

amplifier (n.) An electronic device that boosts signal strength. Amplifiers, or amps, are required to drive speakers for audio output. They are also required at regular intervals in a cable television system between the headend and the subscriber, approximately every 1500 feet.

amplify (v.) To increase the amplitude or power of a given signal. Related to audio, to increase the sound pressure level (SPL). Amplitude is the height of a waveform, or the measurement of a signal from trough to peak.

amplitude modulation See *AM*.

amplitude-shift keying See *ASK*.

analog (n.) A method of representing physical variables, such as voltage, pressure, or motion, that flow and change continuously and are values expressed as the quantitative magnitude of the variables. Analog devices are often controlled by knobs and sliders, and their output is shown by dials, gauges, and meters.

analog RGB (n.) A video signal that sends separate signal lines for red, green, and blue picture information. Each of the signals is encoded as a proportional voltage rather than as digital bits. Video systems for microcomputers employ this system.

analog-to-digital converter See *A/D converter*.

analog video (n.) A continuous electronic signal generated by a camera or a videotape source that represents an infinite number of smooth gradations between video levels. By contrast, a digital video signal assigns a finite series of steps in the gradations and is stored as data.

anchor (n.) In a hypertext environment, such as an HTML document, a word or icon that is colored or underlined and links to another document or location. By clicking on the hypertext link, a user is transported to the new location.

anchor point (n.) In a drawing program, the beginning or ending point of a Bezier curve. See *Bezier curve*.

animatic (n.) A compilation of key scenes used to plan and lay out video spots and motion pictures.

animation

animation (n.) The rapid display of a series of still images or objects that are repositioned in each frame to achieve the effect of movement on a still background.

anonymous FTP (n.) A procedure that downloads files from a public FTP server to the user. It is possible to log on to an anonymous FTP server by using "anonymous" as the login name and an e-mail address as the password.

ANSI (n.) American National Standards Institute.

anti-aliasing (n.) Software alterations in the representation of data that help diagonal or curved lines appear smooth and continuous when displayed from computer-generated sources. In audio applications, the smoothing of steps between discrete samples to reduce the undesirable effects of low bit-rate capture.

anti-aliased letter on left, aliased letter on right

AOL (n.) America Online; a commercial networking service for individual users who have a computer and a modem.

APDA (n.) Apple Programmers and Developers Association; the source for all the tools needed to conduct high-level multimedia development using the Macintosh platform. They may be contacted at 1–800–282–2732 in the United States, or 1–800–637–0029 in Canada.

API (n.) Application Program Interface; software that defines the interface with an operating system or another program via a set of calls or special messages.

Apple Desktop Bus See *ADB*.

Apple Programmers and Developers Association See *APDA*.

Apple Remote Access See *ARA*.

applet (n.) A small application program that performs a specific function or handles media.

AppleTalk (n.) A local area network (LAN) protocol developed by Apple Computer for connecting peripherals and computers. It is a part of the system software from Apple Computer and operates over a variety of wiring types. Technically, it is a CSMA/CD network running at 230 kilobits per second (Kbps) that can connect up to 32 devices using shielded, twisted-pair cable for a distance of approximately 1000 feet.

AppleUNIX See *A/UX*.

Apple Video Compressor (n.) Developed by Apple Computer, this is the original compression and decompression codec used for QuickTime. These algorithms have been updated.

application 1. (n.) A software program that creates or reads a data file. 2. (n.) The set of data and program software contained on a compact disc.

application binary interface See *ABI*.

Application Program Interface See *API*.

application-specific integrated circuit See *ASIC*.

ARA (n.) Apple Remote Access; a communications protocol through which a user can dial up a host Macintosh from a remote modem and share the desktop of the host on the remote computer. Files can be downloaded or uploaded between the two connected computers.

Archie (n.) Available as a UNIX command via Telnet, this tool allows users to search a database of anonymous FTP sites.

architecture (n.) The general design of a computer hardware and software system. A system with "open architecture" allows the addition of internal cards and external peripherals.

archival (adj.) Describes a storage medium that preserves data for an extended period. Archival media must remain stable without degradation over time.

archive (v.) To record information in long-term storage.

archiving (n.) The process of moving data from online storage to nearline (optical disk) or offline (tape) storage. A directory is stored along with the data.

ARCnet (n.) Attached Resource Computer Network; a local area network (LAN) configuration that operates at 2.5 megabits per second (Mbps) over coaxial cable using a token-passing protocol. It features a distributed star topology and is reliable and easily expanded.

ARM 1. (n.) Advanced RISC machine; a miniature reduced instruction set computing processor, such as the one used in the Apple Newton PDA. 2. (n.) Asynchronous response mode; in an unbalanced data connection, a mode in which the secondary station may begin transmission to the primary station without obtaining permission.

ARP (n.) Address Resolution Protocol; a standard used on the Internet that assigns IP addresses to workstations on a local area network (LAN).

ARPA (n.) Advanced Research Projects Agency; a United States government organization that developed packet-switching techniques and created the network that was the precursor to the Internet.

ARQ (n.) <u>A</u>utomatic <u>r</u>equest for retransmission; a case in which the receiver asks the transmitter to resend a frame or a block of information, generally as a result of error correction.

array (n.) A set of coordinates that define rows and columns. A two-dimensional array is described with x and y coordinates, while a three-dimensional array requires x, y, and z coordinates.

artifact (n.) An undesirable distortion that appears in digitized audio or video files as a result of inaccurate information introduced during capture or compression.

artificial intelligence See *AI*.

artwork (n.) Any type of graphics prepared for computer display, printing, or video. This may include drawings, paintings, photographs, maps, graphs, charts, captions, titles, and all elements in which artistic design considerations are of primary concern.

ASCAP (n.) <u>A</u>merican <u>S</u>ociety of <u>C</u>omposers, <u>A</u>uthors, and <u>P</u>ublishers; a licensing agency that controls the rights for broadcast and performance of musical compositions.

ASCII (n.) <u>A</u>merican <u>S</u>tandard <u>C</u>ode for <u>I</u>nformation <u>I</u>nterchange; developed by ANSI, the standardized data character system used internationally to code letters, numbers, and other symbols into the binary values used in most microcomputer applications. It is a seven-bit-plus-parity character code in which each bit can be a one or a zero, and it is capable of representing only 128 items. ASCII files contain text characters only: letters, numbers, and punctuation with no formatting. The other major method of encoding is EBCDIC, an 8-bit code used by mainframe computers. (Pronounced **as-kee**.) *See table.*

Decimal	Hex	Symbol	Acronym	Function
0	0	^@	NUL	Fill Character
1	1	^A	SOH	Start of Heading
2	2	^B	STX	Start of Text
3	3	^C	ETX	End of Text
4	4	^D	EOT	End of Transmission
5	5	^E	ENQ	Enquiry (request response)
6	6	^F	ACK	Acknowledge
7	7	^G	BEL	Bell (sounds a tone)
8	8	^H	BS	Backspace
9	9	^I	HT	Horizontal Tab
10	A	^J	LF	Line Feed
11	B	^K	VT	Vertical Tab
12	C	^L	FF	Form Feed

ASCII

Decimal	Hex	Symbol	Acronym	Function
13	D	^M	CR	Carriage Return
14	E	^N	SO	Shift out (change character set)
15	F	^O	SI	Shift in (change character set)
16	10	^P	DLE	Data Link Escape
17	11	^Q	DC1	Data Control 1 (XON)
18	12	^R	DC2	Data Control 2
19	13	^S	DC3	Data Control 3 (XOFF)
20	14	^T	DC4	Data Control 4
21	15	^U	NAK	Negative Acknowledge
22	16	^V	SYN	Synchronous Idle
23	17	^W	ETB	End of Transmission Block
24	18	^X	CAN	Cancel (ends a command)
25	19	^Y	EM	End of Medium
26	1A	^Z	SUB	Substitute (also end of file)
27	1B	^[	ESC	Escape
28	1C	^\	FS	File Separator
29	1D	^]	GS	Group Separator
30	1E	^^	RS	Record Separator
31	1F	^_	US	Unit Separator
32	20		SP	Space Character
33	21	!		Exclamation Mark
34	22	"		Double Quotes
35	23	#		Pound Sign
36	24	$		Dollar Sign
37	25	%		Percent Sign
38	26	%		Ampersand
39	27	'		Single Quote
40	28	(		Open Parenthesis
41	29	)		Close Parenthesis
42	2A	*		Asterisk
43	2B	+		Plus Sign
44	2C	,		Comma
45	2D	-		Minus Sign, hyphen
46	2E	.		Period
47	2F	/		Slash
48	30	0		Zero
49	31	1		One
50	32	2		Two
51	33	3		Three

ASCII

Decimal	Hex	Symbol	Acronym	Function
52	34	4		Four
53	35	5		Five
54	36	6		Six
55	37	7		Seven
56	38	8		Eight
57	39	9		Nine
58	3A	:		Colon
59	3B	;		Semi-colon
60	3C	<		Less-than Sign
61	3D	=		Equals Sign
62	3E	>		Greater-than Sign
63	3F	?		Question Mark
64	40	@		At Sign
65	41	A		
66	42	B		
67	43	C		
68	44	D		
69	45	E		
70	46	F		
71	47	G		
72	48	H		
73	49	I		
74	4A	J		
75	4B	K		
76	4C	L		
77	4D	M		
78	4E	N		
79	4F	O		
80	50	P		
81	51	Q		
82	52	R		
83	53	S		
84	54	T		
85	55	U		
86	56	V		
87	57	W		
88	58	X		
89	59	Y		
90	5A	Z		

ASCII

Decimal	Hex	Symbol	Acronym	Function
91	5B	[		Open Bracket
92	5C	\		Backslash
93	5D	]		Close Bracket
94	5E	^		Caret
95	5F	_		Underscore
96	60	'		
97	61	a		
98	62	b		
99	63	c		
100	64	d		
101	65	e		
102	66	f		
103	67	g		
104	68	h		
105	69	i		
106	6A	j		
107	6B	k		
108	6C	l		
109	6D	m		
110	6E	n		
111	6F	o		
112	70	p		
113	71	q		
114	72	r		
115	73	s		
116	74	t		
117	75	u		
118	76	v		
119	77	w		
120	78	x		
121	79	y		
122	7A	z		
123	7B	{		Open Curly Bracket
124	7C				Bar
125	7D	}		Close Curly Bracket
126	7E	~		Tilde
127	7F			

ASIC

ASIC (n.) Application-specific integrated circuit; a gate array or logic array. This type of chip has its gates configured to perform a particular function.

ASK (n.) Amplitude-shift keying; a form of digital modulation in which discrete changes in the amplitude of the carrier signal convey a digital signal.

aspect ratio (n.) The resolution expressed in relative height and width values. The standard ratio for computer screens is 3:4. This is the basis for the standard resolutions of 120:160, 180:240, 240:320, 480:640, or 600:800 used by video monitors. The aspect ratio for television monitors is wider, and the problem of overscan introduces variables related to the safe viewing area around the edges. The ratio of modern motion pictures varies from 3:5 to 3:7, creating a problem when a wide-format motion picture is transferred to a 3:4-ratio screen. A 35mm photograph has dimensions of 24 × 36mm, resulting in a 2:3 ratio. A letterbox effect occurs when photos are ported to the computer screen. *See illustration.*

ASPI (n.) Advanced SCSI Programming Interface; developed by Adaptec, a protocol used to configure devices and media on a SCSI chain.

assemble editing (n.) The placement of video sequences back-to-back without a constant reference signal, a process that is prone to minor timing errors. Insert editing, or placing sequences on top of an existing reference track, is more stable.

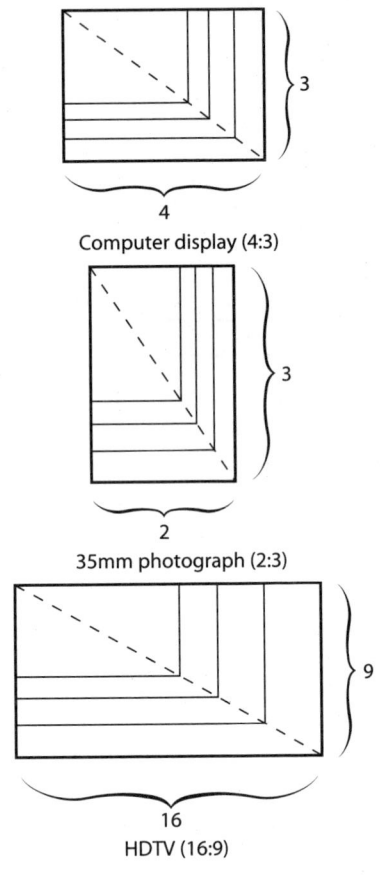

Computer display (4:3)

35mm photograph (2:3)

HDTV (16:9)

aspect ratios

assembly (n.) The conversion of instructions and data written in a computer programming language into lower-level machine code.

assembly language (n.) A lower-level programming language that consists of words and phrases that are used to control a microprocessor. An assembler converts the subroutines of assembly language into machine code that a computer can read. The source code consists of statements, while machine code consists of binary digits.

asset (n.) Any piece of data used in a multimedia program, such as an audio, graphic, text, or video file.

Association for Computing Machinery See *ACM*.

asymmetrical compression (n.) Any video or audio compression process in which more time and resources are required to encode than to decode.

asynchronous 1. (adj.) Describes the performance of computer operations in sequential stages, rather than in a continuous variable stream. 2. (adj.) The opposite of "real-time" conferencing in e-mail applications, where more than one person can participate in a conversation at the same time from different locations. In asynchronous communication they must take turns. 3. (adj.) In telecommunications, a mode in which two devices are free to send data in a continuous stream at any time. Each byte begins with a start bit and ends with a stop bit. It is the most common mode of communication between computer modem users.

Asynchronous Digital Subscriber Line See *ADSL*.

Asynchronous Response Mode See *ARM*.

Asynchronous Transfer Mode See *ATM*.

ATAPI (n.) AT Attachment Packet Interface; an enhancement to the original ATA hard disk controller system that allows packets to be sent to a CD-ROM player.

ATDT (n.) Attention dial tone; a modem command.

ATM 1. (n.) Adobe Type Manager; a utility that extrapolates a screen-resolution character (72 dots per inch) from a PostScript character. 2. (n.) Asynchronous transfer mode; a means of transmitting data that combines different data types (audio, video, or text) with a sophisticated formula for allocating bandwidth and shuttling packets, or cells, of a fixed length (53 bytes). It provides a common means of transporting all types of data, some of which exist as streams that are reassembled on reception.

Attached Resource Computer Network See *ARCnet*.

attachment (n.) Any file linked to an e-mail message that can be opened and viewed by an application resident on the recipient's computer.

attachment unit interface See *AUI*.

attention dial tone See *ATDT*.

attenuate (v.) To reduce the strength of a signal. In audio applications, attenuators often appear as faders or sliding switches that control the decibel levels of output channels on mixing boards.

audio (adj.) Related to sound, as in audio tape, audio track, or audio file.

audio bridge (n.) An electronic device that controls multiple telephone lines connected for two-way audio and data transmission; commonly used for audioconference applications.

audioconference (n.) A meeting over telephone lines with participants in different geographic locations who speak with one another simultaneously. Full-duplex systems allow users to hear other voices while they speak into their headsets. Half-duplex systems allow either reception or transmission of a signal at any given moment, but not synchronous two-way communication.

Audio Engineering Society/European Broadcast Union See *AES/EBU*.

audio frequency See *AF*.

audio frequency-shift keying See *AFSK*.

audio graphics (n.) A hardware and software system that permits computer users in different locations to connect over telephone lines and share data, graphics, and audio information. With an audiographic connection, users can work on the same application or document simultaneously, both can see the data on their computer screens, and they can discuss their progress over a voice channel.

In the most basic application, it refers to any single-frame transmission of graphics with audio signals.

audio interchange file format See *AIFF*.

audio track (n.) The section or layer of an audio/videotape or disc that contains the sound signal that accompanies the video signal. Systems with two separate audio tracks can produce stereo sound or two independent tracks.

audio-video interleaved See *AVI*.

AUI (n.) Attachment unit interface; a 15-pin connector used to couple computers on an Ethernet network.

AUP (n.) Acceptable use policy; an Internet service provider's statement of permissible uses.

author 1. (v.) To create an interactive computer program with the use of an authoring language or system. Developers without formal programming skills can prepare applications for computer systems or CD-ROMs by "scripting" commands. Authoring requires a disciplined approach to preparing the elements of a multimedia program with careful planning and design. 2. (n.) A person who participates in the creation of a multimedia program or an interactive CD-ROM.

authoring software (n.) A program that facilitates the development of interactive multimedia. Systems vary widely in their capabilities, and factors such as the platform, audience, and desired results are taken into consideration when selecting the appropriate tool. It requires less time to develop interactive multimedia with the aid of an authoring system than it does to program it in compiled code. The methods used to develop graphics, text, video, audio, animation, and other media objects generally are not affected by the choice of an authoring system. Software designed for the creation and editing of specific media types is used to refine objects to be imported into the authoring environment, although an authoring tool may have some rudimentary editing features. The following is a description of the primary types of authoring paradigms:

Scripting language: An approach similar to traditional programming. File names identify multimedia elements, sequencing, and hot spots. An object-oriented version of the scripting language is usually implemented.

Flow control with icons: Rapid prototyping and short development time are characteristic. A palette of icons presents the tools for interaction, and a flow line connects the icons. Runtime speed may be slower than with other development tools.

Frame-based system: Uses screens, frames, or cards as the work place and brings media types onto each frame. A way to control the timing of a presentation and the layering of assets generally is provided. An icon palette is available, and conceptual links are made between objects that represent media types, such as graphics, audio, and video files. A scripting language is provided to set up interaction. With this type of tool it is difficult to see the connections while building a program. Some frame-based systems provide a matrix, or a score, that shows the progression of frames on the horizontal axis and the media channels, or tracks, on the vertical axis.

Hierarchical object: A system that defines relationships with metaphors represented by embedded objects (media types or events) and iconic properties (controls or conditional statements), similar to an object-oriented programming language.

Hypermedia linking: A tool that allows conditional relationships to be built between elements and gives the author a means to direct traffic. Most programs show the relationship between elements but do not offer a visual map of the connections.

The table on the following page lists widely used authoring programs, identifies the publisher, indicates the platforms on which programs may be developed or run, and describes the authoring paradigm and prominent features. Programs that offer a cross-platform "player" require that the authoring be done in the original environment. After development, the program may be ported to the player platform as a self-contained module. *See table on following page.*

authoring software

Tool	Platform	Features
Apple Media Tool, Apple Computer	Macintosh, Windows player	Frame-based; Powerful and extensible
Authorware, Macromedia	Macintosh, Windows	Flow control with icons; broad external media support; optimal for CBT and rapid prototyping; ports to Shockwave for the WWW
CourseBuilder, Discovery Systems Int'l.	Macintosh, Windows player	Flow control with icons; creates interactive courseware without scripting
cT, Carnegie Mellon University & WorldWired	Macintosh, Windows, UNIX	Scripting system with Web player; handles video, hot-text, and response tracking
Digital Chisel, Pierian Spring	Macintosh	Frame-based; Hypercard tool with pre-written HyperTalk scripts, library of media
Director, Macromedia	Macintosh, Windows, other players	Frame-based with scripting; animation; object-based scripting language; creates Shockwave files for the WWW
Grasp, Paul Mace Software	DOS	Scripting language
HyperCard, Apple Computer	Macintosh	Frame-based with scripting; the original card metaphor; HyperTalk language
HyperWriter, Ntergard	DOS, Windows	Frame-based, document metaphor; Pro version uses Autolinker, encryption, CBT
IconAuthor, AimTech	Windows, OS/2, NT, UNIX, Macintosh Player	Flow control with icons; data-handling features are a plus for CBT tracking; portable to the WWW
MediaForge, Strata	Windows	Iconic; extensible with Visual Basic adaptation; flexible and powerful
mTropolis, mFactory	Macintosh, Windows player	Hierarchical object system; completely visual, no scripting
Oracle Media Objects, Oracle	Macintosh, Windows	Frame-based with scripting
Quest, Allen Communications	Windows	Frame-based with scripting; language is "ANSI C"
Scala MM100, Scala Inc.	Windows, DOS	Interface is event list with timing controls
ScriptX, Kaleida Labs	Macintosh, Windows player	Scripting language; powerful

Tool	Platform	Features
SuperCard, Allegiant	Macintosh, Windows player	Frame-based with scripting; 24-bit color; hypertext; external media handling
Toolbook II, Asymetrix Corporation	Windows	Frame-based with scripting; database linking; MCI compliant; macros perform interactive functions; ports to the WWW, outputs JAVA; optimized for CBT
Visual Venue, Cinemar Corp.	Windows	Frame-based; navigable three-dimensional environment for controlling media

auto-assembly (n.) In video post-production, the use of an edit decision list, or EDL, as well as a computerized edit controller to automate the process of making a final edited master tape.

autochanger (n.) An optical media system that can store and retrieve data from multiple discs; similar to a jukebox that plays phonograph records.

Autodesk Animator (n.) Developed by Autodesk, a collection of PC animation tools that create files in the Autodesk proprietary "FLC" and "FLI" formats.

autoexec.bat (n.) A batch file, or command set, that is automatically executed by a PC running MS-DOS whenever the system is turned on or booted.

autofeed (n.) A mode in which a scanner can operate continuously. A new page is loaded automatically when the scan of the previous page is completed.

automatic call distribution See *ACD*.

automatic dialog replacement See *ADR*.

automatic frequency control See *AFC*.

automatic gain control See *AGC*.

automatic request for retransmission See *ARQ*.

AutoPlay (n.) A CD-ROM standard developed by Microsoft that allows Windows 95 to detect a disc and load its program automatically.

auto-repeat (n.) A feature of many media playback devices, this is a mode that allows continuous replay of program material until interrupted.

A/UX (n.) Apple UNIX; a version of UNIX that runs on networked Apple computers.

auxiliary data field (n.) A 288-byte field that precedes the data field in a CD-ROM sector. It contains error-correction codes in a Mode 1 disc, but it may contain data on a Mode 2 disc.

AVC (n.) Association of Visual Communicators.

AVI (n.) <u>A</u>udio-<u>v</u>ideo <u>i</u>nterleaved; developed by Microsoft, this is a digital video architecture for use in Microsoft Windows. It is a common standard for synchronized audio/video delivery on IBM-compatible computers, known as Video for Windows. In this file format, blocks of audio data are woven into a stream of video frames.

AWE (n.) <u>A</u>dvanced <u>W</u>ave <u>E</u>ffects; a proprietary method of sound synthesis employed by the 32-bit Sound Blaster card.

backbone (n.) The primary trunk or high-speed connection within a network that connects shorter, often slower circuits or LANs. It carries the heaviest traffic and is central to any network design.

background 1. (n.) The area of a screen or frame over which images or objects are placed; the most distant element in composite layering. 2. (n.) During shared processing in a multitasking environment, less critical events or operations are conducted here. Print spooling while a document is being edited is an example, as is the ability to receive a facsimile while performing other computing functions.

back up (v.) To create an archival copy of data recorded on a storage medium.

backup (n.) The copy of data that is recorded for archival purposes, typically to offline tape storage.

balanced line (n.) A two-conductor line with a ground present is balanced if the two conductors carry equal voltages that are opposite in polarity. In a balanced-to-ground line, the impedance-to-ground levels in both conductors are equal in strength.

bandpass filter (n.) A device that blocks all frequencies not in a specified range. It may be used to process audio signals.

bandwidth (n.) The transmission capacity of an electronic medium, such as network wiring, fiber-optic cable, or microwave links; also the range of signal frequencies where a piece of audio or video gear can operate, or the difference between high and low limiting frequencies. *See the table on the following page for commonly accepted definitions of bandwidths in telecommunications and broadcasting.*

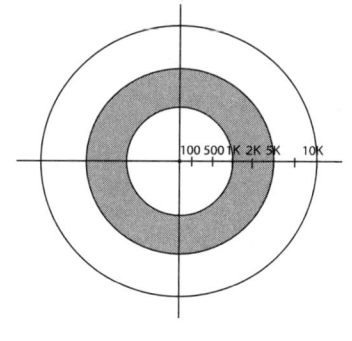

bandwidth between 1K and 5K is shaded

21

bar code

Acronym	Definition	Frequency Range
ELF	Extremely Low Frequency	under 300 Hz
ILF	Infra Low Frequency	300 Hz–3 kHz
VLF	Very Low Frequency	3 kHz–30 kHz
LF	Low Frequency	30 kHz–300 kHz
MF	Medium Frequency	300 kHz–3 MHz
HF	High Frequency	3 MHz–30 MHz
VHF	Very High Frequency	30 MHz–300 MHz
UHF	Ultra High Frequency	300 MHz–3 GHz
SHF	Super High Frequency	3 GHz–30 GHz
EHF	Extremely High Frequency	30 GHz–300 GHz

bar code (n.) A pattern of parallel lines whose variable thickness and separation encode a message that can be read by an optical scanner or wand for decoding by a computer. Many businesses use it as a universal product code (UPC) on retail items, and libraries use it to catalog books. It may be used to control videodisc playback as well.

barrel distortion

bar code

barrel distortion (n.) The opposite of pincushioning in a video display. The vertical sides of the display area curve outwards. *See illustration.*

baseband (n.) A method of transmitting digital information over short distances. The complete bandwidth of the cable is used to transmit a single signal. No modulation of signals exists, and they are transmitted individually. Simultaneous transmission of signals is possible using time-division multiplexing. This is a less expensive, simpler means to transmit information than broadband transmission.

base multitimbral specification (n.) A synthesizer subsystem standard that Multimedia PC audio board manufacturers follow in implementing MIDI playback. According to this specification, three pitched tones are available at once to play up to six notes, and two percussive timbres can play two percussive notes.

BASIC (n.) Beginners' All-purpose Symbolic Instruction Code; an algebraic computer programming language that was developed at Dartmouth College. The language employs if-then logic statements and other English commands as well as mathematical formulas.

basic input/output system See *BIOS*.

basic rate interface See *BRI*.

batch file (n.) In MS-DOS, a text-based file using the file extension .bat that carries out commands when executed. Batch files can be used to avoid retyping commands, to load other programs, or to change a computer's parameters. Batch processing consists of the continuous execution of a series, or batch, of commands.

bay (n.) In the physical frame of a microcomputer case, a space where an internal drive or a peripheral is installed.

baud (n.) A unit of transmission speed named for Jean-Maurice-Emile Baudot that defines the number of discrete signaling elements per second. One baud is approximately equal to one bit per second, but at high speeds, one signal can contain more than one bit. Common baud rates are 300, 1200, 2400, 9600, 14 400, and 28 800 bits per second (bps).

Bayonet-Neill-Concelman See *BNC*.

BBS (n.) Bulletin Board System; a system that provides computer users with access to files for downloading and areas for e-mail. Usually developed for local users, many of these systems are accessible through the Internet and FidoNet mail.

BCC (n.) Block check character; when data is transmitted in blocks, each packet has a control character, or BCC, appended so that the receiver can check for errors and request retransmission if necessary.

BCD (n.) Binary-coded decimal; each digit in this binary number system is represented by four bits. The weighting of each column is 8, 4, 2, 1.

0	=	0000
1	=	0001
2	=	0010
3	=	0011
4	=	0100
5	=	0101
6	=	0110
7	=	0111
8	=	1000

B-channel (n.) An ISDN user channel that carries digital data at 64 kilobits per second (Kbps). It may carry a mixture of data types, including PCM-encoded voice data.

Because It's Time Network See *BITNET*.

Beginners' All-Purpose Symbolic Instruction Code See *BASIC*.

Bell 43401 (n.) A publication from Bell that defines the requirements for data transmission over dc-continuous, private metallic circuits provided by the telephone company, primarily for limited-distance applications.

Bell standards (n.) A set of standards defined by AT&T for modem communications, numbered as follows:

Bell 103: Any AT&T 0–300-bps modem that provides asynchronous transmission with originate and answer capabilities. (FSK type.)

Bell 113: Any AT&T 0–300-bps modem that provides asynchronous transmission with either originate or answer capabilities, not both. (FSK type.)

Bell 201, 201B, and 201C: Any AT&T 2400-bps modem that provides synchronous transmission. 201B applies to full-duplex, public telephone line operation; 201C applies to half-duplex public telephone line operation. (DPSK type.)

Bell 202: Any AT&T 1800-bps modem that provides asynchronous transmission and uses a 4-wire circuit for full-duplex operation; also describes an AT&T 1200-bps modem that provides asynchronous transmission and uses a 2-wire circuit for half-duplex operation. (FSK type.)

Bell 208, 208A, and 208B: Any AT&T 4800-bps modem that provides synchronous transmission. 208A refers to leased-line applications, while 208B was designed for public telephone line operation. (PSK type.)

Bell 209: Any AT&T 9600-bps modem that provides synchronous transmission and uses a 4-wire leased-line circuit for full-duplex operation. (Combined PSK and ASK type, or quadrature amplitude modulation.)

Bell 212 and 212A: Any AT&T 1200-bps modem that provides synchronous transmission and uses a public telephone line for full-duplex operation. (PSK type.)

benchmark (n.) A task or series of tasks used to test capabilities of a processor or system for speed and performance.

BER (n.) <u>B</u>it <u>e</u>rror <u>r</u>ate; a unit of measurement that defines the number of bit writing errors compared to the total number of bits received during a transmission, or the percentage of bits in error found in a given volume or area of storage medium.

bespoke (adj.) Describes custom-made computer-based training software or courseware.

beta *or* **betamax** (n. or adj.) A consumer videotape format developed by Sony. Beta uses .5-inch (12.65 mm) tape in a 6-inch × 3.75-inch (155 mm × 95 mm) cassette. Although the format offers superior resolution, it was eclipsed in popularity by the VHS system developed by Matsushita and JVC.

betacam (n.) A professional-quality .5-inch video recording and playback format developed by Sony. Betacam is portable and provides video quality comparable to 1-inch videotape. Betacam SP is a higher-quality version that uses true component video signals.

beta test (n.) A second and final test for a software product, usually done by actual users in real-world situations with the "beta release."

bezel (n.) The housing that encases the front of a video monitor. Touch screens usually have a large bezel for their controlling electronics.

Bezier curve (n.) A graphic element defined by a formula consisting of two anchor points and two vector values, as opposed to a bitmap. See *vector data*.

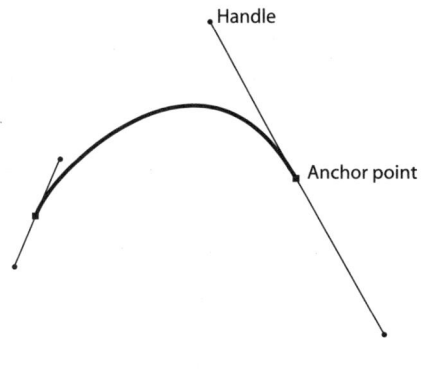
Bezier curve

bilinear filtering (n.) A means of predicting the most appropriate texture pixel for the screen based on interpolation from the four adjacent pixels in the texture.

binary code (n.) Each element in binary code has one of two possible values, a one or a zero, expressed by the presence or absence of a pulse or a high or low voltage level.

binary-coded decimal See *BCD*.

binary digit (n.) A numeral in the binary system, base-two; a one or a zero.

binary file (n.) A file that contains non-textual data, such as an image or an application.

binary notation (n.) The base-two numbering system that uses the digits one and zero. It may be used to represent any type of data. Logic circuits can define these two digits as different states in many ways.

binary synchronous communication See *BSC*.

binary transfer (n.) A method of transferring information between computers that involves the use of error-correction protocol, such as XMODEM or SNA. This is useful if the data is not purely text-based ASCII characters.

binaural audio (n.) Two audio tracks that are recorded with special microphone placement for each track to provide the listener with a perception of depth, or three-dimensional sound, when the tracks are played back together. This is different from simple stereo audio.

BinHex (n.) A standard Macintosh format for converting a binary file to an ASCII file for network transfer.

BIOS (n.) Basic input/output system; the BIOS file contains system control instructions for a microcomputer. Instructions in the ROM of the BIOS help start up a system and define the existing input and output connections.

bipolar (n.) A signaling method used in digital transmission in which a signal carrying a binary value alternates between positive and negative polarities. The signal amplitude can represent a zero or one at either polarity, and the spaces with no value are represented by zero amplitude.

bis (n.) The second version of an original Consultative Committee on International Telegraphy and Telephony (CCITT) standard. In common usage, it appears after the "V.x" designation, as in "V.42 bis," which refers to a modem specification. The third version in a succession is referred to as "V.x ter," as in "V.27 ter."

B-ISDN (n.) The second generation of the International Telephone and Telegraph Consultative Committee's (CCITT) ISDN. It is designed for transmission of real-time multimedia via plain old telephone service (POTS).

bit (n.) A contraction of the words binary digit that represents a unit (either zero or one) of data equal to one binary decision; it is the smallest unit in computer information handling. Computer processing capability is evaluated by the number of bits handled at once. PCs use 8-, 16-, 32-, or 64-bit microprocessors.

bit-block transfer (n.) A technique for moving pixel blocks in memory onto a monitor. It is more efficient than moving individual bits or bytes and is referred to as "blitting."

bit depth (n.) On computer monitors, each pixel can be represented by a variable number of bits used to describe the color of the pixel. Bit depth is the number of bits used in this capacity. A bit depth of two means that only black or white pixels can be shown; a bit depth of four allows the display of 16 colors; a bit depth of eight allows 256 colors; a bit depth of 16 represents 65 536 colors, and 24-bit color yields 16.7 million colors.

bit error rate See *BER*.

bitmap 1. (n.) An image defined by discrete values that are assigned to each pixel. 2. (n.) A common PC graphics file format whereby the image is stored as a pattern of dots with the extension .bmp.

BITNET (n.) Because It's Time Network; widely used by educational institutions in the 1980s, this network had nodes on hundreds of college campuses. It was officially discontinued in 1996.

bit rate (n.) The speed at which data is moved expressed as bits per second (bps). A bit rate expressed in megabits per second is a factor of 8.192 times the same rate expressed in kilobytes per second (KBps) because a kilobyte is equal to 1024 bits times 8. If a file size is known and the data transfer rate at which it streams is known, it is possible to determine the duration of time that an audio or video file will play based on its size. To convert an existing MPEG file of known size and bit rate into the duration for which it will play back, divide the file size in megabytes (MB) by the data transfer rate in KBps. A 5-MB file equals 5000 KB. Divide this by 150 KBps to arrive at 33 seconds of running video.

bits per second See *bps*.

bit stream transmission (n.) The transmission of characters at a fixed rate of speed. No stop and start elements are used, and no pauses exist between bits of data in the stream.

black box (n.) An electronic circuit or assembly that can be isolated from a system in order to perform a special function, such as controlling an external peripheral.

blanking interval 1. (n.) In a video display, the short duration at the end of a scan line when the signal is suppressed and the beam repositions. 2. (n.) The time it takes a video player to locate the next frame to display. See *illustration*.

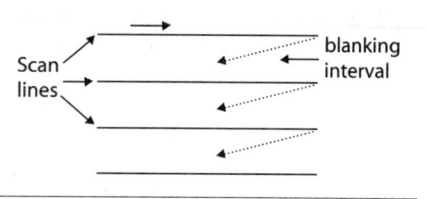

blanking interval between scan lines

blending (n.) The combination of two pixels in the context of a graphic.

block 1. (n.) In CD-ROM or CD-i, the user data portion of a logical sector. 2. (n.) Any group of bits transmitted as a unit or packet. It contains control delimiters at the beginning and end, a header, the data stream, and check characters used for error correction.

block check character See *BCC*.

block error correct (v.) To add 276 bytes of error correction code to the end of each block of data during premastering of a CD-ROM, allowing errors in the user data block to be corrected.

Blue Book (n.) The format used by compact discs that are designed for laser disc players.

blue screen (n.) A solid blue background used in the process of shooting video with special lighting so that the background may be "keyed" out, leaving only the subject, which may be placed over any background of the compositor's choice. This is the technique used by television weather reporters, who appear with a map juxtaposed behind them.

BMP (n.) A three-character MS-DOS extension at the end of a file name that identifies the file contents as a bitmapped pattern. A graphics format (filename.bmp).

BNC (n.) <u>B</u>ayonet-<u>N</u>eill-<u>C</u>oncelman; a round connector attached to the end of a coaxial cable and used in video applications. It is pushed onto the receptacle and then locked by twisting clockwise.

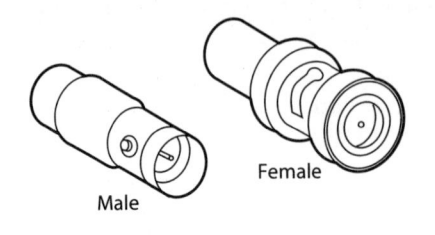

BNC connectors
Male
Female

board (n.) Short for "printed circuit board," an internal plug-in unit with printed-circuit wiring and components. It may either control some essential function of the computer's central processor or provide a special feature such as telecommunications, audio, or video control and display. Also known as a card.

Boolean operator (n.) A qualifying term that refines a definition; examples include AND (items that include both terms that appear in a query), NOT (items that contain one term but not another), and OR (items that are derived from either class defined). In general, it is a variable that can accept only true or false values.

Boolean search (n.) A type of search for information in which qualifiers such as "and," "or," and "not" are used.

boot (v.) To start a computer and prepare it to process commands by loading the operating system.

boot record (n.) Under the ISO 9660 standard, the record that identifies the location of a boot file on a CD-ROM. This file contains an operating system that can be loaded.

boot sequence (n.) The sequence whereby a microprocessor receives instructions from ROM to check its circuits and then to try to load files from a disk drive. It initially tries the A: (floppy) drive, and if the necessary files are not found, it tries to read from the first hard disk drive (C:).

bot (n.) Contraction of robot; a term most often found in multiuser dungeons (MUDs) and chats (IRCs). It refers to a character that is not a person, but rather a collection of responses from a computer program.

bounce 1. (v.) To mix two or more audio tracks into one. Also called ping-ponging. 2. (v.) To return a piece of e-mail because of a delivery error.

bps (n.) <u>B</u>its <u>p</u>er <u>s</u>econd; a measurement that reflects the speed at which data is sent over transmission lines. It should not be confused with a baud rate, which is a measurement of signal elements that may include more than one bit at high speeds.

Bps (n.) <u>B</u>ytes <u>p</u>er <u>s</u>econd; a rate of data transfer, not to be confused with bps, which refers to bits per second.

branch 1. (v.) To leap from one location in a program to another based on programmed responses to user input.

branching point (n.) An optional path which a user may choose, given two or more directions or destinations.

BRender (n.) A three-dimensional API provided by Argonaut, a British game developer.

BRI (n.) <u>B</u>asic <u>r</u>ate <u>i</u>nterface; one of the common interfaces used in integrated services digital network (ISDN). It consists of two bearer B-channels at 64 kilobits per second (Kbps), full-duplex, along with a data D-channel at 16 Kbps. The B-channels can accommodate videoconferencing, voice, or facsimile data, while the D-channel handles private data. The BRI "U" interface uses two wires, while the BRI "T" interface uses four wires.

bridge (n.) A connecting device between two or more subnetworks, or LANs, that are running similar cabling and protocols. It uses the bottom two layers of the OSI model to create an extended network on which workstations on different subnetworks can share data.

bridge disc (n.) A technique for storing data on a CD-ROM XA disc that allows the data to be played back on several platforms. A Photo-CD can be played on a CD-i or Photo-CD player, and also on a 2x multiple session CD-ROM drive.

bridge/router (n.) A sophisticated networking device that performs the functions of a bridge, a router, or both simultaneously. It can route multiple protocols, such as TCP/IP and XNS, while bridging other traffic.

broadband (n.) Broadband transmission is often in the range of 1 megahertz (MHz) or more, and it can accommodate multiple channels. At the minimum, it is used to describe bandwidth capability greater than voice, which telecommunications standards have set at 4 kilohertz (kHz). ISDN is considered a broadband medium. Cable television employs broadband techniques to send multiple channels over a single cable.

Broadband Integrated Services Digital Network See *B-ISDN*.

broadcast (v.) To transmit television and radio programs through the air. In network applications, it means to forward a message to all destinations.

broadcast quality (adj.) Loosely defined, this describes the level of quality that television stations will transmit, adhering to the NTSC format in the United States. This format calls for 525 lines of video at a rate of 60 fields per second, with the appropriate levels of brightness and color (luma and chroma).

browse (v.) To scan networked information with no particular target in mind.

browser (n.) Software that allows a user to search through information on a server; commonly refers to universal client applications, such as Netscape Navigator or Microsoft Internet Explorer. It is the name used by Eastman Kodak on Photo-CD discs for the database program that lets users search for images by keyword or title.

BSC (n.) Binary synchronous communication, or "bisync"; an industry-standard IBM communications protocol that is character- or byte-oriented. A defined set of control characters is used to synchronize the transmission of binary-coded data between two stations, both of which must be synchronized prior to data transmission.

B-spline (n.) A basic spline from which an approximated curve is derived, typically used in the creation of wire-frame models for a dimensional figure.

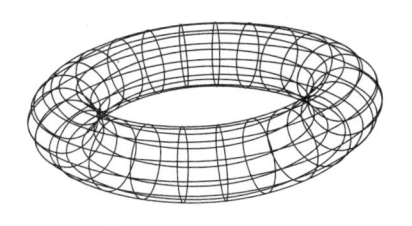

torus formed by a bicubic B-spline surface

bubble memory (n.) Memory technology that uses magnetic bubbles that are generated from a single-crystal sheet. It is nonvolatile and requires very low power levels.

buffer 1. (n.) Memory space that temporarily stores a small amount of data to help compensate for differences in the transfer rate of data from one device to another. It can also be used to store small bits of data that may be used repeatedly (such as a digitized beep or other sound). Most CD-ROM drives have buffers. 2. (n.) A storage space where data is held temporarily until it is passed to or from a host computer or peripheral device.

bug (n.) An error in a computer program or a problem with the system.

build (n.) An interim version of software in which bugs are resolved and features refined prior to release.

Bulletin Board System See *BBS*.

bump map (n.) A texture map that may be applied to the surface of a three-dimensional image to simulate natural surfaces, patterns, or imperfections.

bundled title (n.) A CD-ROM that is packaged with hardware components, peripherals, or entire systems and is not priced separately.

burst (n.) In reference to color television reception, a signal which provides a reference for the 3.58-megahertz (MHz) oscillator. The signal is sent during the video blanking interval.

burst error (n.) An error that contains a group of consecutive bits, often due to scratches on the surface of a CD-ROM.

bus 1. (n.) A connection or path between a central processing unit (CPU) and the input/output devices, or the connection between two processors. Types of buses that have been used in IBM-compatibles include ISA, VESA, and PCI. The Nubus system was used on older Macintosh computers. In 1995, Apple Computer replaced the Nubus with the 64-bit PCI bus in selected Power Macintosh models. 2. (n.) A signal or power-transmitting conduit that allows two or more lines to be connected and their signals mixed.

button (n.) A graphic component of an interface that represents some embedded function. When clicked, buttons can branch the user to another location in the program.

buyout music (n.) Audio tracks that are sold with a license that allows the purchaser to duplicate and use them in productions without paying royalties.

bypass mode (n.) An operating mode on ring networks, such as FDDI and token ring, in which an interface is removed, or bypassed, from the ring.

byte (n.) A measurable number of consecutive binary digits that are usually treated as a unit. Bytes of eight bits usually represent either one character or two numerals. A computer's storage capacity or memory is figured in kilobytes (KB). One kilobyte is equal to 1024 (2^{10}) bits.

byte aligned (n.) Information stored in memory that is located an exact multiple of eight bits from the starting point.

bytes per second See *Bps*.

C (n.) A high-level, procedural programming language that runs faster than other high-level languages because it allows embedding of instructions. It is highly portable to platforms for which there is a C compiler.

cable 1. (n.) All types of wires and cords used to transmit signals or connect equipment. Cables may contain single or multiple wires and may be shielded to reduce interference. Most cables allocate at least one wire to be used as a ground. Coaxial cable is used for video applications. 2. (adj.) Describes local television service delivered over cable rather than broadcast through the air.

cable modem (n.) A device that enables a user to connect a computer with a special circuit board to existing coaxial cable provided by a cable TV network and access digital services inserted into the vertical blanking interval of a television signal. Each interval is able to carry the amount of data approximately equivalent to a 9600 baud modem. Transmission is one-way from the cable provider and is not interactive unless a modem on a telephone line is connected simultaneously.

cable tap (n.) In an Ethernet network, a device that connects a transceiver to the main cable.

cable television See *CATV*.

cache (n.) A temporary block of computer memory that is allocated for frequent or rapid data access.

caching (n.) The use of memory or disk storage to speed data processing by storing data that will be accessed later.

CAD/CAM (n.) Computer-aided design/computer-aided manufacturing; software applications used by engineers for the graphic design of components and systems. Once components are built, they may be manipulated on screen and evaluated. CAM applications extrapolate manufacturing specifications from the CAD designs and may control manufacturing processes.

CADD Computer-aided design and drafting.

caddy (n.) The case or cartridge that protects CD-ROM discs while they are

Category 4

inserted in the drive. Late model drives are typically caddiless, and the disc rests in an open tray.

CAI <u>C</u>omputer-<u>a</u>ided <u>i</u>nstruction. See *CBT.*

CAL Computer-aided learning See *CBT.*

call (v.) In computer programming, to invoke a procedure or subroutine, and to transfer control to it. Ordinarily, control is returned to the program at the instruction immediately following the point from which the call was made.

CAM <u>C</u>omputer-<u>a</u>ided <u>m</u>anufacturing. See *CAD/CAM.*

camcorder (n.) Contraction of camera/recorder; portable videotaping gear. The usual formats are VHS and 8mm, along with their higher resolution versions, S-VHS and Hi-8. VHS-C is a compact version of VHS.

capacitance 1. (n.) The degree to which a substance or device conducts or passes electricity. 2. (n.) The ability to store an electric charge, measured in farads.

capacitor (n.) One of the components in a circuit that stores voltage, like a holding tank. The charge is released later as it is triggered.

capstan (n.) A roller or spindle that controls the speed and movement of magnetic tape through a recorder or player. See illustration.

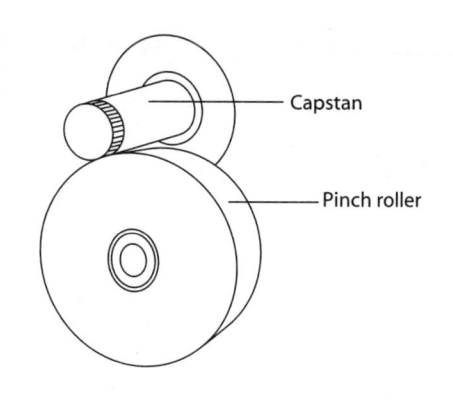

capstan — Capstan, Pinch roller

card (n.) A printed circuit board. See *board.*

carriage return See *CR.*

carrier sense multiple access with collision detection See *CSMA/CD.*

carrier signal (n.) A constant sine wave that can be modulated with a second signal that contains data. The high-pitched tone that a modem emits is an audible carrier signal. Changes, or modulation, in the amplitude, frequency, or phase of the carrier can convey information.

cascade (v.) To connect numerous multiple-port devices in order to expand the number of ports or available I/O lines.

cast 1. (n.) The actors who appear in a production. 2. (adj.) Describes the overemphasis of one hue or tint in an image.

Category 4 (n.) A standard for wiring that

must be met when connecting networks with a bandwidth of 20-megabits per second (Mbps) and 16-Mbps token ring networks.

Category 3 (n.) A standard for wiring that must be met when connecting 10-megabit per second (Mbps) 10BASE-T Ethernet and 4-Mbps token ring networks.

cathode-ray tube See *CRT.*

CATV (n.) Cable television; local television service that is delivered over cable rather than broadcast through the air. It was defined as Community Antenna Television before the installation of cable.

CAV (n. or adj.) Constant angular velocity; a type of videodisc player that spins the disc at a constant speed regardless of the position of the reading head, so that tracks nearer the center pass under the reading head more slowly than the tracks nearer the perimeter. Each frame is separately addressable. The standard speed for CAV discs is 1800 rpm (NTSC) or 1500 rpm (PAL), and the disc makes one revolution for each frame. The maximum program duration is approximately 30 minutes per side on a 12-inch disc.

C-band (n.) A high-frequency spectrum used for satellite transmission. Uplink is at 6 gigahertz (GHz); downlink is at 4 GHz.

CBI (n.) Computer-based instruction. See *CBT.*

CBL (n.) Computer-based learning. See *CBT.*

CBT (n.) Computer-based training; the use of computers to facilitate learning. Also called computer-aided instruction (CAI), computer-aided learning (CAL), computer-based instruction (CBI), and computer-based learning (CBL).

CCD (n.) Charge coupled device; a light-detecting component used by digital cameras.

CCIR (n.) Consultative Committee for International Radio; in addition to the name of the committee, refers to the 625-line TV system used in Western Europe.

CCIR-656 (n.) A recommendation of the CCIR that is the standard for digital component electrical interfaces. It defines synchronizing signals and blanking, and parallel and serial interface specifications.

CCIR-601 (n.) A recommendation of the CCIR that is the standard for digital component video. It specifies color difference coding (Y,R-Y,B-Y) and the 4:2:2 format.

CCITT (n.) Comité Consultatif International de Télégraphique et Téléphonique (International Telephone and Telegraph Consultative Committee); a worldwide standards organization that defines communications protocols. The recommendations enable global compatibility for voice, data, and video transmission over telecommunications devices. The CCIT has been replaced by the ITU.

CCITT Group III (n.) A compression standard used for facsimile transmission.

CCITT Group IV (n.) A compression standard widely used for storing images on optical disc. It is based on a two-dimensional compression scheme in which every scan line is the reference line for the next scan line, and only the changes or deltas are stored.

CCL (n.) Connection Control Language; a set of commands used to identify and manage data connections.

CD (n.) Compact disc; usually refers to a compact audio disc, a 4.75-inch (12 cm) optical disc containing information encoded digitally in the CLV format. This format is popular for high fidelity music that offers a 90+ decibel signal/noise ratio and 74 minutes of digital sound. The standard for this format is the Red Book. The official designation is CD-DA (compact disc-digital audio). The following illustration shows the evolution of compact discs and the relationship between different types of compact discs. *See illustration on following page.*

CD-A (n.) Compact disc-audio. See *CD-DA*.

CD-DA (n.) Compact disc-digital audio. See *CD*.

CDDI (n.) Copper Distributed Data Interface; the implementation of Fiber Distributed Data Interface (FDDI) network protocols using twisted pair copper wiring.

CDEV (n.) Control panel device; a piece of system code used in the Macintosh OS to extend functionality. (Pronounced see-dev.)

CD-i (n.) Compact disc-interactive; developed in 1991 by Philips, this CD-ROM format holds audio, digital data, still graphics, and MPEG video. These discs adhere to the Green Book standard. An infrared remote control device, a mouse, or a track ball allows users to interact with the content on the disc by clicking a cursor over hot spots on the video display.

CD-i audio levels (n.) Levels of audio encoding that are part of the Green Book specification. Level A is a method of recording audio that offers fidelity comparable to that of standard CD audio, but it compresses the data to about half as much space on disc. Level B is used in both the CD-i and CD-ROM XA formats, a method of recording audio that offers medium fidelity but that is more highly compressed than level A. Level C is used in both the CD-i and CD-ROM XA formats, a method of recording audio that offers fidelity sufficient for speech. It is highly compressed.

CDMA (n.) Code Division Multiple Access; a method of concurrent transmission whereby packets of data are coded to differentiate them from other packets. This is related to TDMA, a popular, but slower transmission technique.

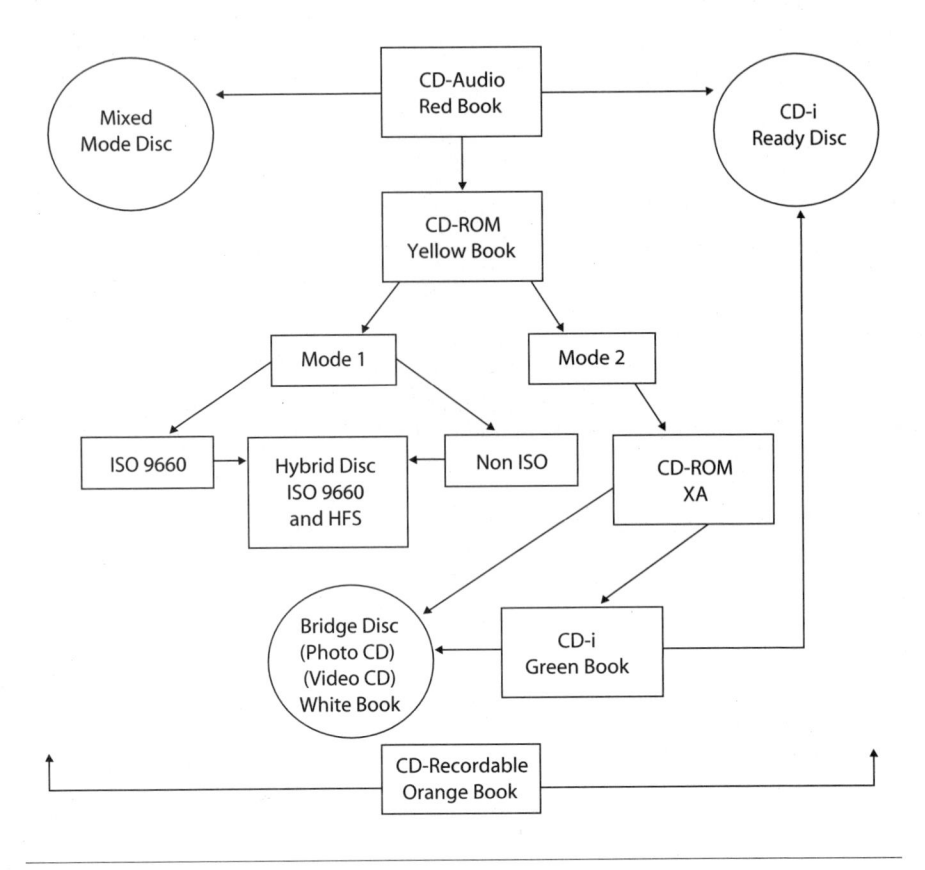

CD family

CDPD (n.) Cellular Digital Packet Data; the standard for 19 200 bits per second (bps) data communications over unused analog cellular voice channels.

CD Plus (n.) A CD-ROM format from Sony and Philips that plays Red Book audio, written on the first tracks, and also includes graphics and data files readable by a microcomputer on later tracks. Windows 95 supports the CD Plus format.

CD + G (n.) Compact disc + graphics; developed by Warner New Media, this format is not readable by standard CD-ROM players. It is a CD format that includes extended graphics capabilities as well as some limited video graphics written to the CD subcode area. The primary use is for *karaoke*, in which the lyrics of a song are displayed and the music without vocals is played to accompany the person who sings the song.

CD + MIDI (n.) Compact disc + Musical Instrument Digital Interface; developed by Warner New Media, this CD format adds Musical Instrument Digital Interface (MIDI) information to the digital audio data.

CD-R (n.) Compact disc-recordable; developed in 1990 by Philips and Sony, this standard is called the Orange Book. It permits the writing of CD-Audio, CD-ROM, CD-ROM XA, and CD-i block structures to a CD-ROM blank by a CD recorder. The primary applications are for prototype production discs, or "one-offs," and for archiving data. In 1992, a second generation of CD recorders became standard, and they were capable of "multisession," or writing to a disc on more than one occasion. To read a multisession disc, readers must be able to identify a complex Table of Contents, but not all readers can do this. The original ISO 9660 logical file structure does not handle multisession discs because it was created before their invention.

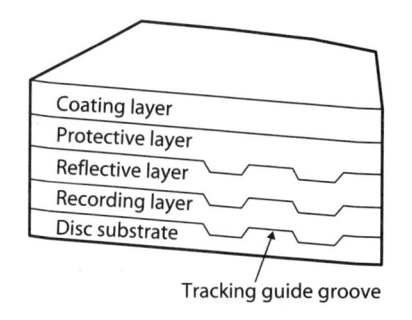

CD-R layers

Coating layer
Protective layer
Reflective layer
Recording layer
Disc substrate
Tracking guide groove

CD-ROM (n.) Compact disc-read-only memory; a 4.75-inch disc onto which optical memory storage is encoded. CD-ROMs hold about 620 megabytes of data. The standards for this format are called the Yellow Book. The logical level standard is called ISO 9660. The UNIX extension is called the Rock Ridge proposal.

CD-ROM drive (reader, player) (n.) Any playback device for data encoded on CD-ROMs. Compared to an audio CD player, it performs more error correction. Usually controlled by a computer to read text, graphic, video, and audio files, it also reads the Red Book audio format. *See illustration on following page.*

CD-ROM extensions (n.) Software routines that connect MS-DOS with specific CD-ROM drivers and compatible computers to read discs in the ISO 9660 and High Sierra formats.

CD-ROM upgrade kit (n.) A package with software, interface card, cables, and the drive for installation in a computer.

CD-ROM XA (n.) Compact disc-read-only memory extended architecture; an extension of the Yellow Book standard, generally consistent with the ISO 9660 format. It is designed to add better audio (ADPCM) compression along with the ability to stream interleaved video with audio for multimedia applications.

CDTV (n.) Commodore Dynamic Total Vision; an interactive multimedia system designed for consumer use. It reads programs on special CD-ROM discs.

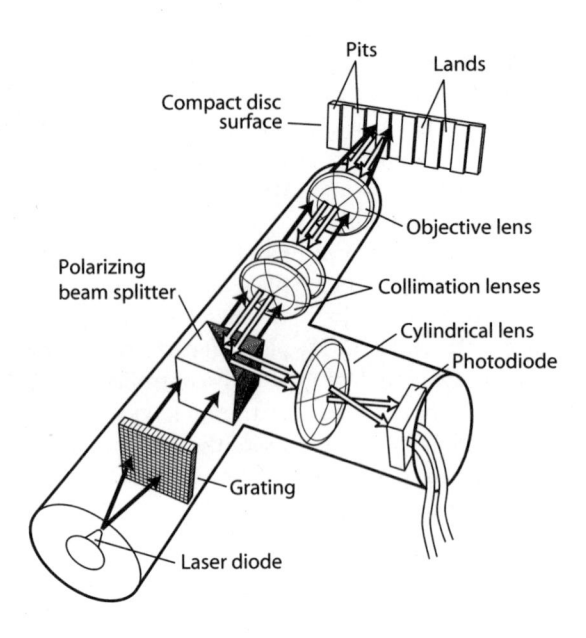

laser beam path on a CD-ROM player

CD-WO (n.) <u>C</u>ompact <u>d</u>isc-<u>w</u>rite <u>o</u>nce; another name for CD-recordable (CD-R).

cell 1. (n.) In spreadsheets, the point where a row and a column intersect. 2. (n.) In animation, a transparent piece of film onto which images are drawn. 3. (n.) In data transmission, a packet of information containing 53 bytes of address information combined with data.

Cello (n.) The trademark name for a freeware Internet browser. Cello allows access to the World Wide Web, Gopher, and FTP. It does not, however, accommodate e-mail messages to newsgroups.

cellular (adj.) Describes a means of dividing an area into regions, or cells, so that each region becomes a network in which every point exists within the range of a central transmission facility.

Cellular Digital Packet Data See *CDPD*.

central processing unit See *CPU*.

Centronics parallel (n.) A standard 36-pin parallel interface that permits the connection of printers and other peripherals to a computer.

CERN (n.) <u>C</u>onseil <u>E</u>uropean pour la <u>Re</u>cherche <u>N</u>ucléaire (European Particle Physics Laboratory); the Swiss research center at which the World Wide Web was developed.

CGA (n.) <u>C</u>olor <u>G</u>raphics <u>A</u>dapter; one of the IBM PC graphics standards.

CGI (n.) <u>C</u>ommon <u>G</u>ateway <u>I</u>nterface; a standard that defines the automatic creation of forms and responses on the Web in the form of HTML documents. CGI scripts convert data input by a visitor to a Web site into a page of information, and they are used to allow access to a database or to accept an order from users.

CGM (n.) <u>C</u>omputer <u>G</u>raphics <u>M</u>etafile; an object-oriented graphic file format used by many software applications.

channel (n.) Either of two independent signals in a stereo audio system, designated right and left. Most audio, video, and computer playback devices provide separate channels for these signals.

chapter (n.) Each independent segment on a videodisc.

chapter cue (n.) A signal in the vertical blanking interval of a master tape identifying the first frame of a new chapter. On a videodisc pressed from this master, a chapter stop is encoded on the corresponding disc frame.

chapter number (n.) The number displayed on the screen that identifies videodisc chapters.

chapter stop (n.) Codes embedded in videodiscs to signal the break between two separate chapters, allowing access to a specific chapter.

character user interface See *CUI*.

chat (n.) An online forum for real-time, text-based discussion by participants who are logged on simultaneously.

check disc (n.) A prototype videodisc or compact disc produced prior to quantity replication to confirm the accuracy and integrity of the data.

checksum (n.) A number representing the sum of a set of data bytes. It is sent with the data set, and error correction schemes use it to determine whether the data has been accurately received.

child directory (n.) In MS-DOS, the directory that resides within a parent directory in the logical format.

chip (n.) A silicon wafer onto which circuit paths are etched or printed photographically in layers, connecting active and passive devices within the solid structure. *See illustration on following page.*

chroma key (n.) A video effect created by shooting objects against a monochrome background, the color of which is "keyed" out so it can be replaced with images from another source. Foreground objects appear to be juxtaposed over the new background in the composition. This color-based video matting (overlay) technique drops all areas of a selected color (usually blue) from the foreground image, and it substitutes corresponding areas of the new background.

chrominance (chroma) (n.) The color and saturation information in a video signal. Luminance must be present to make it visible. Low chroma levels appear to be washed out and high levels are too vivid, causing bleeding between different colors. See *luminance*.

chunk (n.) A block of a type of data that is used in TIFF and RIFF standards.

Chyron 1. (n.) A manufacturer of video character generators. 2. (n.) A word applied in the computer industry to any character generator or to lettering on the screen.

CinePak (n.) A video compression algorithm that was developed by SuperMac and was previously referred to as Compact Video.

CIRC (n.) Cross-Interleaved Reed-Solomon Code; the first level of error correction that is used in every compact disc (CD), and the only one that is used for audio CDs. It consists of two Reed-Solomon Codes interleaved crosswise.

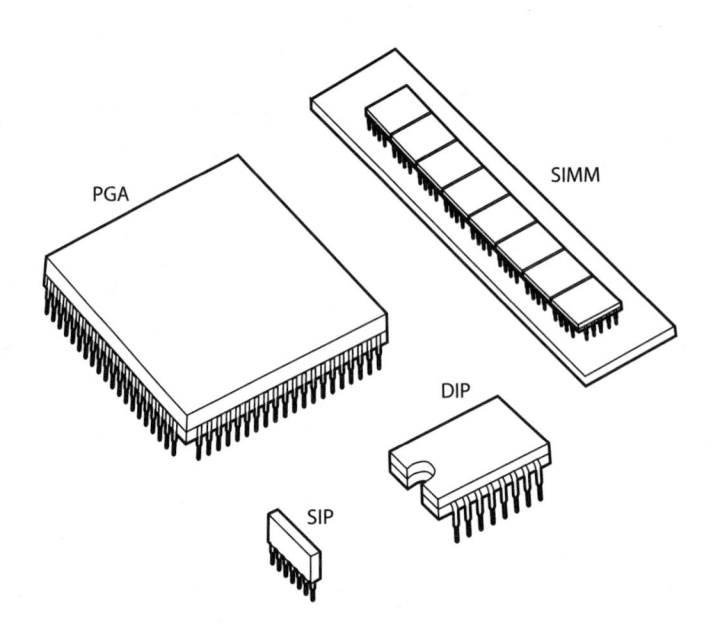

chip formats

circuit switching (n.) A network configuration in which a continuous connection is established between two devices, providing uninterrupted flow of information, as opposed to packet switching.

CISC (n.) <u>C</u>omplex <u>i</u>nstruction <u>s</u>et <u>c</u>omputing; a method of processing in which complex instructions are used at the assembly language level.

CIX (n.) <u>C</u>ommercial <u>I</u>nternet E<u>x</u>change; a group of Internet service providers who provide a backbone service free from acceptable use policies (AUPs) and dedicated to commercial use.

cladding (n.) A material that surrounds the core of a fiber-optic cable, providing insulation and protection.

clean boot (n.) The process of bypassing the config.sys and autoexec.bat files on startup.

cleanroom (n.) A room in which semiconductors are manufactured and CDs are pressed. It is maintained virtually dust-free to reduce particle contamination.

Clear To Send See *CTS*.

click (v.) To press and release a mouse button rapidly, usually over a hot spot or icon on the screen in a graphical user interface (GUI).

client (n.) In the "client/server" model, the system that initiates requests to the server, database, or processing engine. The client uses its own intelligence to further process the results for display.

client/server (n.) A network architecture that distributes computing responsibility between a front-end and a back-end program. Prior to client/server, the burden of data processing was placed on either the client (early PC environments) or the server (a typical mainframe). In the client/server model, clients share data and processing functions with the server.

clip art (n.) Illustrations or artwork files that are made available for use in productions and projects. Catalogs of clip art categorized by subject are widely distributed, and users who purchase them are typically granted permission to use the images without copyright infringement.

clipboard (n.) A memory location in which data that is selected and copied or cut from a document resides until it is pasted or cleared; a form of memory buffer available in most GUIs.

clipping (n.) The process of operating a device in a nonlinear amplitude region and producing distortion so that peaks of waveforms are cut off. Clipped waveforms consist mostly of odd harmonics.

clock speed (n.) The shortest amount of time that is required for a central processing unit (CPU) to perform a single instruction. A computer clock generates regular timing pulses in a range from 25–200 megahertz (MHz).

clone (n.) A computing system based on the IBM design that runs software such as Microsoft DOS and Windows.

closed architecture (n.) A system with software and hardware that is compatible with only one manufacturer or developer, which may not be freely extensible. By contrast, open architecture uses open standards for compatibility.

cluster (n.) A logical storage unit on a hard disk, floppy, or other media.

CLUT (n.) Color look-up table; a selection of colors assigned a digital value and held in a table. A program decodes a color picture for display by matching the code stored for each pixel with the associated color value in the look-up table. This process is also called "indexed color."

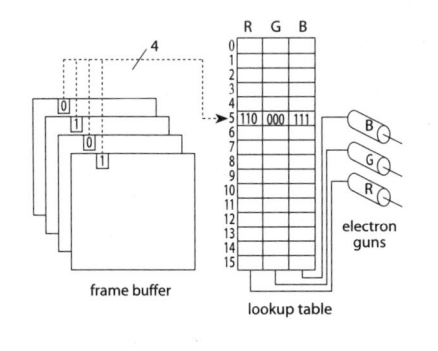

color look-up table components

CLV (n.) Constant linear velocity; a type of videodisc player with variable rotation speed, so that all data sectors pass under the reading head at the same rate. The disc rotates faster when the head is closer to the center of the disc, and more slowly as the head moves away from the center of the disc. Referred to as "extended-play" discs, they will play twice as long per side as CAV discs, or up to one hour. Some of the control features of a CAV disc are lost in the CLV format, such as freeze-frame capability. Compact discs of all types spin at a constant linear velocity and exhibit a constant sector size.

CMOS (n.) Complimentary metal-oxide semiconductor; a MOS device containing both N-channel and P-channel MOS active elements. CMOS is one of two basic processes (MOS and bipolar) used to fabricate integrated circuits.

CMYK (adj.) Describes a type of color representation based on the cyan (C), magenta (M), yellow (Y), and black (K) inks used in color printing. The first three inks form all available colors using subtractive color mixing, while black is used to add tonal range and to define edges.

coaxial cable (n.) A standard video cable with a single center conductor surrounded by insulation and an outer conductor made of woven metal. If the cable is run underground or exposed to water, it is enclosed by another layer of insulation. It is referred to as "coax."

code (n.) Any representation of information using numbers, letters, or symbols.

CODEC (n.) Compression-decompression or compressor-decompressor. This may be either a software-only, or a hardware-assisted scheme that is used to process digital video and/or audio files. The amount of data required to represent moving pictures with sound is reduced by a CODEC, which normally discards redundant data on compression. Some of the more widely used CODECS are Indeo, MPEG, and CinePak.

Code Division Multiple Access See *CDMA*.

coded order (n.) In video compression, the order in which frames are stored and decoded, not necessarily the same as the order in which they are displayed.

coherent light (n.) A light beam that is made up of a single frequency where the light waves are in phase. It is emitted from a laser or light-emitting diode.

color balance (n.) The process of matching the strength of red, green, and blue signals to make an accurate white color from the mixture.

color bars (n.) A video test signal consisting of solid blocks of the three primary colors and their combinations, referred to as "bars." Most frequently, the SMPTE version is used.

color cycling (n.) An animation technique in which a special effect is created by swapping colors in and out of a color look-up table (CLUT).

Color Graphics Adapter See *CGA*.

color look-up table See *CLUT*.

color map (n.) A set of relationships in a table format that defines RGB color components to be displayed based on graphic data from a computer.

color model (n.) A means of defining the color of an image with components in three or four dimensions. The most frequently used models include RGB (red, green, and blue light), HLS (hue, lightness, and saturation), HSV (hue, saturation, and value) and CMYK (cyan, magenta, yellow, and black).

color perception (n.) The sensation of hues created by the human eye as it defines the frequencies of electromagnetic waves. The graph below illustrates the color perceived by each bandwidth in the spectrum, measured in nanometers.

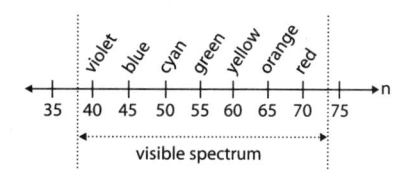

```
          violet blue cyan green yellow orange red
     ├─────┼────┼────┼────┼────┼────┼────┼──→ n
     35   40   45   50   55   60   65   70  75
          ←·············visible spectrum·············→
```

the color spectrum nanometers

colorYCC (n.) Developed by Eastman Kodak for Photo-CD, a device-independent color encoding process. Each color pixel is separated into two 8-bit chroma components and one 8-bit luma component, for a total of 24 bits. The process can also convert RGB color to

YCC, and vice versa. It provides image compression and high resolution for video or print graphics.

Comité Consultatif International de Télégraphique et Téléphonique See *CCITT*.

Command key (n.) On a Macintosh keyboard, a special key that has a flower-shaped diagram and performs functions when combined with other keys. Common functions are global menu choices:

Command-A	Select All
Command-C	Copy material to clipboard
Command-F	Find
Command-G	Find again
Command-I	Get info
Command-M	Make alias
Command-N	New folder or document
Command-O	Open
Command-P	Print
Command-Q	Quit from application
Command-S	Save file to current folder
Command-V	Paste from clipboard
Command-W	Close file or folder
Command-X	Cut to clipboard
Command-Z	Undo last command or typing

command line (n.) In operating systems that require keyboard characters for instructions, such as MS-DOS or UNIX, this display line prompts the user to input keyboard instructions.

Commercial Internet Exchange See *CIX*.

Commodore Dynamic Total Vision See *CDTV*.

Common Gateway Interface See *CGI*.

Common Intermedia Format (n.) A video conferencing standard with a resolution of 352 × 288 pixels.

Common Object Request Broker Architecture See *CORBA*.

Common User Access Architecture See *CUA Architecture*.

compact disc See *CD*.

compact disc digital audio See *CD-DA*.

compact disc-interactive See *CD-i*.

compact disc + graphics See *CD + G*.

compact disc + Musical Instrument Digital Interface See *CD + MIDI*.

compact disc-read-only memory See *CD-ROM*.

compact disc-read-only memory extended architecture See *CD-ROM XA*.

compact disc recordable See *CD-R*.

compact disc-write once See *CD-WO*.

compact video (n.) Developed by SuperMac, this is a CODEC can compress QuickTime movies in 320 × 240 resolution at high frame rates for CD-ROM playback.

companding (n.) The process of compressing data for transmission, and expanding it on reception.

compatibility (n.) Related to compact discs, the extent to which different types of discs can be read by different types of disc drives or players. For example, all CD-DA discs are fully compatible with all CD-DA players, so any player can interpret and reproduce music from any disc, regardless of the manufacturer.

compatible (adj.) Describes the ability to run the same software, such as MS-DOS, on various hardware configurations.

compiled language (n.) Unlike an interpreted language, which is translated into machine code every time it is run, a compiled language is converted into machine language once. This code is stored and called each time the program is run. The collection of symbols used to write the program is called source code. The translated machine language is called object code. Examples of compiled languages are Pascal and C++.

compiler (n.) A computer program that translates higher-level language instructions into machine code readable by a computer.

complex instruction set computing See *CISC*.

complimentary metal-oxide conductor See *CMOS*.

component video (n.) A video signal in which the chrominance (color) and the luminance (brightness) components have been recorded separately. The result is better picture quality. S-VHS and Hi-8 offer two-part component, or Y/C. This format offers higher resolution than composite video, which mixes the Y and C components, because it yields increased bandwidth in the luminance portion of the signal. "Color-under," or limited color bandwidth, is the method used in Y/C. The common Betacam component system further divides color into three components (Y, R-Y, B-Y), which provide better luminance, color accuracy, and lower noise than Y/C.

composite (v.) To build the final version of a production with layers drawn from video, graphics, and audio content that is integrated according to the production plan. 2. (n.) In telecommunications, the side signal of a concentrator, or a multiplexor that includes the multiplexed data.

composite video (n.) A video signal in which all the information about color, brightness, line, field, sync, and blanking are mixed together. Cross-color artifacts become apparent in composite video. See *RGB*.

compound document (n.) A collection of multiple data types, each linked to the application that created it, connected by a navigable interface.

compress (v.) To reduce a file to a significantly smaller size without altering the substantive information. This is accomplished by the elimination of redundant data. Related to analog audio, compression limits the bandwidth and reduces the differences in amplitude between the softest and loudest sounds in a program. In most multimedia applications, digital video must be compressed in order to stream smoothly at an acceptable frame rate.

compressed audio (n.) Related to digitally encoded sounds, a special processing technique that reduces the quantity of data required to define the sounds.

compressed video (n.) A video clip that is digitally encoded with computer algorithms to reduce the amount of data needed to define the video content.

compression (n.) The conversion of digital data, typically video and audio, into a more compact form by using complicated algorithms.

compression-decompression See *CODEC*.

compression ratio (n.) A comparison between the size of an uncompressed data file divided by the size of the compressed version of that file, expressing the degree to which a compression algorithm can reduce file size as a ratio. The MPEG video compression algorithm typically achieves a ratio of 180:1. JPEG still-picture compression formulas achieve less than 20:1 ratios, and at higher ratios exhibit noticeable artifacts and blockiness.

compressor-decompressor See *CODEC*.

computer (n.) Programmable digital equipment that performs computations and manipulates data.

computer-aided design/computer-aided manufacturing See *CAD/CAM*.

computer-based instruction See *CBT*.

computer-based training See *CBT*.

computer graphics (n.) Any and all images that are digitally generated by a computer. Graphics adapter cards are required by IBM-compatible PCs to drive a monitor. Some of the common standards for personal computer graphics are CGA, EGA, VGA, and SVGA.

Computer Graphics Metafile See *CGM*.

concatenate (v.) In programming, to combine character strings.

concentrator (n.) In telecommunications, a device that enables a shared transmission medium to accommodate more data sources than there are channels available within the transmission medium.

condenser microphone (n.) A microphone that translates acoustical signals into electrical signals by using a variable capacitor. Power must by supplied to the capacitor, either by a battery or a phantom power supply.

conditional branching (n.) In computing, when a specified set of conditions is satisfied, previously programmed instructions take a user to a different location in the program. The destination to which the program branches is conditional upon the nature of a user's input. If specific conditions are not met, the computer follows the normal sequence.

conference (n.) An asynchronous online discussion area where a group of users may post information and comments for others with access.

confetti (n.) Small, colored dots on a video screen caused by signal drop-outs or video noise. See *noise*.

config.sys (n.) A file of commands read by MS-DOS each time a PC boots, since it holds the instructions for configuration parameters, device drivers, buffers, and other necessary information.

Connection Control Language See *CCL*.

constant (n.) In programming, a value that does not change, as opposed to a variable.

constant angular velocity See *CAV*.

constant linear velocity See *CLV*.

consumer market (n.) Also called the domestic market, this is the segment of the audio/video market where equipment is used mostly in private homes and software consists of movies and games. The professional market uses industrial gear.

content (n.) The story, information, graphics, audio, and video material that is incorporated in a digital production.

contention (n.) In telecommunications, a method of access used by PBX or public telephone systems where numerous devices are served on a first-come, first-served basis by a limited number of ports.

context-sensitive (adj.) Depending on a user's actions, a context-sensitive program responds with help or prompts that are specifically related to activities in which the user is engaged.

contiguous (adj.) Related to data storage, describes a file whose elements are grouped together and not fragmented in separate locations on a disk. If a file is fragmented, it may not stream smoothly since the heads of the drive have to move around during transmission. Video files will drop frames on playback if they are not contiguous. To make all the files on a disk contiguous, execute the "defrag" command in MS-DOS, or "optimize" with a Macintosh utility.

continuous branching (n.) A feature of an interactive program that modifies the environment constantly in response to the user, rather than only at predetermined branching points or menus.

contrast (n.) The range between the darkest and brightest components in an image. Displays often provide hardware adjustments for controlling contrast, and scanners permit software controls. Adjusting contrast in a selective manner can make relatively light or dark areas of an image become visible while increasing detail.

control code (n.) One of the 32 ASCII codes reserved for issuing hardware control commands, such as advancing a printer page.

controller 1. (n.) Related to hardware, a processing component in a computer that controls the flow of data between the computer and peripheral devices. 2. (n.) The input device for a video game that moves and manipulates objects on the screen. A mouse is a controller for a computer with a graphical user interface.

control panel (n.) In a graphical user interface (GUI), this is a utility program that may be used to adjust parameters for system settings, such as volume, color, and rate of response to input devices.

control panel device See *CDEV*.

Control Program for Microcomputers See *CP/M*.

control track 1. (n.) A track on video recorders that is imprinted with pulses to set timing and align the tape with the recording and playback heads. 2. (n.) A rudimentary method of video positioning that counts pulses on the tape rather than reading time-stamped data that identifies the location of a frame.

convergence (n.) Alignment of the red, green, and blue light beams aimed at phosphors in a triad. The simultaneous firing of the red, green, and blue beams excites the three corresponding phosphors to generate the color white. Slight deviation of the beams due to magnetic misalignment of the electron trajectory causes colored shadows around pixels, and the beams have poor convergence. If the beams are perfectly aimed at the pixels on the screen, the monitor has good convergence.

Copper Distributed Data Interface See *CDDI*.

coprocessor (n.) Frequently referred to as a "math coprocessor," this chip is designed to rapidly execute floating point calculations and other mathematical functions. Many spreadsheets and CAD applications are constructed to take advantage of the presence of a coprocessor in a microcomputer's circuitry.

copyright (n.) The ownership rights to an idea, document, graphic, sound, or other reproducible event or object. This right belongs to the creator unless creation is done under a work-for-hire contract. A copyright may be transferred to another party, or it may be licensed with limitations or contractual conditions.

copy stand (n.) A table or flat surface with a photographic or video camera stationed overhead. Lamps are mounted on the sides to brightly illuminate an image or object placed on the stand, which is the focal point of the camera.

CORBA (n.) Common Object Request Broker Architecture; a network architecture in which clients send messages to objects, and the object performs the requested service.

core (n.) In fiber optics, the center part of an optical waveguide through which light passes. In single-mode fiber, the core diameter is 8–12 microns, while in multimode fiber the diameter may range up to 100 microns.

corrupted data (n.) Data that has lost its integrity and is partially damaged. The loss of any data can cause an entire file to become corrupted and can render it unreadable.

cost per megabyte (n.) A measure of the price for each megabyte of usable storage received. The common formula is to divide the cost of the drive and/or the cost of the media by the number of megabytes. This measure alone ignores performance, which is a more significant factor in evaluating storage devices.

courseware (n.) The aggregate of discs, books, illustrations, tapes, and computer programs required for the delivery of an instructional module. The name implies that there is a software component.

C++ (n.) An advanced, object-oriented version of the C language developed by Bjarne Stroustrup in 1982.

CP/M (n.) Control Program for Microcomputers; a specific microcomputer operating system developed by Digital Research Incorporated.

CPU (n.) Central processing unit; the primary computing device, or the brain of a computer system in which data is manipulated and calculations take place. Physically, it consists of a single microprocessor chip.

CR (n.) Carriage return; a control character in ASCII or EBCDIC that positions the cursor at the left margin.

crawl (n.) The steady, controlled display of text, horizontally or vertically. Rolling credits at the end of a movie is an example of text crawl. Sometimes the term is used as slang to describe thin undulating lines along the edge of a video monitor that appear to "crawl" like a snake.

CRC (n.) Cyclic redundancy check; an error-detection scheme in reading, writing, or transmitting data. The value of the CRC character in a block of data received must match the value transmitted.

crop (v.) To cut off one or more sides of an image to make it smaller or to eliminate unneccessary material.

cross-hatching (n.) A method of filling or shading an area of a graphic with evenly spaced intersecting lines. *See illustration on following page.*

Cross-Interleaved Reed Solomon Code See *CIRC*.

cross-hatching

cross-platform (n.) The capacity of software to run on different operating systems and hardware. Cross-platform development means that assets are captured or prepared on a different platform than the one on which they are delivered.

crosstalk (n.) Undesirable sound that bleeds into a connection or into an isolated audio track from an adjacent track on a tape. On an optical disc, the adjacent track data picked up by the laser head as it attempts to hold the desired signal track being played, possibly caused by inaccurate focus or a warped disc.

CRT (n.) Cathode-ray tube; a graphic display that produces an image by directing a beam of electrons to activate a phosphor-coated surface in a vacuum tube, used by television and video monitors.

CSMA/CD (n.) Carrier sense multiple access with collision detection; a network protocol.

CTS (n.) Clear To Send; a control signal used in a switched half-duplex circuit in an RS-232 modem interface to notify the computer that it has line control. In a full-duplex circuit, this is a constant signal.

C2 (n.) A Reed-Solomon Code that corrects burst errors and detects other errors.

CUA Architecture (n.) Common User Access Architecture; developed by IBM, this is the style of user interface used in OS/2 and Microsoft Windows.

cue (n.) An identifying element placed in the vertical blanking interval of video. Frame numbers, picture codes, chapter codes, flags, and closed captions are examples.

cue inserter (n.) A specialized device used in conjunction with videodisc mastering equipment to identify the field in which the frame ID code should be placed when recording from video. It places cues in the vertical blanking interval of the master tape for transfer to disc.

cue, still (n.) A signal in the vertical blanking interval of a master tape that identifies a still frame on a videodisc.

CUI Character user interface; an interface in which only characters are displayed on the screen, as opposed to graphics in a graphical user interface (GUI).

cursor (n.) An image, arrow, or an I-beam on a computer screen that shows where information may be entered or the location of a mouse or light pen on the screen. It may be represented by any icon.

cut 1. (n.) In audio and video, the term often refers to a segment or scene taken from a production. 2. (v.) In video editing, to change scenes abruptly without the use of a transition.

cut-and-paste (n.) The process of repositioning a segment of a document or an image to another location on screen, to another document, or to a file created by a completely different application from the source of the segment. Clips are usually stored on the "clipboard" during this process.

cybernetics (n.) The study of nervous systemcontrols in the brain, compared to information processing and communications technologies.

cyberspace (n.) An environment made possible by computers that is designed for exploration and communication with both data structures and other humans.

cyclic redundancy check See *CRC*.

cylinder (n.) In reference to a hard disk, a vertical stack of platters with aligned tracks.

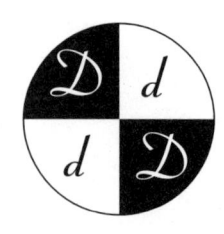

D/A (adj.) Digital-to-analog; a circuit that interprets data representing changes in motion, pressure, or light over time and converts that data into changing voltages over time.

DA (n.) Distribution amplifier; in video post-production, a device that is used to deliver a signal to multiple receiving devices.

DAC (n.) Digital-to-analog converter; a microprocessor chip or circuit that converts numerical data represented by a string of discrete numbers into analog information represented in continuous form, such as a signal that speakers may render into sound.

daisy chain (v.) To link several personal computer peripherals to a single CPU. In a more general sense, it refers to connecting electronic devices in a series.

daisy-wheel printer (n.) An impact printer that prints individual letters arranged around the edge of a disk that serves as the print head. The disk resembles a daisy with many petals or a wheel with spokes. *See illustration.*

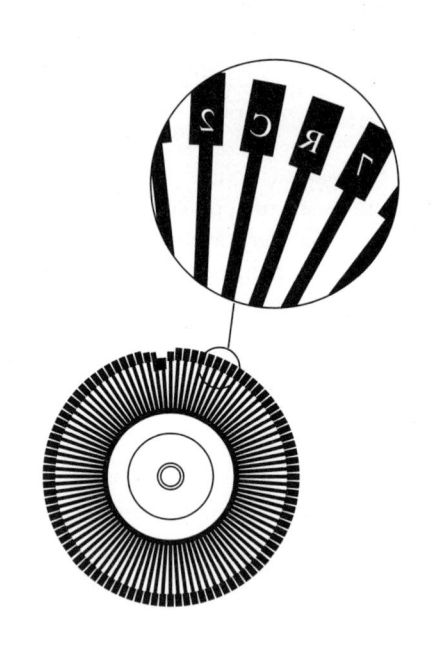

daisy wheel from a printer

DAT (n.) Digital audio tape; a professional-quality audio format developed by Sony. It records and plays back digital audio on magnetic tape cassettes that are smaller than common audio cassettes. Because of their high signal-to-noise ratios, DAT tapes often are used as masters. The signal-to-noise ratio of DAT tape far exceeds that of analog tape. The recording time for a single DAT tape may be as long as 120 minutes.

data (n.) Digital information processed and produced by computers; a collection of numerals, letters, and symbols that define something. The object defined could be an idea, document, image, condition, situation, or event.

data area (n.) According to ISO 9660, the space on a CD-ROM where user data is written, immediately after the "system area." It begins at 00:02:16 absolute time.

database (n.) A file of information assembled in an orderly manner by a program designed to record and manipulate the data. A telephone directory is an example of output from a database.

database management system See *DBMS*.

data bus (n.) Circuitry for transferring data between computer components, connecting the I/O ports, memory, drive controllers, the microprocessor, and other parts of the system. See *bus*.

data capture (n.) A process by which analog material is read, often by an optical sensor, and converted to digital data that can be processed by a computer. The original captured content comes from a graphic, video, or text source. In audio applications, the capture device is a sampler. To capture data is to digitize it.

data channel (n.) The path through which data travels between the input/output devices and computer memory. More than one I/O operation may be performed concurrently, and the flow of information is bidirectional.

data encryption standard See *DES*.

Data Exchange Format See *DXF*.

data glove (n.) A specialized input device that senses the position of a user's hand and then manipulates objects in a virtual reality scenario in a manner that corresponds to the hand movements.

datalink layer (n.) The second lowest layer in the ISO model responsible for assembling and disassembling data packets sent over a network.

data rate (n.) The speed at which data flows; it is often a critical measurement when dealing with streams of audio or video information that require high bandwidth and must not be interrupted.

data set (n.) Synonym for modem.

data suit (n.) A body suit with electrodes that is worn by a user when exploring a virtual world; an extension of the data glove idea.

data terminal equipment See *DTE*.

daughterboard (n.) An auxiliary circuit

DAVIC

board that plugs into a connector on a motherboard or adapter card and adds functionality.

DAVIC (n.) <u>D</u>igital <u>A</u>udio <u>V</u>isual <u>C</u>ouncil; an international group of approximately 250 companies developing an "End-to-End" standard for Interactive Digital Media including interfaces and requirements for applications, systems, and networks. The group includes members of the original MPEG/JTC.

dB <u>D</u>eci<u>b</u>el; 1. (n.) In acoustics, a unit used to measure the amplitude of sound. 2. (n.) In audio engineering, a unit that expresses the difference in intensity between two signals. In 1939, the electronics industry adopted a standard value for zero dB—a one milliwatt reference signal at 1000 hertz (Hz) in a 600-ohm line. This .001-watt reference, known as "dBm," represents a level of 0.7746 volts. Doubling or halving the power of a signal represents a 3-dB difference. An order of magnitude power difference is equal to 10 dB.

DB connector (n.) A data bus hardware link that is available in a variety of configurations. The initials DB are followed by a number that indicates how many pins, or wires, may be connected. Common types of connectors are the DB-9, DB-15, DB-19, DB-25, DB-37, and DB-50. Standards have been established that define pin assignments to ensure compatibility among hardware manufacturers. *See illustration.*

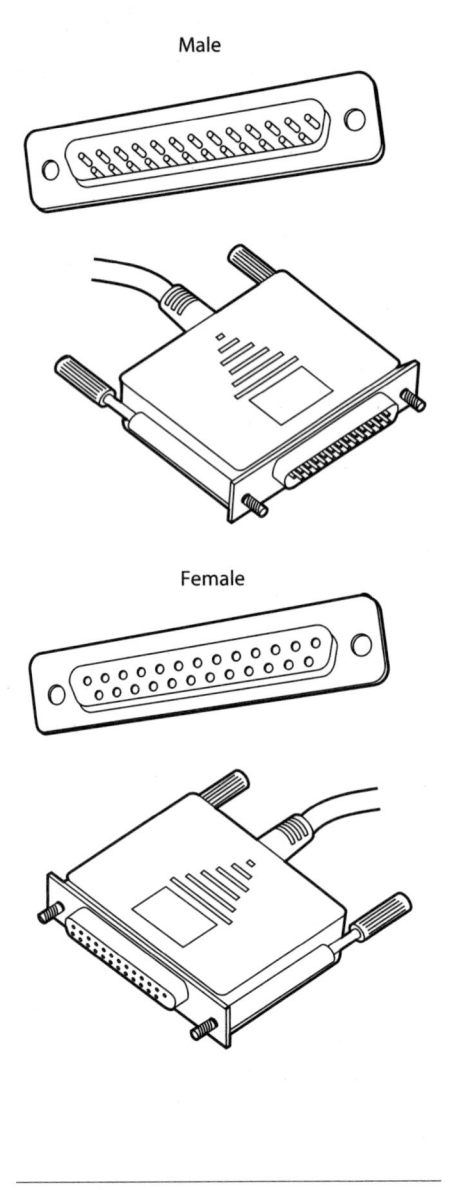

Male

Female

DB connectors

DBMS (n.) Database management system; a program that organizes information in a database and defines access privileges.

DB-9 plug (n.) A 9-pin RS-232-C serial port on an IBM-compatible computer.

DCC 1. (n.) Data Communication Channel. 2. (n.) Digital compact cassette; developed by Philips, this audio medium employs a proprietary recording scheme that uses specially designed tapes. DCC decks will play conventional analog cassettes, but they can make digital recordings on special tapes only.

DCE 1. (n.) Data communications equipment; an intermediary device in a serial RS-232-C communication system that receives, modulates, and parses a signal. 2. (n.) Data circuit-terminating equipment; the terminal device in an RS-232-C data communication system.

D-channel (n.) The channel that carries control signals and call data in a packet-switched mode via an ISDN interface. It typically operates at 16 kilobits per second (Kbps) over a Basic Rate Interface, with 9600 bits per second available for a voice link.

DCI (n.) Display Control Interface; in an IBM-compatible computer video system, an enhancement that moves graphic data directly to the video card and bypasses the processor.

DCT (n.) Discrete cosine transform; a video encoding technique that is similar to Fourier transform, a method of representing a two-dimensional audio signal with a reduced data set. DCT uses the same approach to reduce the data required to represent color or gray-scale levels in video signal, applying equations that require very few pieces of information to identify the content.

DCT coefficients (n.) In video capture, an 8 × 8 block sample is translated into 64 two-dimensional spatial frequencies that define the spectrum of the input signal. The output amplitudes of these signals are DCT coefficients. The value of each coefficient is defined by the 64-point input signal and can be regarded as the relative amount of the 2-D spatial frequencies contained in the signal. The coefficient with zero frequency in both dimensions is the DC coefficient, and the remaining ones are AC coefficients.

DDE (n.) Dynamic Data Exchange; an exchange format that allows two or more programs running simultaneously in Microsoft Windows or OS/2 to communicate with one another. Multitasking is enhanced by the use of programs that can take advantage of this access to data across applications.

DDP 1. (n.) Digital data processor; an example is Sony's SFA/DDP standard. 2. (n.) Distributed data processing; the use of more than one networked computer to run an application at multiple sites simultaneously.

DDR (n.) Digital disk recorder; post-production studios often use DDRs to record frames of video or animation since they have hardware that is capable of capturing a large field of data at once. Abekas is a popular brand of DDR.

DDS (n.) Digital dataphone service; a telecommunications network that typically transmits synchronous data at 56 kilobits per second (Kbps) requiring special interface equipment at both ends.

debug (v.) To isolate and correct errors or malfunctions in computer software or hardware.

DEC (n.) Digital Equipment Corporation; makers of the VAX computer and VMS operating system.

decibel See *dB*.

decimate (v.) To discard portions of a signal for the purpose of reducing the amount of information to be encoded or compressed. Lossy compression algorithms ordinarily decimate while subsampling.

decoder (n.) Any hardware or software system that translates data streams into video or audio information.

decompression (n.) The process of restoring compressed data to its original condition.

decrement (v.) To decrease incrementally, or reduce by a single step.

dedicated (adj.) Describes any computing system that performs one function exclusively.

default (n.) The standard setting of an optional parameter. Factory defaults are the original settings for most equipment.

defragment (v.) To place all data on a hard disk in contiguous sectors, avoiding gaps between parts of a file or pieces of files spread geographically on the disk. When digitizing audio or video direct to disk, the disk must be defragmented so that a continuous stream of data may be recorded to the disk.

degauss (v.) To remove a magnetic field.

delimiter (n.) Any character or symbol that marks the beginning or end of a data segment.

delivery system (n.) The combined hardware and software used to present or play back media, whether it be audio, video, text, images, or a combination of data types, in an interactive environment.

delta modulation (n.) A process for the conversion of analog audio to digital form, similar to pulse code modulation (PCM). It is the sampling of an audio signal at 32 kilobits per second (Kbps) at 1-bit resolution, as opposed to creating eight each 8-bit samples per second in PCM at the rate of 64 Kbps.

delta YUV See *DYUV*.

demo reel (n.) An audio or videotape with samples of a performer's work.

demonstration right (n.) The right to publicly display a copyrighted work. Contractors who create work for hire can preserve these rights for the purpose of showing their work to prospective clients.

density (n.) Related to computing, the degree to which data is spatially distributed on a storage medium. Higher density indicates more compact storage.

depth cueing (n.) In three-dimensional graphics creation, a process that results in the illusion that objects fade into the distance.

dequantization (n.) The reverse process of quantization. Quantization maps many points to one point, and information lost in that mapping cannot be completely recovered in dequantization.

derivative product (n.) A work that adapts material from a previous creation. The original creator owns and may license the rights to derivative products.

DES (n.) Data encryption standard; a security scheme for data communications specified by Federal Information Processing Systems (FIPS) publication 46 and approved by the National Bureau of Standards (NBS).

desktop (n.) In graphical user interfaces, the background screen on which icons and menus appear.

desktop computer (n.) A microcomputer that physically fits on top of a desk. Desktop systems have become popular for publishing and audio/video production due to the miniaturization and proliferation of peripherals.

desktop publishing (n.) (DTP) A broad term for the use of a microcomputer with software to create text and graphics for print. Desktop publishing implies the use of page layout programs.

desktop video (n.) The processes of creating, editing, producing, or viewing video on microcomputer systems.

Deutsche Industrie Norm See *DIN*.

developer (n.) A person or company that creates an entertaining or educational product, such as a game or a reference CD-ROM.

device driver (n.) A software program that controls data transfer between a computer and peripheral device, such as a printer, CD-ROM, or cartridge drive. It may control internal system features, such as digital video or audio playback.

device-independent bitmap See *DIB*.

diagnostics 1. (n.) Procedures for evaluating software and hardware performance with the objective of troubleshooting computer systems. 2. (n.) An application that automates the scheduled maintenance and repair of complex systems.

dialog (n.) A question/answer session between an operator and a computer program that occurs in a "dialog box" where the user chooses an option or enters data. Continuing interaction between an operator and technology is called a dialog.

dial-up (n.) Any line or connection that can be addressed by modem and is established by a switched-circuit connection using the telephone system.

DIB (n.) Device-independent bitmap; a file format used for 256-color bitmapped graphics in Microsoft Windows.

die (n.) A rectangular piece of semiconductor material onto which electronic circuits have been fabricated; any semiconductor not yet packaged.

differential phase-shift keying See *DPSK*.

digital (adj.) Describes anything that uses a set of discrete numerical values to represent data or signals, as opposed to a continuously fluctuating flow of current or voltage, which is analogous to the data it represents. A computer processes digital data that may represent text, sound, pictures, animations, or video content.

digital audio (n.) Audio program material that is represented by binary code rather than by an analog recording. Analog audio is converted to digital using sampling techniques that store a numerical definition of the signal. Higher sampling rates and bit rates result in a more accurate digital representation of the signal. In order to reproduce digital audio, a D/A converter is required.

digital audio tape See *DAT*.

Digital Audio Visual Council See *DAVIC*.

digital compact cassette See *DCC*.

digital compositing (n.) The art of combining video frames as digital rather than as analog signals. This allows computer images to be applied to video frames. Most current offline systems incorporate digital video frames and animations.

digital data processor See *DDP*.

digital disk recorder See *DDR*.

Digital Equipment Corporation See *DEC*.

Digital Multiplexed Interface See *DMI*.

digital satellite system See *DSS*.

digital service (n.) Refers to what a telephone company calls a telecommunications line for data transmission that has rates of data transfer specified at predetermined levels. Examples of the common transfer rates for various levels of service are shown in the following list:

DS-0	64 kilobits per second (Kbps), standard speed for one channel.
DS-1	1.544 megabits per second (Mbps) in North America, 2.048Mbps everywhere else in the world.

DS-1C   3.152 Mbps in North America, over T-1.
DS-2   6.312 Mbps in North America, over T-2.
DS-3   44.736 Mbps, equal to 28 T-1 channels, over T-3.
DS-4   273 Mbps, over a T-4 facility.

digital signal processor See *DSP*.

digital subscriber line See *DSL*.

digital-to-analog converter See *DAC*.

digital video (n.) A video signal represented by binary digits that describe a set of colors and luminance levels which can be converted to moving pictures in the analog domain. Factors that define digital video are resolution (i.e., 240 × 320 pixels), color bit depth (i.e., 8-, 16-, or 24-bit), and frame rate (i.e., 15, 25, or 30 frames per second).

digital video cassette See *DVC*.

digital video disc See *DVD*.

digital video interactive See *DVI*.

digitize (v.) To encode images or sound in a format that may be processed by a computer; to convert analog information, such as an audio signal, into data.

DIMM (n.) Dual in-line memory module; a high-density RAM package, similar to a SIMM, but with dual rather than single connections to the motherboard.

DIN (n.) Deutsche Industrie Norm; a type of connecting plug and mating socket with numerous pins that enable more than one function or channel to be handled by a single connector. A MIDI cable has a 5-pin DIN plug on each end.

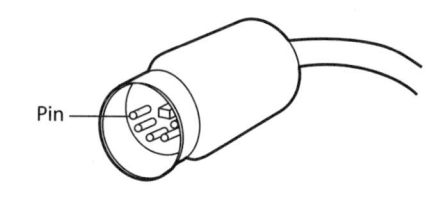

5-pin DIN plug

DIP switch (n.) Dual in-line package switch; a miniature two-position switch mounted on a circuit board to set parameters or control functions.

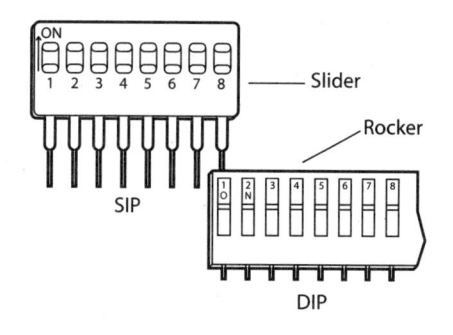

surface mount switches

direct data entry See *DDE*.

Direct Draw (n.) A graphics feature of Windows 95 that permits rapid calls to the display, rather than routing them through the graphical device interface.

direct memory access See *DMA*.

directory (n.) A listing of information about data files and their locations on a storage medium. In the logical format of a disk or a disc, this "branch" of the information tree contains other directories (subdirectories) and/or files.

directory service (n.) Networking software that has the capacity to provide information about resources available on the network, including files, printers, data sources, applications, or other users. It provides users with access to resources and information on extended networks.

Direct3D (n.) The name for the three-dimensional API that is part of the DirectX package for multimedia applications. Direct3D was developed by Microsoft.

DirectTV (n.) A dish receiver and decoding system that receives television channels via satellite transmission, rather than by cable.

disc (n.) Any thin, round platter that stores various types of information in analog or digital formats. It is often used as the short form for CD-ROM, laser disc (analog videodisc), or compact audio disc (CD-A). The data is written in a spiral from the center to the edge. Data on a disc is read by an optical sensor that picks up reflections from a laser beam.

disc geography (n.) The relative location of files, applications, or media assets and data on discs. Closer proximity of related segments results in faster access time *See illustration.*

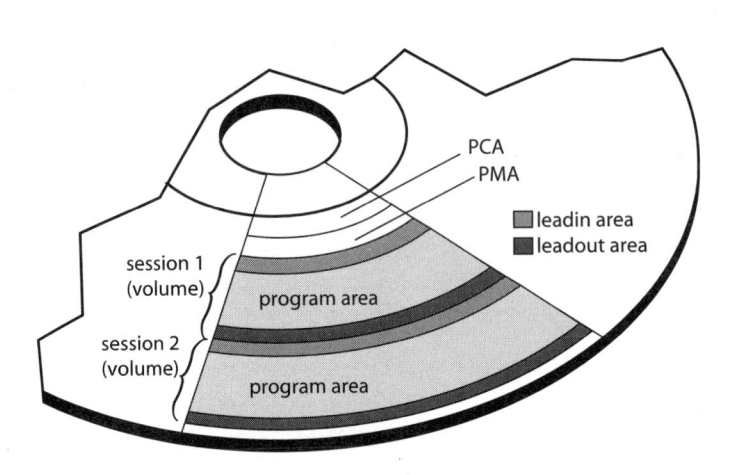

geography of a multisession disc

discrete (adj.) In digital applications, describes separate and distinct pieces of data, each of which may be part of a larger stream of information.

discrete access (n.) In network technology, an access method that requires each workstation to have a separate, individual connection to the host.

discrete cosine transform See *DCT*.

discrete wavelet transformation See *DWT*.

disk (n.) A circular, enclosed magnetic storage medium on which information may be accessed randomly, as opposed to sequentially. Floppy disks are small, portable storage vehicles; hard disks, or fixed disks, are capable of storing more data.

disk cache (n.) A segment of RAM that is allocated to speed up access to data on a disk drive. It holds a copy of recently read data from the disk, including sector information, anticipating that it will be needed again soon.

disk mirroring (n.) The process of writing a pair of disks simultaneously, providing a mirror-image backup if one disk fails. Both disks attach to a host controller.

Disk Operating System See *DOS*.

disk spanning (n.) The method of attaching multiple drives to a single host adapter whereby all of the drives appear as a single contiguous logical unit.

disk striping (n.) The writing of data across multiple disks rather than on one drive. Data is divided into segments, each of which is written to successive drives.

display (n.) A video monitor device, or cathode-ray tube (CRT), that presents numbers, characters, graphics, video, or any other visual information.

Display Control Interface See *DCI*.

display order (n.) The order in which digital video frames should be shown. It is usually the same as the order of input to encoder.

dissolve (n.) The gradual disintegration of a video image, or a means of transition to another frame. Fade outs and fade ins are examples of dissolves to and from a black screen. Dissolves between two video clips require two source VCRs in an A/B-roll configuration.

distance learning (n.) Any learning that occurs at a site other than the classroom where an instructor is located. The transmission of satellite or cable television courses for education and training is often associated with the term. The meaning has expanded to encompass many training activities and other technologies. It is assumed that guidance and course work are specified by an instructional program—that the activity is structured and not self-motivated independent study without external influence.

Other terms for this type of education are flexible learning, student-based learning, and student-centered learning. The latter is particularly accurate, in that it identifies the location of the student as the learning site. It is common for student-centered learning activities to occur on a campus where classroom activities are enhanced by network access and other learning technologies that are accessed by students in a library or computer lab.

distortion (n.) Related to audio, any alteration in a given waveform, resulting in frequencies at the output of a signal processing device that were not present at input. It typically occurs when a signal is digitally processed or amplified.

distributed file system (n.) A file system that accesses data from remote locations across a network. It recognizes multiple servers, manages itself, and can be accessed from any location on the network.

distribution amplifier See *DA*.

dithering (n.) A form of smart conversion from a higher bit depth to a lower bit depth used in audio and graphic files. The process attempts to improve the perceived quality of onscreen graphics when the color palette is reduced. In the conversion from 24-bit color to 8-bit color (millions of colors reduced to 256), dithering adds patterns of different colored pixels to simulate the original color. The technique is also known as "error diffusion" and is applied to both audio bit rate reduction and graphic resolution.

dithered image

DLL (n.) Dynamic-link library; a feature of Microsoft Windows that loads and links pieces of code when called upon.

DMA (n.) Direct memory access; in computing, the process of moving data to and from memory without routing it through the central processing unit.

DMA channel (n.) A logical pathway in a microcomputer for exchanging data between peripherals and memory or just between peripherals without passing the data through the central processing unit (CPU).

DMI (n.) Digital Multiplexed Interface; a voice and data PABX standard for the use of T1 transmission with 64-kilobit per second (Kbps) channels, allowing a more open ISDN architecture.

DNS (n.) Domain name service; software running on an Internet server that

domain name service

translates between domain names and IP addresses. Referred to as resolution, the translation enables users to keep their domain name even though the IP address of the server could change.

documentation (n.) Materials, such as an instruction manual, that explain how to operate software or hardware. There is a trend toward putting documentation online.

Document Type Definition See *DTD*.

dolby (n.) A process that increases the signal-to-noise ratio by raising the volume of quiet passages during recording and lowering them to their original levels during playback. The lowering reduces noise, such as tape hiss, that may be introduced during recording. *See illustration.*

domain (n.) In an Internet address, the part of the naming hierarchy that consists of a sequence of characters separated by dots. The four most common types of domains are .com for company, .org for nonprofit organization, .edu for educational institution, and .gov for government agency. The domains are administrated by InterNIC, and each has a primary and secondary domain name server associated with it. The primary DNS is located on a machine in the associated network, and the server may be determined through the "nslookup" command.

domain name service See *DNS*.

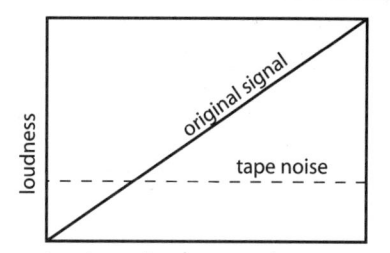

Loud sounds overpower the inherent noise and hiss on an audio tape. However, during soft passages the noise is much stronger in relation to the signal.

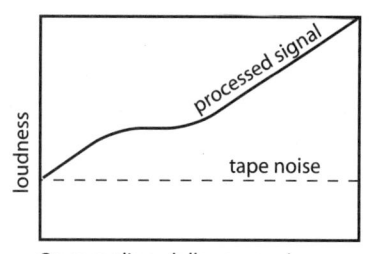

On recording, dolby processing increases the level of quiet sounds in the high-frequency range, but it does not alter loud sounds.

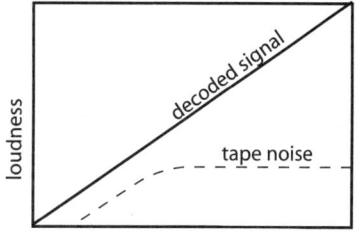

On playback the tape noise is reduced along with all the high-frequency quiet sounds that are restored to their original levels in the decoding process.

dolby signal processing

domestic market (n.) The consumer market in a particular country or geographic area, as opposed to the industrial or professional markets.

D1 (n.) Developed by the Society of Motion Picture and Television Engineers, this component-digital videotape format is a professional recording standard based on the CCIR-601 recommendation. It separates the signal into two color channels and one brightness channel (Y, R-Y, B-Y). Multiple copies may be dubbed without noticeable loss of quality in successive generations using this tape format, which is 19 mm wide and holds up to 94 minutes of program material.

dongle 1. (n.) Jargon for "server key," a small piece of hardware connected to the serial port that permits a secure application to run. 2. (n.) An adapter or connector used to interface video monitors or peripherals.

DOS (n.) <u>D</u>isk <u>O</u>perating <u>S</u>ystem; a computing environment designed for use with a floppy or hard disk. It permits data to be transferred between a computer's memory and disk storage. "DOS" usually refers to the Microsoft Disk Operating System (MS-DOS) designed for the IBM Personal Computer and compatibles.

DOSKey (n.) A utility program that permits a user to customize MS-DOS commands, create stored macros, type more than one DOS command on a line, and personalize the computing environment.

dot matrix 1. (n.) A two-dimensional pattern of dots that defines graphic elements. 2. (adj.) (*dot-matrix*) Describes a type of computer printer that uses pins to print dots on paper. The combined dots form text characters and graphic images.

dot pitch 1. (n.) The smallest distance between adjacent points of color on a monitor. A small dot pitch means that the image is sharp.

dots per inch See *dpi*.

double buffering (n.) The process of writing a graphical frame into memory at the same time that another frame is being displayed. It allows smoother transitions between frames in an animation.

double-speed (adj.) Describes second-generation CD-ROM drives that transfer data at twice the rate of earlier drives. They are usually capable of a sustained rate of approximately 300 kilobytes per second (KBps).

downlink 1. (n.) A transmission link from a satellite to an earth station. 2. (v.) To receive signals from a satellite broadcast with a microwave dish.

downsample (v.) To reduce the amount of data in a stream by selecting only certain pieces of the original content.

downstream (n.) The direction a signal travels from the transmitter, or origination point, to the receiving site.

downward compatible (adj.) Describes software that is capable of being used on older computing systems. It is the capacity to read files created with an earlier version of a software application.

dpi (n.) Dots per inch; a measurement of resolution that defines the output of a display or printer. A screen font usually appears at 72 dpi, while a laser printer usually prints at 300 dpi minimally.

DPSK (n.) Differential phase-shift keying; a modulation technique used in modems.

drag-and-drop (adj.) Describes a feature of Microsoft Windows 95 and the Macintosh OS that permits users to perform functions by dragging icons or selections around the screen with the mouse button down, and dropping them by releasing the button while the icon is over a folder or application. The procedure also applies to moving text blocks in a word-processing program.

DRAM (n.) Dynamic random-access memory; a type of memory component in which the memory cells require periodical recharging. Information that is stored in the memory cells as positive or negative charges may be accessed randomly. It consists of an integrated circuit (IC) that uses a charged capacitor.

Drawing Interchange Format See *DXF*.

drawing program (n.) A program that produces graphical objects rather than bitmaps, which are created by paint programs. Drawing programs use mathematical formulas to define lines that can be scaled and resized without distortion.

drift (n.) Unwanted motion in horizontal lines of video caused when an electronic component, such as a capacitor, becomes unstable and the image scrolls up slowly.

drill-down map (n.) A series of progressively more detailed graphics that serves to enlarge an area of a map or larger image. An example is an interactive city map that displays a neighborhood when the user clicks on it. A subsequent click might show a square mile in an area of the neighborhood; a click on that map might bring up a square block.

drive (n.) Any hardware component of a computer system that spins and reads floppy disks, fixed disks, tapes, CD-ROMs, laser discs, or other media.

drive letter (n.) A letter of the alphabet used to identify a disk drive or peripheral connected to a microcomputer. The primary hard drive is generally called the "C" drive, floppies are usually "A" and "B," and a CD-ROM might be "D."

driver (n.) A software control program that integrates with the computer operating system to give instructions to and interface with a device such as a CD-ROM player or a video card.

drop-down menu (n.) A window that

pops up below a topic selected from the menu bar, offering additional choices or functions.

drop frame (n.) A time code format for video that periodically skips a pulse to account for the difference between the 30 frames per second (fps) standard and the actual 29.97 fps rate found in the NTSC format. Correction for this inconsistency is accomplished by dropping two frames each minute, except on frames that are multiples of ten.

drop-out (n.) The temporary loss of signal, either in data transmission or from an analog tape playback device. By technical telephony standards, a period of at least 4 milliseconds during which a signal has dropped more than 12 decibels.

drop shadow (n.) A graphic effect used with typefaces that creates the illusion of a light source shining on an object or a letter from above so that a shadow appears to be cast behind and below.

drum scanner (n.) A data-capturing device that incorporates a cylindrical drum for mounting original images.

DSL (n.) Digital subscriber line; a twisted-pair copper wire connection with a special modem at either end that filters out background noise and interference and allows high-speed data transfer. It is limited to a transmission distance of 18 000 feet. ISDN is a DSL application with transfer rates of 160 kilobits per second (Kbps), compared to the peak rate of 33.4 Kbps that analog modems can achieve. Typically, high data-rate DSL (HDSL) is used to implement T1 connections. The Asynchronous DSL (ADSL) application is a further advance in this technology, since it supports up to 9 megabits per second (Mbps) throughput, compared to the maximum of 2.048 Mbps handled by ISDN.

DSP (n.) Digital signal processor; an integrated circuit that performs complex operations on data. The data that is processed is usually an audio signal in the form of a digitized waveform. Effects processors perform functions such as digital delay, reverb, filtering, equalization, and stereo chorusing. The term is not limited to audio processing and applies to the treatment of video and other data types.

DSS (n.) Digital satellite system; marketed to consumers as an alternative to cable television, a satellite receiving system with a small dish about 18 inches in diameter that can be used to tune in a wide range of microwave frequencies.

DTD (n.) Document Type Definition; a refinement of the SGML designed by Tim Berners-Lee and Dan Connolly to identify the unique features of HTML.

DTE (n.) Data terminal equipment; any computers or other devices that send and receive data and are connected to modems or other data communications equipment (DCE). The designation as either DCT or DCE determines the role of the device on the network.

D3 format (n.) The telecommunications Digital Service level 1 format with 24 8-bit channels, each of which has a bandwidth of 8 kilohertz (kHz). Its data rate of 1.544 megabits per second (Mbps) is an old Bell System standard in North America, not the CCITT standard of 2.048 Mbps used elsewhere.

D2 format (n.) A digital videotape composite format for mastering that permits multiple generations of dubbing without apparent loss of picture quality. It is based on an 8-bit digital version of NTSC or PAL composite video. Since it is composite, it does not have the pristine quality of D1, which is component digital. The tape itself is 19 mm wide and can record up to 208 minutes of programming.

dual-channel audio (n.) A system that possesses two audio channels and is capable of playing them simultaneously or independently.

dual in-line memory module See *DIMM*.

dual in-line package switch See *DIP switch*.

dub 1. (v.) To copy a tape, producing a second generation. 2. (v.) To copy and combine visual and/or audio elements on an existing tape to produce a composite, mixed master tape.

dump 1. (v.) To transfer digital data from one source to another 2. (v.) To remove data or to empty a container.

duplex (adj.) Describes a transmission line capable of two-way communication in both directions simultaneously.

DVC (n.) Digital video cassette; this video storage medium uses .25-inch metal tape with a digital format similar to CCIR-601, combined with an adapted form of JPEG compression.

DVD (n.) Digital video disc; a second-generation compact disc developed by Toshiba, Sony, Philips, and several other leading manufacturers. The medium consists of a double-sided disc that holds 4.2 gigabytes (GB). High quantities of data and low transfer times are made possible by the use of a red laser beam, which has a shorter wave length. Several hours of high-quality digital video compressed in the MPEG-2 format may be stored on a single disc.

DVI (n.) Digital video interactive; developed by RCA's David Sarnoff Research Center and subsequently purchased and marketed by Intel Corporation, this technology allows real-time compression/decompression and display of full-motion video with audio using hardware assistance on desktop computers. The highest video quality, production level video, or PLV, is achieved by using offline, non real-time compression on powerful parallel processing computers. Lesser-quality real-time video (RTV) compression may be achieved on a desktop computer. Although the quality of DVI is high and it is capable of 100:1 compression ratios, the proprietary hardware decoder board is not in widespread use, nor is it expected to be a platform of future development.

Dvorak keyboard (n.) A keyboard layout designed for speed. The most commonly used letters in the English language are positioned on the center row of keys. It was designed in the 1930s by August Dvorak and William Dealy.

Dvorak keyboard

DWT (n.) Discrete wavelet transformation; a video compression algorithm in which spatial data is converted to frequency data and assigned to quadrants.

DXF (n.) Drawing Interchange Format; a format for CAD programming files developed by Autodesk for its AutoCAD program. It is platform-independent and is also called "Data Exchange Format."

dye polymer See *polymer*.

dynamic data exchange See *DDE*.

dynamic filtering (n.) A process that eliminates the electronic emissions of a computing system that are picked up by sensitive circuitry and can appear as noise in the sound board output.

dynamic-link library See *DLL*.

dynamic microphone (n.) A microphone that converts an acoustical signal into an electrical signal by using a coil moving in a magnetic field. This type of microphone is generally less sensitive than a condenser microphone.

dynamic random-access memory See *DRAM*.

dynamic range (n.) In an audio program, the difference between the lowest and the highest levels of amplitude, or loudness, expressed in decibels.

dynamic storage allocation (n.) While a program that uses storage space is running, this process reserves space for data that it may generate and store in allocated blocks.

DYUV (n.) Delta YUV; this digital video compression format measures the differences between adjacent pixels, rather than differences between consecutive frames. If the contrast between adjacent pixels is high, definition is lost. CD-i employs DYUV compression. Since normal vision is less sensitive to color than to intensity, DYUV encodes luminance (Y) information at full bandwidth and chrominance (UV) information at half bandwidth, then stores the difference, or delta, between adjacent values.

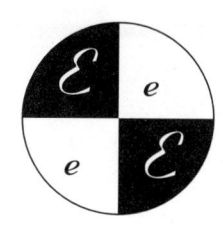

Easter egg (n.) An often humorous message buried in an application by its programmers with no documented access.

EBCDIC (n.) Extended Binary-Coded Decimal Interchange Code. Code that is capable of identifying 256 8-bit characters, as opposed to the 128 character set available in ASCII code. (Pronounced eb-suh-dik.) *See table for examples.*

EBU (n.) European Broadcast Union; a group of organizations that work together to coordinate joint technical interests and advise on the establishment of standards.

EBU time code (n.) European Broadcast Union standard for time-stamping data on audio/videotape; similar to SMPTE time code.

Decimal	Hex	Acronym	Function
0	0	NUL	Null
1	1	SOH	Start of Heading
2	2	STX	Start of Text
3	3	ETX	End of Text
4	4	PF	Punch Off
5	5	HT	Horizontal Tab
6	6	LC	Lower Case
7	7	DEL	Delete
8	8		
9	9		
10	A	SMM	Start of Manual Message
11	B	VT	Vertical Tab
12	C	FF	Form Feed
13	D	CR	Carriage Return
14	E	SO	Shift Out
15	F	SI	Shift In
16	10	DLE	Data Link Escape

EBCDIC

Decimal	Hex	Acronym	Function
17	11	DC1	Device Control 1
18	12	DC2	Device Control 2
19	13	TM	Tape Mark
20	14	RES	Restore
21	15	NL	New Line
22	16	BS	Backspace
23	17	IL	Idle
24	18	CAN	Cancel
25	19	EM	End of Medium
26	1A	CC	Cursor Control
27	1B	CU1	Customer Use 1
28	1C	IFS	Interchange File Separator
29	1D	IGS	Interchange Group Separator
30	1E	IRS	Interchange Record Separator
31	1F	IUS	Interchange Unit Separator
32	20	DS	Digit Select
33	21	SOS	Start of Significance
34	22	FS	Field Separator
35	23		
36	24	BYP	Bypass
37	25	LF	Line Feed
38	26	ETB	End of Transmission Block
39	27	ESC	Escape
40	28		
41	29		
42	2A	SM	Set Mode
43	2B	CU2	Customer Use 2
44	2C		
45	2D	ENQ	Enquiry
46	2E	ACK	Acknowledge
47	2F	BEL	Bell
48	30		
49	31		
50	32	SYN	Synchronous idle
51	33		

EBCDIC

Decimal	Hex	Acronym	Function
52	34	PN	Punch On
53	35	RS	Reader Stop
54	36	UC	Upper Case
55	37	EOT	End of Transmission
56	38		
57	39		
58	3A		
59	3B	CU3	Customer Use 3
60	3C	DC4	Device Control 4
61	3D	NAK	Negative Acknowledge
62	3E		
63	3F	SUB	Substitute
64	40	SP	Space
65	41		
66	42		
67	43		
68	44		
69	45		
70	46		
71	47		
72	48		
73	49		
74	4A	¢	Cent Sign
75	4B		
76	4C	<	Less-than Sign
77	4D	)	Open Parenthesis
78	4E	+	Plus Sign
79	4F	|	Logical OR
80	50	&	Ampersand
81	51		
82	52		
83	53		
84	54		
85	55		
86	56		

EBCDIC

Decimal	Hex	Acronym	Function
87	57		
88	58		
89	59		
90	5A	!	Exclamation Mark
91	5B	$	Dollar Sign
92	5C	.	Period
93	5D	)	Close Parenthesis
94	5E	;	Semi-colon
95	5F		
96	60	-	Minus Sign, hyphen, dash
97	61	/	Slash
98	62		
99	63		
100	64		
101	65		
102	66		
103	67		
104	68		
105	69		
106	6A		
107	6B	,	Comma
108	6C	%	Percent Sign
109	6D	_	Underscore
110	6E	>	Greater-than Sign
111	6F	?	Question Mark
112	70		
113	71		
114	72		
115	73		
116	74		
117	75		
118	76		
119	77		
120	78		
121	79		

EBCDIC

Decimal	Hex	Acronym	Function
122	7A	:	Colon
123	7B	#	Number Sign
124	7C	@	At Sign
125	7D	'	Single Quote
126	7E	=	Equal Sign
127	7F	"	Double Quote
128	80		
129	81	a	
130	82	b	
131	83	c	
132	84	d	
133	85	e	
134	86	f	
135	87	g	
136	88	h	
137	89	i	
138	8A		
139	8B	{	Open Curly Bracket
140	8C		Bar
141	8D	}	Close Curly Bracket
142	8E	~	Tilde
143	8F		
144	90		
145	91	j	
146	92	k	
147	93	l	
148	94	m	
149	95	n	
150	96	o	
151	97	p	
152	98	q	
153	99	r	
154	9A		
155	9B		
156	9C		

EBCDIC

Decimal	Hex	Acronym	Function
157	9D		
158	9E		
159	9F		
160	A0		
161	A1		
162	A2	s	
163	A3	t	
164	A4	u	
165	A5	v	
166	A6	w	
167	A7	x	
168	A8	y	
169	A9	z	
170	AA		
171	AB		
172	AC		
173	AD		
174	AE		
175	AF		
176	B0		
177	B1		
178	B2		
179	B3		
180	B4		
181	B5		
182	B6		
183	B7		
184	B8		
185	B9		
186	BA		
187	BB		
188	BC		
189	BD		
190	BE		
191	BF		

EBCDIC

Decimal	Hex	Acronym	Function
192	C0		
193	C1	A	
194	C2	B	
195	C3	C	
196	C4	D	
197	C5	E	
198	C6	F	
199	C7	G	
200	C8	H	
201	C9	I	
202	CA		
203	CB		
204	CC		
205	CD		
206	CE		
207	CF		
208	D0		
209	D1	J	
210	D2	K	
211	D3	L	
212	D4	M	
213	D5	N	
214	D6	O	
215	D7	P	
216	D8	Q	
217	D9	R	
218	DA		
219	DB		
220	DC		
221	DD		
222	DE		
223	DF		
224	E0		
225	E1		
226	E2	S	

ECC

Decimal	Hex	Acronym	Function
227	E3	T	
228	E4	U	
229	E5	V	
230	E6	W	
231	E7	X	
232	E8	Y	
233	E9	Z	
234	EA		
235	EB		
236	EC		
237	ED		
238	EE		
239	EF		
240	F0	0	Zero
241	F1	1	One
242	F2	2	Two
243	F3	3	Three
244	F4	4	Four
245	F5	5	Five
246	F6	6	Six
247	F7	7	Seven
248	F8	8	Eight
249	F9	9	Nine
250	FA		
251	FB		
252	FC		
253	FD		
254	FE		
255	FF		

ECC (n.) Error correction code; in CD-ROM writing, a system of scrambling data and recording redundant data onto a disc as it is premastered. On playback, this redundant data helps detect and correct errors that arise during data transmission. See *block error correction*.

echo (n.) In telecommunications, the reflection of a signal back to the sending station.

EDAC (n.) Error detection and correction; an encoding technique that detects and corrects bit errors in digital data.

EDC (n.) Error detection code. On a CD-ROM, code that has 32 bits of information per sector. The code is used to detect errors in the data of the sector.

EDI (n.) Electronic Data Interchange; a networking protocol that allows encrypted data to be sent between two parties over the Internet securely.

edit 1. (v.) To connect audio or video segments from multiple media sources and create a master program tape. 2. (v.) To remove undesirable content from the source tape or file.

edit controller (n.) A complex system that controls the actions of video and audio recording or playback machines, positioning them at the appropriate points and changing modes as needed, to assemble an edited production.

edit decision list See *EDL*.

EDL (n.) Edit decision list; in an offline, nonlinear video editing process, a record of edits that is made with Society of Motion Picture and Television Engineers (SMPTE) beginning and ending frames identified. It consists of a series of entry points that are recorded in order to allow the user to recreate or modify a video program. It lists the time code where cuts are to be made and special effects introduced. The list can be logged from a window dub, an offline editing system, or a computer.

edutainment (n.) Entertaining and educational digital media products.

EEPROM (n.) Electronically erasable programmable read-only memory; a special type of PROM that can be erased with an electric current for reloading. See *PROM*.

EFM (n.) Eight-to-fourteen modulation; the process that turns each 8-bit byte of data into 14 "channel" bits during the mastering of a compact disc.

EGA (n.) Enhanced Graphics Adapter; an IBM Personal Computer display adapter that supports 16 colors from a palette of 64 colors at 640 × 350 pixels.

EHF (n.) Extremely high frequency; in the 30–300 gigahertz (GHz) range.

EIA (n.) Electronics Industries Association; the recommendations of the EIA are identified by the prefix "RS-", as in RS-232 and RS-422.

EIAJ (n.) Electronics Industries Association of Japan.

EIDE (n.) Enhanced integral drive electronics; a controller for up to four storage devices connected to a computer.

EIDS (n.) Electronic Information Delivery System; a microcomputer- and videodisc-based A/V training system, contracted by the United States Army in November 1986 as the Army-designated standard stand-alone CBT system. EIDS refers to both the hardware configuration, provided by Matrox Electronics under the initial contract, and the standard for courseware (i.e., EIDS-compatible). With 14 000 units installed, EIDS is the largest videodisc implementation.

8-bit audio (n.) The process of using an 8-bit sample to digitize and play back sound. The quality is inferior to 16-bit samples. It is adequate for speech but relatively useless for music. The other factor that significantly impacts audio quality, in addition to the bit depth, is the frequency at which the sound is sampled. Common frequencies are 11.025, 22.050, 44.1, and 48 kilobits per second (Kbps).

8-bit color (n.) A monitor setting that allocates 8 bits of memory to each pixel and yields up to 256 different colors simultaneously.

8mm videotape (n.) A videotape format that is 8 millimeters wide and used in camcorders. Hi-8, which employs S-video separation of color and luminance, is a higher-quality version.

eight-to-fourteen modulation See *EFM*.

EISA (n.) Extended Industry Standard Architecture; an enhancement of 8/16-bit ISA (IBM PC/AT) architecture, developed by nine personal computer manufacturers in 1988 as a response to IBM's Micro Channel bus. It offers full compatibility with ISA bus and boards and a 50 percent improved data transfer rate with a 32-bit data path over Micro Channel. (Pronounced **ee-sah**.) See *ISA*, *Micro Channel architecture*.

electroluminescence (n.) The process of subjecting solid phosphor to an alternating current field, causing it to emit light. This technology is implemented in flat-panel displays for notebook computers because it is energy-efficient.

electromagnetic interference See *EMI*.

electronically erasable programmable read-only memory See *EEPROM*.

Electronic Data Interchange See *EDI*.

Electronic Information Delivery System See *EIDS*.

electronic mail (e-mail) (n.) Any system for transmitting messages or information digitally through a communications network. A microcomputer with a modem and telecommunications software can connect with a network, an online service, or another computer using ordinary telephone lines.

electronic publishing (n.) The creation and distribution of computer-generated media, similar to traditional print publishing, except the product is delivered as digital data. Content is distributed on storage devices or over networks for computer-based delivery.

Electronics Industries Association See *EIA*.

ELF emission (n.) An extremely low frequency magnetic field that is generated by monitors and other common appliances and can be hazardous to frequent computer users.

e-mail See *electronic mail*.

EMI (n.) Electromagnetic interference; emissions from electronic devices and lighting that interfere with the performance of other devices.

emoticon (n.) A face made with keyboard characters, called a "smiley." :-)

emphasis (n.) In imaging, a mid-range control that can cause tones to be exaggerated or minimized. It is the equivalent of a loudness control in an audio amplifier. If parts of an image are too dark and too bright, the middle tones become subdued. The detail of an image becomes clearer as the middle tones are enhanced.

EMS (n.) Expanded Memory Specification; bank-switching in early IBM-compatible systems that permits 8088 chips to use more than one megabyte (MB) of physical memory. It has been replaced by extended memory.

emulator (n.) A computer system used to test programs under development, typically simulating performance.

Encapsulated PostScript See *EPS*.

encode 1. (v.) To translate images or sound into a digital format. Encoding is the final step in converting an analog signal into a data representation. Other steps are sampling and quantizing. 2. (v.) To combine three-color signals into one composite video signal.

encoder 1. (n.) A microprocessor-based hardware system that converts analog video signals into a series of binary numbers that define the signal content. 2. (n.) A device that transforms the original red, green, and blue (RGB) video signals into a luminance signal (Y) and a chrominance signal (I and Q) for NTSC transmission.

encryption (n.) A process used to encode data. Encryption makes it difficult to decode without proprietary software, thus protecting data from unauthorized access. Encrypted data is usually ciphered by the application of an algorithm that must be reapplied to translate it.

end of file See *EOF*.

end of message (n.) A control character that identifies the last bit of data in a message.

Energy Star (n.) An energy-efficiency guideline established by the Environmental Protection Agency (EPA) to identify an upper limit for wattage that an inactive computing device may draw. Compliance is voluntary, and manufacturers whose equipment meets the guidelines may display the Energy Star logo.

engine (n.) A software shell that controls the way media is presented and how a user can interact with a multimedia program.

Enhanced Graphics Adapter See *EGA*.

Enhanced Small Device Interface See *ESDI*.

entropy (n.) The measure of randomness or chaos; the ability of a system to undergo spontaneous change.

entropy encoder/decoder (n.) A type of encoder that compresses quantized DCT coefficients more compactly based on spatial characteristics. The decoder decompresses DCT coefficients according to the same principle.

envelope (n.) In audio engineering, a curve created by connecting the amplitude parameters of a sound over time. A simple envelope might consist of the attack, decay, sustain, and release levels, or ADSR. Changing the ADSR settings changes the shape of a tone but not its basic pitch. An envelope generator is a device used to shape these four elements.

EOF (n.) End of file; a control character that identifies the last bit of data in a block, packet, or stream.

EPROM (n.) Erasable programmable read-only memory; a type of PROM that can be erased through exposure to ultraviolet light and then reloaded. See *PROM*.

EPS (n.) Encapsulated PostScript; the graphic format designed by Aldus to describe an image in Adobe's PostScript page-description language. A bitmapped version of the image generally is placed in the header of the file in TIFF format for indexing and previewing.

equalization (n.) In audio recording and processing, the use of filters or attenuators to adjust output levels in specified frequency ranges.

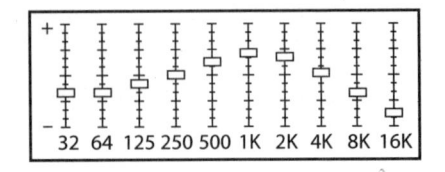

graphic equalizer

erasable programmable read-only memory See *EPROM*.

erase (v.) To delete previously recorded data from a storage medium, such as a floppy disk. Generally, data is not removed from the medium, but rather the pointers to it are rendered invisible. Most data can be recovered after being erased, unless the medium is reformatted.

error correction code See *ECC*.

error detection and correction See *EDAC*.

error detection code See *EDC*.

ESDI (n.) Enhanced Small Device

Interface; an interface for transferring data between a mass storage device, or other peripheral, and a microcomputer. An ESDI board has a buffer and can transfer data at 10 megabits per second (Mbps). (Pronounced **ez-dee**.)

establishing shot (n.) A scene used in video to make the viewer comfortable with the environment.

etch (v.) In semiconductor manufacture, to remove specific portions of a layer by chemical reaction.

Ethernet (n.) A widely-used local area network (LAN) specification for data communication that is an IEEE 802.3 standard, typically implemented as thin net or 10BASE-T, consisting of a physical link with a data link protocol that operates up to 10 megabits per second (Mbps) over twisted pair or coaxial cable. The data over an Ethernet LAN is distributed in packets.

EtherTalk (n.) The Ethernet protocol used by Apple computers.

European Broadcast Union See *EBU*.

exchange (n.) In telecommunications, a coordination point established by a common carrier in a geographical area where the central office support and the equipment for communications services are provided.

executable program (n.) A type of computer program, typically found in DOS with the extension .exe that performs a function or carries out a series of commands.

execute (v.) To carry out software commands.

exit strategy (n.) The means by which capital investors may receive a return on their investment. Acquisition by another company and the sale of shares in a public offering are two common strategies.

expanded memory manager (n.) In MS-DOS, the emm386.exe program that converts extended memory into expanded memory.

Expanded Memory Specification See *EMS*.

expansion bus (n.) A circuit or pathway that allows components to interact with a computer's processing unit. Types of buses are identified below with the width of the data path and the clock speed.

Bus	Processor	Data Path	Clock Speed
ISA	(PC/XT)	8-bit	8.33 MHz
	(PC/AT)	16-bit	8.33 MHz
EISA	(PC/80486)	32-bit	8.33 MHz
MCA	(IBM PS2)	32-bit	10 MHz
NuBus	(Mac)	32-bit	10 or 20 MHz
VESA	(PC/80486)	32-bit	40 or 66 MHz
PCI	(PowerPC/ Pentium)	32/64-bit	131MHz (max)

expansion slot (n.) A socket on a microcomputer motherboard into which an expansion board may be inserted.

Half-sized circuit boards fit into an 8-bit ISA slot, while full-sized boards use a 16-bit slot. PCI boards pass 64 bits of data simultaneously and require a special type of socket for their edge connector. Examples of expansion boards that fit into slots include sound cards, video adapters, internal modems, and host controllers. The slots in multimedia computers are often filled with cards that perform special digitizing functions.

expert system (n.) A program that calls on information stored in a knowledge base to make decisions using an inference engine. Data is processed in a manner similar to human reasoning, and problems are solved by accessing the IF/THEN statements in the knowledge base.

extended architecture See *XA*.

extended attribute (n.) Data that further identifies a file in Windows NT and OS/2, adding information about the original application that created the file and the names of other related files.

extended attribute record See *XAR*.

Extended Binary-Coded Decimal Interchange Code See *EBCIDIC*.

Extended Graphics Adapter See *XGA*.

Extended Industry Standard Architecture See *EISA*.

Extended Multitimbral Specification (n.) A synthesizer subsystem standard followed by Multimedia PC audio board manufacturers. It permits the playing of 16 melodic notes and 16 percussive notes at once, given a palette of nine different melodic tones and eight percussive tones.

extension 1. (n.) Any small program that plugs into a larger one and provides increased functionality. Extensions allow operating systems to control CD-ROM drives. 2. (n.) The letters that appear after the dot (.) in the name of an MS-DOS file to classify the file type. Some extensions frequently encountered in PC multimedia applications are listed below:

.avi	Audio video interleaved
.bmp	Bitmap
.fli	Animation format
.gif	Graphic interchange format
.jpg	Joint photographic expert group
.mid	MIDI format
.mov	QuickTime for Windows
.mpg	Moving pictures expert group
.tif	Tagged image file format
.wav	Windows audio format

The Macintosh file-naming system uses two hidden extensions, called file attributes, that are each four letters long. One is for the file type and the other is for the creator.

extent (n.) A set of logical blocks on a CD-ROM that are numbered in ascending order and contain one file section.

extract (v.) To decode a file encoded for network transmission, usually with reference to the uuencode/uudecode UNIX utility.

extremely high frequency See *EHF*.

extremely low frequency emission See *ELF emission*.

extrude (n.) A graphic effect that gives two-dimensional objects a three-dimensional look by extending solid shadows from 2-D lines and shapes. Extrusion is often applied to boldfaced print.

face (n.) In three-dimensional animation, a plane in a wire-frame model.

facility 1. (n.) In telecommunications, the line and all equipment required to furnish a completed circuit. 2. (n.) A capability offered by hardware or software that provides functionality for the user.

facsimile (**fax**) 1. (n.) A digital document or scanned image that is transmitted to another fax machine or computer using telephone lines; a form of e-mail.

fade-in (v.) In a video or audio context, to bring the levels up to normal brightness or volume gradually. When video is digitized and compressed, undesirable artifacts and "blockiness" often result from very slow fades. Quick cuts are preferred for this reason.

fader (n.) A sliding volume control or potentiometer, often used to control the amplitude of signals on a mixing board.

FAQ (n.) Frequently Asked Questions; on the Internet, a list of commonly asked questions and answers relating to specific topics.

FAT 1. (n.) File allocation table; a map of a hard disk or CD-ROM that defines the exact location of tracks, sectors, and clusters on the storage medium. 2. (adj.) Describes a Macintosh application that is accellerated for the Power Macintosh CPU and also runs on a 680×0 CPU.

fault-tolerant (adj.) Describes a system that is resistant to failure. An example is a RAID 1 mirrored system, which is fault-tolerant since it provides disk input/output even if one of the drives fails.

fax See *facsimile*.

FCC (n.) Federal Communications Commission; the United States government agency that regulates telephone services, radio, and satellite communications. Regarding electronic devices, a "Class A" certification is required for industrial applications, while home electronics must comply with a "Class B" certification, which specifies lower levels of radiation.

F-connector (n.) A threaded coaxial cable connector used with video equipment. *See illustration on following page.*

Female / Male

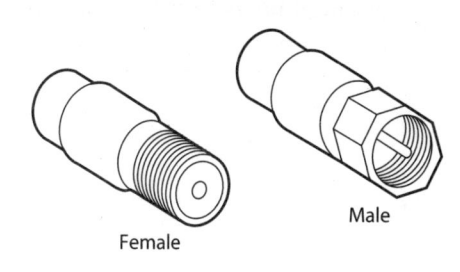

F-connectors

FCS (n.) Frame check sequence; a 16-bit field containing error-checking information that appears at the end of a frame in a bit-oriented protocol.

FDDI (n.) Fiber Distributed Data Interface; a standard for transmission of high bandwidth traffic via fiber optics at 100 megabits per second (Mbps). It is a local area network (LAN) specification from ANSI that uses token-ring topology.

FDDI-II (n.) An advanced, 200-megabits per second (Mbps) version of the Fiber Distributed Data Interface (FDDI).

FDHD (n.) Floppy drive high density; a disk drive used in Macintosh computers that can read and write to 3.5-inch disks in both double-density and high-density formats and can accept DOS formatted disks for cross-platform applications.

feature connector (n.) On graphics adapters for IBM-compatibles, a connector with 20–26 pins that permits access to the video signal path and allows video signals to be mixed, or "overlayed," with computer graphics.

FED (n.) Field emission display; a flat-panel electronic display that employs a matrix of cathodes, control electrodes, and phosphor elements to produce an electronic image.

Federal Communications Commission See *FCC*.

feedback 1. (n.) The electronic signal that occurs when the output of a system becomes its own input in real time. An example is the high-pitched squealing that occurs when a microphone is placed in front of a loudspeaker. 2. (n.) In an interactive instructional system, the positive or negative reinforcement of responses made by the user.

FET (n.) Field-effect transistor.

Fiber Distributed Data Interface See *FDDI*.

fiber optics (n.) The transmission of signals or data in the form of light pulses through a strand of glass fiber.

Fidonet (n.) Management software for a private bulletin board system (BBS) that provides procedures and data exchange standards for e-mail, file transfer, conferencing, and other functions.

field (n.) 1. The horizontal lines created during one pass of an electronic beam from the top to the bottom of a screen. A field is the same as a frame in computer video because the lines are drawn sequentially. However, two interlaced fields are used to draw each frame in broadcast video formats. A single field fills every other horizontal line of resolution only. This equals one-half of a complete television scanning cycle (1/60 of a second NTSC; 1/50 of a second PAL/SECAM) per frame. 2. (n.) In database applications, the location of data within a record.

field dominance (n.) The order in which video fields are recorded on a videotape during edits or transfers. Given two fields per frame, field one dominance places a new picture in the first field of each frame, while field two dominance places it in the second.

field-effect transistor See *FET*.

field emission display See *FED*.

field frequency (n.) The rate of display for each field in a video format, typically 59.94 times per second in NTSC. This number is rounded off to 60 hertz (Hz).

FIFO (n.) First-in-first-out.

file (n.) Any collection of information that is recorded and given a unique name. It may contain text, images, sound, or an application. In computing terms, a container for data.

file allocation table See *FAT*.

File Manager (n.) In Microsoft Windows, an application program that allows the user to organize and view the files and directories on a disk. It typically resides in the "Main" program group located in the Program Manager application.

file server (n.) In a computer network, the central computer that controls network functions and manages shared files.

File Transfer Protocol See *FTP*.

fill 1. (n.) A supplementary light source that softens shadows and brings out the background missed by the key light in a video shoot. 2. (n.) A color or pattern occupying a graphic region 3. (v.) To put a color or pattern in a graphic region.

film chain (n.) Referred to as telecine, this collection of equipment is used to transfer frames of film to electronic frames or videotape, incorporating projectors, multiplexers and a camera.

FILO (n.) First-in-last-out.

filter 1. (n.) In a visual context, a partially transparent material that passes or blocks light of a particular color or orientation. 2. (n.) In an audio context, an electronic circuit that passes or blocks signals of a specified frequency. 3. (n.) Any device that shapes or conditions a signal, including anti-aliasing, diffusing, equalizing, and sharpening filters applied in the process of editing digital images.

Finder (n.) In a Macintosh OS, the application that manages the graphical user interface (GUI). It is used to open, copy, delete, or move files represented by icons.

Finger (n.) A software program that detects information about a user on a network, including information about patterns of usage.

firewall (n.) On a local area network (LAN) connected to a larger network, the security system that prevents outside intrusion as well as inside information from getting out. Typically, all traffic must pass through a single machine, where the firewall is implemented.

FireWire (IEEE 1394) (n.) The designation for an interface standard that specifies a transmission method, media, and protocol. This high-performance serial bus defines a point-to-point cable-connected virtual bus and a backplane physical layer. The cable version supports data rates of 100, 200, and 400 megabits per second (Mbps) over a cable medium supported by the standard. The backplane version operates at 12.5, 25, or 50 Mbps. Both versions are fully compatible at the link layer and above. Features include multimaster capabilities, live connection and disconnection (hot plugging), and transmission speed scaleable from 100–400 Mbps.

The technology was developed by Texas Instruments to address the need for mass information transfer. Ordinary networks do not provide adequate connection capabilities and bandwidth for future demands. Parallel high-speed communications, such as SCSI, are not suited to long distance transmission and do not support live connection and disconnection of peripherals, such as digital video cameras, scanners, or printers. This capability is provided by the 1394 standard. The cable version integrates I/O connectivity in personal computers using a scaleable, high-speed serial interface.

The standard is a transaction-based packet technology for both chassis and peripheral devices. The serial bus behaves as though it were memory space interconnected between devices, or as if devices resided in slots on the main backplane. Device addressing is 64 bits wide, allocating 10 bits for network IDs, 6 bits for node IDs, and 48 bits for memory addresses. It is capable of addressing 1023 networks of 63 nodes, each with 281 terabytes of memory.

Memory-based addressing views resources as registers, or memory that can be accessed with processor-to-memory transactions. A bus entity is referred to as a "node," which may be individually identified, addressed, and reset. Multiple nodes may be in a single module, and multiple ports may be in a single node.

The distance between each node should not exceed 4.5 meters, and the maximum number in a chain is 16, for a total maximum end-to-end distance of 72 meters. Cable distance between each node is limited primarily by signal attenuation. A cable with 28-gauge signal pairs may be up to 4.5 meters in length, while a cable with 24-gauge signal pairs may be 14 meters long. A maximum of 16 cable hops is allowed between the most widely separated nodes. The end-to-end distance may vary from 72 to 224 meters, depending on the configuration.

Signals transmitted on cable and backplane environments are NRZ with Data-Strobe (DS) encoding. DS encoding allows only one of the two signal lines to change each data bit period, doubling the tolerance jitter. DS encoding is licensed from SGS-Thomson/INMOS.

The FireWire IEEE 1394 standard supports asynchronous and isochronous data transfers. The asynchronous format transfers data and transaction layer information to a specific address, while the isochronous format broadcasts data based on channel numbers rather than specific addressing. Both non-real-time critical applications, such as scanners and printers, and real-time critical applications, such as video and audio, are capable of operating on the same bus because the interface provides both formats.

The serial bus 1394 could replace other peripheral connection communication methods in use today, such as the Centronix parallel, RS232, SCSI, and Apple Computer's Desktop Bus (ADB). It would enable a single high-performance serial bus. New interfaces, such as direct connect video I/O, will employ this technology for its advantages. Memory space addressing is a good solution for "slotless" systems, such as PDAs.

Communications at different speeds between 100 and 400 Mbps may occur simultaneously on one medium. The "hot plugging" and dynamic reconfiguration abilities make it a user-friendly environment. This standard will allow connecting an expansion system and providing communications on demand without having to shut down and reconfigure whenever devices are added or removed.

firmware (n.) A device or machine component with a microprocessor on board. It is characterized by data in ROM that controls hardware components.

fixed disk See *hard disk*.

fixed repetition (n.) An instructional design feature that repeats a lesson or module in the same way.

flag (n.) A bit of data set to "0" or "1" that represents a particular piece of information, position, or status.

flame (v.) To criticize or heap indignities upon an individual on the Internet, often resulting from an inappropriate or uninformed remark made by the individual who is flamed.

flash memory (n.) An EPROM, or erasable programmable read-only memory. It is nonvolatile, with a fast access rate, and it can be erased with ultraviolet light; the term also applies to EEPROMs, which are electronically erased. They are used to provide data to equipment that can accept and read a small EPROM card.

flat 1. (adj.) Describes images of low contrast. 2. (adj.) Describes an image with objects shaded in uniform color and brightness for each small polygon, rather than varying the shading at edges or across the polygon.

flat-file database (n.) A database that holds records in a single file. Flat-files are not as fast or as powerful as relational databases.

flatten (v.) To remove the Macintosh binary headers from a QuickTime file to make it compatible with QuickTime for Windows. After flattening, a file must be renamed to conform to MS-DOS conventions, with up to eight characters followed by the ".mov" extension.

FLC (n.) A sophisticated version of the Autodesk Animator FLI format animation file that supports 640 × 480 images in up to 8-bit color. Viewers for FLC files are available for most computers.

FLI (n.) The acronym for the original Autodesk Animator animation file format. This file format supports 320 × 240-pixel images in up to 8-bit color. FLI viewers are available for most microcomputers.

flicker (n.) An "interfield" flicker, also known as jitter, which is caused when two fields that comprise a single video frame are not identical; two different pictures will alternate 60 times per second when viewed in a still frame mode. This flicker is also introduced by low vertical refresh rates in a TV screen, preventing the eye from retaining a continuous perception of successive images.

floating point arithmetic (n.) The use of scientific notation in order to reduce the number of digits required to express a quantity. An example is the expression of 200 000 000 000 as 2×10^{11}.

floating point unit See *FPU*.

floppy disk (n.) A storage medium commonly used in all types of microcomputers. A floppy disk consists of a paper-thin flexible diskette, usually 3.5 or 5.25 inches in diameter, coated with magnetic material. The 3.5-inch disks have replaced the larger size, and they hold up to 1.44 megabytes (MB) of uncompressed data. The capacity of the diskette is determined by whether the medium is single-sided (SS), double-sided (DS), double-density (DD), or high-density (HD).

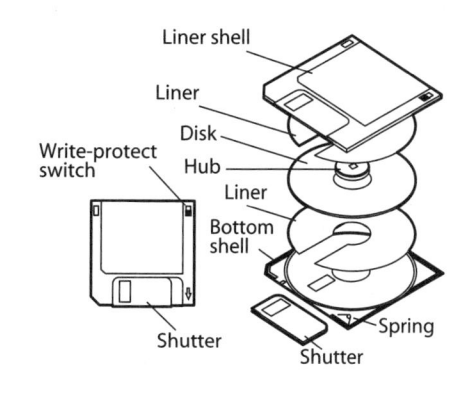

3.5-inch floppy disk

floppy drive high density See *FDHD*.

FLOPS (n.) F̲loating point o̲perations p̲er s̲econd.

flowchart (n.) In an interactive design, a map of the user's options and corresponding responses to input. It outlines branching and shows program segments and decision points.

flying erase head (n.) In a helical scan video recorder, an erase head that rotates along with the recording heads so that it can erase a single line of video. With this technology, new segments can be added to existing footage seamlessly.

FM (n.) F̲requency m̲odulation. Change in the frequency of a carrier signal that is used to express information based on the rate and degree of change.

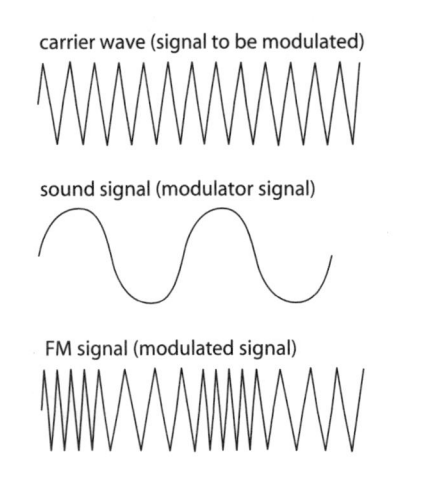

carrier

modulator

FM sound (modulated sound wave)

FM-generated wave forms

carrier wave (signal to be modulated)

sound signal (modulator signal)

FM signal (modulated signal)

FM broadcast signal

FMV (n.) F̲ull-m̲otion v̲ideo; moving pictures that play at the full resolution and frame rate in which they were encoded, resulting in a smooth, continuous display. Following broadcast video standards, this is usually considered 30 frames per second (fps) in the NTSC format and 25 fps in PAL format.

folder (n.) The equivalent of a directory in a graphical user interface (GUI); an image that represents a container for files or applications.

foley artist (n.) A sound-effects specialist in the film industry.

folio (n.) A page number in a document.

font (n.) A typeface or family of alphanumeric characters and symbols in a single style, such as Times, Roman, or Helvetica. It was originally used to define print and has been applied to computer-generated characters.

footprint 1. (n.) The amount of space on a desktop or table required for the base of a computer or peripheral. 2. (n.) In satellite communications, the territory covered by the transmitting beam of the satellite.

format 1. (v.) To prepare a storage medium by defining tracks and sectors where data will be placed in compliance with a specific operating system's requirements. Disks formatted for the Macintosh are not readable in Microsoft DOS or Windows without a cross-platform utility that translates data. 2. (n.) The specifications of a software/hardware platform, or a unique means of formatting.

formula translator See *FORTRAN*.

FORTRAN (n.) Formula translator; developed by IBM, this computer compiling language was originally invented to solve scientific problems, but is also used for commercial applications. The syntax consists of algebraic expressions and arithmetic statements.

4:2:2 (n.) The ratio of the sampling rates used for turning three components of an analog video signal into a digital signal. It is also referred to as CCIR-601, a standard used for professional video production equipment and D1 format digital videotape. See *A:B:C notation*.

fps (adj.) Frames per second; in video or animation, the number of times each second that a new picture is drawn on the screen.

FPU (n.) Floating point unit; a math coprocessor chip that performs floating point arithmetic, and by doing so, offloads this computationally intensive function from the central processing unit (CPU). Programs that are optimized to take advantage of a math coprocessor run much faster when one is present.

fractal (n.) A set of points, or coordinates, with a fractional dimension. In digital compression, a fractal model may be applied to an image to preserve its original shape. The model can later be used to generate repetitive features found in the image.

fractional T1 (n.) A telecommunications service that offers customers the use of one or more channels in a T1 connection, as opposed the all 24 channels. Charges are billed according to the number of channels used.

fragmented file (n.) A file that has been written to a disk in discontiguous sectors.

frame 1. (n.) A single video image that belongs to a stream of moving pictures. In an interlaced system, such as NTSC, it consists of two interlaced fields. A video frame in NTSC consists of 525 lines, while a frame in SECAM/PAL consists of 625 lines. In multimedia applications, a frame may be a still image on the screen that is just one in a sequence of frames. 2. (n.) In telecommunications, a transmission block. 3. (n.) A feature of the later releases of Netscape Navigator that displays different parts of a Web page in the same window. An example is a list of terms in a frame on one side of the open window, and a graphic image or a paragraph defining the term on the other side of the window in a frame.

frame-accurate (adj.) Describes professional video editing equipment that can locate and process a specified single image. Consumer products generally have the capacity to locate approximate locations only.

frame address code (n.) Time-stamped data that identifies a frame of video by its location. It is placed in the blanking interval prior to the frame.

frame buffer 1. (n.) A random-access memory allocation dedicated to storing a frame of digital video and used to refresh a raster image. The buffer may include some processing ability. As with all digital video descriptors, the number of bits per pixel determines picture quality. 2. (n.) A component that records and stores the lines of a video frame and functions as a time base corrector.

frame check sequence See *FCS*.

frame dropping (n.) The inability of a decompression system to play all the encoded frames in a stream of digital video. Since playback algorithms preserve the integrity of the audio track at the expense of video frames, some frames may not be displayed on playback in order to sustain the audio track.

frame grabber (n.) A device that captures and stores a single video frame to be edited or printed later.

frame rate (n.) The number of times per second a video image is redrawn, scanned, or displayed on a monitor. The rate for NTSC format is about 60 frames per second (fps); for PAL/SECAM format it is 25 fps. Film runs at 24 fps.

frame relay (n.) A packet network service that depends on the integrity of the data in a signal to increase the speed of transmission. A frame relay circuit begins to check for errors as soon as it receives the header, unlike older X.25 networks. The service is offered with T1 and DDS connections.

frames per second See *fps*.

freeze-frame (n.) A display of a single frame or image, held motionless, that is selected from video or film footage; an image drawn from a longer motion sequence.

frequency modulation See *FM*.

frequency-shift keying See *FSK*.

Frequently Asked Questions See *FAQ*.

front-end (adj.) Describes a visual interface used to access information in a database or menu-driven multimedia program.

FSK (n.) F̲requency-s̲hift k̲eying. In telecommunications, the assignment of different audio frequencies to binary digits. Transmission of a bit stream causes tones to change in pitch, representing a zero or a one.

f-stop (n.) In photography, a number that represents a logarithmic value for the intensity of light in a given lens. It is a factor of the ratio between the focal distance and the diameter of the iris, or lens opening. A lens with a focal distance of 70 mm and a diaphragm diameter of 20mm has an f-stop value of 7:2, or 3.5:1, expressed as f3.5. Lower ratios indicate larger lens openings and a shorter focus depth. In photography, the f-stop is set initially for the depth of field, and each increasing stop doubles the amount of light that is emitted.

FTP (n.) F̲ile T̲ransfer P̲rotocol; a method of passing data from one computer to another over networks or telephone lines, usually involving a modem. Error detection, compression, and translation are features of some protocols. Some of the common protocols are Xmodem, Ymodem, Zmodem, and Kermit.

fulfillment (n.) Services that entail warehousing, order processing, and shipping of products, such as CD-ROMs; typically performed by a duplicator or manufacturer.

full-duplex (n.) Bidirectional, simultaneous two-way communication over telephone lines, preferably on a four-wire circuit.

full-frame ID (n.) A code placed in a video stream that identifies the first video field of a new film frame; also referred to as a "white flag."

full-frame time code (n.) Society of Motion Picture and Television Engineers coding on videotape that accounts for all frame numbers chronologically; also known as "nondrop frame" time code.

full-motion video See *FMV*.

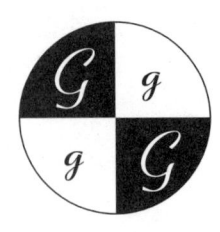

gaffer (n.) A stage hand who constructs and dismantles sets for film or video productions.

gain (n.) In audio, the increase in signal provided by an amplifier between input level and output level. It may be positive, negative, or null (unity gain).

game port (n.) A serial connection on a computer that is used for interfacing input devices such as joysticks.

gamma (n.) A value that identifies the degree of contrast in a photograph or electronic image. Gamma values are determined according to a gradation curve. A steep curve indicates a high gamma value and high contrast. Gamma may be adjusted by component, color, halftones or highlights, or across an entire image. Gamma correction is the adjustment of contrast in an image.

gateway (n.) A dedicated computer that connects to two or more networks and routes information between them. Networks connected to a gateway may be running different protocols, such as TCP/IP and SNP, and the gateway converts between protocols operating in the top three layers of the OSI model.

General MIDI (n.) A standard configuration for MIDI digital music systems. It refers to the assignment of particular sounds to specified preset locations. MIDI sequencer files should sound roughly equivalent when executed by a variety of sound cards or synthesizers. This is not always the case, given the extreme differences between the sound of FM synthesizers and wavetable sample players.

Specifically, MIDI is a mapping structure that assigns instrument sounds, or voices, to each of the 128 different presets, programs, or patch locations. In a multitimbral MIDI sequence, each musical part or voice is sent to a different preset according to a "patch map." General MIDI defines the type of sound that resides at each patch location. There are 16 groups of eight instrument types. MIDI programs may be assigned to MIDI channels, and a sequence of note-on and note-off events may be sent to each discrete channel. The determination of which voice responds to which channel is controlled by a system message that sets up the receiver.

General MIDI specification sets the first nine channels for instruments and the tenth for percussion. The remaining channels, 11 through 16, are left open for user configuration. Since early generations of sound cards were unable to support all 16 channels, Microsoft devised a proprietary system for assigning MIDI voices in Windows. In this scheme, "Basic MIDI" devices use MIDI channels 13, 14, 15, and 16. In a more evolved system called "Extended MIDI," devices use channels 1 through 9 for instruments, channel 10 for percussion, and no assignments are possible for channels 11 through 16. The following is the General MIDI instrument program map:

#	Group	Instrument
1	Piano	Acoustic Grand
2	Piano	Bright Acoustic
3	Piano	Electric Grand
4	Piano	Honky-Tonk
5	Piano	Electric Piano 1
6	Piano	Electric Piano 2
7	Piano	Harpsichord
8	Piano	Clav
9	Pitch perc	Celesta
10	Pitch perc	Glockenspiel
11	Pitch perc	Music Box
12	Pitch perc	Vibraphone
13	Pitch perc	Marimba
14	Pitch perc	Xylophone
15	Pitch perc	Tubular Bells
16	Pitch perc	Dulcimer
17	Organ	Drawbar Organ
18	Organ	Percussive Organ
19	Organ	Rock Organ
20	Organ	Church Organ

General MIDI

#	Group	Instrument
21	Organ	Reed Organ
22	Organ	Accordian
23	Organ	Harmonica
24	Organ	Tango Accordian
25	Guitar	Acoustic Guitar (nylon)
26	Guitar	Acoustic Guitar (steel)
27	Guitar	Electric Guitar (jazz)
28	Guitar	Electric Guitar (clean)
29	Guitar	Electric Guitar (muted)
30	Guitar	Overdriven Guitar
31	Guitar	Distortion Guitar
32	Guitar	Guitar Harmonics
33	Bass	Acoustic Bass
34	Bass	Electric Bass (finger)
35	Bass	Electric Bass (pick)
36	Bass	Fretless Bass
37	Bass	Slap Bass 1
38	Bass	Slap Bass 2
39	Bass	Synth Bass I
40	Bass	Synth Bass 2
41	Strings	Violin
42	Strings	Viola
43	Strings	Cello
44	Strings	Contrabass
45	Strings	Tremolo Strings
46	Strings	Pizzicato Strings
47	Strings	Orchestral Strings
48	Strings	Timpani

General MIDI

#	Group	Instrument
49	Ensemble	String Ensemble 1
50	Ensemble	String Ensemble 2
51	Ensemble	Synth Strings 1
52	Ensemble	Synth Strings 2
53	Ensemble	Choir Aahs
54	Ensemble	Voice Oohs
55	Ensemble	Synth Voice
56	Ensemble	Orchestra Hit
57	Brass	Trumpet
58	Brass	Trombone
59	Brass	Tuba
60	Brass	Muted Trumpet
61	Brass	French Horn
62	Brass	Brass Section
63	Brass	Synth Brass 1
64	Brass	Synth Brass 2
65	Reed	Soprano Saxophone
66	Reed	Alto Saxophone
67	Reed	Tenor Saxophone
68	Reed	Baritone Saxophone
69	Reed	Oboe
70	Reed	English Horn
71	Reed	Bassoon
72	Reed	Clarinet
73	Pipe	Piccolo
74	Pipe	Flute
75	Pipe	Recorder
76	Pipe	Pan Flute

General MIDI

#	Group	Instrument
77	Pipe	Blown Bottle
78	Pipe	Shakuhachi
79	Pipe	Whistle
80	Pipe	Ocarina
81	Synth lead	Lead 1(square)
82	Synth lead	Lead 2 (sawtooth)
83	Synth lead	Lead 3 (calliope)
84	Synth lead	Lead 4 (chiff)
85	Synth lead	Lead 5 (charang)
86	Synth lead	Lead 6 (voice)
87	Synth lead	Lead 7 (fifths)
88	Synth lead	Lead 8 (bass+lead)
89	Synth pad	Pad 1 (new age)
90	Synth pad	Pad 2 (warm)
91	Synth pad	Pad 3 (polysynth)
92	Synth pad	Pad4 (choir)
93	Synth pad	Pad 5 (bowed)
94	Synth pad	Pad 6 (metallic)
95	Synth pad	Pad 7 (halo)
96	Synth pad	Pad 8 (sweep)
97	Synth fx	FX 1 (rain)
98	Synth fx	FX2 (soundtrack)
99	Synth fx	FX 3 (crystal)
100	Synth fx	FX 4 (atmosphere)
101	Synth fx	FX 5 (brightness)
102	Synth fx	FX 6 (goblins)
103	Synth fx	FX 7 (echoes)
104	Synth fx	FX 8 (sci-fi)

General MIDI

#	Group	Instrument
105	Ethnic	Sitar
106	Ethnic	Banjo
107	Ethnic	Shamisen
108	Ethnic	Koto
109	Ethnic	Kalimba
110	Ethnic	Bagpipe
111	Ethnic	Fiddle
112	Ethnic	Shanai
113	Perc	Tinkle Bell
114	Perc	Agogo
115	Perc	Steel Drums
116	Perc	Woodblock
117	Perc	Taiko Drum
118	Perc	Melodic Tom
119	Perc	Synth Drum
120	Perc	Reverse Cymbal
121	Sound fx	Guitar Fret Noise
122	Sound fx	Breathing Noise
123	Sound fx	Seashore
124	Sound fx	Bird Tweet
125	Sound fx	Telephone Ring
126	Sound fx	Helicopter
127	Sound fx	Applause
128	Sound fx	Gunshot

In addition to the 128 instruments listed in the table above, the General MIDI specification assigns 47 drum sounds to a "key map." The following table shows the General MIDI percussion "key map." The percussion instrument that is assigned to each note number is named in table on the following page. For your reference, middle "C" is note number 60.

General MIDI mode

Note #	Instrument
35	Acoustic Bass Drum
36	Bass Drum 1
37	Side Stick
38	Acoustic Snare
39	Hand Clap
40	Electric Snare
41	Low Floor Tom
42	Closed Hi-hat
43	High Floor Tom
44	Pedal Hi-hat
45	Low Tom
46	Open Hi-hat
47	Low-mid Tom
48	High-mid Tom
49	Crash Cymbal 1
50	High Tom
51	Ride Cymbal 1
52	Chinese Cymbal
53	Ride Bell
54	Tambourine
55	Splash Cymbal
56	Cowbell
57	Crash Cymbal 2
58	Vibraslap
59	Ride Cymbal 2
60	High Bongo
61	Low Bongo
62	Mute High Conga

Note #	Instrument
63	Open High Conga
64	Low Conga
65	High Timbale
66	Low Timbale
67	High Agogo
68	Low Agogo
69	Casaba
70	Maracas
71	Short Whistle
72	Long Whistle
73	Short Guiro
74	Long Guiro
75	Claves
76	High Wood Block
77	Low Wood Block
78	Mute Cuica
79	Open Cuica
80	Mute Triangle
81	Open Triangle

General MIDI mode (n.) The mode a Microsoft Windows audio system operates in if its MIDI Mapper matrix sets patches and channels to default MIDI Manufacturers Association standards.

general protection fault See *GPF*.

generation 1. (n.) In storage media, particularly magnetic tape, the number of times a dub is removed from the master.

A copy of the first copy is second-generation. The quality of each successive generation on magnetic tape is degraded. With digital formats, there is no difference between generations. 2. (n.) In hardware, a stratification reference to major evolutionary stages in development. Successive generations incorporate significant improvements and changes.

generational loss (n.) Reduced quality in audio or video clarity as a result of successive duplication. See *generation*.

generic courseware (n.) Educational material that appeals to a broad market, rather than custom courseware for a specific audience.

genlock (n.) A machine that aligns the data rate of a video image with that of a digital device to ensure accurate timing in the digital copy. An abbreviation for "synchronization generator lock."

geographic information system See *GIS*.

geosynchronous satellite (n.) A satellite that orbits at the same rate as the earth's rotation, so that it remains in a stationary aspect to a given point on earth.

GHz (n.) Gigahertz; one billion cycles per second.

GIF (n.) Graphic Interchange Format; a file format used to store most graphic images for online distribution; it is used by CompuServe forum libraries and other online services. (Pronounced **jiff**.)

giga (n.) Prefix meaning "one billion." A gigabit (Gb) is one billion bits. A gigabyte is equal to 1 073 741 842 bytes, or one billion 8-bit bytes.

GIS (n.) Geographic information system; the digital storage of demographic data.

glass master (n.) The mold from which discs are stamped. It is made of glass, and the data is stored as pits in the mold.

global file specification See *wildcard*.

global key (n.) A keyboard character that performs a specific global function, regardless of program context. The "Esc," or escape key, might be an example.

GND (n.) Ground; an electrical connection between equipment and a zero voltage point. A ground loop occurs when equipment is grounded at more than one point.

gold disc (n.) A CD-R; the blank disc has a lower layer of polycarbonate with a preformed track spiral, which the recording laser beam follows and inscribes. A translucent layer of green recordable material adheres to the polycarbonate, with a reflective layer of gold on top. These resilient discs are coated with lacquer.

Gopher (n.) An information retrieval system on the Internet that was created by the University of Minnesota.

Gouraud shading (n.) An efficient three-dimensional rendering algorithm that averages the luma and chroma values at each corner of a polygon.

GPF (n.) General protection fault; an error message that occurs when software is trying to read or write memory that it does not own or have access to.

gradient (n.) A method of filling or shading an object that incorporates the blending of two different shades or patterns across the surface of the object.

graphical user interface See *GUI*.

Graphic Interchange Format See *GIF*.

graphics (n.) The visual content prepared for a production. Computer-generated letters, symbols and drawings, photographs, scans, slides, and all other still visuals belong to this broad category.

graphics accelerator (n.) A specialized circuit board that contains a coprocessor which enhances the graphical performance of a computer. It is inserted into an expansion slot and relieves the CPU from graphics processing.

graphics input (n.) The use of a peripheral, such as a drawing tablet, mouse, touch screen, or light pen to create or alter a graphics display.

graphics input device (n.) Any digitizer that feeds a computer x-y coordinates and in some cases, color data.

graphics output device (n.) Any device that displays or records an image; monitors and printers are examples.

graphics tablet (n.) This type of drawing surface, often with pressure-sensitivity, feeds a computer data defining x-y coordinates from a hand-held input device, such as a light pen.

grayscale (adj.) In a computer graphic, the number of levels of gray that exist between black and white. With a minimum of 256 levels, the quality of a black-and-white photograph can be achieved.

Green Book standard See *CD-i*.

grip (n.) In a film or video production, the person who mounts or positions the camera according to the director's instructions. It may be mounted on a dolly, a crane, or on any other surface that provides a desirable camera angle.

ground See *GND*.

guard band (n.) A narrow bandwidth of dead space between two adjacent channels; space inserted between tracks of recorded material on audio or videotapes to prevent crosstalk between tracks.

GUI (n.) Graphical user interface; an environment in which icons represent objects that an operator can manipulate with a pointing device. Initially designed by Xerox, it serves as the basis for the Macintosh operating system and has been deployed in a similar context by Microsoft in Windows. See *user interface*.

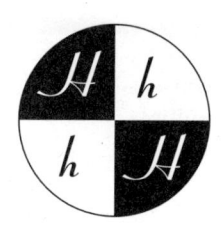

hacker (n.) A person who has developed sophisticated computer programming skills and can break codes and access restricted data without access privileges.

half-duplex See *HD*.

half-height (adj.) Describes a floppy disk drive, CD-ROM drive, or other peripheral that is approximately 1.75 inches tall and may be mounted in a short drive bay.

half-inch (n.) Jargon for .5-inch videotape used in Betacam, S-VHS, and VHS video formats.

halftone (n.) Related to a graphic display or a printed document, a color value that is created with dots. The degree of color intensity is determined by the density and diameter of the dots. Printers, scanners, and monitors use halftone graphic techniques. This method of depicting color is different from gray scale, which defines actual shades of gray. *See illustration.*

handle (n.) In a graphical environment, the corner or edge of an object onto which the user may click and drag to reposition or resize an image.

halftone image

handshake (n.) The exchange of signals between two devices that establishes connection as a part of the communication protocol.

handwriting recognition (n.) A hardware/software system that converts handwritten letters into data files. It can be implemented on the touch screen of a personal digital assistant (PDA) with a light pen on a graphics tablet, or by a scanner with OCR software.

HARC-C (n.) <u>H</u>ouston <u>A</u>dvanced <u>R</u>esearch <u>C</u>enter-<u>C</u>; a video compression algorithm based on wavelet theory and programmed in C language.

hard copy (n.) Documents and images in printed, concrete form, such as slides, prints, transparencies, and plots.

hard disk

hard disk (n.) A fixed, magnetic disk drive that stores large amounts of data. Winchester is a common type. It consists of a stack of rigid platters with multiple read and write heads.

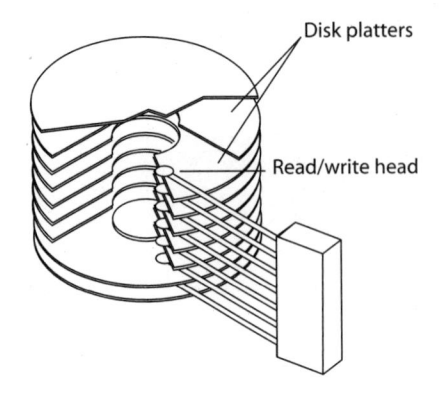

hard disk mechanism

harmonics

hardware (n.) The electromechanical segment of a data processing system.

hardware key (n.) A small connector that plugs into the parallel port of a computer. It typically contains code required for the computer to perform a certain function, such as run proprietary software. It may be referred to as a "dongle," but that word is also commonly used to describe a special adapter for a video monitor.

harmonic (n.) A tone whose frequency is a multiple of another lower tone or fundamental. Musical sounds consist of a fundamental and a number of harmonic overtones.

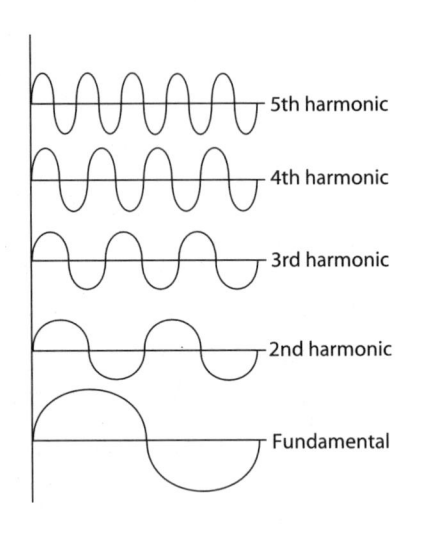

Hayes AT command set (n.) Standards developed by Hayes Corporation for controlling intelligent modem parameters. This set of commands has become the de facto standard in the industry.

HBI (n.) Horizontal blanking interval; the length of time required for the beam of a cathode-ray tube (CRT) to return from the right side of a line of pixels to the left side of the next line while scanning. The interval is included in the signal for each of the 525 lines in an NTSC picture. See *VBI*.

HD 1. (adj.) Half-duplex; describes a telecommunications circuit that provides data transmission in two directions, but it can transmit in only one direction at a time. 2. (n.) Hard disk. 3. (adj.) High-density.

HDSL (n.) High-data-rate digital subscriber line; a technique developed by Bellcore Research to filter out background interference in twisted-pair copper wires using a DSL modem in T1 applications. A unit is required at each end of the connecting wire, and the transmission distance is limited to 18 000 feet.

HDTV (n.) High-definition television; a video format with higher resolution than normal NTSC, PAL, or SECAM broadcast standards. HDTV formats range from 655 to 2125 scanning lines, with an aspect ratio of about 5:3 and a video bandwidth of 30 to 50 megahertz (MHz), which is over five times greater than standard NTSC. The most typical implementation of HDTV will provide 1125 lines of resolution rather than 525 in NTSC, and it will offer a 16:9 aspect ratio. It will also be equipped with surround-sound and CD-quality audio. The bandwidth of digital HDTV will exceed 300 MHz.

head (n.) An electromagnetic assembly that reads and writes data to any type of media, such as magnetic tape, an optical disc, or the platter in a hard disk drive.

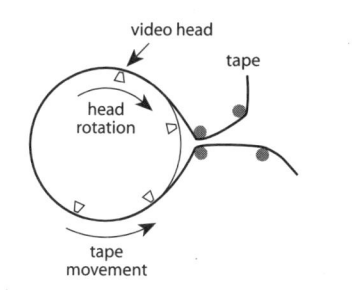

read and write head in a VCR

headend (n.) The site in a cable system or broadband coax network where the programming originates and the distribution network starts. Usually, the signals are received off the air from satellites, microwave relays, or fiber-optic cables at the headend for distribution.

header 1. (n.) In telecommunications and computing, information recorded at the beginning of a packet of data being transmitted that may identify what follows. On a CD-ROM it is recorded at the beginning of a sector, containing the address of the sector (logical block number) as well as the mode in which it is recorded. 2. (n.) With reference to hardware, a row of pins on a circuit board that will accept a connector.

header field (n.) In CD-ROM terms, the address of a sector, or logical block number. It consists of four bytes recorded at the beginning of each sector, identifying the address of the sector and the mode in which the sector is recorded.

headroom (n.) The amount of excessive amplitude an analog tape recorder can accept, past the point where the meters peak, before distortion occurs. Headroom is valuable when recording live sounds that could peak unexpectedly.

head slot (n.) A small aperture in the jacket or casing of a floppy disk that exposes the media to read and write heads.

Heidi (n.) An API developed by Autodesk that supports multiple renderers of three-

helical scan

dimensional images and allows access to multiple output devices.

helical scan (n.) A tape playback system with two video heads mounted on opposite sides of a revolving drum. The head drum spins at a single frame per revolution, so each head scans one field or half a frame per revolution. High tape speeds are achieved by moving the tape and the heads. The tape moves in a helical path as it winds around the video head drum.

helper application (n.) Related to a Web browser, a program that enables a browser to play multimedia file types, such as audio, video, or animation. A file will play automatically from the browser if the correct MIME type is specified and it is available on a system.

hertz See *Hz*.

heuristic (adj.) Describes a trial-and-error method of solving problems with evaluation of the progress made at various steps in the process.

heuristic routine (n.) A software methodology that solves problems by trial-and-error rather than by an algorithmic procedure. A computer may be said to engage in learning during this process.

Hewlett-Packard Graphics Language See *HPGL*.

hexadecimal (n.) A numbering system with numbers 0–9 and letters A–F, which together are called "hex" digits. *See table.*

Hexadecimal	Decimal	Binary
01	1	00000001
02	2	00000010
03	3	00000011
04	4	00000100
05	5	00000101
06	6	00000110
07	7	00000111
08	8	00001000
90	9	00001001
0A	10	00001010
0B	11	00001011
0C	12	00001100
0D	13	00001101
0E	14	00001110
0F	15	00001111
10	16	00010000
11	17	00010001
12	18	00010010
13	19	00010011
14	20	00010100
15	21	00010101
16	22	00010110
17	23	00010111
18	24	00011000
19	25	00011001
1A	26	00011010
1B	27	00011011
1C	28	00011100
1D	29	00011101
1E	30	00011110
1F	31	00011111
20	32	00100000
21	33	00100001
22	34	00100010
23	35	00100011
24	36	00100100
25	37	00100101
26	38	00100110
27	39	00100111
28	40	00101000

HFC (n.) Hybrid Fiber Coax; a broadband network, such as cable TV, that uses optical fiber from a centralized location to a point downstream where the signal continues via coaxial cable.

HFS (n.) Hierarchical File System; an Apple Macintosh operating system convention for storing data.

hidden attribute (n.) A feature that prevents files from being displayed in the directory list when running MS-DOS.

hidden file (n.) A file whose attributes are set so that it is not normally shown in a directory listing. System files in MS-DOS are hidden so that they are not deleted accidentally by the user.

Hi-8 video (n.) An improved version of the Sony 8 mm format. Hi-8 video yields higher luminance levels and better quality than standard 8 mm, with Y/C component S-video connections.

hierarchical link (n.) A "parent-child" relationship is set up in this type of link between two objects, where changes made to the parent are automatically inherited by the child, but changes made to the child object will not necessarily be reflected in the parent.

hierarchical structure (n.) A system of tree-structured directories, built in layers and based on pathways between root directories and subdirectories.

high-definition television See *HDTV.*

High-Level Data Link Control See *HLDLC.*

high-level language See *HLL.*

High Sierra format (n.) A standard CD-ROM format for file and directory placement. It was developed by computer vendors, software developers, and CD-ROM system integrators. Twelve companies began work on the format proposal in 1985 at the High Sierra Hotel in Lake Tahoe, Nevada. The ISO 9660 format is a revised version of the High Sierra format adopted by the International Organization for Standardization.

HLDLC (n.) High-Level Data Link Control; the standard protocol that was established by the ISO for international communications.

HLL (n.) High-level language; any programming language in which a single statement may be translated to numerous assembly language or machine code instructions. High-level languages are designed to be machine-independent, in contrast to an assembly level language. C++, BASIC, Pascal, and FORTRAN are examples of high-level languages.

HLS (n.) Hue, luminance, and saturation.

hologram (n.) An image with a layered, three-dimensional appearance that is produced by a laser-based system rather than lenses.

home page (n.) A document that is accessed via the World Wide Web by using a browser, or universal client. A home page, or Web page, is typically written in Hypertext Markup Language (HTML), which provides the capacity to link "hot words" to other words, graphics, or pages.

horizontal blanking interval See *HBI*.

host adapter (n.) A controller card (such as a SCSI adapter) that routes data between the CPU and peripherals, such as CD-ROM drives, printers, or disk drives.

host computer (n.) Any computer that provides the processing power for terminals and peripherals connected to it.

hot 1. (adj.) Describes a defined region on the monitor (in an interactive program) that responds to a mouse click or a touch. Activating the area initiates an action or causes a process to be performed. 2. (adj.) In audio terms, describes a tape recorded at the maximum possible signal level. 3. (adj.) In video production, describes a camera that is in use, or "on air."

hot fix (n.) A "hot swap"; the replacement of a failed disk drive in a multiple drive system with a "hot spare," while the remaining drives are online.

hot links 1. (n.) This includes text, buttons, or icons that are specially tagged in an interactive program, making it possible to connect instantly to information in another location or to execute instructions simply by clicking on them or otherwise activating the links. 2. (n.) A connection between two or more programs that updates data in linked programs automatically when it is changed in one of the associated programs. For example, making a change in a database file linked to a graph will cause a corresponding change in the graph representing the data.

Houston Advanced Research Center-C See *HARC-C*.

HPGL (n.) Hewlett-Packard Graphics Language; a bitmapped graphic file format used by IBM-compatible graphics programs.

HQX (n.) A Macintosh program that converts binary files into the 7-bit BinHex format so they can be transferred to another user as text.

HSV (n.) Hue, saturation, and value; a system of defining colors.

H.320 (n.) The standard that applies to a broad range of video conferencing applications. It defines how data flows among conferencing devices over network or telephone lines. The image size, or resolution, under this standard is 352 × 288 pixels, and it is sometimes referred to as Common Intermedia Format.

HTML (n.) Hypertext Markup Language; a set of commands for marking a document so that it can be read by a

Web browser, such as Netscape Navigator. All home pages on the World Wide Web are HTML documents. HTML is a subset of Standard Generalized Markup Language (SGML). HTML codes, or tags, specify the function of a text string (title, heading, body, etc.), but they do not instruct a parser on how to display information. As a result, different browsers format documents differently.

HTTP (n.) <u>H</u>yper<u>t</u>ext <u>T</u>ransfer <u>P</u>rotocol; a standard on the Internet that enables the creation of hyperlinks between documents. A hyperlink automatically and transparently transfers a file to the user when it is activated.

H.261 (n.) A common International Telephone and Telegraph Consultative Committee (CCITT) standard for compressed video.

hub (n.) A network repeater that does not provide retiming functions.

hue (n.) A color, such as cyan, yellow, magenta, red, blue, or green.

Huffman coding (n.) A type of compression that requires one or more sets of Huffman code tables to be specified by the application for coding as well as decoding to decompress data. The Huffman tables may be predefined and used within an application as defaults or computed specifically for a given file. It is a lossless algorithm.

hybrid disc 1. (n.) A CD-ROM that is in the logical disc format and contains ISO 9660 and HFS data structures. 2. (n.) Usually, it is the term for a CD-ROM in the Orange Book format, a multisession disc. Developed by Philips and Eastman Kodak, this format allows information to be added to previously recorded data. A Kodak Photo-CD is an example.

Hybrid Fiber Coax See *HFC*.

HyperCard (n.) An interactive authoring environment developed by Apple Computer. HyperTalk is the scripting language that consists of English commands and creates the links between words, buttons, and diverse media. Programs (stacks) consist of frames (cards) with routines (scripts). XCMDs (external commands) and XFCNs (external functions) are used to extend the functionality.

hypermedia (n.) Another word for multimedia, new media, or digital media. It refers to a dimensional environment with text, graphics, audio, animation, and video elements that are linked.

hypertext (n.) Indexed words that are linked to graphics, audio, or other words not located in close proximity. Theodore Nelson is credited with the first usage of the term in 1963. The World Wide Web is based on Hypertext Markup Language, or HTML. The hypertext links are like the strands of a spider web.

Hypertext Markup Language See *HTML*.

Hypertext Transfer Protocol See *HTTP*.

Hz

Hz (n.) <u>H</u>ert<u>z</u>; a unit of frequency measurement that was named for German physicist Heinrich Rudolph Hertz (1857–1894). One Hz is equal to one cycle per second (cps). One kilohertz (kHz) is equal to 1000 cps, and one megahertz (MHz) is equal to 1 000 000 cps.

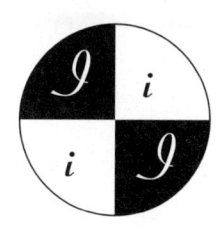

IBM-compatible (adj.) Describes a personal computer that runs MS-DOS and is often referred to as a PC, as opposed to a Macintosh.

IBM PC (n.) <u>IBM</u> <u>P</u>ersonal <u>C</u>omputer; a common microprocessor-based computer employing the Intel style 16-bit CISC processor. It includes the IBM PC-XT and the IBM PC-AT (ISA bus), an earlier generation of the Personal System/2 (PS/2). An expanded definition of the term "PC" includes any microcomputer that runs Microsoft DOS or Windows.

IBM PS/2 (n.) <u>IBM</u> <u>P</u>ersonal <u>S</u>ystem/<u>2</u>; replaced the IBM Personal Computer series in 1987. It uses 8088, 80286, or 80386 processors and implements IBM's Micro Channel Bus. It runs MS-DOS and OS/2 and is compatible with most PC programs.

IC (n.) <u>I</u>ntegrated <u>c</u>ircuit; a self-contained circuit module that passes electric current in predetermined paths. The circuit is created by arranging chemicals on the surface of a semiconductor, such as crystalline silicone. ICs may contain transistors, resistors, and many other types of processing components in their circuitry.

ICIA (n.) <u>I</u>nternational <u>C</u>ommunications <u>I</u>ndustries <u>A</u>ssociation.

ICMP (n.) <u>I</u>nternet <u>C</u>ontrol <u>M</u>essage <u>P</u>rotocol; TCP/IP procedures that enable the functions used for network layer management and control.

icon (n.) Any graphic symbol that represents an object, function, or task. Most often, it represents a file or application in a graphical user interface. When the cursor appears on top of an icon, a mouse click will generally initiate an action.

ICW (n.) <u>I</u>nteractive <u>C</u>ourse<u>w</u>are (United States Army).

ID (n.) <u>Id</u>entification.

IDE (n.) <u>I</u>ntegrated <u>d</u>rive <u>e</u>lectronics; an interface between AT-style computers and hard disk drives. It is commonly used to describe an interface that connects disk drives, CD-ROM drives, and tape drives to IBM-compatible personal computers.

It has been replaced by the SCSI interface in many multimedia applications.

IEEE (n.) Institute of Electrical and Electronics Engineers; a professional society with committees that have established standards for communications interfaces.

IEEE 488 (n.) An 8-bit parallel interface bus between a host computer and a graphics terminal.

IETF (n.) Internet Engineering Task Force; a group that assumes responsibility for managing and maintaining the Internet.

IGES (n.) Initial Graphics Exchange Specification; a cross-platform format for CAD programming, an industry standard defined by the American National Standards Institute (ANSI).

IIA (n.) Information Industry Association.

IICS (n.) International Interactive Communications Society; a grass-roots organization of multimedia developers that has supported the growth of the multimedia industry since its inception. The home office is in Portland, Oregon, USA.

illegal character (n.) A character that may not be used in a command or statement because it is reserved for another use. For example, an MS-DOS file name may not contain a period since that character is used by the operating system to separate the file name from its extension.

IMA 1. (n.) Interactive Multimedia Association; a group of corporations with products based in the multimedia industry. Their home office is located in Arlington, Virginia. 2. (n.) International MIDI Association; the policy-setting group that establishes the standards incorporated in the MIDI specification.

image processing (n.) The manipulation of data to produce a display or to alter a previously defined graphic using digital means.

impedance (n.) The combined effect of capacitance, inductance, and resistance on a signal. According to Ohm's Law, voltage is equal to the product of current and resistance at a given frequency. Microphones are differentiated by whether they operate on a high or low impedance circuit. A low-impedance condenser microphone is more sensitive than a high-impedance dynamic microphone. A low-impedance microphone requires phantom power or a battery.

import (v.) To move data into an open file from memory. The data may be any compatible file type, such as a graphic, and it may exported from a different application. For example, an AIFF sound file may be imported into a Macromedia Director movie and either linked to the movie or combined with all the other assets in the movie file.

inbetweening (tweening) (n.) A function incorporated in some computer animation programs that draws images on the screen automatically to create simulated motion between two coordinates.

inches per second See *ips*.

incremental backup (n.) An archival procedure that copies only files that have changed since the last backup was performed. It is a common way to save recent work from a hard disk to a floppy disk without saving information that has been archived in a full backup.

Indeo (n.) A software-based digital video compression/decompression standard developed by Intel Corporation. Frequently used to facilitate and improve delivery in the Video for Windows or QuickTime formats, it can achieve software decompression at 320 × 240 resolution, at 12–15 frames per second (fps) on a 486DX66 processor; better resolution and frame rates can be achieved on faster processors. The individual video display system, particularly the video card drivers that are installed, will impact decoding to a large degree. It is software-based, so the quality improves with processor speed and computing power.

indexed color systems (adj.) Color systems that obtain data from the user or a file and point to a table of output colors called a color look-up table (CLUT).

individualized instruction (n.) Software that modifies the teaching approach or content based on student feedback to optimize learning.

industrial market (n.) The segment of video and multimedia markets that addresses training, marketing, sales, and communications for businesses rather than home consumers.

Industry Standard Architecture See *ISA*.

inference engine (n.) Related to artificial intelligence, the technology that controls the reasoning process in a knowledge-based system.

infotainment (n.) Interactive CD-ROM programs that blend entertainment with informational, educational activities.

infrared (n.) A spectrum of electromagnetic radiation with wavelengths longer than visible light waves, but shorter than microwaves. It consists of the bandwidth between 0.75 and 1000 microns, a spectrum used for fiber-optic transmission and through-the-air transmission for short distances. Remote control devices typically rely on infrared technology.

in-house (adj.) Describes production or development conducted in a company or organization, without inviting external resources, facilities, or consultants. Developing media in-house is the opposite of out-sourcing production.

INI file (n.) A file with the extension .ini that contains data specific to a certain application in Microsoft Windows, usually defining the configuration and default settings for the application.

INIT (n.) In the Macintosh OS, a utility program that initializes on startup. Conflicting INITs may cause the mouse to freeze and the system to crash. To avoid this, a Macintosh may be started while holding down the Shift key, which disables all INITs, and they may be enabled one by one until the conflict is isolated.

Initial Graphics Exchange Specification See *IGES*.

initialization (n.) A set of routines run by a device or program. Blank media must be initialized for the platform on which they will be used. Printers on a network must be initialized for access. Microcomputers set up registers and memory locations on initialization.

injection molding (n.) The process of forcing melted plastic (polycarbonate) into a mold; the method used to create the substrate of a compact disc.

in-point (n.) The first frame of a video segment or the beginning of an audio track that is chosen for editing.

input 1. (v.) To send information to a computer or processor. 2. (n.) The data sent to a processor or storage device. 3. (n.) A terminal, jack, or receptacle provided for the introduction of an electrical signal into a device.

insert editing (n.) Editing in which new video or audio material is inserted into pre-existing material on a master tape. Time code is not altered.

insertion point (n.) The position on the screen where a blinking cursor is located and characters are entered when typed.

Institute of Electrical and Electronics Engineers See *IEEE*.

instructional design (n.) Computer-aided methods of presenting material that result in learning. Aspects related to interactive programming include questioning strategy, levels of interaction, reinforcement, and branching routines.

instructional designer (n.) An educational training developer.

Instructional Systems Design See *ISD*.

Instructional Television Fixed Service See *ITFS*.

integrated circuit See *IC*.

Integrated Services Digital Network See *ISDN*.

intellectual property (n.) Content or knowledge that may be protected by copyright. Protection of the owner's rights to intellectual property has become a significant concern in multimedia, given the ease with which content can be digitized and transferred.

interactive laser disc levels (n.) Three degrees of interactivity were proposed by the Nebraska Videodisc Design/Production Group in 1980. They are as follows:

Level One: A consumer-model player with still/freeze frame, picture stop, chapter stop, frame address, and dual-channel audio, but limited memory and processing power.

Level Two: An industrial-model player with Level One features, plus programmable memory and faster access time.

Level Three: Level One or Two players interfaced to a computer or peripheral.

interactive media (n.) Types of media that allows users to control the flow of program material. Media may be produced with varying degrees of interactivity.

Interactive Multimedia Association See IMA.

interactive services (n.) Services that allow a subscriber to send messages to a programming source, or content provider, to control the flow of information and engage in two-way communications such as polling, shopping, and banking.

interactive television (n.) A system with the capacity to send information to a broadcast television provider via another communications device, such as a telephone, keypad, or touch screen, allowing viewers to send messages back to the televised source.

interactive video (n.) The use of digital technology to control the flow of video content. In interactive video, the user's choices and decisions determine how a program is presented.

interactivity (n.) Reciprocal communication between a user and a playback device or digital media system.

interchange levels (n.) Under the ISO 9660 standard, the three nested levels at which a CD-ROM file may be named and recorded. Many operating systems and their extensions that read discs require Level 1 restrictions to be observed. The levels may be described as follows:

Level 1: The files consist of a single File Section in one Extent, recorded as a continuous stream and not interleaved. File and directory names must adhere to the strict ISO 9660 naming conventions.

Level 2: The files consist of one File Section in one Extent with no interleaving, but no naming restrictions apply.

Level 3: The files are not restricted.

interconnect (n.) In cable television, a microwave circuit, or cable, that links headends or distribution hubs so that they can exchange programs or services.

interexchange carrier (n.) A long-distance telecommunications service provider that connects multiple local access transport areas (LATA).

interface 1. (n.) A device that connects two pieces of hardware, such as the link between a computer processor and peripherals. 2. (n.) In programming, the means by which a computer user gives instructions and receives information from a computer.

interference (n.) Undesirable energy that is received with a signal and may appear as noise caused by electromagnetic fields.

interfield frames (n.) Frames that result from 3:2 pull-down, the film-to-tape conversion process in which a video frame contains two fields from different film frames.

interframe coding (n.) A method of video compression in which a portion of the data that defines a stream of images is eliminated by discarding redundant data shared between consecutive frames.

interlaced (n.) The combination of two separate field scans joined to form a single video frame. In a video stream, the first field contains even-numbered scan lines, while the second field consists of odd-numbered lines. The two complementary fields lace together to form a single, complete frame. This practice, common to most video systems, is based on the concept of video persistence. The human eye holds the image of the first field while the second field is displayed and blends the two.

interleaving 1. (n.) The nonsequential storage or transmission of information in an alternating series of frames or chunks. A sequence is reassembled on playback to present a continuous flow in the original order. Data files are not always stored in one contiguous block of memory. On a compact disc, files may be split so that small image and audio chunks are discrete, but near in proximity. With interleaving, the laser reading head moves smoothly between the file locations. Without interleaving, gathering information alternately from the two files would require many seeks and excessive head movement. 2. (n.) A method of error detection and correction for CD-ROMs in which a sequence of data is read into a grid vertically and read out again horizontally so that wrong lines are rearranged into individual wrong bits. This process facilitates isolation and correction of errors.

International Interactive Communications Society See *IICS*.

International MIDI Association See *IMA*.

International Telecommunications Union See *ITU*.

International Telecommunications Union-Telephony Sector See *ITU-T*.

International Telecommunications Union-Telecommunications Standardization Sector See *ITU-T*.

International Television Association See *ITVA*.

Internet (n.) A packet-switched network developed by the Advanced Research Project Agency (ARPA) of the Department of Defense to give researchers access to databases and computers. The beginnings of the Internet date from 1969, when the ARPANET was started. The Internet has grown into a large, diverse community of online users that is self-governing and develops its own procedures. Physically, it is the interconnection of many small networks at campuses, research institutes, corporations and military installations sharing a common TCP/IP addressing interface. The Internet spans most countries in the world, several thousand networks, and millions of users. It is expected that distributed multimedia over the Internet will rapidly increase, allowing the delivery of sounds and video over the network as bandwidth increases for more users. Internet activities include sending messages over e-mail, conducting group discussions over Usenet, accessing databases, and "surfing" World Wide Web documents, or pages, that are linked to one another.

Internet acronyms (n.) A form of shorthand for commonly used phrases, consisting of the first letter of each word in the phrase. In some instances, the sound of the letter itself represents a word. The following is a list of common acronyms:

AFK	Away from keyboard
BCNU	Be seein' you
BRB	Be right back
BTW	By the way
CUL8R	See you later
ENQ?	Are you there?
FOAF	Friend of a friend
FYI	For your information
IMHO	In my humble opinion
LTNS	Long time, no see
OIC	Oh, I see
OTOH	On the other hand
ROFL	Rolling on the floor laughing
RTFM	Read the fine manual
TIA	Thanks in advance
TMK	To my knowledge
TNX	Thanks
TTFN	Ta ta for now

Internet address (n.) A 32-bit address assigned to hosts using TCP/IP.

Internet Control Message Protocol See *ICMP*.

Internet country codes (n.) Country abbreviations that identify the top-level domain of a machine. *See tables on following page.*

Internet Engineering Task Force See *IETF*.

Internet Protocol See *IP*.

Internet Relay Chat See *IRC*.

InterNIC (n.) A consortium that is contracted by the National Science Foundation (NSF) and provides services to Internet users. Two entities that are involved are AT&T and Network Solutions, Inc.

Internet country codes

Code	Country
.ae	United Arab Emirates
.am	Armenia
.ar	Argentina
.at	Austria
.au	Australia
.be	Belgium
.bg	Bulgaria
.bh	Bahrain
.br	Brazil
.ca	Canada
.ch	Switzerland
.cl	Chile
.cn	China
.co	Columbia
.cr	Costa Rica
.cy	Cyprus
.cz	Czech Republic
.de	Germany
.dk	Denmark
.do	Dominican Republic
.ec	Ecuador
.ee	Estonia
.eg	Egypt
.es	Spain
.fi	Finland
.fr	France
.gb	Great Britian (UK)
.gl	Greenland
.gr	Greece
.hk	Hong Kong
.hr	Croatia
.hu	Hungary
.id	Indonesia
.ie	Ireland

Code	Country
.il	Israel
.in	India
.is	Iceland
.it	Italy
.jp	Japan
.kr	Korea (South)
.kw	Kuwait
.li	Liechtenstein
.lu	Luxembourg
.lv	Latvia
.mo	Macau
.my	Malaysia
.mx	Mexico
.nl	Netherlands
.no	Norway
.nz	New Zealand
.pe	Peru
.ph	Phillipines
.pl	Poland
.pt	Portugal
.ro	Romania
.ru	Russian Federation
.se	Sweden
.sg	Singapore
.si	Slovenia
.sk	Slovakia (Slovak Republic)
.th	Thailand
.tr	Turkey
.tt	Trinidad and Tobago
.tw	Taiwan
.us	United States
.uy	Uruguay
.ve	Venezuela
.za	South Africa

interpolation (n.) Related to graphics, the process of computing intervening values within a numerical range and applying those values to fill the spaces between given values. When a picture is enlarged, this is the process through which higher resolution is accomplished.

interpreted language (n.) Program code that is converted into machine-readable format and processed simultaneously; it is slower than a compiled language, but more flexible.

interrupt (n.) A computer instruction that momentarily stops the normal operation of a routine. Usually the operation can be resumed from the interruption point later. As the peripheral units interface with the CPU, interrupts occur frequently. Devices are each assigned an interrupt request, or IRQ, and conflicts result when two or more channels are assigned the same IRQ number on a personal computer. See *IRQ*.

interrupt request See *IRQ*.

intraframe coding (n.) Related to video compression, a technique that allocates more data to the coding of highly detailed parts of a single frame at the expense of less detailed areas.

intranet (n.) The use of a dedicated file server running TCP/IP in a local area network (LAN) to provide HTML documents and other files that are accessed by clients using a Web browser as their interface. The intranet may provide users with an external connection to the Internet, facilitating communication with both local and distant Web servers. The advantages of an intranet are the speed with which streaming data can be delivered locally, the security of an internal LAN with a firewall, and the use of a single user-friendly interface for both internal and external communications.

intuitive (adj.) Describes "user-friendly" software that instinctively provides options or information the user needs.

inverted tree structure (n.) A way to provide access to a wide range of data pages, offering a series of menus until the desired page of information is reached.

IP (n.) Internet Protocol; the networking standard for sending a basic unit of data, an IP datagram, via the Internet.

IP address (n.) Internet Protocol address; a unique number that identifies a specific Internet server. It is formatted as a series of digits separated by periods, such as 123.45.678.9.

ips (n.) Inches per second; the running speed of a tape player, such as 3¾, 7½, or 15 ips.

IPX/SPX (n.) The transport protocol that is used in most Novell NetWare environments. In client-server environments in which the server engine is a network loadable module (NLM), communication between the client and the server is generally conducted over IPX/SPX.

IRC

IRC (n.) Internet Relay Chat; a global multiuser chat system that allows people to discuss topics over "channels" on the Internet. Written in 1988 by Jarkko Oikarinen, IRC is constantly evolving with the conventions pertaining to its use. To access an IRC, it is necessary to run a "client" program that connects to an IRC network. Telnet may not be used. Source code for an IRC client is available by anonymous FTP to the following sites:

Windows	cs-ftp.bu.edu:/irc/clients/pc/windows
UNIX	ftp.funet.fi /pub/unix/irc
Macintosh	ftp.funet.fi /pub/unix/irc/mac
MS-DOS	ftp.funet.fi /pub/unix/irc/msdos

A few of the many IRC servers available for connection:

USA	irc.bu.edu
	piglet.cc.utexas.edu
Canada	irc.mcgill.ca
Europe	irc.funet.fi
	cismhp.univ-lyon1.fr
	stork.doc.ic.ac.uk
Australia	troll.elec.uow.edu.au
Japan	endo.wide.ad.jp

All IRC commands start with a "/" and most are one word. Typing "/help" calls for help information. Typing "/names" calls for a list of names. The list of names may be limited by typing "/names -min 20" and only a list of channels with 20 or more people on it will be called. The output of "/names" appears as follows:

Pub: #hack	@brillo rascal mon
Pub: #Nippon	@jellyroll @molli_R

"Pub" means public (or "visible") channel; "hack" is the channel name; "#" is the prefix. A "@" indicates the "Channel operator" who controls the channel.

To join a particular channel, type "/join #channelname". New users benefit from visiting the channel "#irchelp". To join a conversation, type a line of text and send it by striking the [return] key. IRC will automatically insert <nickname> before all of your channel messages. To leave a channel, type "/part #channelname". To access a list of channels and topics, type "/list -min 30" (on ircII), which will show channels with 30 or more members. Many IRC operators visit #Twilight_Zone frequently. Some widely used foreign language channels are:

#nippon	Japanese channel, with Kanji characters
#espanol	Spanish channel
#russian	Russian channel

An IRC users' manual is available from cs-ftp.bu.edu:/irc/support. This IRC primer is recommended reading before joining any list. Addresses for IRC-related mailing lists are shown here:

"operlist"   Discusses server code, routing, and protocol. To join, mail: operlist-request@kei.com with Subject: subscribe

"ircd-three"   Discusses protocol revisions of the ircd (irc server). To join, mail: ircd-three-request@kei.com with Subject: subscribe

For more technical information, refer to the IRC RFC (rfc1459), available at all RFC FTP sites, such as cs-ftp.bu.edu:/irc/support/rfc1459.txt. Other online IRC information sources are:

cs-ftp.bu.edu:/irc/support/alt-irc-faq
ftp.kei.com:/pub/irc/alt-irc-faq
http://www.kei.com/irc.html

If the Netscape Navigator 2.0 or later browser is used to access the Internet, the Netscape Chat plug-in, which is an IRC client, is available. A copy of this plug-in can be downloaded from ftp://ftp20.netscape.com/pub/chat. It should be placed in a separate directory before it is installed. More IRC servers are listed below:

Port	Address	Country
6667	iapp.netscape.com	USA
6667	austin.tx.us.undernet.org	USA
6667	sanjose.ca.us.undernet.org	USA
6667	washington.dc.us.undernet.org	USA
6667	oxford.ok.eu.undernet.org	UK
6667	Montreal.qu.ca.undernet.org	Canada
6667	caen.fr.eu.undernet.org	France
7000	xgw.dal.net	Finland
7000	liberator.dal.net	UK
7000	uncc.dal.net	USA
7000	skypoint.dal.net	USA
7000	cin.dal.net	USA

IRIX (n.) An operating system for Silicon Graphics systems.

IRQ (n.) Interrupt request; an internal signal sent in a PC to indicate that a software routine, peripheral device, or circuit needs attention from the central processor (CPU). The term also refers to a signal line or channel used to carry the interrupt signal from hardware devices to the PC's interrupt controller chip. The original PC provided 8 such lines, while later models provide 16. IRQ lines cannot ordinarily be shared, so it may be problematic to configure a new device.

Sound cards require one or more interrupt channel assignments. The best choice for their interrupt is usually the Sound Blaster default, IRQ 5. MS-DOS reserves this channel for a second printer port. If another device is assigned to interrupt 5, move an 8-bit sound card interrupt to IRQ 7. Move a 16-bit sound card interrupt to any available IRQ between 8 and 15. The standard interrupt assignments are listed below:

Number	Function
IRQ 0	Timer Output 0
IRQ 1	Keyboard (Buffer Full)
IRQ 2	Cascade from IRQ 9
IRQ 3	Serial Port 2; Serial Port 4; SDLC Communications; BSC Communications; Cluster Adapter; Network (Alternate); 3278/79 (Alternate)
IRQ 4	Serial Port 1; Serial Port 3; SDLC Communications; BSC Communications; Voice Communications Adapter
IRQ 5	Parallel Port 2, Sound Blaster Default
IRQ 6	Floppy Disk Controller
IRQ 7	Parallel Port 1; Cluster Adapter (Alternate)
IRQ 8	Real-time Clock

ISA

IRQ 9	Software redirected to INT 0A(Hex); Video; Network; 3278/79 Adapter	CLIP	Calling line identification presentation (displays the caller's number).
IRQ 10	Reserved	CLIR	Calling line identification restriction (prevents caller's number display).
IRQ 11	Reserved		
IRQ 12	Reserved	DDI	Direct dialing in (to an individual user on a private exchange).
IRQ 13	Coprocessor		
IRQ 14	Hard Disk Controller	MSN	Multiple subscriber number.
IRQ 15	Reserved	TP	Terminal portability.

ISA (n.) **I**ndustry **S**tandard **A**rchitecture; the name for the common bus architecture in an IBM-compatible personal computer.

ISD (n.) **I**nstructional **S**ystems **D**esign.

ISDN (n.) **I**ntegrated **S**ervices **D**igital **N**etwork; an international digital telecommunications standard that accommodates voice, data, and signaling and brings high bandwidth to the microcomputer desktop. The typical basic rate interface (BRI) uses two common twisted pairs, unshielded, to deliver two 64-kilobits per second (Kbps) bearer (B) channels and one data signaling (D) channel at 16 Kbps. The two bearer channels may be used simultaneously. The telephone connection may be a distance of approximately one mile from the central office switch, which will limit access. The primary rate interface (PRI) carries 24 bearer channels and a 64 Kbps data channel, with a capacity of nearly 2 megabits per second (Mbps). Among European countries, a memorandum of understanding (MOU) has been established that defines "Priority 1" ISDN facilities and services as follows:

"Priority 2" ISDN facilities and services are defined as follows:

AOC	Advice of charge.
CCBS	Completion of calls to busy subscriber.
CD	Call deflection.
CFB	Call forwarding busy.
CFNR	Call forwarding no reply.
CFU	Call forwarding unconditional.
COLP	Connected line identification presentation.
COLR	Connected line identification restriction.
CONF	Add-on conference call.
CUG	Closed user group.
CWL	Call waiting.
ECT	Explicit call transfer.
FPH	Freephone supplementary service.
HOLD	Call hold.
MCID	Malicious call identification.
MMC	Meet me conference.
3PTY	Three-party service.
SUB	Subaddressing.
UUS	User-to-user signaling.

ISO (n.) Greek for "the same as" or "equal to." It is used as the name of the **I**nternational **S**tandards **O**rganization. This organization, founded in Geneva in 1946, is involved in the development and definition of worldwide standards. In multimedia, they have defined CD-ROM formats, compression algorithms, communications specifications, and standards for a wide range of technical software applications. They serve most fields except electrical or electronic applications, which are dealt with by the IEC (International Electrotechnical Commission). Members from 80 countries staff the Joint Technical Committees (JTC), on which the ISO and IEC combine. (Pronounced **eye-soh**.)

isochronous (adj.) Describes a type of data transmission in which characters are separated by a whole number of bit-length intervals. Timing information is embedded in the data stream. This is in contrast to asynchronous transmission, in which characters may be separated by random-length intervals.

ISO image (n.) An exact representation of the entire set of data and programs as it will appear on a CD-ROM, including content and logical format, simulated on another medium. It is sent to a disc manufacturer for premastering and mastering. It is also referred to as a CD-ROM image or disc image.

ISO 9660 (n.) An international standard that specifies the logical file format for CD-ROM files and directories. It is directly derived from the High Sierra Group Proposal. ISO 9660 discs can be read by most PC CD-ROM drives if the proper software driver has been loaded into the system.

ITFS (n.) Instructional Television Fixed Service; a broadcast system that operates in a specified band of microwave frequencies established by the FCC exclusively for educational programs. ITFS operates within a radius of approximately 20 miles, or "line-of-sight." A special converter is required to receive and translate the broadcast audio, video, or data into standard television signals.

ITU (n.) International Telecommunications Union; a Geneva-based organization that addresses standards, such as those for video teleconferencing.

ITU-T (n.) International Telecommunications Union-Telecommunications Standardization Sector; an international body that sets telecommunications standards; formerly known as the International Telephone and Telegraph Consultative Committee (CCITT).

ITVA (n.) International Television Association; a professional organization of producers, technicians, engineers, and others who participate in the development of broadcast video and film.

jack (n.) Related to audio, video, or computing gear, a connecting point that accepts the plug on a cable or line. It is a female connector in most cases.

jaggies (n.) Undesirable artifacts that appear in a graphic display or printout as a result of a lack of adequate resolution to portray lines that are not on the horizontal or vertical axis. See *aliasing*.

jewel box (n.) The plastic box in which audio CDs and CD-ROM discs are packaged. The printed matter enclosed usually consists of a booklet and tray card.

jitter (n.) A shift in phase of digital pulses in transmission, causing lack of synchronization. It results in unstable video signal reception.

jog (v.) To change position in a video clip, or shuttle it, by a single frame or small number of frames when editing.

Joint Photographic Expert Group See *JPEG*.

joystick (n.) An input device that rotates on an axis and controls the position of a cursor. It may be equipped with a button that sends messages that a program can interpret. Video and arcade games are often enabled by the use of a joystick.

JPEG (n.) Joint Photographic Expert Group; an international consortium of hardware, software, and publishing interests who, under the auspices of the International Organization for Standardization, defined a universal standard for the digital compression and decompression of still images for use in computer systems. The format itself is also called JPEG, and it is a lossy compression scheme that uses DCT and quantization to encode still images. The technique may be used to compress images with moderate detail up to about a 15:1 ratio before visible degradation occurs. An 800-kilobyte (KB) file may be compressed to approximately 80 KB with the application of JPEG compression in a 10:1 ratio, and relatively little necessary data will be lost. When the same 800-KB file is reduced to 40 KB, a 20:1 ratio, artifacts may be noticeable. The process is based on identifying a block of pixels that are all approximately the same color with a single chroma descriptor and multiplying that information by a factor that defines the area of the block. Hence, high compression ratios result in a "blocky" end product, and simple images with little detail and few gradients lend themselves to higher compression ratios.

jukebox (n.) An optical or magnetic storage unit that holds multiple discs, any of which may be selected and automatically loaded into the play station. It usually refers to a stack of CD-ROMs.

jump (v.) In an interactive program, to branch to another location.

jump cut (n.) An abrupt type of video edit that shows a new camera angle, a different frame size, or a notable change in the placement of the subject. Jump cuts may be remedied with cover shots and cutaways, but are they generally avoided.

jumper (n.) A small patch cable, or a clip that completes or breaks a circuit.

justification (n.) The process in which space is allocated in a line of text so that both ends meet a pre-established margin.

Ka Band (n.) This bandwidth of the electromagnetic spectrum lies in the high microwave range.

Kaleida (n.) The name adopted by collaborators from Apple Computer and IBM with the intent to develop and promote new multimedia software technologies with applications for computers, personal electronics, and communications. Kaleida seeks to create a cross-platform multimedia environment. See *ScriptX*.

karaoke (n.) "Empty orchestra" in Japanese. A performer sings into a microphone to music provided by a laser disc or video-CD while lyrics are displayed as subtitles on a screen. It is a popular activity in homes and nightclubs in Japan.

Kb (n.) Kilobit; one thousand bits or binary digits, as opposed to bytes (8-bit words).

KB (n.) Kilobyte; in reference to binary data, this is 2^{10}, or 1024 bytes. For example, DOS has a limit of 640 KB of conventional memory.

Kbps (n.) Kilobits per second; a measurement of data transfer in thousands of bytes each second. The time required to transfer a 1-megabyte (MB) file at 14.4 Kbps = 9.7 minutes; at 128 Kbps = 66 seconds; at 10 megabits per second (Mbps) = .8 seconds.

KBps (n.) Kilobytes per second; a measurement of data transfer or movement in thousands of bytes each second.

Kermit (n.) A file transfer protocol and terminal emulation program used to download files from a host to a local computer by modem. It can transfer binary files over Telnet and other connections without corrupting data.

kernel (n.) The portion of an operating system that controls basic functions, such as resource allocation and memory management.

kern (v.) To control the spacing between letters in a document. Certain letter combinations require more or less space between them to become legible and pleasing to the eye, such as the letters AV, an example of negative spacing.

key 1. (n.) A button on an input device that sends data to the computer program to which it is connected. 2. (n.) Jargon for "keyframe," an image used at the beginning or end of an animation sequence. 3. (n.) Jargon for "keylight," often the brightest light shining on the main character in a scene of a video or film production. 4. (v.) To switch between two or more video sources, based on a control signal, or the control signal itself. An example is chroma keying, where a color is used as a key to eliminate or block objects of that color in a video composition.

keyboard 1. (n.) Any device that contains alphanumeric, symbol, and function keys that can input text or instructions to a computer. The version that resembles a typewriter is referred to as a "QWERTY" keyboard because of the layout of the keys. 2. (n.) A piano, synthesizer, or MIDI keyboard with black-and-white keys that is used to perform music.

keyer (n.) In video-editing, a video switcher that cuts a hole in the background and fills it with material from another source. Text and graphics are frequently "keyed" over NTSC video. The keyer superimposes two or more images by alternating among inputs during the scans across the screen defining the video image. With the aid of this technique, a weather forecaster appears to be standing in front of a map, when in reality, she is standing in front of a blue screen.

key frame 1. (n.) An image that is used at the beginning or end of an animation sequence or as a reference point in a video stream. 2. (n.) In compressed video, a frame that contains complete information rather than just data about changes made in the previous frame.

keypad (n.) A small keyboard that typically consists of numeric and function keys only.

keywords 1. (n.) Words written in a high-level computing language that call subroutines. 2. (n.) In some training applications, "keyword" tests help evaluate a learner's comprehension.

kHz (n.) Kilohertz; one thousand cycles per second.

kilo (n.) A prefix meaning one thousand.

kilobit See *Kb*.

kilobits per second See *Kbps*.

kilobyte See *KB*.

kilobytes per second See *KBps*.

kilohertz See *kHz*.

kiosk (n.) A free-standing, interactive multimedia system, that typically has a touch screen for input. It is often located in a public access area, and it may be used to convey information or to collect data.

knockout

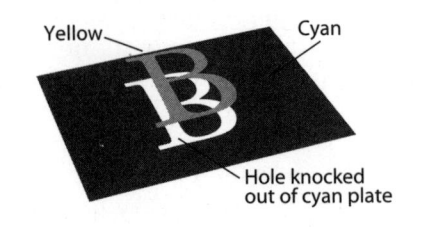

knockout

knockout (n.) The removal of an element in a multilayered graphic so that the underlying color does not tint overlapping layers. *See illustration.*

KU Band (n.) A bandwidth of the electromagnetic spectrum that is used by satellites, ranging from 12 to 14 gigahertz (GHz).

Lambert shading (n.) A method of applying a graduated shade to a surface by filling small polygons with different colors, or shades, resulting in a faceted appearance; also called "faceted shading."

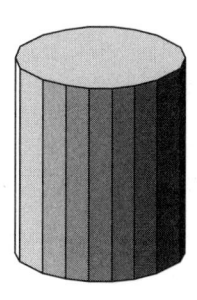

Lambert-shaded cylinder

LAN Local area network 1. (n.) A system of cables and interfaces controlled by a communications protocol that connects two or more microcomputers for sharing resources and peripherals. Connection is also possible with an infrared link. 2. (n.) Any physical network technology that operates at high speed over short distances, such as several thousand yards. Technologies that play roles in a LAN include Ethernet, Token Ring, ATM, FDDI II, 10Base-T, and SNA.

LANC (n.) Local Application Numerical Control; developed by Sony, this machine control protocol for videotape recorders and players can carry control-S data. It is implemented by a variety of camcorders in the 8mm and S-VHS format and is capable of transferring Hours:Minutes:Seconds:Frames information to and from digital controllers.

land (n.) The space between pits on the surface of a compact disc.

landing zone (n.) The cylinder number at which the head is parked when a hard disk drive is idle or off.

landscape (n.) A layout in which the width of a printed page is greater than the height. In a "portrait" layout, the height is greater than the width.

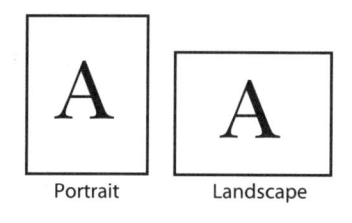

landscape and portrait layouts

language (n.) In programming, a set of instructions specified by a programmer that can be carried out by a computer. BASIC, COBOL, Pascal, FORTRAN, and C++ are common languages.

LAPD (n.) **L**ink **A**ccess **P**rocedure-**D**; a link-level protocol for ISDN connections that has a different framing sequence than the LAP Balanced (LAPB) protocol.

laptop (n.) Any portable computer. Since portables are becoming smaller and lighter, it is more common to refer to them as "notebook" computers.

large-scale integration See *LSI*.

laser (n.) **L**ight **a**mplification by **s**timulated **e**mission of **r**adiation; a laser generates and amplifies energy in the optical spectrum into a beam. The focused beam consists of a single wavelength of light, so when it passes over an uneven surface (like the data spiral of a compact disc), changes in the wavelength due to reflection can be detected and converted into a stream of binary data.

laser disc (n.) (LD) A reflective optical medium, also called a videodisc. "Laser Disc" is a trademark of Pioneer, USA and has been used freely to describe all types of videodiscs.

laser pickup (n.) A mechanical subsystem in an optical disc player that holds and positions the laser.

laser printer (n.) Any printer that uses laser optics to produce text and images on photosensitive paper. Desktop laser printers require toner cartridges and typically range from 300 dots per inch (dpi) to 600 dpi in resolution.

laser rot (n.) The degradation of an optical disc caused by the use of contaminated raw materials or improper process controls.

Laservision (n.) A trade name for the videodisc format supported by manufacturers such as Pioneer, Philips, and Sony.

Laservision read-only memory See *LV-ROM*.

LATA **L**ocal **A**ccess and **T**ransport **A**rea; there are 161 local telephone service areas in the United States, and calls made point-to-point within a single LATA are the responsibility of the local telephone company. InterLATA calls are processed by an interexchange carrier.

latency (n.) Time spent waiting for a response; a component in the measurement of access time in hard disk and CD-ROM drives.

layering (n.) A concept applied in multimedia production to create dimensionality. In sound design, a mix may contain numerous channels, or layers, with different audio tracks on each channel. A layered graphic design typically shows objects in the foreground with others in the background. In the process of editing a video production, materials from various sources are layered. Complex three-dimensional animations employ a high degree of layering.

L-band (n.) A bandwidth of the electromagnetic spectrum that lies in the 1-gigahertz (GHz) range and is used for satellite transmission and microwave applications.

LCD (n.) Liquid crystal display; an array of liquid crystal cells that are electronically turned on and off, modulating light that shines from behind the display. Large LCD panels can simulate computer graphic output when used with an overhead projection system. Because LCDs consume very little power, they are often used for numbers and letters on calculators, watches, and hand-held games.

LD (n.) See *laser disc*.

leader (n.) In the process of storing analog recordings on magnetic tape, a clean, blank segment of tape-like material that is spliced before the first cut and between programs. Sometimes the term is used loosely to refer to a few seconds of blank tape at the head of a reel.

leadin (n.) In videodisc programs, the 40 seconds of video black preceding the active program.

lead-in area (n.) A space reserved at the beginning of a recordable compact disc (CD-R) that is left blank for the disc's table of contents (TOC). The table is recorded in this space when the disc is filled, or when it is permanently closed and finalized.

leading (n.) In desktop publishing programs, the distance between the baseline on which type rests between two consecutive lines; composed of the height of the type and the space between the lines. (Pronounced **ledding**.)

leadout (n.) In videodisc programs, the 30 seconds of video black with no audio following the active program.

lead-out area (n.) A space reserved at the end of a session on a recordable compact disc (CD-R), which indicates the end of the data has been reached and the session has been finalized.

leased line (n.) A dedicated telephone connection that links two or more points without passing through switching equipment.

LED (n.) Light-emitting diode; a semiconductor diode that emits light when current passes through it. The most common LED application is the alphanumeric display on a calculator. A laser is a type of LED that can serve as the source for optical data transmission.

Lempel-Ziv-Welch See *LZW*.

letterbox (v.) To crop the top and bottom of the screen while displaying video. Programs recorded in the original aspect ratio of film, which is proportionately wider than a computer or television monitor, will often appear with a black band above and below the viewing area. This results in a rectangular frame with the edges cropped.

letterbox effect

level (n.) In audio terminology, the amplitude or strength of a signal, usually expressed in decibels related to a reference signal. In video, levels are measured in IRE units.

LFO (n.) Low-frequency oscillator. In sound synthesis, a device capable of subsonic frequency generation, used most often as a controller for other functions, such as vibrato or tremolo.

library (n.) In programming, a list of procedures and/or functions that can be accessed and implemented. It consists of a collection of previously built code or routines.

light-emitting diode See *LED*.

light pen (n.) A stylus that controls the position of a cursor on a monitor. It has a light-detecting tip and is used for graphics input or as a user interface device.

linear (adj.) Describes a medium in which content is arranged sequentially and the user must move through the material in either forward or reverse motion without entry points or branching. A videotape is linear, while digital media is interactive.

linear audio (n.) The use of a separate track on a videotape dedicated to recording audio. This technique may result in low fidelity, but the audio may be edited separately from the video.

line art (n.) Images that contain only black-and-white information with no grayscale or blended tones. This category includes halftone images that appear gray but consist of tiny black dots on a white background.

line level (adj.) Describes an audio signal that ranges from 100 millivolts (mV) to approximately one volt for full signal, typically the output of a preamplifier rather than the low-level signal from a microphone.

Lingo (n.) A scripting language used for authoring in Macromedia Director. It is similar to HyperTalk, the language used in HyperCard scripting.

link 1. (n.) A connection between two pieces of data, such as between an icon and the information it represents. 2. (n.) A connection between network nodes.

Link Access Procedure-D See *LAPD*.

link layer (n.) In the OSI reference model, this is Layer Two, the Data Link Layer.

liquid crystal display See *LCD*.

LISP (n.) List processor; a programming language developed by John McCarthy that consists of expressions that are lists of instructions to a computer. The lists establish relationships between themselves, and the values created by the relationships become part of the data in a LISP program. It is commonly used in artificial intelligence applications.

listserv (n.) A program that automates mailing lists on the Internet or any large network.

lithography (n.) The transfer of a pattern or image from one medium to another, such as from a mask to a silicon wafer.

load (v.) To transfer a computer program from storage into RAM.

Local Access and Transport Area See *LATA*.

Local Application Numerical Control See *LANC*.

local area network See *LAN*.

local bus (n.) In microcomputer architecture, a data bus with a short signal path between the main processor and I/O processors, frequently used for fast video functions.

local exchange (n.) A telecommunication provider's central office where a subscriber's line is terminated.

localize (v.) To tailor the content of piece of media to fit the cultural requirements of a specific region or population.

LocalTalk (n.) The hardware that is used to connect Macintosh computers and peripherals for AppleTalk communications.

location 1. (n.) The address where data is recorded or located in computer memory. 2. (n.) A place where a film is shot, usually outdoors or in a "real world" environment, as opposed to in a studio where backgrounds are created.

logic (n.) The application of truth tables, relational propositions, and gated circuits used for computation. Logic circuits are used to control the operation of IC devices.

logical codes (n.) Tags that provide general directions in an HTML document. For example, the tag <em> means emphasis, which could be translated as italic or bold. By contrast, physical codes have specific meanings. The tag <b> indicates bold.

logical device (n.) A device that exists in the logic of a computer, whether or not it is physically connected or even exists.

logical expression (n.) In computer logic, a comparison between two variables or values that yields a true or false answer. For example, the statement "1>0" is true, or correct.

logical file format (n.) In reference to data stored on a compact disc or hard drive, a structure in the shape of a virtual "tree" of directories and files, facilitating access to information. It is also referred to as the "logical format."

log on (v.) To enter a networked multiuser environment, typically by submitting a username and password to the host computer.

log out (v.) To exit from a networked multiuser environment. Typing "logoff" will usually send a message to the host that the session initiated by the most recent "logon" is terminated.

longitudinal redundancy check See *LRC*.

longitudinal time code (n.) Time code information that is recorded, or "stamped" in the form of an audio signal, on an available track of a videotape. It provides a means of precisely locating any point on the tape, which enables frame-accurate machine control.

loop 1. (n.) A complete electrical connection that is self-contained. 2. (n.) The repeated display of a series of still frames, an audio file, a video segment, or the execution of a series of instructions without interruption. 3. (v.) To repeat.

loop through (n.) A feature of an audio, video, or data circuit that provides an output connector that sends the same signal the unit receives as input. This makes it possible for an auxiliary unit to receive the signal at approximately the same time.

lossless compression (n.) Compression technique that reduces the storage requirements of a file, yet completely preserves the original information contained in images or other data.

lossy (adj.) Describes coding methods that do not preserve all the original data, so that it cannot be recovered later. However, data lost in the quantization of high-frequency components of an image are virtually imperceptible to the human eye, so the data that is discarded may be relatively insignificant.

lossy compression (n.) A compression technique that greatly reduces the quantity of data reduction by discarding redundant and unnecessary information in images and data files, while maintaining the basic content. See *DCT*.

low-frequency oscillator See *LFO*.

low-level language (n.) An assembly language that translates each statement into a single machine instruction.

LPT (n.) Line printer; a parallel port on an IBM-compatible computer where a printer is often interfaced through a 25-pin connector. See *parallel port*.

LRC (n.) **L**ongitudinal **r**edundancy **c**heck; a procedure that tests the accuracy of networked data or information stored on a data tape.

LSI (n.) **L**arge-**s**cale **i**ntegration; in a microprocessor, generally more than 1000 and fewer than 10 000 operations.

LTC (n.) **L**ongitudinal **t**ime **c**ode; a method of time-stamping videotape.

lumen (n.) A unit of luminous flux emitted by a light source, measured in candelas. A candela is the intensity radiated by a single candle.

luminance (n.) The degree of brightness; one of the three image characteristics coded in a video signal (represented by the letter Y) and measured in lux or foot-candles.

luminance bandwidth (n.) The frequency range representing the degree of brightness that a video system can record or transmit. Shape detail is determined largely by this factor.

luminance key (n.) A signal used to switch between two or more video images based on the brightness of one of the signals.

lux (n.) A unit of measurement equal to one lumen covering the surface of one square meter.

LV See *Laservision*.

LV-ROM 1. (n.) **L**aser**v**ision **r**ead-**o**nly **m**emory; developed in 1986 by Philips, this laser disc format combines analog video with digital data and audio on a 12-inch laser disc. It has been called Advanced Interactive Video (AIV). An updated version of the format was reintroduced in 1990 by Pioneer. It provides for digital data in the ISO 9660 (High Sierra) CD-ROM format to be encoded along with the normal stereo audio and video information on a standard 12-inch laser videodisc.

Lynx (n.) A UNIX text-based Web browser.

LZW (n.) **L**empel-**Z**iv-**W**elch; a lossless compression algorithm developed in 1977. It relies on identifying similarities between character codes and recording that data in an abbreviated format.

MAC (n.) <u>M</u>edia <u>a</u>ccess <u>c</u>ontrol; a media-specific access control protocol within the IEEE 802 specification. It defines the lower sublayer of OSI link layer, which complements the Logical Link Control (LLC). It includes variations for token ring, token bus, and CSMA/CD.

machine-independent (adj.) Describes software designed to work on more than one kind of computer. It offers similar performance or output when run on different types or models of machines.

machine language (n.) Binary code that expresses computer instructions and data in an executable form at the lowest level. No further translation is required for computer processing.

Macintosh (n.) Developed by Apple Computer in 1984, this popular microcomputer was based on the Motorola 68000 series CPU. It evolved into the Power Macintosh based on a RISC processor in 1994. Its operating system is the Finder, a GUI designed by Xerox. Multimedia features such as sound generation, QuickTime video, and interactive icons have been built into the hardware and software of Macintosh computers since their inception, establishing a model in this regard for other system designers.

Macintosh Programmer's Workshop See *MPW*.

macro (n.) A small block of code, or a series of commands, batched together and executed by a keystroke or combination of function keys; used to replace or automate frequently performed tasks.

magnetic storage (n.) Any medium used to save information encoded as variations in magnetic polarity. Common examples of magnetic storage are audio and videotapes and floppy diskettes.

magnetic tape (n.) Typically made from a mylar base, this tape is thin and not elastic. It is coated with a ferromagnetic emulsion and used to record and store audio tracks, video programs, and computer data.

magneto optical See *MO*.

magneto-optical disc (n.) A high-density, read-and-write optical storage media. Access speed is slower than a hard disk but faster than a CD-ROM. Discs are written by a laser that heats a spot on the disc surface; the spot is polarized by an electromagnet from the other side of the disc. When read, the change in polarity changes the reflection of light from the reading laser at that spot, and the difference is interpreted as a data value. These discs may be written and read many times, like a large floppy disk. See *MO*.

mail gateway (n.) A connection between multiple electronic mail systems that transfers mail between them; applies to machines that bridge dissimilar main systems on different networks.

mainframe computer (n.) The primary framework of a large computer's central processing unit (CPU).

main processing unit (n.) The computational core of a system which provides the logical, arithmetic, and control functions that access, process, or output data.

management information systems See *MIS*.

Mandelbrot set (n.) A subset of a complex plane whose boundary is a fractal of great detail and variety. It is named for Benoit Mandelbrot, who performed the first research on the subject in the 1970s. See illustration.

Mandlebrot set

mapping (n.) In graphic design, the process of specifying how a texture is applied to the surface of an object. In three-dimensional animation, how a texture follows an object is a function of its mapping, as well as the scale and orientation of the surface image.

markup (n.) The instructions embedded in a text document that specify formatting features, such as headings and paragraphs. Since many proprietary versions exist, Structured Generalized Markup Language (SGML) is the proposed universal standard.

mask (n.) 1. The area on a graphic screen on which nothing may be imaged. 2. (n.) A chrome and glass pattern used in the photolithography process for etching a layer of silicon in chip manufacturing.

master 1. (n.) The final edited version of a program, recorded on high-quality audio tape, videotape, or film, that is intended for broadcast or as the source for duplication. 2. (v.) To produce stamper molds used for replication. In compact disc manufacturing, it refers to the creation of a glass master from which copies are reproduced. A laser beam "engraves" the pits representing binary data into a photo-resistant surface.

matrix (n.) A predetermined array of quantities or elements.

Mb (n.) Mega<u>b</u>it; one million bits, not bytes. Bytes are typically 8-bit words.

MB (n.) Mega<u>b</u>yte; the quantity of 20^{20}, or 1 048 576 bytes not bits.

M-bone (n.) <u>M</u>ulticast back<u>bone</u>; an Internet provision for video transfer.

MCA 1. (n.) <u>M</u>edia <u>C</u>ontrol <u>A</u>rchitecture (Apple). 2. (n.) <u>M</u>icro <u>C</u>hannel <u>a</u>rchitecture (IBM); the revised bus for PC architecture introduced by IBM in its PS/2 series microcomputers. It is incompatible with original PC/AT architecture.

MCI (n.) <u>M</u>edia <u>C</u>ontrol <u>I</u>nterface; a platform-independent multimedia specification published by Microsoft and others in 1990. It provides a consistent way to control devices such as CD-ROMs and video playback units. See *RIFF*.

MCI drivers (n.) Drivers that direct the recording and playback of multimedia objects. The syntax requires that a MCI command "open" a device, give it instructions, and "close" it. A set of commands is shared by all MCI devices for basic functions, such as "play" and "stop." Microsoft has defined 11 MCI devices that drivers control, including an undefined classification. *See table below.*

MCI Device	Command Syntax
Animation player	MCI_DEVTYPE_ANIMATION
Audio CD player	MCI_DEVTYPE_CD_AUDIO
Digital audio tape	MCI_DEVTYPE_DAT
Video in a window	MCI_DEVTYPE_DIGITAL_VIDEO
Undefined	MCI_DEVTYPE_OTHER
Video overlay	MCI_DEVTYPE_OVERLAY
Image scanner	MCI_DEVTYPE_SCANNER
MIDI sequencer	MCI_DEVTYPE_SEQUENCER
Videocassette recorder	MCI_DEVTYPE_VCR
Videodisc player	MCI_DEVTYPE_VIDEODISC
Waveform player	MCI_DEVTYPE_WAVEFORM_AUDIO

MDI (n.) <u>M</u>ultiple <u>d</u>ocument <u>i</u>nterface; a feature of Microsoft Windows that permits more than one document to be open simultaneously. The borders of the application window contain all open documents. Program Manager is a typical MDI application in Windows 3.1.

mean time between failure See *MTBF*.

media (n.) The plural form of "medium"; anything that is used for storage or transmission of information, such as disks or networks.

media access control See *MAC*.

Media Control Interface See *MCI*.

media-independent (adj.) Describes any software program that delivers the same content on different playback systems.

Media Player (n.) In the Accessories Directory of Microsoft Windows, there is a viewer, or player, for all types of audio and video data streams. This applet is called Media Player, and if the drivers are loaded for a particular media type, such as Video for Windows (.avi), it provides a way to view and hear a stream of data. This is an easy way to access any type of multimedia on a Windows-based system.

medium (n.) In a digital context, the substance or object on which information is stored or transmitted. The plural form is media. Examples in telecommunications of transmission media include fiber optic, wire, cable, air, and water.

mega (n.) Prefix meaning one million. In the decimal system 1 000 000 is expressed as 10^6. In the binary system, which used to quantify data, this is expressed as 2^{20}, or 1 048 576.

megabit See *Mb*.

megabyte See *MB*.

megaflop (n.) One million floating-point calculations per second; a measurement of the speed of a workstation or a mainframe.

megahertz See *MHz*.

Memorandum of Understanding See *MOU*.

memory (n.) The place where data is recorded and stored, either permanently or temporarily. It is usually measured in kilobytes, megabytes, or gigabytes. Memory is placed in tracks and sectors on formatted media.

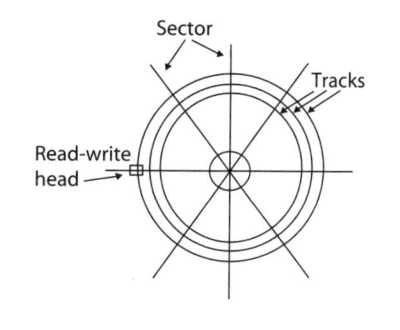

memory configuration on a magnetic disk

menu (n.) A list of options from which

users may choose. The options are often available through a drop-down menu bar at the top of a graphical user interface (GUI) screen.

menu-driven (adj.) Describes a type of interface that allows the user to navigate by selecting choices from a menu of options on the screen, rather than typing characters on a command line.

mesh (n.) In three-dimensional modeling, an object defined by a series of points between which planes are defined.

metafile (n.) A means of storing objects by defining their shapes mathematically in a file that contains both bitmap and vector data. An example of a metafile is the Windows graphics file type with the extension .wmf. The format is useful to move graphics between applications, such as PowerPoint and Director.

metal-oxide-semiconductor See *MOS*.

MHz (n.) Megahertz; one million cycles per second.

Micro Channel architecture See *MCA*.

Microcom Networking Protocol See *MNP*.

microcomputer (n.) A self-contained computer system with a microprocessor, input devices, display, and memory. Also called a desktop or personal computer.

micron (n.) One-millionth of a meter; also known as a micrometer.

microphone patterns (n.) The sensitivity of a microphone to the direction of sound sources in relation to the axis of the microphone body. Sounds that originate directly in front of the microphone's diaphragm have greater intensity and fuller frequency response than sounds that emanate from the side. Note the patterns illustrated. The cardioid microphone has excellent off-axis rejection, which is desirable in some recording situations. *See illustration on following page.*

microprocessor (n.) Any integrated circuit containing the central processing unit (CPU) for a small computer. Intel has manufactured 80286, 80386, 80486, and Pentium chips for IBM-compatibles, and Motorola has made 68000, 68020, 68030, 68040 chips for the Macintosh. These are all CISC chips. A new generation of RISC-based chips was designed by Apple Computer, Motorola, and IBM, and they are used in PowerPC and Power Macintosh computers.

microsecond (n.) One-millionth of a second.

Microsoft Compact Disk Extension See *MSCDEX*.

Microsoft Disk Operating System See *MS-DOS*.

Microsoft Network See *MSN*.

personal computers running MS-DOS. It is loosely based on the point-and-click, icon-based interface invented by Apple Computer and deployed on all Macintosh computers. Version 3.1 incorporates device drivers needed for multimedia functionality. See *GUI*.

microwave (n.) This bandwidth of high-frequency radio waves lies between 890 megahertz (MHz) and 20 gigahertz (GHz). Microwaves are used for line-of-sight, point-to-point, and omnidirectional transmission of audio, video, and data signals within a terrestrial range of 20 to 30 miles.

MIDI (n.) Musical Instrument Digital Interface; an industry-standard hardware/software system for microprocessor control of musical instruments and devices. It defines a protocol for the interchange of musical information between computers, digital musical instruments, and sound boards. MIDI is a simple serial communications bus, like a SCSI bus. The signal is a serial voltage transmission at the rate of 31 250 bits per second. The messages are bytes encoded to define status (the type of message) and data (information regarding the preceding status byte). The cable is a shielded, twisted pair of wires connected to pins 4 and 5 of a 5-pin DIN plug. Pin 2 is the ground. Any device with a MIDI port can communicate with another one with similar connections. A MIDI interface and software is all that is needed for a computer to control MIDI-compatible

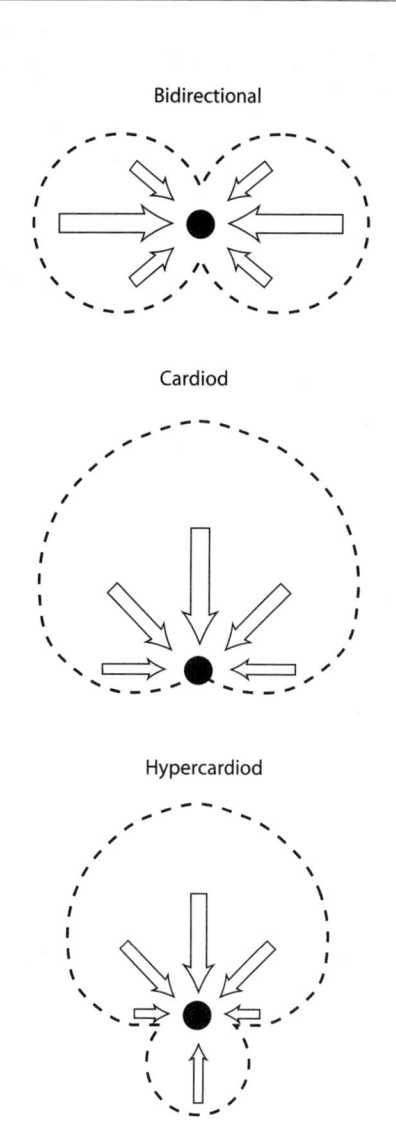

microphone patterns

Microsoft Windows (n.) A graphical user interface, or operating system, patented by Microsoft for use with

digital instruments. The file extension is .mid. See *General MIDI*.

MIDI modes (n.) The four ways in which MIDI equipment may be configured. Mode 1 is OMNI ON/Polyphonic; mode 2 is OMNI ON/monophonic; mode 3 is OMNI OFF/polyphonic; mode 4 is OMNI OFF/monophonic. Channel mode messages set an instrument's mode to OMNI on or off, which determines the channels that will be read. OMNI ON means all channels are read, and OMNI OFF means just one assigned channel will be read. Channel mode messages further qualify the OMNI setting to respond polyphonically, playing more than one note at a time, or monophonically, playing only one note at a time. In monophonic modes no chords are possible.

MIDI 1.0 specification (n.) The International MIDI Association (IMA) defined this original specification for the use of MIDI communications in collaboration with manufacturers of digital synthesizers. The five types of messages in the specification can be divided into two groups: system messages and channel messages. While system messages send information to an entire MIDI system, channel messages send it to selected channels. Channel messages are most common, and they follow a status byte that identifies which of the 16 MIDI channels is to receive the data. They may be one of two varieties; channel voice or channel mode messages. Channel voice messages carry information such as "note on" or "note off" signals for any given key number with velocity values.

MIDI system messages (n.) Unlike channel voice or mode messages, system messages are read by all devices connected to the system. The three types of MIDI messages are System Common, System Real-Time, and System Exclusive. They are defined as follows:

Real-Time: Messages include the MIDI Clock timing pulse; Start, Stop, or Continue a sequence; Active Sensing to confirm a connection; and System Reset to return all devices to their default status.

System Common: Messages include MIDI Time Code (MTC) or Quarter Frame, Song Position, Song Select, and Tune Request.

System Exclusive: Messages carry a manufacturer ID that is recognized only by one brand of equipment. This type of message includes the Sample Dump Standard, which allows nonexclusive descriptions of waveforms which can be edited and played back on different brands of sample players. It also includes MIDI Time Code messages, which can be used to synchronize with SMPTE devices. The MIDI Files Standard allows a sequence to be read by any type of MIDI device, regardless of the platform. This file type is the Standard MIDI File (SMF).

migration (n.) Automatic or program-controlled movement of data between slower storage media and faster storage media. The rules of migration determine when objects are moved.

mil (n.) A unit of measurement equal to one-thousandth of an inch, or 25.4 microns.

million instructions per second See *MIPS*.

millisecond (n.) One-thousandth of a second.

MIME (n.) Multipurpose Internet Mail Extensions; a protocol for sending sound, graphics, and other binary data over the Internet as attachments to e-mail.

minicomputer (n.) A parallel binary system with more storage and a faster processor than a microcomputer, but one that is smaller and less costly than a mainframe computer.

minidisc (n.) An audio compact disc format developed by Sony for use with its Data Discman portable system. Invented in 1991, a minidisc holds 200 megabytes (MB) of data. The format was revised in 1992 and introduced as a rewritable magneto optical disc format for music. The media resembles a 2.5-inch floppy disk.

minimize (v.) In a graphical user interface, to reduce an open window to an icon, or a very small representation of the contents.

mip mapping (n.) The storage of several different resolutions of a texture map to avoid recalculating texture images as a viewer zooms closer to or further away from a textured surface.

MIPS (n.) Million instructions per second; a measurement of computer performance, or processing speed.

mirror site (n.) An FTP site on the Internet that contains the same information held by another site, so that demand on the original site is distributed.

MIS (n.) Management information systems; the application of computers to perform business functions, such as information retrieval and representation of a database, projecting and forecasting, communications, tracking accounts, and assisting in decision-making regarding resource allocation.

mission-critical (adj.) Describes system resources that would seriously impair the ability of an organization to function if they failed.

mixed-mode disc (n.) A compact disc including computer data and CD-DA tracks. Typically, computer data is placed in the first track, and the audio is placed in one or more of the following tracks.

MMA (n.) MIDI Manufacturers Association; the organization of digital synthesis and studio equipment makers that collaborate on standards and related issues.

MMC (n.) Multimedia Marketing Council; owners of the MPC trademark; a group of hardware vendors collaborating with Microsoft. Specifications established by the MMC are marked with the MPC trademark.

MNP (n.) Microcom Networking Protocol; an asynchronous communications protocol that permits packet retransmission, data compression, and speed negotiation between two modems. The CCITT V.42 standard specifies the four classes of MNP as a backup error-correction scheme for the link access procedure for modems (LAPM).

MO (n.) Magneto optical; the use of a laser beam to heat special magnetic recording media and reduce its resistance to the reversal of magnetic polarity while a magnet is used to change polarity in selected spots. The media becomes stable at normal temperatures, makes a relatively permanent record, and is housed in a protective cartridge. Most rewritable optical drives employ this technology.

mode (n.) Related to compact discs, there are two basic modes. In Mode 1, used with CD-ROM applications, 288 bytes of each sector is used to store error-correction code, and the remaining 2048 bytes per sector is used for data. Mode 2, used in CD-i and CD-ROM XA, has two forms. Form 1 is similar to Mode 1, with Red Book error correction. Form 2 discs provide an area of 2336 bytes per sector of non-error-corrected data for information storage, which is used most commonly for graphic and audio content.

modeling 1. (n.) In three-dimensional animation, the first step in creating a 3-D object. 2. (n.) An educational process in which a computer system simulates a process. A user can input values and learn from the resulting changes in the process.

modem (n.) A shortened version of modulator/demodulator; a device that converts digital data into audio signals for transmission over telephone lines and translates the audio signals back into data on reception.

modular (adj.) Composed of individual components that can stand alone or work together.

modular code See *OOP*.

modulation (n.) Change; a carrier signal that is modulated, or encoded with information that is analogous to another signal, transmits both signals. If the carrier signal is of a constant level that does not change, the changes represent the signal it is carrying. The opposite process is demodulation, or decoding of the data.

moiré patterns (n.) In a display with limited resolution, undesirable optical effects created by overlapping grids and lines. An example is the display of a striped shirt on a television monitor where the scan lines do not align with the stripes. (Pronounced **moi-ray**.)

monitor (n.) A picture tube or screen that can display video signals and/or computer graphics.

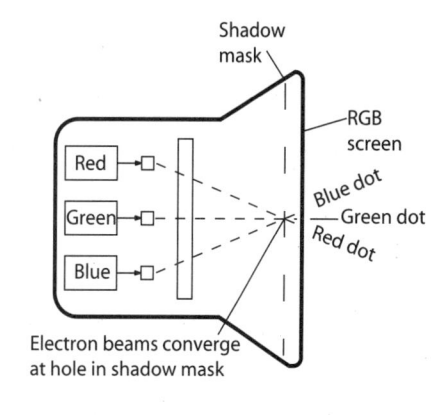

RGB monitor

monochrome display (n.) A black-and-white monitor capable of shades of gray but no colors.

monospace font (n.) A set of letters and symbols in which each character has the same fixed width, or pitch, as opposed to a proportional font.

MOO (n.) MUD Object-Oriented; a visual version of a Multi-User Dungeon.

morph (v.) To melt one image into another by smoothly moving points from their original positions to new locations in another image. Morphing is done with graphic effects software packages that create a smooth transition from one image to another.

MOS (n.) Metal-oxide semiconductor; a silicon wafer with channel transistors that is used to create integrated circuits or discrete components.

Mosaic (n.) Developed at the National Center for Supercomputing Applications, this was the first popular browser, or universal client, for the World Wide Web. It has evolved into Netscape Navigator.

mosaic filter (n.) An image processing technique that divides a graphic into small squares, each of a single hue.

motion blur (n.) A blending or streaking effect deliberately added to images to simulate the appearance of moving objects. It is commonly used in animation sequences to show the path of an object without a strobing effect.

motion choreography (n.) In animation and computer graphics, the process of determining the displacement, or change in position, of each object over time.

motion compensation (n.) A video compression scheme used in MPEG. Motion vectors are used to increase efficiency in predicting pixel values, and vectors are used to provide offsets based on the positioning of objects that move between I and P frames. The difference between the actual image and the predicted image is the information encoded. See *MPEG frame types*.

motion-JPEG (n.) A proprietary extension of the JPEG compression standard for still images used to compress a stream of moving pictures at a constant frame rate. It provides much lower compression ratios than video compression standards, such as MPEG, that capitalize on similarities between successive frames. Motion-JPEG files are editable, but generally are not transportable to different hardware platforms for playback. Motion-JPEG is implemented differently depending on the hardware used to encode, and there is no universal standard for decoding motion-JPEG.

motion video 1. (n.) Video sequences with frame rates (number of pictures per second) that are high enough to appear as continuous moving pictures rather than as a succession of still images. 2. (n.) The type of video image produced by a camera rather than still video, animation, or computer graphics.

MOU (n.) Memorandum of Understanding; in Europe, telephone companies that provide ISDN services created this document. It specifies facilities required for "Priority 1" service.

mouse (n.) An input device for a computer that rolls on a smooth surface and determines the location of a cursor on the screen. It has one or more buttons used to "click" on icons or hotspots on the screen. These mouse clicks are interpreted as instructions by the computer. *See illustration.*

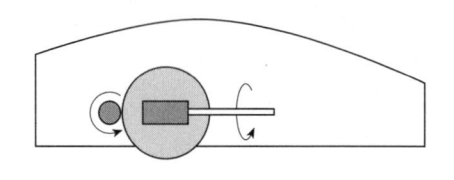

cross-section, mechanical mouse

MoviePlayer (n.) An applet used by the Macintosh to view QuickTime movies. The user interface is a standard Play Bar Controller that allows one to start, stop, and pause a movie, adjust the volume, and watch the progress on a slider.

Moving Picture Expert Group See *MPEG.*

MPC (n.) A trademarked abbreviation for Multimedia Personal Computer. The original MPC specification was developed by Tandy Corporation and Microsoft as the minimum platform capable of running multimedia software. In 1993, the MPC Marketing Council introduced an upgraded MPC-2 standard.

MPC-1 (n.) A specification that defines the following minimum standard requirements for a multimedia computing system: a 386SX or 486 CPU; 2 megabytes (MB) of RAM; 30 MB hard disk; VGA video display; 8-bit digital audio subsystem, CD-ROM drive; system software compatible with Windows 3.1 or higher APIs.

MPC-3 (n.) A specification that defines the following minimum system functionality for Level 3 compliance in a multimedia computing system: a 75-megahertz (MHz) Pentium CPU with 8 megabytes (MB) of RAM; a 520-MB hard disk; a 16-bit, wavetable-capable sound card with multitimbral MIDI playback; a 24-bit color display with MPEG-1 playback capability in hardware or software with a resolution of 352 × 240 at 30 frames per second (fps); a quad-speed CD-ROM drive with a 600-kilobytes per second (KBps) sustained transfer rate capable of playing all common CD-ROM formats, including Photo-CD and Video CD; stereo speakers; system software compatible with Microsoft Windows 3.1 and Microsoft DOS 6.0 or higher APIs.

MPC-2 (n.) A specification that defines the following minimum standard requirements for a Level 2 multimedia computing system: 25 megahertz (MHz) 486SX with 4 megabytes of (MB) RAM; 160 MB hard disk; 16-bit sound card; 65 536 (16-bit) color video display; double speed CD-ROM drive; system software compatible with Windows 3.1 or higher APIs.

MPEG (n.) Moving Picture Expert Group; the working committee which, under the auspices of the ISO, defined standards for the digital compression and decompression of motion video/audio for use in computer systems. These standards consist of MPEG-1, MPEG-2, and later versions. The MPEG-1 standard delivers decompressed data in the range from 0.6 to 5.0 megabits per second (Mbps), allowing CD players to play full-motion color movies at 30 frames per second (fps). MPEG-1 compression ratios as high as 200:1 are attainable. Source Image Format (SIF) is the reduced resolution obtained in MPEG-1 by decimating the 720 × 480 input to 360 × 240 prior to compression. The final resolution of MPEG-1 is 352 × 240. For compression bit rates below 3.5 Mbps, MPEG-1 SIF resolution is preferable to higher resolutions that require greater bandwidth. Captured from an NTSC source, MPEG-1 operates at 30 frames per second (fps) and 30 fields. MPEG-1 processes audio in 16-bit stereo at 44.1 kilohertz (kHz), the same rate as audio CD or at higher rates. Building on the MPEG-1 standard is MPEG-2, which extends to the higher data rates (6–15 Mbps) needed for broadcast quality signals. MPEG-2 is designed to support a range of picture aspect ratios, including 4:3 and 16:9. It adheres to the CCIR-601 standard of 720 × 486 and 60 fields, as opposed to 30 fields in MPEG-1. However, the minimal bit rate needed to pass such a large amount of data is 5 Mbps for high resolution. As the compressed bit rate is reduced, output video quality declines.

MPEG compression (n.) The conversion of an analog videotape or live video source into a stream of digits that represents the original product in the MPEG digital video format. It is a complex combination of video and audio compression techniques that reduce the size of a data file at ratios up to 200:1.

MPEG frame types (n.) Three basic types of frames created by an MPEG encoder exist. 1. Intra-coded frames (I-frame): A picture coded using only information drawn from itself; I-frames, like key frames, provide access points in the data stream. 2. Bidirectionally predictive frame (B-frame): A picture coded using motion-compensated prediction from previous and future reference frames. B-frames provide an efficient means of coding but require a memory buffer for future reference frames. 3. Predictive-coded frame (P-frame): A picture coded using motion-compensated prediction from the previous reference frame.

MPEG layers (n.) In hierarchical order, the different layers in an MPEG stream are as follows:

Block: An 8-column × 8-row block of pixels; the unit to which DCT is applied.

Macroblock: The four 8 × 8 blocks of luminance data and the corresponding 8 × 8 blocks of chrominance data coming from a 16 × 16 section of the luminance component of the picture; the basic unit for motion-compensation prediction.

Slice: A series of macroblocks that serves as the synchronizing unit for reconstruction of the image data; typically, all the blocks in one horizontal picture interval; usually 16 lines of the picture.

Picture: Source image or reconstructed data for a single frame, consisting of three rectangular matrices of 8-bit numbers that represent the luminance and chrominance signals.

Group of pictures (GOP): A self-contained sequence of pictures that starts with an I-frame and contains a variable number of P-frames and B-frames; SMPTE time code may be added to mark the first picture in a group at this layer.

Sequence: A video sequence beginning with a "sequence header" followed by one or more groups of pictures and ending with a "sequence end" code.

MPEG-1 (n.) A version of the MPEG compression method that is optimized for data rates in the 1 to 1.5 megabits per second (Mbps) range, such as the transfer rate of CD-ROM drives and T-1 communications links.

MPEG-2 (n.) A form of MPEG compression that is optimized for data rates above 5 megabits per second (Mbps) and intended for applications such as broadcast video.

MPW (n.) Macintosh Programmer's Workshop; the environment in which application development for the Apple Macintosh system takes place.

MSAU Multistation Access Unit; a wiring concentration in an IBM token ring network that connects up to eight lobes to a ring.

MSCDEX (n.) Microsoft Compact Disc

Extension; drivers for CD-ROM readers connected to a computer.

MS-DOS (n.) Microsoft Disk Operating System; the Disk Operating Systems of IBM Personal Computers that was developed by Microsoft. See *Disk Operating System*.

MS-DOS CD-ROM extensions (n.) A set of routines that connect the MS-DOS operating system to the driver routines for specific models of CD-ROM players. The extensions allow machines running these operating systems to read CD-ROM discs formatted in the ISO 9660 and High Sierra format.

MSN (n.) Microsoft Network; (n.) A host for Internet activity that is supported by Microsoft.

MTBF (n.) Mean time between failure; a measure of how long a computer peripheral, such as a hard drive, can be expected to function before a failure.

MTC (n.) MIDI time code; a regular pulse wave used to synchronize MIDI tracks with sequences, video, and other devices.

MUD (n.) Multiuser Dungeon; an online environment that provides a setting for role-playing games for more than one user at once. Text-based commands are often used to navigate and communicate.

MUD Object-Oriented See *MOO*.

mu-law (n.) Digital encoding of voice based on pulse code modulation. It is used in the United States and Japan for telephony.

multicast backbone See *M-bone*.

multifrequency monitor (n.) A display unit that can respond to a fixed number of video signal frequencies, supporting various resolutions and standards.

multimedia (n. or adj.) A synthesis of digital media types combining text, graphics, audio, animation, and video. Interactivity is a feature of most multimedia, which is also referred to as digital media, new media, or hypermedia.

multimedia extensions (n.) (MME) A set of software routines and specifications for running multimedia programs in Microsoft Windows 3.0, which were absorbed into Windows 3.1.

Multimedia Marketing Council See *MMC*.

Multimedia Personal Computer See *MPC*.

multimedia platform (n.) Devices used to deliver diverse media types including text, graphics, audio, animation, and video in an interactive environment.

multiplatform (adj.) Describes the ability of software to perform on more than one hardware platform. Such software is sometimes referred to as "cross-platform," particularly if it has been ported to run with a different operating system and equipment than the one on which it was created.

multiple document interface See *MDI*.

multiplex See *MUX*.

multiplexor (n.) In broadcast and telecommunications, a device used to divide a transmission facility into multiple subchannels. This is accomplished by allotting a common channel to several different transmitters alternately, or by splitting the total frequency bandwidth into narrower bands and transmitting different signals simultaneously.

multiprocessor (n.) A computer that combines two or more similar microprocessors, providing more speed and power for complex procedures and multitasking than a computer with a single central processing unit (CPU).

Multipurpose Internet Mail Extensions See *MIME*.

multiscan monitor (n.) A video display that accepts a range of horizontal and vertical timings, including those that correspond to VGA and RGB computer graphics. Some multiscan monitors automatically adjust to the appropriate timing based on the video source.

multisession (adj.) Describes a CD-ROM format that allows information to be recorded incrementally in different recording sessions. During each session the TOC (Table of Contents) is updated.

Multistation Access Unit See *MSAU*.

MultiSync (n.) A registered trademark of NEC Technologies, Incorporated, for their class of monitors designed to work with a wide range of video input frequencies and formats.

multitask (v.) To process more than one task at a time, typically with two or more applications running at once, and transfer information between them. Both Microsoft Windows and the Macintosh OS are multitasking operating systems.

multitimbral (adj.) Describes the capacity for more than one instrument, or MIDI patch, to play simultaneously. A sequence of MIDI tracks may be created with a different voice assigned to each track for multitimbral playback.

multiuser (adj.) Describes a computing environment that may be accessed by more than one person simultaneously. UNIX was designed to support such an environment.

Multiuser Dungeon See *MUD*.

Musical Instrument Digital Interface See *MIDI*.

mute (v.) To silence an audio track.

MUX (v.) **Mu**ltiple**x**; to combine audio and video program data along with private data in layers that provide timing information, similar to the process of interleaving. In general, to multiplex is to deliver two or more distinct signals combined on a single channel.

MX (n.) **M**ail e**x**change; a DNS record used to define hosts that are able to accept mail.

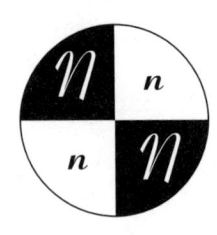

NAB (n.) National Association of Broadcasters.

NAK (n.) Negative acknowledgment; a code returned by a receiving unit when inaccurate information is received.

named pipes (n.) An interprocess protocol used by OS/2 and UNIX. Named pipes act as temporary files on disk or in memory and can be accessed by two processes to exchange information.

NAMM (n.) National Association of Music Merchants.

nano (adj.) Prefix meaning one-billionth.

nanosecond (n.) One-billionth of a second.

NAP (n.) Network access point; one of the main hubs through which Internet traffic in the United States flows.

NAPLPS (n.) North American Presentation Level Protocol Standard; a videotext protocol that permits pictures to be compressed into small blocks of data for low-bandwidth storage and transmission.

narration (n.) An audio commentary, or voice-over, that is frequently used in multimedia productions to provide spoken instructions, explain concepts, and "host" interactive programs.

narrowband (n.) Any transmission link that is limited to a low data rate, such as a 4-kilohertz (kHz) voice channel, as opposed to broadband.

narrowcast 1. (v.) To direct a program to a small, well-defined proportion of the potential audience. 2. (n.) A program directed to a narrow audience.

National Bureau of Standards See *NBS*.

National Information Infrastructure See *NII*.

National Research and Education Network See *NREN*.

National Television Systems Committee See *NTSC*.

native signal processing (n.) A type of computing in which a powerful microprocessor performs the work of a digital signal processor (DSP) chip in real time, allowing activities, such as video decoding, to be integrated with other functions in a single processing system.

navigation (n.) The means by which a user explores and controls graphic, text, audio, and video elements in a multimedia program.

NBS (n.) National Bureau of Standards; a group who makes recommendations to the United States government concerning federal data communications specifications.

N-connector (n.) A threaded coaxial cable connector named after Paul Neill.

NCSA (n.) National Center for Supercomputing Applications.

NCTA (n.) National Cable Television Association.

NDIS (n.) Network Driver Interface Specification; a standard that was created by Microsoft for writing hardware-independent drivers.

nest (v.) To embed instructions, data, or subroutines within another structure sequentially.

NetBIOS (n.) Network basic input/output system; software developed by IBM that interfaces between a computer operating system and an IBM token ring network.

netiquette (n.) Well-mannered network communications.

Netscape Navigator (n.) A popular universal client, or browser, that is used to access the World Wide Web.

Netware (n.) An operating system for a LAN developed by Novell.

network (n.) In general, a group of computers, peripherals, or other equipment connected to one another for the purpose of passing information and sharing resources. Networks may be local or remote. The topology of a network is the geographic arrangement of links and nodes, which may be arranged in the shape of a star, a tree, or a ring.

network access control (n.) Circuits in a local area network that determine when individual workstations may transmit messages.

network basic input/output system See *NetBIOS*.

Network Driver Interface Specification See *NDIS*.

network file system See *NFS*.

network interface card (n.) (NIC) A printed circuit board that is installed in an expansion slot on a computer to allow it to be connected to a network.

network layer (n.) The third layer in the

network loadable module

OSI model responsible for network routing of information packets. The network layer adds a header to define the routing addresses.

netware loadable module See *NLM*.

network topology (n.) The logical and physical relationship between nodes on a network, defined by the layout of links and nodes. Common topologies are similar in shape to a star, tree, or ring. *See illustration.*

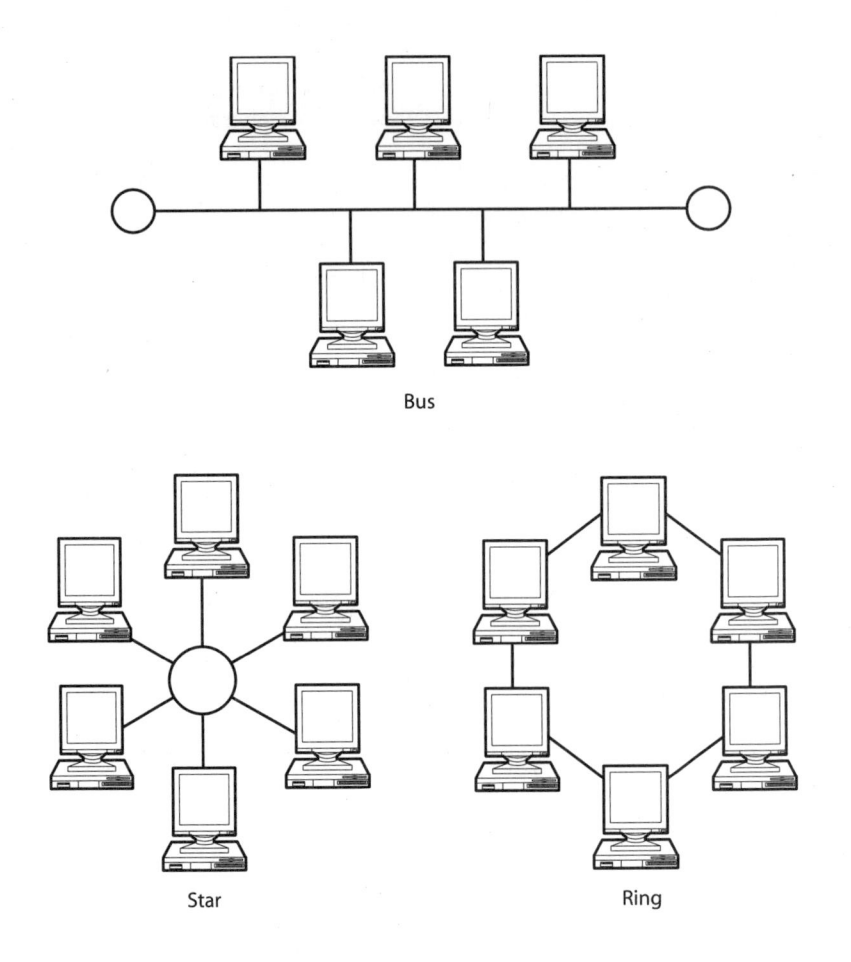

Bus

Star

Ring

network topologies

network user identification See *NUI.*

newsgroup (n.) A conference that is located in the Usenet area of the Internet.

New Technology See *NT.*

Newton (n.) A hand-held computer manufactured by Apple Corporation and known as a personal digital assistant (PDA). Information is entered with a stylus, and handwriting recognition is built into the operating system.

NeXTstep (n.) A UNIX-based object-oriented operating system developed for the NeXT computer and ported to the Intel pentium family of processors.

NFS (n.) Network file system; a method of file sharing data on a LAN or on the Internet. NFS is an extension to TCP/IP that lets files on remote network nodes appear to be connected locally.

NIC See *network interface card.*

NiCad (n.) Nickel cadmium; a compound used in rechargeable batteries for notebook computers and portable devices. This type of battery suffers from the "memory effect," wherein a battery recharged after only partial discharge will lose the capacity to hold a full charge. (Pronounced **nye-cad**.)

nickel cadmium See *NiCad.*

NII (n.) National Information Infrastructure; the broad interconnection of computer, telephone, and cable networks. Often referred to as the "Information Superhighway."

NLM (n.) Netware loadable module; an application program that can be dynamically loaded and unloaded on a Novelle NetWare 3.x or 4.x server. Examples of NLMs are Lotus Notes NLM, Sybase's SQL Server, and Oracle Server.

node (n.) A point of connection on a network, or the equipment that is attached at that point.

noise (n.) Bursts of interference that are not part of the signal. In video, continuous noise may produce a random salt-and-pepper pattern on the picture, called "snow." In audio, RF noise produces unwanted hiss or disturbances.

non-disclosure agreement (n.) A common legal instrument used to keep a contractor from sharing confidential information with competitors, or from making public any information addressed after the agreement.

noninterlaced (adj.) Describes video systems that draw horizontal lines across the screen in succession, as opposed to interlaced scanning in which even and odd lines are drawn alternately in two sweeps. A noninterlaced scan is also known as a "progressive scan." Computer monitors are typically noninterlaced, while television video monitors are interlaced, and their signal content contains two fields for each frame.

nonlinear (n.) In the field of digital media, files or events that are indexed may be accessed immediately by a user. In linear media, such as an audio or videotape, the user must shuttle forward or backwards in time to an event or a frame. The characteristic of nonlinearity is a key distinction between media and is leveraged in well-conceived multimedia programs.

nonlinear editing (n.) Digital video editing techniques that record source clips on hard disk, allowing an editor to jump directly to any segment without shuttling through other clips.

nonlinear quantization (n.) In MPEG compression, the process of assigning more bits to define low-frequency spectrum data than to the high frequencies. The human eye is more sensitive to lower frequencies. Some data is lost in the high-frequency spectrum, but the technique is extremely efficient in reducing the amount of data needed to define images. In general, this type of quantization attaches priorities to data based on its relative value on decoding, and less significant information may be discarded.

non-recalibrating (adj.) Describes a hard drive that does not pause periodically for a few milliseconds to perform thermal recalibration, or a cool down. Many hard disk drives are unsuitable for capturing video files direct to disk because they have thermal sensors that interrupt the process when the drive reaches a certain temperature. Special "AV" drives are non-recalibrating.

nonvolatile memory (n.) Read-only memory whose contents are maintained by batteries when the main power is switched off. It is useful for keeping boot sequence and BIOS instructions constantly accessible. Generally, all storage mediums other than dynamic RAM are nonvolatile.

normalize (v.) In audio engineering, to expand the highest peaks of amplitude to their greatest allowable levels, raising the amplitude of softer sounds proportionally. This treatment is typically done as a standard procedure in processing digital audio. It lends presence to a track and improves the signal-to-noise ratio.

North American Presentation Level Protocol Standard See *NAPLPS*.

NREN (n.) National Research and Education Network; a five-year project approved by the United States Congress in 1991 to create a national electronic education "superhighway."

NRZ (n.) Non-return-to-zero; a method of recording binary data in real time.

NSFnet (n.) The national backbone network funded by the National Science Foundation.

NSP (n.) Native Signal Processing.

NT (n.) New Technology; in the phrase "Windows NT," this is the version of Microsoft Windows.

NTSC (n.) National Television Systems Committee; a committee of the Electronics Industries Association (EIA) that prepared the standard specifications approved by the Federal Communications Commission in December 1953 for commercial color broadcasting in the United States. The specifications define a color television format having 525 scan lines, a field frequency of 59.94 hertz (Hz), a broadcast bandwidth of 4 megahertz (MHz), a line frequency of 15.75 kilohertz (kHz), a frame frequency of 1/30 of a second, and a color subcarrier frequency of 3.58 MHz.

NuBus (n.) A 32-bit bus architecture that was developed by Apple Computer for use in the Macintosh series of computers.

NUI (n.) Network user identification; a combination of the user's address and password on an X.25 packet-switched network.

null modem cable (n.) An RS-232-C cable wired in such a way that two computers can be connected and communicate without a modem.

NURBS (n.) Non-Uniform Rational B-Spline; basic spline functions used to construct curves from a set of control points that do not share the periodic properties of a uniform B-spline.

nybble (n.) Four bits, or half of a byte.

Nyquist frequency (n.) In digitizing audio, a sample rate equal to twice the speed of the highest frequency component in the content being sampled, including harmonics. The rate must be at least this high to avoid aliasing or "foldover" in the sampled audio file.

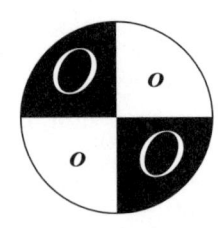

object (n.) In programming, a corporal body or an abstraction with well-defined constituents and interpretations. An object is an identifiable, encapsulated entity that provides one or more services requested by a client. In object-oriented programming, an object is an instance of a class. In general multimedia terms, an object is a stored data element such as a video clip, an audio file, or the graphic representation of an object.

object code (n.) The machine language code that is output by a compiler or assembler, as opposed to source code which is converted into object code. Object code can stand alone if a library of functions is available for linking.

object identity (n.) The property of an object that distinguishes it from other objects. In an object-oriented system, this property is independent of content, type, and addressability. Object identity is the only property of the object maintained irrespective of time or modifications.

object linking and embedding See *OLE*.

object management (n.) The storage, retrieval, and archival of objects in an object-oriented system.

Object Management Group See *OMG*.

object-oriented database (n.) A database that stores data in the form of encapsulated objects and provides an object-oriented application development and data manipulation interface.

object-oriented programming See *OOP*.

Object Packager (n.) A small application that is part of the Microsoft Windows system software and is used to process raw files into objects for use with OLE. It is located in the Accessories directory and permanently links an object icon to the file name with which it is associated.

object reference (n.) An object name that reliably denotes a particular object in the Common Object Request Broker Architecture (CORBA).

object request broker See *ORB*.

object server (n.) An object-oriented

networked database server that provides for storage and retrieval of objects.

OCR (n.) Optical character recognition; software used with a scanner to convert printed pages into text files.

OC x (n.) Optical Carrier at a multiple of 51.84 Mbps. An OC 12 connection moves digital data at 622 megabits per second (Mbps).

OEM (n.) Original equipment manufacturer; a manufacturer of hardware that may be modified or included in a system marketed by a value-added reseller (VAR).

offline 1. (adj.) Describes an operation that occurs independently and is not under the control of a computer. Also refers to the act of processing information while disconnected from a network so the data can be distributed when the connection is made. 2. (adj.) In video post-production, describes a type of editing that occurs separately from the final assembly and mastering process. The term also refers to a system that can make an edit decision list (EDL) or simple cuts only, rather than one that performs a full range of editing and video effects.

ohm (n.) The unit used to express electrical resistance. One ohm of resistance allows one amp of current to flow when one volt of electromotive force is applied.

OLE (n.) Object linking and embedding. Developed by Microsoft in collaboration with other software companies in 1990, this software specification allows developers to integrate information created by different applications. It accomplishes this by making simple extensions to existing graphic applications running under Microsoft Windows, Macintosh System 7.0, or OS/2 Presentation Manager. OLE is a standard that defines how objects interact, and it provides a software channel for passing objects. A program called STORAGE.DLL manages the OLE files as well as the links between originators and users. In Windows, the "clipboard" is a handy way to implement OLE capabilities. In any application that supports OLE, the copy-and-paste operations will transparently link objects to documents. An embedded voice annotation in a text document is a practical application of OLE, which results in a crude but effective form of multimedia. Audio files must be packaged as objects, since OLE does not work with raw files. The "Object Packager" application found in the Accessories directory is required to process raw files into objects for use with OLE. (Pronounced **oh-lay**.)

OMDR (n.) Optical memory disc recorder; a Matsushita/Panasonic write-once analog videodisc recorder that writes to 8- or 12-inch blanks. The format is not compatible with laser videodisc players from Pioneer, Philips, or Sony.

OMF (n.) Open Media Framework; a de facto standard developed by Avid

Technologies and a group of partners for specifying multimedia data and control in an open manner for digital editing and playback.

OMG (n.) Object Management Group; an organization that has developed standards and products associated with Object Management in a distributed networked environment, recognized for work on object request brokering (CORBA).

one-off (n.) A CD-recordable blank disc on which program data has been written.

online 1. (adj.) Describes the condition in which computers and peripherals are in direct interactive communication with one another on a network. Online services such as America Online and CompuServe are popular networks with millions of users whose computers can be connected to a central file server, and who can then exchange information among themselves. 2. (adj.) A traditional video editing term that describes a comprehensive system that can edit, record, and add special effects. Online systems are expensive, so rough edits or edit decision lists are typically compiled using offline systems. In video postproduction, the online edit is the final editing process that integrates all the elements created and specified earlier by the offline edit.

online service (n.) A provider that offers dialup electronic mail, conferences, information resources, and other communication services for users who have a computer, modem, and telephone line. Examples are America Online, CompuServe, Prodigy, and Microsoft Network (MSN).

OOP (n.) Object-oriented programming. Each element, or object, in a logic program of this type is self-contained, stands alone, and holds all the data and instructions related to a particular task. Any element can call up any other object or element, and the recipient can perform the task for itself. The paradigm provides for object classes, methods, and inheritance. It is also referred to as modular code, where the modules are independent and easily cross-linked.

open architecture (n.) Related to microcomputers, a hardware configuration that allows the addition of circuit boards, which are typically plugged into slots on a motherboard, to expand the functionality of the original system. This may be accomplished by connecting outboard gear or peripherals to internal expansion buses or external ports. Software that integrates the expanded hardware with existing features is required.

OpenGL (n.) An API developed by Silicon Graphics. It was intended to be an open standard for three-dimensional CAD applications and visualization of images.

Open Media Framework See *OMF*.

OpenScript (n.) The scripting language

used by the Asymetrix ToolBook multimedia authoring program for Microsoft Windows.

Open System Interconnection See *OSI*.

operating system (n.) Software loaded into RAM when a computer boots up, controlling fundamental processes such as saving and retrieving files. Operating systems may have command-based interfaces, like DOS, or graphical user interfaces (GUIs), like the Macintosh OS or OpenLook for UNIX, developed by Sun Microsystems.

operator (n.) Any character that represents an operation, or action performed on a number or variable. Common operators include (+) addition, (−) subtraction, (*) multiplication, and (/) division. In query languages used to locate information in databases, Boolean operators (AND, OR, NOT, NOR) are used. Another type is the relational operator, such as (<) less than and (>) greater than.

OPL (n.) Developed by Yamaha, this type of synthesizer chip is used in the Creative Labs Sound Blaster and other popular sound boards. These chips use frequency modulation (FM) synthesis.

optical character recognition See *OCR*.

optical disc (n.) A disc that stores digital data which can be read with reflected laser light.

optical disc player (n.) Any playback device that can read data from optical media by using reflected laser light.

optical memory (n.) Any technology incorporating storage devices that use laser light to record or read data.

optical memory disc recorder See *OMDR*.

optical read-only memory See *OROM*.

optoisolator (n.) A miniature device that converts electrical signals into light, transmits the light across a small gap, and converts it back into electrical signals. It makes a circuit immune to interference and ground-loop problems because no electricity flows across the gap.

Orange Book (n.) The specification for compact disc recordable (CD-R), or "write once" systems, developed by Philips and Sony. It includes specifications for the Hybrid Disc technology on which Eastman Kodak's Photo-CD is based.

ORB (n.) Object request broker; an implementation of a common interface that allows multiple clients to access services provided by multiple objects following a standardized interface. The standard, Common Object Request Broker Architecture (CORBA), has been defined by the Object Management Group, an industry association.

original equipment manufacturer See *OEM*.

OROM (n.) Optical read-only memory; media that can be read by an optical reader but may not be recorded.

orthographic projection (n.) The visible outline of an object that is projected onto a surface in which the projection vector is parallel to the z axis.

OS 1. (n.) Operating system. 2. (n.) Optical storage.

oscillator (n.) Any device that vibrates internally to generate a signal at a specified frequency, such as an audible tone, usually for test purposes. Oscillators are used to produce musical tones as well.

OSI (n.) Open System Interconnection; a standard and a model for data communications. In this model a component is identified at each of the following seven layers:

1. Physical layer (hardware, medium)
2. Data linking layer (linking protocols)
3. Network layer (type of network)
4. Transfer layer (protocol for transfer)
5. Session layer (way to communicate)
6. Presentation layer (adaptation of connections)
7. Application layer (specific implementation of defined facilities)

OS-9 (n.) A "real-time" operating system on which the CD-i development system is based.

OS/2 (n.) Operating System/2. A multitasking, higher-level operating system developed by IBM and Microsoft for the PS/2 series of microcomputers equipped with 80386 or later microprocessors. See *IBM PS/2*.

outboard (adj.) Describes external, rack-mounted audio signal processing equipment, such as an equalizer, compressor/limiter, aural exciter, or digital delay.

out-point (n.) The final frame of a segment of audio/video media to be edited or dubbed.

output 1. (v.) To send data from a computer or processor to another device, such as a printer or disk drive. 2. (n.) The digital data sent from memory for display or transfer, or any signal that is generated or passed on by any means.

outsource (v.) To hire specialists, consultants, or an external production company to produce segments of media types.

overdub (v.) To add a signal or channel to an existing audio mix, such as a new vocal or instrumental track.

overflow error (n.) A buffer over-run, in which data is received too fast to be captured completely and accurately. It may also occur when the memory allocation is not large enough to accept a unit of data that is sent to it.

overlay 1. (n.) The ability to superimpose text or graphics onto still or motion video by digital means, such as with a character generator. 2. (v.) To show one video image positioned on top of another. To overlay two analog video signals cleanly, they must be synchronized to the same timing signal, or genlocked.

oversample (v.) To read data at a higher rate than normal to produce more accurate results, or to make it easier to sample.

overscan (n.) A condition in which a video signal bleeds off the edges of a monitor. When computer images are sent to a monitor in the overscan mode, up to 20% of the content around the edges may be lost.

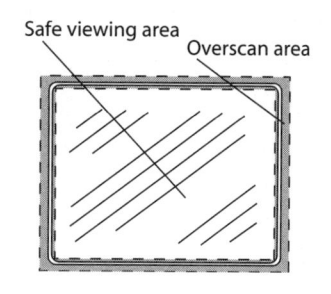

overscan

PABX (n.) Private automatic branch exchange; an automatic telephone exchange that is owned by a user and routes calls to and from the public telephone network.

package 1. (n.) Any software application or set of computer programs needed to perform a task. 2. (n.) A combination of hardware and software that constitutes a complete multimedia delivery system. 3. (v.) To combine media, printed matter, and casing for the purpose of distributing a product.

packet (n.) A chunk of binary data organized in a block for transmission including control data about the type of data and length of the packet, the data itself, and error detection and correction bits.

packet switching (n.) A method of transferring data by addressing blocks of information, committing channels only while data is being transmitted. After transmission, a channel is free to transfer other packets. The data network determines the routing during the transfer of a packet. In circuit switching, the routing is determined prior to transfer, rather than during transfer. Packets do not always arrive in the order in which they are sent. For data that must stream over a network in order, such as audio files, circuit switching is used.

packet-switching data network See *PSDN*.

page (n.) A predetermined segment of expanded memory that can be swapped in and out of the page frame. The page frame is the physical location in conventional memory where expanded memory pages are stored.

Paged Memory Management Unit See *PMMU*.

page description language See *PDL*.

pagination (n.) The process of dividing a document into pages, which can be done automatically or manually by a word processing program.

paired cable (n.) Any cable consisting of conductors that are all twisted pairs. It is the most common communications wiring.

PAL (n.) Phase alternation line; the European standard for color television, which operates at 25 frames per second (fps), with a resolution of 768 pixels by 576 lines. See *NTSC, SECAM*.

palette 1. (n.) In digital imagery, the number of predefined colors available for display or printing. 2. (n.) Within a software application, the onscreen display of tools, options, or modes available for selection by the user, most often in a rectangular grid display.

palette flash 1. (n.) An undesirable event during which the current palette used by an application is instructed to change and a momentary bright flash occurs. For example, consecutive frames in a Multimedia Director movie could contain different palettes, and a flash will appear on the monitor between the two frames while the movie is played.

pan 1. (v.) In video and film production, to rotate a camera horizontally across a panorama, changing the angle of view. 2. (v.) In computer graphics, to move in one direction along the plane of the drawing, keeping the same scale and orientation. 3. (v.) In audio production, to shift the position of a sound between the right and left stereo channels.

Pantone Matching System See *PMS*.

parallel 1. (n.) A general term for a computer port usually used to connect printers. The transmission of data through a parallel port is done by sending a byte, or eight bits at once. This is in contrast to a serial port, which sends bits one at a time. 2. (adj.) Describes the simultaneous processing of individual parts of a larger job in computer applications.

Parameter RAM See *PRAM*.

PARC (n.) Palo Alto Research Center; a facility operated by Xerox where early experiments were conducted in graphical user interfaces (GUIs), pointing devices, and object-oriented languages.

parent directory (n.) In MS-DOS, a subdirectory that lies one step above the child directory.

parity (n.) A technique used to determine whether bits of data were altered in transmission. A parity bit is appended to an array of bits to make the sum of all the bits always odd or even and checked on reception.

parser (n.) A program that translates English language commands into machine-readable instructions. In an interactive program, it interprets user input and determines the response.

particle animation (n.) An animation technique used when natural forces, such as wind or gravity, control the movement of small objects in a sequence.

partition (n.) A section of storage addressed by the operating system separately. Drives may be divided into multiple partitions.

Pascal (n.) A programming language based on ALGOL, designed for systems programming. It is also used to teach programming as a systematic discipline since it emphasizes structured aspects of programming.

passive matrix (adj.) Describes a type of liquid crystal display (LCD) that uses one transistor for each row and one for each column of pixels. By contrast, an active matrix display uses transistors for each pixel.

password (n.) Any string of characters or numbers a user enters into a computing system to gain access to protected files or to be granted privileges when it is accurately recognized by the system.

paste (v.) To retrieve text or a graphic from a clipboard or memory buffer and insert it into a document.

patch 1. (v.) To connect circuits with a patch cord or cable, typically done on a patch bay. 2. (n.) Last minute instructions or commands added to a software program that are required to make it run but are not part of the formal plan.

path 1. (n.) A set of descriptors in MS-DOS that identifies the location of a file. For example, the path "C:\graphics\project\filename.bmp" leads to a specific graphics file on the "C" drive. 2. (n.) Linked curves in a vector-oriented image.

path name (n.) The name of a file, along with the names of any directories, that must be opened to access it in a hierarchical file system. In MS-DOS, the letter that represents the drive in which the media is located is part of the path name.

PBX (n.) Private branch exchange; a phone system that connects lines internally in a business and provides a link to an outside line. Users must dial 9 to access the outside line.

PC (n.) Personal computer; a relatively low-cost, portable computer system for business and home use that was popularized by IBM and Apple Computer. Strictly defined, only IBM-compatible models are called PCs.

PCA (n.) Program calibration area; the area on a recordable disc reserved for the CD-R drive to calibrate the laser power for recording on the disc.

PC/AT architecture (n.) Personal Computer/Advanced Technology; acronym for the IBM 80286-based computer that uses a 16-bit data bus. It evolved from the 8088-based PC/XT with an 8-bit bus, retaining compatible hardware features.

PCB (n.) Printed circuit board. See *board*.

PCD See *photo-CD*.

PC-DOS (n.) Personal Computer-Disk Operating System; the IBM version of the operating system.

PCI (n.) Peripheral component interconnect; a standard, 64-bit bus architecture that is found in IBM-compatible and Macintosh microcomputers.

PCM (n.) Pulse code modulation; a standard means of encoding audio information in a digital format by sampling the amplitude of the audio waveform at regular intervals and representing that sample as a digital numeric value. Current standards are based on International Telephone and Telegraph Consultative Committee (CCITT) Recommendation G.711:1988, which specifies more codes for low frequency components and fewer codes for high frequency components. Telephone systems in the United States and Japan use mu-law encoding, while Europe and the rest of the world use A-law encoding. See *ADPCM*.

PCMCIA (n.) Portable Computer Memory Card Industry Association; the PCMCIA card is an industry-standard compact storage device and interface mechanism for use with notebook computers. There are three types of cards. Type 1, which is 3.3 mm thick, is most often used for memory enhancements. Type 2, which is 5.0 mm thick, is used for modem and LAN interfacing. Type 3, which is 10.5 mm thick, is used for mass storage I/O.

PC Speaker Driver (n.) A Microsoft Windows program that produces sounds using software and the computer's onboard speaker. It is not a substitute for a sound board, but it is functional.

PCX (n.) This common graphics format in Microsoft Windows was developed by ZSoft for the PC Paintbrush program.

PDA (n.) Personal digital assistant; Apple Computer initially used the term to describe its Newton technology. Generically speaking, it is any battery-powered hand-held device providing digital information management and communications, capable of calculating, scheduling, notetaking, maintaining address files, data transfer via modem, and other similar activities.

PDF (n.) Portable Document Format; a document type created by Adobe Acrobat from PostScript files that can be accessed by virtually any type of computer. This format provides a cross-platform solution to distribution of information.

PDL (n.) Page description language; a programming language used to control the formatting and layout of a printed page and send instructions that a printer with processing capabilities can interpret. An example is Adobe PostScript.

peer-to-peer network (n.) A network in which each computer is independent and can serve the others or act as a workstation. Peripherals connected to any computer networked in this fashion are available to any of the other peer computers connected.

Pel (n.) Picture element; the smallest unit defined on a display; a pixel.

Pentium (n.) The name given to the Intel processor that succeeds the 80486. It is characterized by a 64-bit data bus and superscalar CISC architecture.

performance objective (n.) In computer-based training (CBT), a narrowly-defined goal that is clearly stated for students in an interactive environment.

peripheral (n.) A device that is controlled by a computer but is a separate unit interfaced with the computer, such as a printer, scanner, and an external modem.

peripheral component interconnect See *PCI*.

personal computer See *microcomputer* and *PC*.

Personal Computer-Disk Operating System See *PC-DOS*.

personal digital assistant See *PDA*.

perspective correction (n.) A technique in three-dimensional texture mapping that evaluates the appearance of a texture from different points of view, then draws and illuminates the texture automatically.

PERT/CPM (n.) Program evaluation and review technique/critical path method; a complex project management process for determining the effectiveness of a system or a program.

PGA (n.) Pin grid array; a square-shaped integrated circuit that has connecting pins surrounding the bottom edges on all four sides. It is the form factor that is frequently used for microprocessor chips.

phantom power (n.) A method of powering condenser microphones by sending a direct current (DC) signal over audio lines, usually between 12 and 48 volts.

phase alternation line See *PAL*.

phase modulation (n.) A method of modifying, or changing, the phase of a sine wave carrier signal so that it contains the modulating signal information.

phase shift (n.) The degree to which the starting point of a waveform is early or late in relation to a reference.

phase-shift keying See *PSK*.

phone plug (n.) A male audio connector measuring .25 inches in diameter that is used to terminate cables connecting most high-impedance and line level instruments and signal processors, such as electric guitars, synthesizers, and amplifiers. The monophonic (mono) version allows two wires to be connected to a tip and sleeve. A stereo version permits connection of three wires, with a tip, ring, and sleeve configuration. A female receptacle for this type of plug is called a phone jack. On consumer audio equipment, such as portable CD players and cassette decks, this style of connector measures .125-inches in diameter and is called a miniature (mini) phone plug.

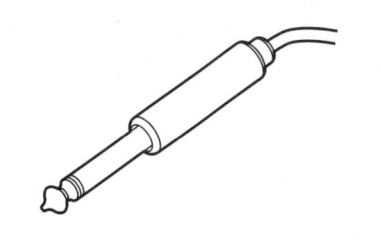

.25-inch monophone plug

Phong shading (n.) A method of specifying the color of each pixel in a three-dimensional model. It offers high quality but is incapable of reflection, transparency, or other advanced effects.

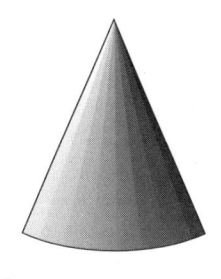

Phong-shaded cone

Photo-CD (n.) Photo-compact disc; developed by Eastman Kodak, this compact disc format is based on the Hybrid Disc specification, used to store scanned photographic images. Photo-CD media can be recorded in multiple sessions, so in this regard they adhere to the Orange Book specification. Film scanners generally are used to capture the graphic content for Photo-CDs. In a basic Photo-CD format, five different resolutions, or "image pacs," appear for each of the 100 images. Expressed in pixels, these resolutions are 128×192, 256×384, 512×768, 1024×1536, and 2048×3072. Note that the aspect ratio is 2:3, as in a photograph, rather than the computer display ratio of 3:4. Images on a Photo-CD are defined in Kodak's proprietary YCC format. In MS-DOS, the extension for this file type is .pcd.

The Portfolio version of the Photo-CD format can accommodate higher-level programming with buttons that can branch to other images or a sequence of frames. An audio clip can be attached to each frame, but it will not play continuously if different images are displayed.

photoconductor (n.) In fiber optics, a transducer that emits current in proportion to the amount of light it receives.

photodiode (n.) A component in a laserdisc player that translates variations in the light reflected from the surface of a disc into the electronic signals, which define the audio, video, and control tracks.

photolithography (n.) A process for transferring a pattern from a mask to a silicon wafer using a photosensitive emulsion and light.

photon (n.) In physics, a unit of light energy. Photons travel through an optical fiber the same way electrons travel through a wire cable.

photo-realism (n.) Computer representation or imaging that seems to be photographically faithful to detail.

physical codes (n.) Tags that define exactly how text should be displayed in an HTML document.

physical format (n.) The standard for how information is physically recorded onto compact discs.

physical layer (n.) The lowest layer of the OSI Reference Model, which governs hardware connections and byte-stream encoding for transmission. It manages physical transfer of information between network nodes.

physical media (n.) Any physical means of transferring signals between two systems. This term is typically used for media connecting the lowest layer (layer 0) of the OSI (Open Systems Interconnection) Reference Model.

physical sector (n.) The location where data is placed on a compact disc or other digital media. For example, the Yellow Book specification requires that each compact disc be divided into 270 000 physical sectors of 2336 bytes each.

PIC (n.) Picture file; a bitmapped graphic file format developed by Lotus Corporation used by IBM-compatible programs.

pickup 1. (n.) An electronic transducer that sends a low-level signal corresponding to the sound produced by a musical instrument, such as an electric guitar or bass. 2. (n.) Related to video or film production, a shot or sequence recorded after the initial shoot, used during editing to update content. 3. (n.) Jargon for a microphone.

PICS (n.) A Macintosh-specific "multimedia" format developed in 1988 by Macromedia and others for exchanging animation sequences. A PICS file is an assembly of several PICT frames in a sequence.

PICT (n.) Picture format; developed by Apple Computer in 1984 as the standard format for storing and exchanging black-and-white graphics files. PICT2 (1987) supports 8-bit color and gray scale. Current PICT specifications do not limit color bit depth.

picture cue (n.) A signal in the vertical blanking interval of a master tape that identifies the beginning of a frame. Each cue is encoded as a frame number on a videodisc pressed from the master tape.

picture depth (n.) The number of bits used to store picture data, or the number of shades of color that can be represented by that number of bits. Settings vary from 1-bit (black and white), 8-bit (256 colors), 16-bit (65 536 colors) to 24-bit (16.7 million colors).

picture element See *Pel*.

picture stop (n.) An index point on a

laserdisc, encoded in the vertical blanking interval, that allows the user to stop at a particular frame.

pincushion distortion (n.) Image distortion caused by the vertical sides of a displayed image curving inward to form concave edges. Most monitors are equipped with controls that will minimize this.

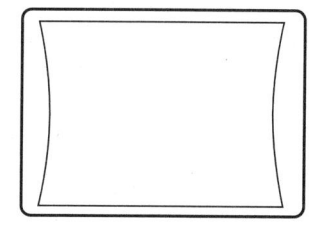

pincushion distortion

ping (n.) A command used to determine whether a networked computer is responding.

ping-pong (v.) To mix several audio tracks on a multitrack tape recorder onto an unused track on the same tape. This yields more individual recorded layers. It is not possible to alter the mix between the tracks that are bounced onto an open track after the original tracks are erased or replaced by new program material.

pink noise (n.) An audio signal with an equal amount of intensity distributed throughout the frequency spectrum.

pinout (n.) A diagram that indicates how wires or pins in a connector are allocated.

pit (n.) A physical indentation in the information layer of a compact disc or laserdisc. Pits determine how a laser beam is reflected. Pits in transmissive discs either block the beam or they allow it to pass through the disc. Pits on VHD discs cause a detectable change in electrical capacitance. The pits on a recordable compact disc are different from those on mastered discs because they are actually mounds created in the dye layer by the laser beam. A pit may also be referred to as the space between "lands" along the data spiral of a compact disc.

pixel (n.) An abbreviated form of "picture element"; the smallest raster display element represented as a screen coordinate with a specified color or intensity level. Picture resolution is measured by the number of pixels used to create an image. A common resolution is 640 × 480 pixels.

placeholder (n.) An item used as a surrogate for the finished product in a production until the final version is completed. It may be a graphic or audio file.

planar (n.) The flat capacitor built between silicon and polysilicon layers in a semiconductor.

plasma display (n.) A flat display with a grid of electrodes in a gas-filled panel. The gas emits light when ionized by the electrodes, yielding high-quality images.

plastic leaded chip carrier See *PLCC*.

platform (n.) A particular hardware and software operating system, such as the IBM-compatible/DOS platform or the Macintosh platform.

PLCC (n.) Plastic leaded chip carrier; a type of semiconductor package.

plotter (n.) An output device similar to a printer that draws or plots a two-dimensional image on paper. Varieties include pen plotters, electrostatic plotters, photograph-plotters, ink-jet plotters, and laser plotters.

plug (n.) The male connector in a plug-and-jack system.

plug and play (n.) The ability of an operating system to identify peripherals or other interfaced components, such as speakers and a CD-ROM reader, and transparently configure the system to incorporate them.

plug-in (n.) A program that is an extension of another program, one that enhances the utility of the original application. Plug-ins for Netscape Navigator allow enhanced media types to be employed, such as realtime audio.

PLV (n.) Production level video; in digital video interactive (DVI), high-quality compression.

PMA (n.) Program memory area; the place on a recordable disc where the information about tracks and sessions are temporarily stored. Information in the PMA eventually becomes the table of contents (TOC) for a session.

PMMA (n.) Polymethyl methacrylate; the rigid, transparent acrylic plastic used to manufacture optical media.

PMMU (n.) Paged Memory Management Unit; an integrated circuit that supports virtual memory by assisting the processor in locating needed data, either on a hard disk or in physical memory.

PMS (n.) Pantone Matching System; a standard trademarked system of identifying over 500 colors by number; a formula created by an exact mixture of the red, blue, and green primary colors. Also known as PMS color.

PNG (n.) Portable Network Graphics; a graphics specification developed by Thomas Boutell and Tom Lane for network transmission; it is used by CompuServe.

point of presence See *POP*.

point of view See *POV*.

point-to-point (adj.) Describes an uninterrupted connection between two pieces of equipment, such as a private telephone circuit or a satellite transmission. *See illustration on following page.*

point-to-point protocol See *PPP*.

polarity (n.) The identification of a positive or negative charge on one side of an electrical circuit.

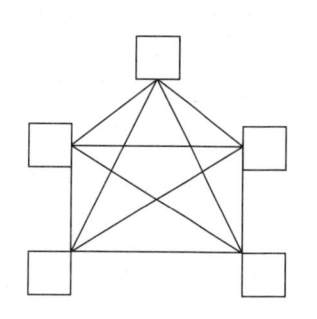

point-to-point network

polling 1. (v.) To connect to a remote computer system to look for e-mail or access information. 2. (n.) A method of controlling the sequence of transmissions by devices on a multipoint line by requiring each device to wait until the controlling processor clears it for transmission.

polycarbonate (n.) A resilient plastic used to manufacture compact discs.

polymer (n.) A compound made of similar molecules that are linked together. A dye polymer layer that can be altered by exposure to lasers is used in optical disc recording systems.

polymethyl methacrylate See *PMMA*.

POP 1. (n.) Point of presence; an interface location in a Local Access and Transport Area (LATA) that connects to inter-LATA carriers. 2. (n.) Post Office Protocol; software that manages mail service on an Internet host.

port 1. (n.) In computing, a socket for connecting peripheral cables to a computer. 2. (v.) In multimedia development, to translate file types and entire programs into versions that will run on a different platform. For example, Macromedia Director movies can be "ported" easily from a Macintosh to Microsoft Windows.

portability (n.) The ability to use the same software on different hardware systems or across platforms. A high degree of portability reduces the need to modify programs for delivery on different hardware.

Portable Document Format See *PDF*.

Portable Network Graphics See *PNG*.

Portable Operating System Interface for Computing Systems See *POSICS*.

portrait (n.) A layout in which the height is greater than the width. In a "landscape" layout, the width of a printed page is greater than the height.

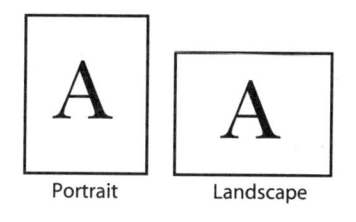

Portrait   Landscape

portrait and landscape layouts

POS (n.) Point-of-sale.

POSIX (n.) Portable operating system

interface in UNIX; an Institute of Electrical and Electronics Engineers (IEEE) standard that defines operating system services based on UNIX, but is easily implemented by other systems.

post (n.) Jargon for post-production, the part of a video or multimedia production performed in a studio after live filming and the construction of basic images.

posterize (v.) To convert an image to a more elementary form by rounding all tonal values to lower settings, creating a surrealistic, stark result.

posting (n.) A message entered into a communications network.

post-production (n.) In creating video programs, a phase that occurs after the original footage is shot. It includes offline and online editing, compositing, sweetening, and the final mix.

PostScript (n.) A universal page layout language developed by Adobe that defines the positioning of images and text.

potentiometer (n.) A component in a circuit that provides varying degrees of resistance. It may take the form of a knob, a thumbwheel, or a slider. In audio equipment a variable potentiometer is often referred to as a "pot." The faders (sliding volume controls) on a mixing board are an example of pots. See *illustration*.

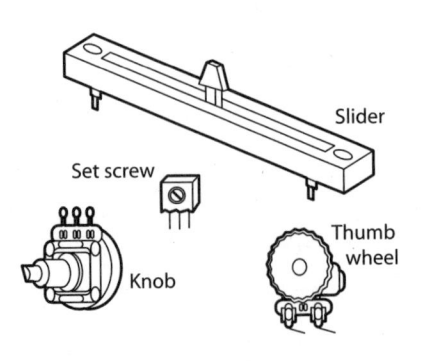

potentiometers

POTS (n.) Plain old telephone service.

POV (n.) Point of view; a video shot that frames a person's face as he or she looks directly into a camera lens.

PowerOpen Association (n.) An organization that was formed to promote the PowerOpen Environment and to provide software developers with support. Founding members include Apple Computer, Bull Systems, Harris Computer Systems, IBM, Motorola, Tadpole Technology, and Thomson CSF. See *PowerOpen Environment*.

PowerOpen Environment (n.) A next-generation, open systems environment that provides software developers and users with a powerful standards-based platform. Specifications include the PowerPC RISC chip and the PowerOpen application binary interface (ABI).

PowerPC (n.) Developed by Apple Computer, IBM, and Motorola in a collaborative effort, a highly-evolved microprocessor chip released in 1994 that replaces the 68000 series as the CPU for the Macintosh series. It is based on reduced instruction set computation, or RISC processing. This family of processors from the PowerPC alliance includes the 32-bit 601, 603 and 604, and the 64-bit 620, which contains 7 million transistors.

PPP (n.) <u>P</u>oint-to-<u>p</u>oint <u>p</u>rotocol; the successor to SLIP, which provides router-to-router and host-to-network connections over both synchronous and asynchronous circuits.

PPT (n.) <u>P</u>ower<u>Point</u> file format; the extension used by Microsoft PowerPoint files. Distributed with the Microsoft Office package of software applications, PowerPoint is widely used as a business presentation program.

PRAM (n.) <u>P</u>arameter <u>RAM</u>; a portion of RAM that is used to store system configuration and startup settings on a Macintosh computer. It is powered by a battery and will automatically default to factory settings if the battery is removed from the computer for a few minutes. This procedure, called "zapping the PRAM," is a last resort when solving system problems. (Pronounced **pee-ram**.)

predictive encoding (n.) In MPEG compression, the storing of the difference between a prediction of the data and the actual data in subsequent frames, which results in higher compression ratios.

pre-groove (n.) The spiral track that is molded into the polycarbonate substrate for the recording laser beam to follow when writing data onto recordable compact discs.

premastering (n.) The process of creating a tape, hard disk drive, or CD-R containing data in the proper format to be recorded onto a master from which compact discs are replicated. Typically, this includes adding error correction and location data, and the disc is reviewed and evaluated before the master disc is made.

Premiere (n.) A nonlinear video editing program developed by Adobe that is used in multimedia development, usually for processing QuickTime.

preproduction (n.) Preparatory tasks, such as flowcharting, storyboarding, script-writing, and graphic design, that are performed prior to shooting material for video or authoring a multimedia program.

pre-roll (n.) In video production, the process of rewinding tape to a point that precedes the beginning a scene, or a specific frame identified by time code. In order to bring the tape up to speed, it is necessary to begin rolling slightly ahead of the first frame of a segment to be dubbed or encoded.

presentation layer (n.) An OSI layer that determines how application data is encoded while it is in transit between two end systems.

PRI (n.) Primary rate interface; an ISDN interface to primary access that operates at 1.544 megabits per second (Mbps). It consists of 23 B-channels at 64 kilobits per second (Kbps) and one D-channel at 64 Kbps. An additional 8 Kbps is used for framing. Specifications for the system vary in Europe, where 30 B-channels are provided along with a 64 Kbps D-channel, and 64 Kbps is used for framing. Data and voice information may be transmitted simultaneously over all channels.

primary rate interface See *PRI*.

primitives (n.) Related to two-dimensional graphics, these are simple shapes such as squares, triangles, and circles. Examples of three-dimensional primitives are blocks, spheres, and tubes.

printed circuit board See *PCB*.

printer (n.) A common output device that prints computer-generated graphics and text on paper. A daisy-wheel printer uses a disc with characters around the outer edge. A dot matrix printer makes a pattern of small dots. A laser printer produces high-quality graphics, typically 300 to 600 dots per inch (dpi), using technology similar to that of a copy machine.

print spooler (n.) Software that schedules printing tasks. Rather than committing all cycles of a computer during printing whenever a print command is issued, it allows the user to be productive and print as time permits later.

private automatic branch exchange See *PABX*.

private branch exchange See *PBX*.

processing 1. (n.) The manipulation of data from one state to another, usually at the request of an operator or user; the basic function that computers perform. 2. (n.) In film work, the photographic development of a film negative.

processor audio (n.) Sound created and played back by computer data manipulation, rather than sound that is digitized from an acoustical environment for playback with standard digital to audio (D/A) converters.

production (n.) In video terms, the activity that takes place while video or film footage is being shot. See *preproduction, post-production*.

production level video See *PLV*.

professional market (n.) A group of customers who purchase software or production equipment for use on the job, as opposed to the consumer market. See *industrial market*.

program 1. (v.) To plan and define a series of computations or processes which are to be executed by a computer. Developing a software program includes writing code and specifying output formats. 2. (n.) Software instructions that control a computer's processes in solving problems and performing tasks.

3. (n.) Any kind of audio or video material on a tape or disc that is prepared for an audience.

program calibration area See *PCA*.

programmable read-only memory See *PROM*.

program memory area See *PMA*.

programmer (n.) Someone who writes code for computers, defining the computational processes.

progressive scan (n.) A video system that creates an image by painting each horizontal line across the screen in succession rather than painting alternate sets of lines in two sweeps down the screen, which is called interlaced scan; also called "noninterlaced."

project evaluation and review technique/ critical path method See *PERT/CPM*.

PROM (n.) Programmable read-only memory; a type of nonvolatile, semiconductor read-only memory component that can be programmed by the user once, and thereafter only read.

prompt (n.) A request shown on the computer monitor for action on the part of the user; in MS-DOS it includes a symbol for the internal hard disk or external memory device that is currently being addressed.

proof-of-concept (n.) A prototype of a piece of media used to prove the viability of the project and attract interest in a full-blown production.

proprietary (adj.) Describes material, owned by an individual or an entity, that is not available for use without permission. Production companies may either produce proprietary products or perform "work for hire," in which the producer is not the owner. Software that is proprietary typically runs only on specific hardware platforms.

prosumer (adj.) Describes high-tech production gear with output quality that falls between professional and consumer. It is used with reference to camcorders and mixers with specifications below broadcast grade but above that of equipment purchased for home use.

protocol (n.) A standard procedure or set of rules with which software and hardware systems must comply in order to be compatible. A network protocol must be observed by all users to allow data communications. Protocols deal with error handling, framing, and line control in transmitting and receiving packets. An example of a telecommunications protocol is X-modem.

protocol converter (n.) A device for translating the data transmission code, or protocol, of one network or device to the corresponding code or protocol of another, enabling equipment with different conventions to communicate with one another.

prototype (n.) A working model of a product used to demonstrate the product, test design ideas, or secure financing for a complete version.

PSDN (n.) Packet-switching data network; a network in which data is transmitted in packets that can be routed individually over network connections and reassembled at the destination.

PSK (n.) Phase-shift keying; a form of digital modulation in which discrete phases of the carrier signal convey a digital signal.

PS/2 (n.) Personal System/2. See *IBM PS/2*.

public access 1. (n.) Time provided for independent producers to air their programs on cable television. 2. (adj.) Describes multimedia kiosks used by the general public or by a wide range of visitors, often with touchscreens for input.

public domain (n.) Intellectual property that is free of copyright or patent and may be duplicated or used without permission. The use of public domain software is unrestricted. It may be used by anyone at no charge.

public network (n.) Any network that is operated by a common carrier and provides packet-switched, circuit-switched, and leased-line circuits to the public.

publish and subscribe (n.) The ability to establish links between documents in the Macintosh 7.0 or later operating system. Subscribing documents are updated automatically when changes are made to the publishing document.

pulse code (n.) An audio signal recorded on each frame of a videotape that allows easy access to individual frames.

pulse code modulation See *PCM*.

Px64 (n.) A conferencing standard introduced by the International Telegraph and Telephone Consultative Committee (CCITT) for compressed motion video with audio. It was devised for transfer over copper or fiber-optic phone lines. Px64 encodes video at 30 frames per second (fps) in real time, with synchronized audio for transmission at speeds up to 4 megabits per second (Mbps). (Pronounced **P times sixty-four**.)

QA (n.) Quality assurance; a discipline that addresses all business activities, with the intention of improving procedures and outcomes, and submits the results of production to a stringent testing regimen.

QAM (n.) Quadrature amplitude modulation; a modulation process that incorporates both amplitude and phase modulation to increase the number of bits per baud.

quadrature amplitude modulation See *QAM*.

quadruplex (n.) Developed by Ampex, "quad" is an industrial videotape format that offers broadcast quality. It has four video heads and uses 2-inch videotape.

quad-speed (adj.) Describes CD-ROM drives with data transfer rates of approximately 600 kilobytes per second (KBps), four times the rate at which first generation CD-ROM drives operated.

quality assurance See *QA*.

quantization (n.) A process that attempts to determine what information can be discarded safely without a significant loss in visual fidelity. It uses DCT coefficients and provides many-to-one mapping. The quantization process is inherently lossy due to the many-to-one mapping process.

quantize (v.) To measure the amplitude of a sample at regular intervals to establish a representative numerical value to encode. Other steps in analog-to-digital (A/D) conversion are sampling and encoding.

quantum (n.) A small, indivisible piece of energy.

query (v.) To request information from a database.

queue (n.) In computing, a series of tasks or operations waiting to be performed.

QuickDraw (n.) A set of software routines that a Macintosh computer uses to display graphics.

QuickTime (n.) Developed by Apple Computer in 1991, this part of the system software architecture integrates audio, video, and animation seamlessly across applications. It provides timing services to maintain synchronization between images and sound. Files in this format may be played by the MoviePlayer applet or any application that can call a movie as long as the QuickTime extension is in the system folder. The format is not restrictive regarding the size of the window or the frame rate, but it is dependent on the processing capabilities and speed of the machine on which it plays back. With Cinepak compression, QuickTime movies can be streamed from a 2X CD-ROM reader to a 320 × 240 window at 12 to 15 frames per second (fps) on a Macintosh Quadra. As is the case with most digital audio/video players, the audio track will command the timing, and video frames will be dropped in order to maintain continuous, smooth sound delivery.

QuickTime video files can be captured with any AV Macintosh, but the quality of this method of capture is much lower than that which is achieved by using a dedicated encoder card, such as the VideoVision or Targa systems. The tools available for editing and manipulating QuickTime are available from APDA, 800–282–2732.

QuickTime for Windows (n.) A version of QuickTime from Apple Computer that has been ported over to Windows. It plays QuickTime movies that have been specially processed, or "flattened," to remove their Macintosh binary headers. QuickTime movies have different brightness and contrast characteristics when viewed on an IBM-compatible as opposed to a Macintosh, due to the fact that the gamma component of images is treated differently by the two systems.

The QuickTime for Windows runtime player is distributed free of charge. It can be downloaded from CompuServe (GO MACDEV) in Section 8 of the Apple System Files. The two files needed are qtdsk1.zip and qtdsk2.zip. Use the "-d" option in pkunzip.exe to decompress the files, copy them to floppies, then install them in Windows.

QuickTime VR (n.) An extension to QuickTime 2.0 from Apple Computer that allows playback of panoramic images. Development requires some advanced resources, including knowledge of the Macintosh Programmer's Workshop (MPW), Lingo scripting, and the capacity to digitize photographs and seamlessly connect them into a single landscape.

qwerty (adj.) Describes a standard typewriter keyboard layout.

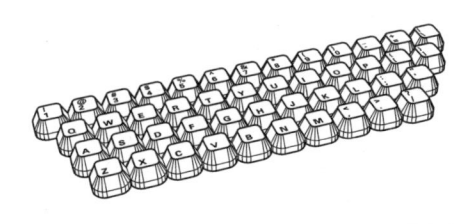

qwerty keyboard layout

RAD (n.) Rapid Application Development; a software development tool that allows a programmer to build a user interface quickly, integrate media types, and create links in Microsoft Windows. With the exception of Visual Basic, these programs are best considered as database development tools, rather than multimedia design tools. Some of the common development systems are listed below:

Delphi: A development tool from Borland that is based on Pascal. It compiles stand-alone machine language .exe and .dll files.

PowerBuilder: A program developed by PowerSoft that applies its own scripting language, PowerScript, which is similar to BASIC.

SQLWindows: A professional tool from Gupta for database development, which can also handle multimedia.

Visual Basic: (VB) From Microsoft Corporation, a preferred programming tool for Windows. The tool makes it easy to build and reuse models with icons, buttons, and toolbars. In some cases, this program is the best choice for multimedia development in Windows, since its products support OLE 2.0 and operating system integration is automated. The program lacks a compiler.

radial (n.) Referring to the geometry of a circle, a line drawn from the center outwards to the edge of a disc.

radio button (n.) An interactive icon that represents a choice or selection. Clicking on a radio button in a GUI selects one option and rejects all others.

radio frequency (n.) (RF) Electromagnetic waves in the bandwidth between 10 kilohertz (kHz) and 3 megahertz (MHz), that are propagated in the air without a guide wire or a cable.

radio frequency identification See *RFID*.

RAID (n.) Redundant array of inexpensive disks; the term dates from 1988, when it was used to describe a type of system that uses two or more hard disk drives to achieve higher data transfer rates and to improve reliability.

Levels for different applications are as follows:

RAID 0: (Disk striping) Data is transferred across an array of disks in parallel fashion for simultaneous read/write operations, with no mirroring and no parity. After a crash, data is not recoverable.

RAID 1: (Disk mirroring) The contents of one disk are copied to another with striping and mirroring, so if one disk goes down, the data is still available.

RAID 2: (Bit interleaving) A less efficient system, with multiple error-correction routines. It stores parity on one or more disks and uses striping.

RAID 3: (Byte interleaving) This system uses an even number of drives, with an added parity drive. It features high throughput, but the drives cannot operate independent of one another.

RAID 4: (Sector interleaving) In this system data can be written to individual drives, but parity information must be updated constantly on each drive.

RAID 5: (Block interleaving) A system that stores the parity data on each drive and allows simultaneous read/write operations. For write-intensive applications it is slower.

RAM (n.) Random-access memory; a memory storage chip installed in a computer that holds information which can be accessed rapidly by the microprocessor. Generally, the operating system and application programs are loaded into RAM. This part of a computer's memory can read (find and display) and write (record) information and can be updated or amended by the user.

RAMP (n.) Remote Access Maintenance Protocol; a protocol used in Internet applications.

random-access (adj.) Describes a hardware delivery system that is capable of leaping to any indexed point nonsequentially in data files that reside in memory.

random-access memory See *RAM*.

rapid application development See *RAD*.

raster 1. (n.) The area illuminated by the scanning beam of a display grid. A raster display device stores and displays data as horizontal rows on a uniform grid. 2. (n.) Bitmap data.

rasterize (v.) To render vector data into a bitmap image.

RAVE (n.) Developed by Apple Computer, the API for QuickDraw 3D. It incorporates the MF3d file format for VRML files and is intended to be multiplatform-compatible.

ray tracer (n.) In rendering an animation, a ray tracer sends hypothetical light beams across a scene and calculates visual effects and reflections from objects in the scene.

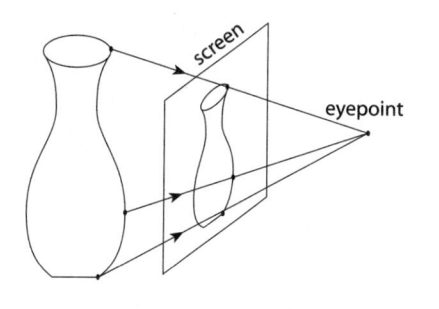

projection in ray tracing

RBOC (n.) <u>R</u>egional <u>B</u>ell <u>O</u>perating <u>C</u>ompany.

RCA connector (n.) A common connector that is used by most consumer audio and video equipment. The male connector consists of an inner pin surrounded by a concentric ring. The female connector is a socket with a raised housing for the ring. It is also known as a "phono" connector, not to be confused with a "phone" jack or plug, which refers to a .25-inch pin with no ring around it.

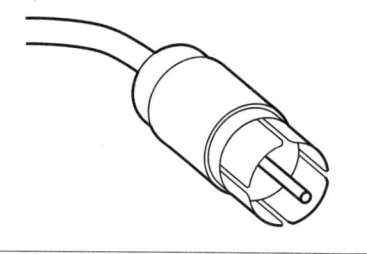

RCA connector

read (v.) In computer terminology, to transfer information from one storage medium to another medium or device. For example, data is read from a disk to a computer screen. See *write*.

read-only memory See *ROM*.

real estate (n.) The space available for data on storage media, or the physical space on the desktop.

real time (n.) The time during which a data processing event occurs. In real time, data is received and processed, and the results are returned so quickly that the process seems instantaneous to the user. The term often refers to simultaneous digitization and compression of audio or video information. The opposite would be offline processing or compression.

Real-Time Operating System See *RTOS*.

real-time video See *RTV*.

reboot 1. (v.) To restart a computer without shutting off the power. It occurs when the "reset" button is pressed or the "restart" option is chosen in software.

receiver 1. (n.) An electronic device that receives a signal, transmitted or delivered by any means, and decodes it. Specifically it refers to equipment designed to receive and display or reproduce a broadcast audio or video signal. 2. (n.) The "earpiece" portion of a telephone headset that converts current into sound waves.

record 1. (n.) In a database, a group of related items, or fields, treated as a single unit of information. 2. (v.) To capture or encode an event on magnetic tape, or in a digital format, so that it can be preserved and reproduced at a later time.

rectifier (n.) An electronic component that converts alternating current (AC) into direct current (DC).

Recycle Bin (n.) A receptacle represented by an icon in Microsoft Windows 95 that is analogous to the "trash can" in the Macintosh OS. Files that are to be removed from a computer's storage system are placed here, and they may be either discarded or restored.

Red Book standard (n.) The audio CD specification, developed by Philips and Sony. Red was the original color of the cover on the specification book that defines the format for audio compact discs. Many of the parameters found in the other books defining CD standards are based on those in the Red Book.

Red-Green-Blue See *RGB*.

redirector (n.) Software that intercepts requests for resources within a computer and analyzes them for remote access requirements. A redirector may assign a local disk identification letter to a logical disk on a NetWare server.

reduced instruction set computing See *RISC*.

redundancy 1. (n.) The process of digitizing or capturing the same data more than once. Compression routines throw out the redundant data 2. (n.) In data storage, the repetition of information to increase the degree of reliability.

redundant array of inexpensive disks See *RAID*.

Reed-Solomon Code (n.) A method of error correction named for Irving Reed and Gustave Solomon, who invented it in 1960.

reference level (n.) An established level, or the starting point for making relative measurements, most often in signal strength or power. The most common example is 0 decibels per milliwatt (dBm), or 1 milliwatt.

refresh rate (n.) The number of times per second, or frequency at which a displayed image is scanned or renewed on a CRT. In NTSC video, that rate is 60 times per second. On computer monitors, rates slower than 75 hertz (Hz) can result in flicker and poor picture quality.

relational database (n.) A collection of data files with at least one field in common, so that there is a means of relating any number of data units by using a common factor.

relay (n.) A type of switch that is electronically opened or closed to connect circuitry.

REM (n.) Remark; a comment used in programming code to describe the purpose, or temporary status of a command.

remark See *REM*.

Remote Access Maintenance Protocol See *RAMP*.

remote bridge (n.) A bridge that connects physically dissimilar network segments across WAN links.

remote control (n.) The ability to issue a command to an interactive program with an independent electronic device from a distance, often employing infrared technology.

remote production unit (n.) A van or a mobile trailer that houses audio/video equipment for production.

removable cartridge (n.) An enclosed data cartridge that can be ejected and inserted into any similar playback device. A SyQuest reader accepts a cartridge that may hold between 44 and 270 megabytes (MB) of data.

render (v.) To calculate attributes of an image that are based on geometric models and result in the production of a dimensional object. In animation applications, to calculate the instructions for a complex series of images.

repeater (n.) An amplifier that is needed at regular intervals to restore the power of an analog signal. Repeaters regenerate digital signals while removing spurious noise. Regeneration and retiming ensure that the signal is clearly transmitted.

replicates (n.) Copies of CDs or other discs pressed from a stamper disc.

replication (n.) Mass reproduction of prerecorded discs or of media in general. Unlike duplication, this is the term used for a process that periodically compares two copies of a database and updates both to reflect changes in the two copies.

report (n.) The output from a database that has been organized according to previously defined specifications in response to a query.

repurpose (v.) To use content in a pre-existing program to perform a function other than the one for which it was originally intended.

request for proposals See *RFP*.

request for technology See *RFT*.

request to send (n.) (RTS) A standard control signal that puts a modem in the "originate" mode, preparing it to send data.

ResEdit (n.) Resource editor; a utility program for the Macintosh that allows a programmer to edit system resources, such as icons and dialog boxes.

resistance (n.) In an electronic circuit, the property of a conductor that resists the flow of current, measured in ohms.

resolution 1. (n.) The number of pixels per unit of area on a monitor screen or dots per inch in a printed graphic. A display with a finer grid has more pixels and higher resolution, hence it can reproduce a more detailed image. 2. (n.) The size of a window used to display video or images, such as 640 × 480 or 320 × 240.

resource fork (n.) One of the two forks in a Macintosh file. The other type is the data fork. Reusable items, such as icons, fonts, dialog boxes, and menus are contained in a resource fork.

Resource Interchange File Format See *RIFF*.

response-based (adj.) Describes a form of computer-based instruction that reacts to input and causes a program to progress at each learner's individual rate.

restore 1. (v.) To copy an archived file from backup into local storage where it can be readily accessed. 2. (v.) To return a window in a graphical user interface (GUI) to its previous dimensions after it has been resized, minimized, or maximized.

reticle (n.) A piece of glass with a chrome pattern for several die used in the photolithography process.

revolutions per minute See *rpm*.

RFC (n.) Request for comments; documents that define standards and proposed standards for Internet operations.

RFI (n.) Radio frequency interference; noise in the radio frequency spectrum that is introduced by electromagnetic radiation and can cause undesirable effects in nearby components.

RFID (n.) Radio frequency identification; a type of integrated circuit that communicates using an integrated microwave transceiver.

RFP (n.) Request for proposals; a formal bidding procedure in which vendors are encouraged to respond.

RFQ (n.) Request for quotations; a formal procedure through which an organization invites bids from vendors for equipment or services.

RFT (n.) Request for technology; a procedure used by standardization bodies for requesting technology that meets industry requirements.

RGB Red-Green-Blue. 1. (n.) A type of computer color display output signal consisting of separately adjustable red, green, and blue signals or components. This is unlike composite video, in which signals are combined prior to output. RGB monitors offer higher resolution than composites. Digital RGB systems are available, but most computers use analog RGB video. 2. (adj.) Describes a type of color model in which colors are represented as the combination of red, green, and blue light. RGB color space is often represented as a square, with one corner black and the opposite corner white. See *composite video*.

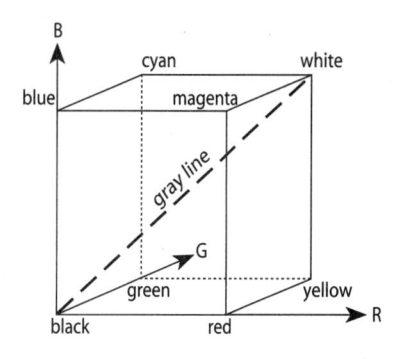

RGB color cube

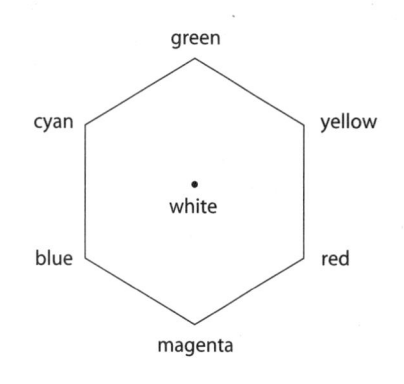

RGB hexagon

RG58 (n.) A specification for thin Ethernet coaxial cable with 50-ohm impedance.

RG62 (n.) A specification for ARCNET coaxial cable with 93-ohm impedance.

rheostat (n.) An electronic component that provides variable resistance.

ribbon cable (n.) A type of cable that has multiple conductors and is flat like a ribbon.

rich text 1. (n.) Text that includes embedded formatting information, such as italics or structural layout descriptors, along with the characters. 2. (n.) The proprietary Rich Text Format (RTF), a format developed by Microsoft to exchange formatted text using only normal alphanumeric symbols.

Rich Text Format See *RTF*.

RIFF (n.) Resource Interchange File Format. Introduced by Microsoft and IBM in 1990, a cross-platform file format for images, audio, and other media types. A RIFF file can store multiple data types as distinct structures, called chunks. See *Media Control Interface (MCI)*.

ring latency (n.) The time required for a signal to propagate once around a ring in a token ring or IEEE 802.5 network.

ring topology (n.) A network topology in which a series of repeaters are connected to one another by unidirectional transmission links to form a single closed loop. Each station on the network connects to the network at a repeater.

RIP 1. (n.) Routing Information Protocol; a routing protocol for TCP/IP networks. 2. (n.) Roster Image Processor; software that converts vector data into a bitmap, typically for printing.

RISC (n.) <u>R</u>educed <u>i</u>nstruction <u>s</u>et <u>c</u>omputing; a simplification of the processor architecture that achieves high performance by reducing the range of instruction sets and executing them faster.

RLE (n.) <u>R</u>un-<u>l</u>ength <u>e</u>ncoding; developed by Microsoft, this CODEC for 8-bit video achieves a relatively low level of quality, particularly on nonrepeating data from frame to frame.

RLL (n.) <u>R</u>un-<u>l</u>ength <u>l</u>imited; a means of storing data on a hard disk that increases the density of the data, creating more compact files.

RLV (n.) <u>R</u>ecordable <u>l</u>aser <u>v</u>ideodisc (Optical Disc Corporation); a dated form of media used to record analog video and audio on a blank videodisc.

RMI (n.) <u>R</u>emote <u>M</u>ethod <u>I</u>nvocation; a JAVA API.

rms (n.) <u>R</u>oot <u>m</u>ean <u>s</u>quared; a formula used to measure the power of an audio amplifier, and a means of qualifying the capacity of loud speakers.

Rock Ridge Format (n.) CD-recordable specifications for UNIX that permit directory structures to be updated when new files are added to the disc. The specifications include the Rock Ridge Interchange Protocol Specification (RRIPS) and the System Use Sharing Protocol (SUSP). The SUSP extension to the ISO 9660 standard allows more than one file system extension to exist on a single CD-ROM disc. The RRIP specification allows POSIX files and directories to be recorded on CD-ROM without requiring modifications to files, such as renaming. Both of these specifications are extensions of the original ISO 9660 format for CD-ROM.

ROM (n.) <u>R</u>ead-<u>o</u>nly <u>m</u>emory; a computer storage medium that allows the user to recall and use information (read) but not to record or amend it (write).

root directory (n.) In MS-DOS, the topmost directory visible on a hard disk. It is under this directory that all subdirectories are nested.

rotational speed (n.) The speed at which the disk spins inside a drive, measured in revolutions per minute (rpm).

Rot-13 (n.) A form of encryption that is frequently used in Usenet postings to transpose the letters A–M with the letters L–Z.

rough cut (n.) A working copy of an edited master tape.

router (n.) A protocol-dependent device that connects networks. It is useful in breaking down a large network into smaller subnetworks. Routers introduce longer delays and have lower throughput rates than bridges. Like a bridge, a router restricts local area network (LAN) traffic and passes data to a routed LAN only when it is intended for that LAN. A repeater indiscriminately passes data along, regardless of the intended destination.

routing bridge (n.) A media-access-control-layer bridge that employs network-layer methods to determine a network's topology.

routing protocol (n.) A protocol that accomplishes routing through the implementation of a specific routing algorithm.

routing table (n.) A table stored in a router or another inter-networking device that keeps track of routes (in some cases, metrics associated with those routes) to specific network destinations.

routing update (n.) The message sent from a router to indicate network accessability and associated cost information. Routing updates most often are sent at regular intervals and after a change in network topology.

rpm (n.) Revolutions per minute; a measurement of the speed at which an object spins.

RRIPS See *Rock Ridge Format*.

RS-530 (n.) The specification of pinout for balanced interfaces, such as RS-422A with a DB-40 connector.

RS-422A (n.) A recommended standard developed by the EIA that defines the physical and functional features of a computer interface with communications equipment. A balanced line and a 40-pin connector are two of its features.

RS-170A (n.) A recommended standard developed by the Electronics Industries Association to specify color video signals for the NTSC format used in broadcast and in most consumer video products.

RS-232C (n.) A serial interface standard developed by the EIA for use in connecting computers and peripherals. The RS-232C port is a feature on most computing devices, and most gears with an RS-232C connector can be interfaced, as long as software drivers exist. This standard defines circuit functions and pin assignments. The physical connector comes in the traditional 25-pin version, or the newer 9-pin model. In data communications, this specification defines the interface between data terminal equipment (DTC) and data circuit-terminating equipment (DCE), using serial binary data.

RTF (n.) Rich Text Format; a format that defines text and is used for cross-platform applications where the characters and limited formatting information must be converted to a different word processing application or file type.

RTOS (n.) Real-Time Operating System; a CD-i operating system developed by Microware.

RTS (n.) Request to send; the signal

generated by a DTE over an RS-232 interface. The DCE responds with a clear to send (CTS) signal.

RTV (n.) Real-time video; a low-level digital video encoding scheme for desktop compression using an Intel i750-based video card.

run-length encoding See *RLE*.

run-length limited See *RLL*.

runtime code (n.) Program code that allows playback or delivery of a program without requiring the parent application to be present. Most multimedia authoring software tools give the developer the option of outputting a program with runtime code. In this format the program cannot be altered or reverse-engineered, and it requires less storage space than the parent application.

runtime license (n.) A type of license that permits the inclusion of runtime code in a replicated product.

safe zone (n.) The area in the center of a video frame that is sure to be displayed on all types of receivers and monitors. The outer edge of a video frame, which may vary from 10 to 20 percent of the total, is not reproduced in the same way on all sets.

SALT (n.) Society for Applied Learning Technology; an association of educators and instructional designers that promotes technology in education.

sample rate (n.) The frequency at which bits of data are recorded in digitizing a sound. Normally, sound is sampled at 44.1 kilohertz (kHz). To reduce the amount of space required to store audio data, 22.050 kHz and 11.025 kHz rates are used. These rates yield lower quality and are not advised for high-fidelity music. When a sample encoded at a given bit rate is converted to a higher or lower rate, some noise is introduced, but this is not nearly as serious as the artifacts generated in bit-rate conversion from 16- to 8-bit audio.

sampled sound (n.) A file containing data that represents an event that has been digitally captured from an acoustic waveform, rather than data resulting from electronic synthesis.

sampling (n.) The process of measuring an analog signal at periodic intervals or obtaining the values of an analog function by making a series of regular measurements of the function. It is a step in the process of converting an analog signal into a digital signal. The three steps are sampling, quantizing, and encoding. Sampling errors can cause aliasing effects and artifacts.

SASI (n.) Shugert Associates System Interface; the original incarnation of the SCSI interface.

satellite (n.) A receiver, repeater, or regenerator for microwave signals in geosynchronous orbit typically 22 300 miles above the surface of the earth. The "footprint" at this distance is approximately one-third of the globe.

satellite transmission delay (n.) The duration it takes for a signal to travel from an earth station to a satellite and bounce back to a receiving station. The delay is approximately a quarter of a second for radio waves at the speed of light (186 000 miles per second) to travel 44 600 miles.

saturated colors (n.) Bright colors, especially reds, that do not reproduce well on a video monitor because of their strong chroma component. They tend to saturate the screen with color or bleed around the edges, producing a blurred image.

SB (n.) Sound blaster; developed by Creative Labs, an audio card for IBM-compatibles that has become a de facto standard in the industry. It also refers to compatibility with SB software drivers, setup, and configuration.

Scalar Processor Architecture See *SPARC*.

scalability (n.) A feature that allows the same content to be displayed at higher resolution on larger monitors while supporting low resolutions on smaller monitors. Usually, scalable video or audio technologies allow the same data to be output over a range of quality levels, with better playback systems producing higher-quality products. A scalable font exists in a vector format and is a series of mathematical calculations that allow type to be resized without sacrificing quality.

scan 1. (v.) To convert a document or graphic on paper to a digital image format. 2. (n.) Related to video terminology, the rapid journey of the scanning spot back and forth across the scan lines on the back side of a screen. 3. (n.) In laserdisc technology, a mode of play in which the player skips over several disc tracks and displays occasional frames as it passes.

scan area (n.) The area to which the movement of the light source and the mirror/lens in a scanner is restricted.

scan contrast (n.) The range of values between white and black areas of an image.

scan conversion (n.) The process of putting data into a grid format for display on a raster device. It is a necessary operation when converting from a computer's non-interlaced VGA format to an NTSC video source which is interlaced. Poor quality scan conversion will cause annoying flicker when an NTSC monitor is used as the output from a computer video source.

scan lines (n.) The parallel lines on a video screen, from upper left to lower right, along which the scanner travels to pick up and lay down video information. NTSC systems use 525 scan lines to a screen; PAL systems use 625.

scanning frequency (n.) The number of sweeps across a video screen per second, either horizontally or vertically.

scanning spot (n.) In a cathode-ray tube, the beam generated by the electron gun that travels across the screen and paints a picture with red, green, and blue dots.

scan resolution (n.) The detail of an image determined by the physical limitations of a scanner as well as by the software settings. It equals the number of dots per inch (dpi) the scanner encodes. Higher resolutions create larger files, and a scanner must collect more information. It is important to scan for the resolution in which the image will be displayed. Screen resolution is typically only 72 dpi, while a standard for laser printing is 300 dpi. High-resolution film scanners can operate at levels above 2400 dpi.

scan threshold (n.) A user-defined setting on a scanner that instructs the detection circuitry to detect the chosen level of pixel brightness.

SCMS (n.) Serial Copy Master System; a function on digital audio tape (DAT) consumer decks that discourages making multiple copies by adding data to the program of dubs that are not first-generation.

score 1. (n.) The written notation that represents a musical composition. 2. (v.) To write a musical composition. 3. (n.) The representation of an animation sequence, or a movie, used in Macromedia Director.

screen 1. (n.) The viewing area on a monitor, or any surface onto which images are projected. 2. (n.) A process used to produce gray levels. In the PostScript language, a screen may be defined by the shape of the spots on the screen, the size of the spots, and the screen angle.

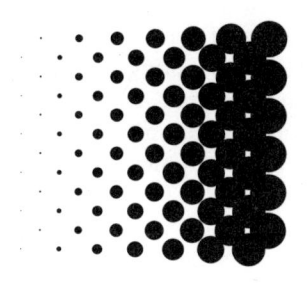

a screen in PostScript

screen dump (n.) The process of saving a graphic image of whatever appears on the monitor as a file or sending it to a printer.

screen saver (n.) A program that replaces the image displayed on monitor with a shifting pattern that prevents a monitor from being etched by a still image. It can be set to begin after a predetermined interval of inactivity and usually remains in effect until the mouse is moved or a key is depressed.

scrim (n.) In video production, a wire mesh screen placed over a lighting source to distribute the light for a scene more evenly.

script 1. (v.) To author in a high-level language that consists of statements in English which serve as commands. The original scripting language was HyperTalk, developed by Apple Computer. 2. (n.) A document that defines all the elements of a video or film production, including dialog, camera position, lighting, and the set itself.

ScriptX (n.) Developed by the Kaleida alliance, this authoring and playback software system provides cross-platform portability of multimedia software and a universal development tool.

scroll (v.) To cause text or graphics on the computer screen to move vertically upwards or downwards, progressively revealing more data. Most word-processing programs allow the user to scroll with an upwards or downwards arrow in a scroll bar on the side of the text field.

SCSI (n.) Small computer systems interface; developed by ANSI in 1986, a standard hardware/software interface system used by a variety of computers and peripherals. The protocol is used by Macintosh computers, IBM-compatibles, and workstations to communicate with up to seven storage devices and other peripherals under SCSI-1, and up to 15 devices under SCSI-2. SCSI-1 at 8 bits allows data transfer at speeds of 1.5–5 megabits per second (Mbps) asynchronously. Fast SCSI-2 at 8 bits permits transfer at speeds up to 20 Mbps synchronously. Wide SCSI-2 at 16 bits allows transfer at 10 Mbps synchronously because it uses twice the number of bits. "Fast, Wide SCSI" allows performance at up to 40 Mbps. All SCSI interfaces require termination at both ends, and devices on a SCSI chain must be set to different ID numbers. (Pronounced **scuzzy**.)

SDK (n.) Software Development Kit; a term used by Microsoft to refer to their applications development packages.

SDLC (n.) Synchronous Data Link Control; the protocol used in the IBM System Network Architecture (SNA).

SEA (n.) Self-extracting archive; an executable file that decompresses itself automatically when it is run.

search engine (n.) A program that locates and presents data, typically associated with a sizable database.

search time (n.) The duration required for a storage device to locate specific data on the medium.

SECAM (n.) Séquentiel Couleurs à Mémoire (sequential color with memory); the French composite video standard also adopted in Russia and many Middle Eastern countries. The basis of operation is the sequential recording of primary colors in alternate lines. Specifications include a 50-hertz (Hz) field frequency and 625 lines of image resolution. See *NTSC, PAL*.

sector (n.) On magnetic recording media, such as hard disks, circular cylinders are divided logically into equal segments, or pie-shaped wedges, each of which is a sector. *See illustration on following page.*

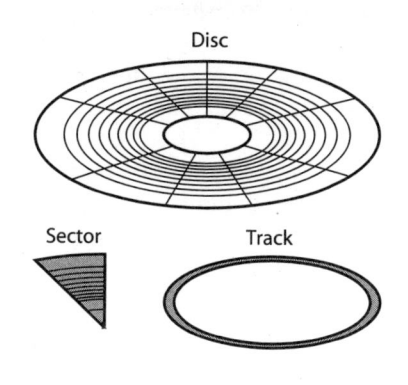

sector layout

secure sockets layer See *SSL*.

seek time (n.) The average time required to locate specific data on a disk. It is often computed as the time necessary to move the read head to the correct track and the time for the disk to spin one half of a rotation.

SEG (n.) Special effects generator; any video signal processor that changes the way images appear onscreen.

segment (n.) A portion of a video or audio program with the first and last frame, or the start and stop points identified, typically by time code; an excerpt from a larger piece from which it is lifted.

segue 1. (n.) A transition between two scenes, events, or musical numbers in a medley. (Pronounced **seg-way**.)

self-diagnostics (n.) Procedures used by a system to check its own operations and identify errors; usually performed when power is turned on.

self-extracting archive See *SEA*.

self-referential (n.) A data reduction technique based on redundancy within an image that is encoded. JPEG (Joint Photographic Expert Group) compression is an example. Intra-coded frames, known as I-frames, apply this concept in MPEG compression.

semiconductor 1. (n.) A material with limited conductivity. 2. (n.) An electronic component with circuitry that directs signals through gates and pathways based on the conductivity of the material. Integrated circuits that perform memory functions, transistors, and diodes are fabricated from semiconductor materials.

sequence (n.) A progression of data, events, images, or sounds that occurs in a specified order.

sequencer 1. (n.) A computer or controlling microprocessor that issues instructions to programmable musical instruments via MIDI. 2. (n.) The software program that enables a user to compose and edit music with a MIDI system.

Séquentiel Couleurs à Mémoire See *SECAM*.

serial (adj.) Describes operations pertaining to a series, or sequential time-based passage of data. Serial ports on computers process data one bit at a time in an orderly fashion as they pass information to or from input and output devices, such as modems and printers. A serial interface implies a single transmission channel.

serial copy master system See *SCMS*.

serial VTR control (n.) A computerized remote control of the functions of a videotape recorder via a normal RS-232 or RS-422 cable connection.

serif 1. (n.) In typography, a decorative flourish or thin line at the top or bottom of a letter that makes it easier to read. Fonts without serifs are referred to as "sans serif."

server (n.) A host computer, or backend application, with a large hard disk drive that shares its resources and storage with other computers on a network. It makes files and services available to clients.

servocontrol (n.) A device that converts weak mechanical force into greater force, which is a particularly useful function for a controlling mechanism that positions a lever, a gear, or a drive head.

session layer (n.) The OSI layer that provides a means for dialogue control between end systems.

SFA (n.) Still-frame audio.

SFX (n.) In audio work, a common abbreviation for "sound effects."

SGML (n.) Standard Generalized Markup Language; a universally recommended language for adding formatting information to text-only documents.

shading (n.) In three-dimensional graphics, the gradation from light to dark, or the blending of colors on a surface. Flat shading is quickly computed but is of low quality. Gouraud shading provides better image quality but takes somewhat longer. Phong shading is of excellent quality but takes a long time to perform the necessary calculations for each pixel.

shadow mask (n.) A method of construction for a display or a cathode-ray tube (CRT). The shadow mask is like a panel with very small holes situated behind the screen. The holes correspond to triad locations on the screen. The shadow mask guides the electron beams to strike one of the three phosphors in a triad.

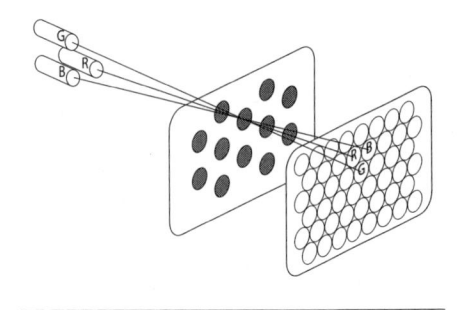

shadow mask

shared access (n.) In network technology, an access method that permits multiple stations to use the same

transmission medium. Contended and explicit access are types of shared access. Discrete access, in which each station has to have a separate connection, is the opposite of shared access.

shared disc (n.) A CD-ROM or laserdisc created through a joint production with a segment of the disc allocated to each contributor.

shareware (n.) User-supported software programs that are transferred or sold with the understanding that a fee will be paid to the program author if it meets the user's needs.

sharpen (v.) To enhance the distinction between darker and lighter pixels. Lines, edges, and other details in an image can be exaggerated through sharpening. Sharpening can enhance blemishes in the original, so it must be used judiciously.

shell (n.) The user interface; an external layer of a program that provides the user with controls and access to information.

shielding (n.) A metallic foil or braid that wraps the conductors in a cable to reduce interference from magnetic fields.

Shift-click (v.) To hold down the Shift key while clicking the mouse. In most Macintosh and Microsoft Windows applications, it allows the user to select a range of text between the original cursor position and the spot where the Shift-click takes place. It may be used to select multiple items on the desktop as well.

short (n.) Any video or film that lasts less than 35 minutes.

shot (n.) In production work, a continuous run with a film or videotape recorder.

Shugert Associates System Interface See *SASI.*

SIF (n.) Source Image Format; a video parameter that specifies a resolution of 352 x 240 at 30 hertz (Hz).

SIG (n.) Special interest group.

SIGGRAPH (n.) Special interest group in computer graphics; an association of computer users who share an interest in graphics. It is supported by the Association for Computing Machinery (ACM).

signal-to-noise See *S/N.*

silicon (n.) A nonmetallic element used in the semiconductor industry as a substrate for multiple layers of material on which electrical circuits are created. It is grown from a crystal to form a cylindrical "log," which is sliced into thin sections (typically 1/40 inch thick) to create bare wafers.

SIMM (n.) Single in-line memory module; a high-density DRAM package with several PLCCs connected to a single printed circuit board.

Simple Management Protocol See *SMP.*

Simple Mail Transfer Protocol See *SMTP.*

simple profile (n.) Streams of MPEG that use only I-and P-frames, using less buffer memory for decoding. It is less efficient than coding with B-frames. See *MPEG frame types*.

simplex (n.) One-way transmission, with the capacity to either send or receive, but not to do both at once.

simulation (n.) The use of images and sound to represent a situation or an event with a degree of realism. The simulation mode is useful in training applications where it enables users to learn the operation of equipment. New techniques and technologies have evolved rapidly for simulating virtual reality with three-dimensional models, walk-throughs, and fly-bys.

single in-line memory module See *SIMM*.

Single Line Internet Protocol See *SLIP*.

single-mode fiber (n.) A type of optical fiber that supports a single mode of light propagation above a cutoff wavelength. The core diameter is typically 5 to 10 millimeters, and transmission rates approach 100 GHz per kilometer.

SIP (n.) Single in-line package; a form factor for a board-level component, such as a transistor whose connections all extend from one side.

SIT (n.) Stuff-it; a Macintosh compressed file format.

site (n.) An address on the World Wide Web or any Internet location where information can be viewed or accessed with a browser or client application. A home page is usually the access point to a site on the Web.

16-bit audio (n.) The use of a 16-bit sample rate to digitize and play back sound. The quality is vastly superior to 8-bit sound. The audio CD standard is 16-bit, with a 44.1 kilohertz (kHz) sample rate. At this rate, a minute of stereo sound requires approximately 10 megabytes (MB) of storage.

16-bit bus (n.) A type of data bus that can exchange 16 bits of data at a time with a microcomputer's processor or memory.

16-bit color (n.) A video monitor setting that allocates 5 bits of memory each for the red and blue components of each pixel and 6 bits to the green, providing up to 65 536 different colors at once.

16:9 (n.) The aspect ratio of the horizontal size of an image to the vertical size, which is proposed for the HDTV video format.

slate (n.) A term derived from the movie industry's use of a slate board held up to indicate the beginning of a new "take." In a recording studio, the slate usually consists of the engineer's voice identifying the take number and an accompanying log sheet with the title, duration, and other particulars about the take.

SLED (n.) <u>S</u>ingle <u>l</u>arge <u>e</u>xpensive <u>d</u>isk.

SLIP (n.) <u>S</u>ingle <u>L</u>ine <u>I</u>nternet <u>P</u>rotocol; a protocol used by the Internet to run IP over serial lines, such as telephone circuits or RS-232 cables, interconnecting two systems.

slot mask (n.) A method of guiding electron beams in a picture. It is made of vertical wires which create the slots. The dot pitch in a slot mask is the space between the slots.

slow motion (n.) Display of frames at a slower than normal rate in either forward or reverse.

small computer systems interface See *SCSI*.

smart hub (n.) A concentrator for twisted-pair Ethernet or ARCNET networks. It has management features that allow an administrator to configure a network and monitor performance.

SMDS (n.) <u>S</u>witched <u>m</u>ultimegabit <u>d</u>ata <u>s</u>ervice; a "fast-packet" service that establishes high-speed connections between sites.

SME 1. (n.) <u>S</u>ociety of <u>M</u>anufacturing <u>E</u>ngineers. 2. (n.) <u>S</u>ubject <u>m</u>atter <u>e</u>xpert.

SMF (n.) <u>S</u>tandard <u>MIDI</u> <u>F</u>ile.

SMP (n.) <u>S</u>imple <u>M</u>anagement <u>P</u>rotocol; a popular standard for network management. SMP may also refer to Symmetrical Multi-Processing or a Symbolic Manipulation Program.

SMPTE 1. (n.) <u>S</u>ociety of <u>M</u>otion <u>P</u>icture and <u>T</u>elevision <u>E</u>ngineers; a professional engineering society that works to develop standards for motion picture and television equipment. 2. (n.) The time code standard itself, which is implemented in professional video editing systems.

SMTP (n.) <u>S</u>imple <u>M</u>ail <u>T</u>ransfer <u>P</u>rotocol; the Internet standard protocol for transferring electronic mail messages from one computer to another. SMTP specifies how two mail systems interact and the format of control messages they exchange to transfer mail.

S/N (n.) <u>S</u>ignal-to-<u>n</u>oise; the relationship between the strength of an audio or video signal compared to the measurable amount of noise, or undesirable interference it has picked up in transfer. Higher S/N ratios mean higher-quality signals, and each generation of a dub results in a lower S/N ratio. Digital media has the capability for much higher S/N ratios than analog media, and degradation does not occur in the dubbing process.

SNA (n.) <u>S</u>ystems <u>N</u>etwork <u>A</u>rchitecture; the protocols, formats, and logical structure for configuring, operating, and controlling a computer network. An SNA network is comprised of network accessible units (NAU), the transport network, gateway functions, boundary functions, and intermediate session routing function components. Systems Network Architecture consists of the following layers supporting the end user:

1. Transaction Services Layer
2. Presentation Services Layer
3. Data Flow Control Layer
4. Transmission Control Layer
5. Path Control Layer
6. Data Link Control Layer
7. Physical Control Layer

SND (n.) A Macintosh audio file format used for system sounds as well as for recording and playback of audio.

SNMP (n.) Simple Network Management Protocol; a protocol used with Transmission Control Protocol/Internet Protocol (TCP/IP) to manage devices from different vendors and solve incompatibility issues.

Society of Motion Picture and Television Engineers See *SMPTE*.

software (n.) All types of code, including logic programs that cause processors to perform computing functions. It refers to the part of a computing system that is not hardware.

Software Development Kit See *SDK*.

Solaris (n.) An operating system for Sun Microsystems computers.

SONET (n.) Synchronous Optical Network; the standards for data communication over fiber-optic cable between 51.84 megabits per second (Mbps) and 13 gigabits per second (Gbps).

SOP (n.) Standard operating procedures; production processes that are followed in order to allow more than one person to contribute to the production.

Sound Blaster See *SB*.

sound card (n.) A circuit board added to the motherboard of a microcomputer. It generates audio signals and provides output to headphones or external speakers.

sound pressure level See *SPL*.

Sound Recorder (n.) An applet, available in in Microsoft Windows, that creates .wav audio files. The quality of the audio is dependent upon the quality of the microphone used and the sampling circuitry on the installed sound card. To ensure the highest signal-to-noise ratio (S/N), audio recordings should always be made by adjusting the input levels so that the meters reach, but do not exceed peak levels. In digital recording, little headroom exists beyond the peak level, and input levels that are too hot will cause ugly distortion.

soundtrack (n.) The audio recording associated with a movie or a videotape production.

source code (n.) The text in which a computer program is written. It is then compiled into machine code which a processor can execute.

spam (v.) To send hundreds of inappropriate postings to individuals or to lists on the Internet.

SPARC (n.) <u>S</u>calar <u>P</u>rocessor <u>Ar</u>chitecture <u>R</u>educed-Instruction-Set <u>C</u>omputer; a fast and powerful workstation that was developed by Sun Microsystems and is based on RISC processing.

spatial resolution (n.) Related to graphic or video display, the number of lines or dots used to define an image. When not otherwise specified, the word "resolution" by itself is means spatial resolution, rather than color or time-based resolution.

special effects generator See *SEG*.

spectrum (n.) A continuous range of frequencies.

speech recognition See *voice recognition*.

speech synthesizer (n.) A device that produces human speech sounds from data in another form, such as a text file.

spikes (n.) Brief, abnormally high voltage fluctuations that can occur on an ordinary electrical line providing power to a facility. They can cause damage to electrical circuits and components.

spindle synchronization (n.) A feature of some hard disk drives in which the rotational position of their spindles is synchronized. It is implemented in the RAID 3 format.

SPL (n.) <u>S</u>ound <u>p</u>ressure <u>l</u>evel; the amplitude of an audio waveform in the atmosphere.

splice (v.) To cut cleanly and bind together pieces of magnetic tape from different sources in order to achieve a seamless whole. Before digital media, it was the only way to edit audio and video content. Modern digital editing equipment allows the user to instantly choose segments from various sources, paste them together in memory, and change the result if it is not desirable.

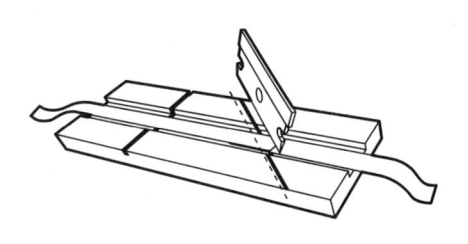

splicing block for audio tape

spline (n.) A smooth curve that interpolates multiple points and is defined by several other curves, or polynomials. The term originally was used to describe the flexible rod used in drafting to draw a curved line.

spline-based modeling (n.) The use of Bezier curves in three-dimensional modeling to bend shapes more smoothly and realistically.

split edit (n.) In postproduction, an edit of only the audio or video portion of a

splitter (n.) A device that accepts a single signal and provides multiple ports through which it may be accessed.

spool (n.) Simultaneous peripheral operations online; the practice of temporarily storing data in a buffer to reduce delays in processing or printing.

spreadsheet (n.) A computer-generated worksheet consisting of columns and rows of numbers, letters, or other symbols. Formulas can be applied to a group of entries, and the results can be calculated automatically. Spreadsheets can be used for scheduling, managing resources, accounting ledgers, balance sheets, grade books, and many other creative purposes.

sprite (n.) A concept applied in Macromedia Director that refers to a graphics element that can be manipulated on-screen as an object.

SQL (n.) Structured Query Language; a widely used programming language for defining, modifying, and accessing information in relational databases. It allows queries to be made from other programs.

square-pixel digitizing (v.) To convert an image from a television signal, which has a different aspect ratio than a computer monitor, and to correct for distortion that would result from

squeezing and cropping rectangular pixels. NTSC signals would be distorted up to 11% if corrections, or square pixels, were not interpolated from the rectangular pixels.

SRAM (n.) Static random-access memory; memory that is contained in an IC that does not require recharging. Unlike DRAM, SRAM retains stored information.

SSL (n.) Secure sockets layer; a protocol for passing private, encrypted information over Internet connections developed by Netscape.

stack (n.) Related to the Apple HyperCard program, this is a set of cards, or frames, with the accompanying programmed "scripts." See *HyperCard*.

stairstepping (n.) The uneven representation of diagonal lines or curves on a computer screen. It can be corrected to a degree by antialiasing software.

stamper (n.) A perfectly flat final mastering disc used to mold replicas.

stand-alone 1. (adj.) Describes a multimedia program that runs without the application that created it being present, requiring no other software support. 2. (adj.) Describes equipment, such as an interactive kiosk, that is independent of a larger network.

Standard Generalized Markup Language See *SGML*.

Standard MIDI File (n.) (SMF) The format that is universally accepted by musical applications for a stream of MIDI data in a file.

standard operating procedures See *SOP*.

standards (n.) Uniform protocols that define communication between devices. Standards are established to reduce incompatibility between competitive technologies. They are often developed by a committee belonging to an industry association, such as the ISO. The EIA sets "RS" standards. ANSI standards for data communications usually begin with the letter "X", such as the ASCII code standard, X3.4-1967. The ITU-T (formerly known as the CCITT) publishes recommendations rather than standards, such as the "V" series, that refer to data transfer over telephone lines.

star topology (n.) A method of connecting devices in a LAN that routes all communications through the central hub or controller. See *network topology*.

start bit (n.) The first bit sent in asynchronous data transmission that alerts the receiving computer that what follows is the beginning of a meaningful character. It is always the binary digit 1.

static random-access memory See *SRAM*.

station (n.) Data terminal equipment that sends and receives messages on a data link, such as a user device on a network node.

step frame (n.) A function in video playback equipment that permits movement, forward or reverse, one frame at a time.

step time (n.) A method of recording discrete MIDI events one by one for playback as a continuous stream later, rather than recording in real time at a set tempo.

STI 1. (n.) Speech transmission index. 2. (n.) Standard tape interconnect.

still frame 1. (n) A single frame of film or video displayed on a monitor as a static image. 2. (adj.) Describes graphical or textual information recorded on a single frame and intended to be displayed as a motionless image.

stop bit (n.) A control bit that signifies the end of an asynchronous character in data transmission. It is always the binary digit 0.

storyboard (n.) A sequence of graphic representations, often with dialog or captions, showing important scenes in a program. It is used to plan a production, to visualize, and to present program ideas. Storyboards are often an artist's sketches in a form similar to a comic strip.

STP (n.) Secure Transfer Protocol; a networking protocol that encrypts data. It may also mean shielded twisted pair, or signal transfer point.

stripe (v.) To record time code, usually SMPTE, on a channel of the tape prior to editing. This procedure allows accurate access to individual frames.

Structured Query Language See *SQL*.

stuff-it See *SIT*.

stylus (n.) An input device in the form of a pen-shaped instrument used to enter text, draw lines, or point to choices on a computer screen.

subassembly (n.) An individually replaceable component integrated with other components to form a system.

subdirectory (n.) A data structure in the Micrsoft DOS and Windows filing systems that represents a division of the root directory. It may be further divided into numerous lower-level subdirectories to provide a means of managing data.

submenu (n.) A lower-level menu, or series of choices, at which the user arrives after selecting a main menu choice that branches to the submenu.

subnetwork (n.) A small network linked with other networks by a router or a bridge.

subsample (v.) When capturing data, to discard portions of a signal for the purpose of reducing the amount of data that must be compressed. Most types of lossy compression perform this operation.

substrate (n.) In a CD-ROM or other optical storage device, the molded plastic base onto which data is encoded.

subtractive color (n.) Assuming a white background, the mixture of various intensities of the colors cyan, magenta, and yellow to produce all visible colors.

Super Video Graphics Array See *SVGA*.

surface (n.) A three-dimensional space defined by the relationship between three variable coordinates—x, y, and z.

surface mount (n.) Related to PC board assembly, a technique for high-density manufacturing using a variety of semiconductor packages.

surge protector (n.) A device used to monitor the level of electrical current between a power source and a computer or other electronic component. When a surge of voltage exceeding a certain limit is detected, the circuit is shut down or the level automatically reduced to prevent damage to the electronics.

surrogate travel (n.) A virtual-reality system in which point-of-view travel is simulated, allowing the user to control the path taken through the environment.

Surround Video (n.) A technology developed by Microsoft for encoding panoramic views into graphics files. It permits users to view their surroundings in any direction from a fixed pivot point or points. It is conceptually similar to QuickTime VR from Apple Computer.

SUSP (n.) §ystem Use §haring Protocol; an extension to the ISO 9660 standard that permits multiple file system extension to exist on a single CD-ROM.

sustained transfer rate (n.) The number of bytes per second a CD-ROM drive or other storage medium can deliver as it reads data objects larger than its internal buffer.

SVGA (n.) §uper Video Graphics Array; a video standard established by the Video Electronic Standards Association. Updated versions allow resolutions of up to 1280 × 1024 with 24-bit color.

S-VHS *or* **Super VHS** (n.) An advancement of the VHS videotape format, featuring higher luminance and more lines of resolution. See *VHS*.

S-video (n.) A type of video signal used in the Hi-8 and S-VHS videotape formats. It transmits luminance and color independently as separate components, avoiding the combination done in composite video and the resulting loss of picture quality. Also known as Y/C video.

swap file (n.) A hidden system file in Microsoft Windows 3.1 that is located on a local hard disk in contiguous space and serves the function of expanding apparent internal RAM. It is also known as virtual memory. Swap files may be permanent or temporary.

sweetening (n.) In video or film postproduction, the development of an audio track with mixed elements such as music, sound effects, and applause. In the process, the signal-to-noise ratio is improved and general quality of the sound track is polished.

swim (n.) A form of drift in which a shadow image appears to move from the top to the bottom of a video screen. It is caused by noise in electronic signals or by noise generated locally in the display electronics.

switch 1. (n.) A device that opens or closes circuits or selects paths. In video production, a "switcher" is used to select the current signal source or camera shot that becomes the output. 2. (n.) In MS-DOS, an argument to control the execution of a command that usually involves a qualifying parameter, typically delimited by a "/" symbol.

Switched 56 (n.) Switched public data transmission service at 56 kilobits per second (Kbps).

switched line (n.) A telecommunications link that may follow a different physical path with each use of the service, as is the case with the public telephone system.

switched multimegabit data service See *SMDS*.

symmetrical compression (n.) In audio/video encoding, techniques for encoding that can be reversed in order to yield the exact same data upon decoding.

sync (n.) (synchronization) The part of a video signal, or a separate signal sent with the video, that carries timing information on each frame.

synchronized (adj.) Describes two or more events that are coordinated exactly in time. It is especially important that audio data and video images be synchronized when they are combined.

synchronous (adj.) Occurring at the same time or in real time, rather than temporarily separated. A conversation or conference in real time is synchronous communication, while responding to e-mail messages at a later date is asynchronous communication. In synchronous transmission, successive bits or events all move at a constant pace, or rate of speed. The characters are spaced by time in a synchronous transmission, rather than by start and stop bits.

Synchronous Optical Network See *SONET*.

sync-locked (adj.) Describes the exact alignment of two signals, which occurs when the sync pulses of a videotape recorder are locked with those of another deck or a camera.

syntax (n.) A legal expression or statement in a computer language. If the statement follows a particular sequence and includes only acceptable characters, it is said to have proper syntax.

synthesized sound (n.) A type of sound consisting of waveforms that are created by the use of mathematical formulas, produced by either analog or digital means, rather than waveforms that are sampled from acoustic sources.

synthesizer (n.) An instrument that creates sounds electronically. Controls on the instrument typically allow the user to change basic sound qualities, such as frequency, amplitude, and the envelope of each timbre. A synthesizer is by definition not a sample player.

SyQuest (n.) Named after the company that manufactures it, a type of removable storage system that employs cartridges and offers a high data transfer rate. Standard SyQuest cartridges hold 44, 88, 135, 200, or 270 megabytes (MB) of data on a 5.25-inch cartridge. A second-generation 3.5-inch cartridge holds 230 megabytes (MB) of data.

SYSOP (n.) System operator; the person who takes responsibility for managing a bulletin board or e-mail service.

system area (n.) The space on a CD-ROM that is located between the addresses 00:00:00: and 00:02:16. This is where data related to the operating system and error correction data is placed.

system operator See *SYSOP*.

System 7.X (n.) Any operating system later than 7.0 used by the Macintosh.

Table of Contents See *TOC*.

tag (n.) A character or string connected to an item of data, often at the beginning and end, that contains identifying information. In HTML, a tag is placed before and after a text string to identify the type size and other features of the data.

Tagged Image File Format See *TIFF*.

tap (n.) A connection to the main transmission line in a cable-based local area network (LAN).

tape archive See *TAR*.

tape storage (n.) A ribbon of magnetic recording media stored on a reel or a cassette. Tapes can hold analog or digital data. When used for data storage, they offer low cost-per-megabyte, but tape deteriorates over time. Another disadvantage is that accessing data from a tape is slow. The primary application in digital media is for archival backups, which are usually done overnight so that hard disk drives can be erased and used the next day for digitizing new data. *See tape transport illustration on following page.*

TAR (n.) Tape archive; a filename extension in the UNIX operating system.

TARGA (n.) Truevision Advanced Raster Graphics Adapter; a 24-bit color image format defined by Truevision, originally for that company's line of TARGA videographics interface cards. It has since been used as an exchange format by many other image-creation and editing programs. The term is also used in reference to a series of graphics cards produced by Truevision for microcomputers. The PC series was among the first to support full-color (24-bit) display.

TB (n.) Terabyte; used to quantify data in bytes, or 8-bit words, this is equivalent to 2^{40}, or 1 099 511 627 776 bytes. The prefix tera also refers to 10^{12}.

TBC (n.) Time base corrector; a device that resets the timing portion of a video signal to the standard values for a given video format. It has the effect of cleaning up the output of videotape players or computer video cards prior to broadcast. It is useful in synchronizing two independent video signals.

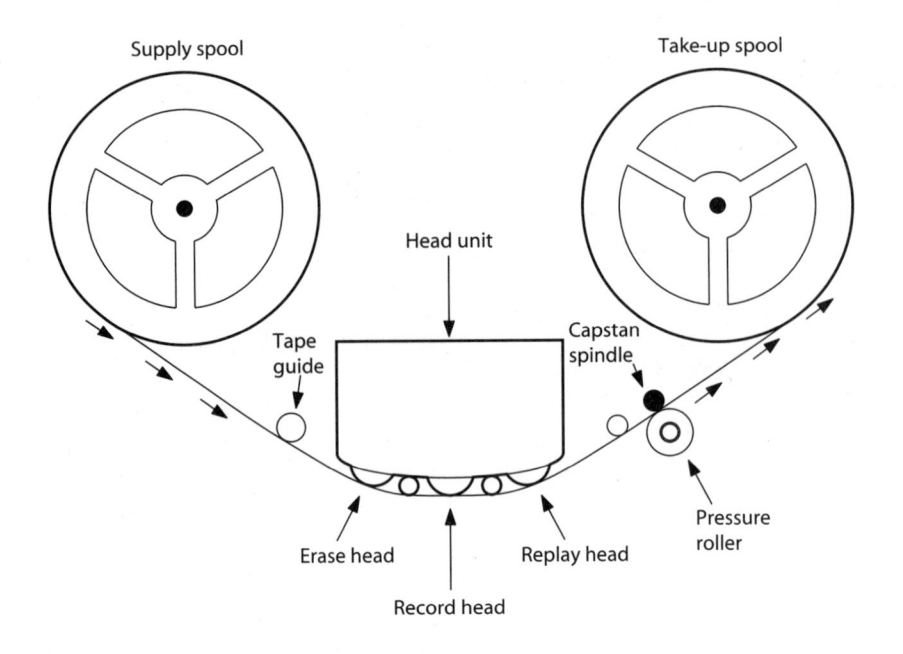

tape transport in a reel-to-reel recorder

TBK (n.) The filename extension for a file that is created by the popular multimedia development application Toolbook.

TCP/IP (n.) Transmission Control Protocol/Internet Protocol; the set of connectionless transport protocols used by the Internet to support services, such as remote login (Telnet), file transfer (FTP), and mail (SMTP). It is the result of ARPAnet development before the Internet was established. IP is a packet-switching protocol, while TCP checks, tracks, and corrects transmission errors.

TDM (n.) Time-division multiplexor; a device that interleaves bits or characters from multiple terminals which are connected over a single transmission line carrying many channels.

TDMA (n.) Time division multiple access; an integrated services digital network (ISDN) that is offered on a bearer channel basis and used for high volume, international public telephone traffic.

tear-off menu (n.) A small menu of frequently used tools that may be repositioned onscreen.

technology without an interesting name See *TWAIN*.

telco (n.) An abbreviation for "telephone company" or "telephone central office."

telecine See *film chain*.

telecommute (v.) To use telecommunications equipment while working at home to maintain contact with an office.

telecommunications (n.) The transfer of signals, sounds, and images over telephone or radio communications systems. It includes passing information between voice systems and computer terminals over cable and wireless connections.

telecomputing (n.) The combination of telephone, television, cable, and computing technologies in a single system that is typically based in the home.

teleconference (n.) A telephone call among several parties, set up by a telecommunications provider, which enables more than two callers to participate in a conversation at once in an "audio conference." The use of video allows participants at remote sites to see and hear, participate in meetings, and share visual data in a "video conference."

telephony (n.) The transmission of electronic signals that represent sounds or data to a remote location with or without wiring.

teletext (n.) Computer-generated characters that are inserted into the vertical blanking interval of a broadcast signal, normally during lines 18 to 21 of a one-way transmission.

television standards (n.) Different countries around the world have adopted one of three standards for television signals used for both broadcast and videotape playback applications. The three formats are PAL, NTSC, and SECAM, and there are significant differences between them. One thing they all have in common is that each frame is made up of two fields. Phase alternating line (PAL) moves at 25 frames per second (fps), with 625 scan lines. It uses amplitude modulation at a channel bandwidth of 8 megahertz (Mhz). The National Television Standards Committee (NTSC) format moves at 29.97 fps, with 525 scan lines, and it uses amplitude modulation at a channel bandwidth of 6 Mhz. The Séquentiel Couleurs à Mémoire (SECAM) format uses the same frame rate and number of scan lines as PAL, but it uses frequency modulated subcarriers at a bandwidth of 8 Mhz. In a few South American countries, hybrid formats that are known as "PAL-M" and "PAL-N" combine features of both NTSC and PAL. In most of Central America, NTSC is the standard, while in most Scandinavian and Western European countries PAL is the standard. The following is a list of some of the countries that adhere to the three popular standards:

NTSC—United States, Canada, Mexico, Japan, South Korea, Philippines

PAL—Great Britain, Germany, Spain, India, Australia, China (PROC)

SECAM—France, Hungary, Poland, Russia, Saudi Arabia, Egypt

Telnet (n.) The Internet standard protocol for remote terminal connection service which allows a user at one site to interact with a remote system at another site, as if the user's terminal were connected directly to the remote computer. NCSA Telnet is the standard on the Macintosh platform.

template (n.) A previously designed structure or shell into which data may be placed. It provides a consistent look for graphic presentations.

temporal redundancy (n.) The duplication of information found at earlier points in a stream of data or in a signal.

ter (n.) The third version of an original CCITT standard, as in V.27ter.

terabyte See *TB*.

terminal 1. (n.) The hardware used in a computer-based information system through which information passes. It often takes the form of a remote work station, such as a VT100, with a visual display and keyboard connected to a central processing unit (CPU). A dumb terminal has no processing capability, while an intelligent terminal has its own processor. 2. (n.) Any point at which information can enter or exit a communication network.

terminate 1. (v.) To place an electrical load at the end of a circuit. 2. (v.) To install a connector on the end of a cable.

terminate and stay resident See *TSR*.

terminated line (n.) A circuit with resistance at the end point equal to the characteristic impedance of the line. This ensures that no standing waves or reflections are present when a signal enters near the end of the line.

tessellation (n.) Changing models that exist as coordinates in space into polygons.

test (n.) A structured type of interaction that elicits a response, allowing measurement of a user's knowledge.

texels (n.) The abbreviation for textured pixels.

text (n.) A string of data that consists of standard ASCII characters and no other information or file types.

texture map (n.) The shading and surface features on a two-dimensional or a three-dimensional object. In addition to being an image, a texture can be a procedure calculated from formulas. *See illustrations on following page.*

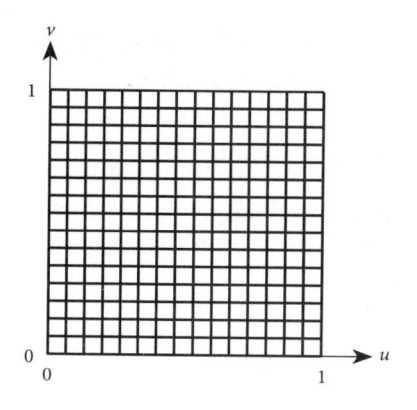

rectangular grid as a texture map

rectangular grid mapped onto a sphere

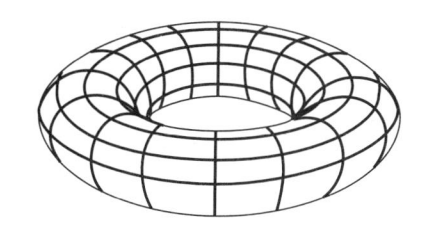

rectangular grid mapped onto a torus

TFT (n.) Thin film transistor; a microminiature integrated circuit formed by thin layers of conductive material on an insulating substrate.

TGA (n.) A Targa format, captured by a TrueVision video card, with the extension .tga.

THD (n.) Total harmonic distortion; a measure of performance in audio gear that monitors hum and other unwanted frequencies. It is expressed as a percentage of noise compared to the total signal. Lower percentages are better.

thermal wax printer (n.) A color printer that creates an image by using heated pins to melt a thin coating of wax on a ribbon, transferring the wax onto the paper.

thin Ethernet (n.) A networking technology that makes use of thinner coaxial cable than standard Ethernet. It is also called "cheapernet" because the cable costs less. It adheres to the IEEE 802.3 standard and is known as "10base2." Transmission is at 10 megabits per second (Mbps) over a maximum distance of 200 meters, and cable ends are terminated with BNC-style connectors.

thin film transistor See *TFT*.

thread 1. (n.) A complete operation, set of instructions, or process executed by software that cannot be interrupted. 2. (n.) A series of interrelated messages sent over a network.

Threaded-Neill-Concelman See *TNC*.

3-DGF (n.) Three-Dimensional Geometry File; a cross-platform format developed by Macromedia for exchanging 3-D geometric data.

3DO (n.) A manufacturer and marketer of an interactive multimedia player capable of high-resolution graphics and fast animation. The player reads specially formatted CDs and is designed to deliver games, movies, and educational applications. (Pronounced **3-dee-oh**.)

¾-inch (adj.) Describes a .75-inch videotape used in Sony U-matic video recorders. This format is used by some video professionals and in many television studios.

3:2 pulldown (n.) The process of converting film at 24 frames per second (fps) into NTSC video at 30 fps.

throughput (n.) The data processing capacity, or rate at which data can be passed by a bus. It is most often expressed in bits per second (bps).

thumbnails (n.) Small versions of larger graphic images. Typically, they are used for indexing a database of graphics or for previewing an image at a larger resolution that would take a great deal of space or time to draw. An encapsulated postscript file carries with it a thumbnail in the TIFF format for previewing.

TIFF (n.) Tagged Image File Format. Developed in 1986 by Aldus, Microsoft, and others, this image format is used to store and exchange graphics on the IBM-compatible and Macintosh platforms.

tiled windows (n.) An arrangement of program windows in a graphical user interface (GUI) in which the windows do not overlap.

timbre (n.) A musical term for the color of a tone, determined primarily by its overtone structure. The difference between an oboe and flute sounding the same note is a difference in timbre. This is not to be confused with pitch (frequency), loudness (amplitude), or the shape of a tone (envelope).

time base corrector See *TBC*.

time code (n.) Address code with time-referenced information recorded on a spare track of videotape, or inserted in the vertical blanking interval of a video signal. It is expressed as an eight-digit number that displays time in hours, minutes, seconds, and video frames in the format hh:mm:ss:ff.

time code generator (n.) A special type of signal generator that outputs SMPTE time code in the form of a regular pulse, which is typically recorded as an audio signal on an unused track of videotape.

time code reader (n.) An electronic device that reads and displays SMPTE time code. It is generally integrated in a professional quality playback or recording deck.

time-division multiplexor See *TDM*.

timeout (n.) A default action performed by a program when a pre-determined period of time expires before a user enters data or offers input of any kind. This may result in initiating a screen saver or automatically looping a sequence.

title (n.) In electronic or digital publishing, a volume, set of volumes, or a program on CD-ROM.

TNC (n.) Threaded-Neill-Concelman; a threaded connector used with coaxial cables.

TOC (n.) Table of Contents; the space on a CD-ROM where information is imprinted about the tracks on a disc, their starting locations, and the total length of the data on the disc.

toggle 1. (v.) To switch between two applications or choices, such as on and off, with a single key or button. 2. (n.) Any two-position switch that may be mechanical or virtual.

token ring (n.) A local area network (LAN) that is configured in a ring, around which a token, or special signal, is passed between terminals over a single channel. The floating message, or token, gives each terminal permission to transmit data. A multistation access unit (MSAU) controls the passage of data around the ring at speeds of up to 16 megabits per second (Mbps). This network structure, an Institute of Electrical and Electronics Engineers (IEEE) standard, was developed by IBM.

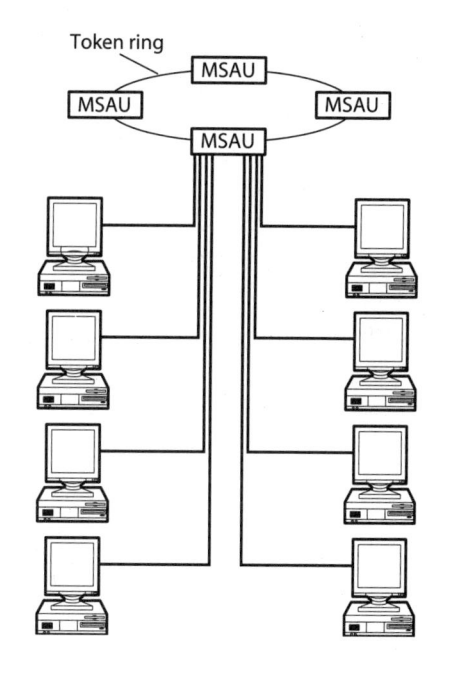

token ring network

T1 (n.) A digital transmission link that can pass data at rate of 1.544 megabits per second (Mbps) over normal twisted-pair wiring. It can handle 24 voice channels at 64 kilobits per second (Kbps), and it is a North American telecommunications standard.

toolbar (n.) A collection of icons that activate program functions in a graphical user interface (GUI). In graphics programs, the tools may represent a lasso selector, text entry, or an eraser. Other tools determine line size, width, color, or shape.

torus (n.) A three-dimensional shape that resembles a donut and is known as an anchor ring. For an example, see the B-spline surface illustration.

total harmonic distortion See *THD*.

touch screen (n.) A display or monitor that serves as a control or input device that responds to the touch of a user. Touch-screen systems employ a variety of technologies such as plastic membranes, infrared grids, capacitance sensors, and acceleration detection devices.

TPI (n.) Tracks per inch, a measurement of density on magnetic media. A DOS-formatted, high-density 3.5-inch floppy disk holds 135 TPI.

track 1. (n.) On an audio tape or videotape, the physical area that contains an individual program or some control information. It could be compared to a lane on the freeway. 2. (n.) The process through which a recorded videotape plays back. A machine that "tracks" well has its heads properly aligned. Videotape tracks are recorded diagonally. 3. (n.) The adjacent bands of the data spiral on a compact disc. The tracks on a hard disk exist as concentric circles rather than in a spiral shape.

trackball (n.) An alternative input device to the mouse; it functions like a mouse upside down and requires little desktop space. Spinning the ball causes a cursor on the screen to move.

track-relative time (n.) A method used to determine start and stop times of audio segments on a mixed-mode disc.

transactional (adj.) Describes a retail kiosk where a customer can make a credit card purchase or conduct business.

transceiver (n.) A system that receives, amplifies, and retransmits a signal without altering the original content significantly.

transcoding (v.) To convert from one video or graphic format to another, as opposed to encoding, which refers to the original capture or digitization of images.

transducer (n.) Any device that converts one form of energy into another, such as a microphone that converts sound pressure levels that vary into an analogous varied stream of voltage.

transfer rate (n.) The rate at which digital information is transferred to or from a storage medium or device. For example, a single speed compact disc reader transfers data at approximately 150 kilobytes per second (KBps).

transistor (n.) A three-terminal, solid-state electronic device that is used for switching or amplification. Integrated logic circuits contain a large number of miniature transistors.

transmission (n.) The electronic transfer of a signal or data from one location or device to another.

Transmission Control Protocol/Internet Protocol See *TCP/IP*.

transmission rate (n.) The rate of speed at which data can be transferred across a communications medium under varying conditions.

transparency (n.) The degree to which a computing system interferes with the process of interaction. Intuitive software running on equipment that is easy to use makes technology transparent.

transponder (n.) A satellite communications device that can receive a signal, convert it to a new frequency, amplify it, and send it back to earth immediately. They are normally contained within re-transmitting satellites.

transport layer (n.) The network entity responsible for end-to-end control of transmitted data in the OSI model.

tree (n.) A local area network (LAN) topology that resembles the shape of a tree with only one route between network nodes.

triad (n.) Related to a RGB display, a set of red, green, and blue phosphors arranged in a triangle. Three guns fire different-colored electron beams at the phosphors on the tube. The phosphors are excited by the gun whose color matches theirs. The triad produces a single color which is a combination of the three excited phosphors.

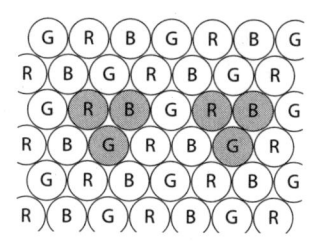

triad—phosphor dot pattern

troubleshoot (v.) To test system components for continuity and performance, and to identify faulty connections and parts. If a visual inspection does not indicate loose connections, voltage levels and logic circuits should be checked. If logic levels are improper, it could be the result of a malfunctioning IC or noise caused by electromagnetic interference. Many systems are equipped with diagnostic test programs, which may identify the cause of a problem. After all hardware components and connections are tested, look for a bug in the software.

true color 1. (n.) A system in which the color information belonging to an image is used directly to determine the output color, rather than as an index to a table of colors in a palette. 2. (adj.) Describes color systems with enough colors to create an image that looks natural to the human eye. It is typically defined as 24-bit color.

TrueType (n.) A scalable font technology, developed by Apple Computer in 1991, which is implemented in Microsoft Windows and OS/2 operating systems, as well as in the Macintosh.

Truevision Advanced Raster Graphics Adapter See *TARGA*.

trunk (n.) A telephone line, or channel, between the telephone company's central office or switching center and another point.

TSR (n.) Terminate and stay resident; in MS-DOS, a program that remains in memory once it has been loaded from a disk.

T3 (n.) A combination of 28 T1 lines at once, with an aggregate data rate of 44.736 megabits per second (Mbps).

TTL (n.) Transistor-transistor logic; bipolar integrated circuit logic that employs transistors with multiple emitters.

turnkey system (n.) An integrated hardware/software program that is ready to run without setup or engineering. The user simply turns a key to operate.

TWAIN (n.) Technology without an interesting name; the programming logic that allows graphic manipulation software to capture images from a scanner in the "twain" format.

tween (v.) To create an interpolated image between two set images, or coordinates, in animation or graphics program. Tweening speeds up the creation of animated sequences by letting the user define just the keyframe images, and then instructing the computer to fill in the intervening pictures.

twisted pair (n.) In telecommunications, standard cable made up of one or more pairs of copper wire twisted around one another to reduce induction and interference between the wires.

2-D graphics (n.) Artwork and designs that exist in a single plane, or two dimensions. Basic drawing applications are two-dimensional, and information is defined on an x-y axis.

two-phase commit (n.) A data notation method, physically located on independent machines, that ensures the success or failure of each machine. If all statements succeed, an action is committed; if any one of the statements fail, all statements within the transaction revert to their original condition.

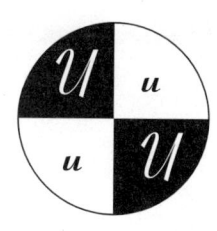

UART (n.) Universal asynchronous receiver/transmitter; an integrated circuit that converts between serial and parallel data formats. For example, a UART is necessary to convert the parallel data from a computer into serial data for asynchronous transmission.

UDTV (n.) Ultra-high definition television; a proposed digital broadcast standard with higher resolution than HDTV. UDTV will provide approximately 3000 lines of resolution, as opposed to 1125 lines in HDTV. No standards have been established to date.

UHF 1. (n.) Ultra-high frequency; the radio frequency from 300 to 3000 megahertz (MHz). 2. (n.) The TV broadcast band located in this range. In the United States, UHF channels 14 through 83 occupy the range from 470 MHz to 890 MHz.

UI (n.) User interface; software that facilitates communication with a computer. It may consist of a singe line on which commands are entered, or it may consist of icons and menu bars in a graphical user interface (GUI).

Ultimatte (n.) A brand name for a chroma key system used to overlay multiple video images. The Ultimatte system transfers the luminance (brightness) image of the dropout color, which enables the transfer of shadows to the composite image.

Ultimedia (n.) The entire line of IBM multimedia tools and technologies. The IBM PS/2 Ultimedia Model M57 SLC was IBM's first PS/2 machine with built-in multimedia capabilities. The Ultimedia line, dating from 1991, complies with MPC computer specifications.

ultra-high definition television See *UDTV.*

ultra-high frequency See *UHF.*

U-matic (n.) The trade name, developed by Sony, for .75-inch videotape recorders and players.

unbalanced (adj.) In audio and telecommunications, describes channels that carry a signal on one wire referenced to ground. While unbalanced wiring is less expensive than balanced configurations which carry the signal as a difference between two wires, unbalanced lines are more susceptible to spurious noise.

underscan (v.) To limit the electron beam in a CRT to scan within the boundaries of the display. This reduces the normal size of a video image by up to 20%. To ensure that the complete image is always visible within a display area, it is advisable to check the boundaries of an image in underscan mode. Computer monitors usually operate in this mode, but the underscanning feature is available on professional video systems only.

undo (v.) To void the last action made by a user in a graphical interface. The Edit menu in most Microsoft programs offers the Undo function, which also may be invoked by pressing the key combination Control-z.

Uniform Resource Locator See *URL*.

universal asynchronus receiver/transmitter See *UART*.

unity gain (n.) In audio engineering, the condition in which input and output levels are equal, with no apparent amplification or attenuation.

UNIX (n.) Developed by AT&T, a 32-bit operating system with excellent multitasking capabilities. It is widely used on powerful computer work stations, such as those made by Sun Microsystems and SGI. UNIX is an alternative to MS-DOS or the Macintosh OS. While it is a complex system with arcane keyboard commands, some of the most elegant graphical user interfaces have been devised to implement UNIX transparently for end users.

UNIX-to-UNIX copy program See *UUCP*.

unshielded twisted pair See *UTP*.

upgrade (n.) A recent release or version of a software program that includes more features or performs better.

uplink (n.) A transmission system that sends signals up to a satellite in orbit.

upload (v.) To send a file to a networked host or to another machine.

upper memory (n.) An area outside of the first 640K of conventional memory that is reserved for system software, where programs cannot store information. Upper memory blocks are typically used for TSRs and device drivers.

UPS (n.) <u>U</u>ninterruptible <u>p</u>ower <u>s</u>upply; a device that can provide electrical power to a system if the normal power source fails, which prevents interrupted service.

upstream (adj.) In a two-way television network, describes the direction a signal travels from a receive site back to an origination site.

URL (n.) <u>U</u>niform <u>R</u>esource <u>L</u>ocator; the address of a home page on the World Wide Web.

USART (n.) Universal synchronous-asynchronous receiver/transmitter. See *UART*.

USB (n.) Universal Serial Bus.

Usenet (n.) A public network on the Internet in which newsgroup participants exchange information by posting messages to the group and following a thread or train of thought.

user (n.) The operator of a computer program.

user bits (n.) Referring to an 80-bit SMPTE time code word, these are undefined bits that are available for uses other than time code.

user-friendly (adj.) Describes programs and systems that are designed for ease of operation.

user interface See *UI*.

utility programs (n.) Programs designed to support the operation of software and hardware. Examples of MS-DOS utilities are CHKDSK and DEFRAG.

UTP (n.) Unshielded twisted pair; standard networking cable under the category 3 specification.

UUCP (n.) UNIX-to-UNIX copy program; a store-and-forward system, primarily for UNIX systems, but currently supported on other platforms, including VMS and some personal computers.

uuencode/uudecode (n.) A program that converts binary files into ASCII files for transmission and decodes them on reception.

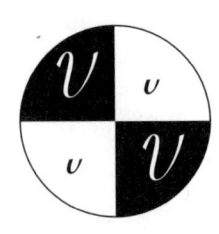

validation (n.) The process of assessing and refining testing procedures and other components of an instructional design.

value (n.) In relation to color, the degree of lightness or darkness, or the intensity.

value-added reseller See *VAR*.

vaporware (n.) Proclaimed software that has not been released or developed.

VAR (n.) Value-added reseller; a company that assembles systems, provides a package for their customers, and offers service after the sale.

variable-length coding (n.) In MPEG compression, the technique of assigning shorter identifiers, or code words, to more common events, and longer code words to less common events. It is also referred to as entropy coding.

varied repetition (n.) A technique used by instructional designers to present a segment of a lesson several times with the same content, but with different modes of presentation.

VAX/VMS (n.) Virtual Address Extension/Virtual Memory System; a computing environment developed by Digital Equipment Corporation (DEC).

VB (n.) Visual Basic; a programming environment developed by Microsoft.

VBI (n.) Vertical blanking interval; period of time during which picture information is suppressed and the scanning beam returns to the top of the picture. Data is placed in this interval to maintain image stability and to provide access to a frame. Technically, the VBI consists of lines 1–21 of video field one and lines 263–284 of field two. Frame numbers, flags, and closed captions are placed in this interval. A cable modem may use this space to send the equivalent of a 9600 baud signal during each scan line. See *horizontal blanking interval*.

VCR (n.) Videocassette recorder; a home videotaping device.

vector data (n.) A set of coordinates that is extrapolated to define lines and shapes. It is infinitely scaleable, unlike bitmap or raster data.

vector graphics (n.) Line drawings. A vector display represents data as line segments identified by the x-y coordinates of their end points.

vectorscope (n.) An instrument that tests a video signal and displays results as displacement in a circular pattern. The location of dots on the scope indicate the timing of various components of the test signal relative to signal reference points. It is widely used to evaluate and adjust the color component of video signals.

Venn diagram (n.) A graphic representation of regions that represent parameters. Overlapping regions represent common parameters, or sets. Logical operations may be illustrated by the intersection, inclusion, or exclusion of regions in a Venn diagram.

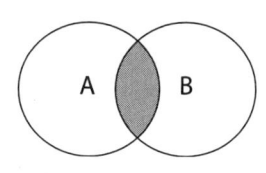

Venn diagram

VERONICA (n.) Very easy rodent-oriented net-wide index to computer archives; a search tool for the Internet.

vertical blanking interval See *VBI*.

vertical interval switching (v.) To alternate rapidly between two video signals during the vertical blanking interval at the end of a scan, leaving no noticeable shift in the output signal.

vertical interval time code See *VITC*.

vertical markets (n.) Special groups that require products suited to their needs. The medical profession is a vertical market with unique information needs. By contrast, office management products are not highly differentiated.

very easy rodent-oriented net-wide index to computer archives See *VERONICA*.

very large-scale integration See *VLSI*.

VESA (n.) Video Electronics Standards Association; an industry trade group formed to codify the software interface for advanced video cards. The term is also used for the interface itself to describe a "VESA slot" on a computer.

VfW (n.) Video for Windows; developed by Microsoft in 1992, this scalable digital video format decodes digital video files of the .avi file type. It runs in all implementations of Microsoft Windows, including version 3.1, Windows NT, and Windows 95. This type of video file can be compressed by several popular codecs, including Indeo and Cinepak, making the files smaller in size and allowing them to stream at higher data rates.

VGA (n.) Video Graphics Array; a standard system for driving an analog monitor with 16 colors at 640 × 480 resolution. In text mode the resolution is

720 × 400, and with 256 colors the resolution drops to 320 × 200. It was developed by IBM in 1987 and has been replaced by SVGA systems. *See table.*

VHS (n.) <u>V</u>ideo <u>h</u>ome <u>s</u>ystem; a popular consumer .5-inch videotape format developed by Matsushita and JVC.

video (n.) The translation of moving images into electronic signals. The term video implies a stream of visual images displayed at a constant frame rate, usually with an audio track. The signals can be broadcast through the air via high-frequency carrier waves or distributed via closed circuit cable. Video applications include commercial broadcasts, corporate communications, marketing, home entertainment, arcade games, security systems, and the moving picture component of multimedia programs.

Graphics Adapters	Resolution	Simultaneous Colors/Mode
EGA	640 x 350	16/text
	720 x 350	4/text
	320 x 200	16/graphics
	640 x 200	16/graphics
	640 x 350	16/graphics
VGA	720 x 400	16/text
	360 x 400	16/text
	640 x 480	16/graphics
	320 x 200	256/text
XGA	640 x 480	65 536/graphics
	1024 x 768	256/graphics
	1056 x 400	16/text
SVGA	800 x 600	16 777 216/graphics
	1024 x 768	16 777 216/graphics
	1280 x 1024	16 777 216/graphics

video bandwidth (n.) The range of frequencies at which pixels may be input to a monitor, measured in megahertz.

video black (n.) A portion of videotape with no images or sound recorded on it; used as a buffer between programs and inserted before and after tape segments.

videocassette (n.) The case that holds magnetic tape used for videotape applications, most often in the VHS format.

videocassette recorder See *VCR*.

Video-CD (n.) A full-motion digital video format on CD-ROM using MPEG-1 video compression and incorporating a Program Control Bar (PCB) with controls similar to a VCR. It conforms to the White Book specification.

video clip (n.) A section of recorded video drawn from a longer video recording.

videoconference (n.) Two or more locations linked by fast telecommunication lines, with all participants able to see and hear one another in real time.

videodisc (n.) An optical laser disc, 9 or 12 inches in diameter, that stores data, text, still images, and full-motion video in an analog format. This may include any platter from which video content can be decoded and displayed on a monitor, including a Video-CD in the White Book format, which contains video compressed to the MPEG-1 specification.

videodisc formats 1. (n.) Optical videodisc or laser disc. 2. (n.) CD-ROM formatted for either CD-i or Video-CD 3. (n.) Digital Video Disk (DVD), a 1995 specification developed through collaboration of Philips, Sony, Toshiba, and Panasonic.

video display (n.) Any CRT (raster format) that displays information from a video source. See *monitor*.

video driver (n.) The software interface between an application program and the physical video card hardware.

Video Electronics Standards Association See *VESA*.

Video for Windows See *VfW*.

Video Graphics Array See *VGA*.

video head (n.) A component in a videotape player over which tape passes. The head reads or records the video signal.

video home system See *VHS*.

video-in-a-window (n.) The placement of a video clip on top of the background on a computer monitor. It may be incorporated in the form of a quarter-screen box playing compressed digital video in one of the popular software codecs, such as QuickTime or Video for

video object

Windows. It may also be input by means of a special video adapter card that can display an NTSC or PAL signal on a VGA monitor.

video object (n.) A file that contains a video clip.

video overlay (n.) The placement of computer-generated video over analog video, including letters produced by dedicated titling systems. It requires a genlock to synchronize the input signals.

videophone (n.) A telephone product used to transmit and receive compressed video and audio over existing telephone lines.

video RAM See *VRAM*.

video reprocessing (n.) A common editing technique in which video from a computer source is keyed over existing video. See *overlay*.

video server (n.) A networked storage device, typically a hard disk, optical drive, or CD-ROM jukebox, that holds video data that is accessible online to delivery systems or workstations. It may perform decoding operations for its clients, or this may be performed at each workstation.

videotape (n.) A particular type of magnetic tape, used to record moving pictures, that can also record synchronized audio signals. See *illustration*.

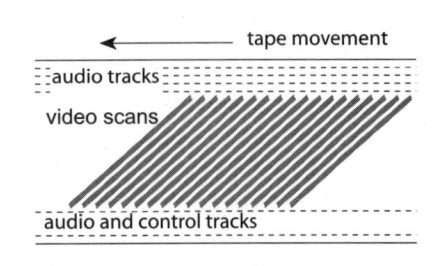

information on a videotape

videotape formats (n.) The analog tape standards used in recording video, informally differentiated by the width of the tape.

1-inch: Used for professional broadcast quality video recording and editing, stored on open reels.

.75-inch: Sony U-matic format, stored in thick cassettes.

.5-inch: Cassette-based; VHS and Sony Beta are low-end consumer formats. Super-VHS and Super Beta are higher-quality versions in the .5-inch format.

8mm: Consumer format that provides good-quality recording on small tape cassettes, popular in hand-held camcorders. An enhanced version called Hi-8 has improved resolution and is comparable to S-VHS quality. Hi-8 and S-VHS have 400 lines of resolution and S-video (YC) separation, but the greater width of S-VHS tape makes it less prone to drop-outs.

Many professionals prefer the Sony

Betacam SP for shooting and D-2 (digital composite) for editing masters. Two digital formats, D-1 (digital component) by Sony, and D-5 by Panasonic, are used in professional studios.

videotext (n.) A distribution system for information that uses screens of text as the primary content. Videotext services can be distributed through cable or broadcast television systems, or they can be sent over telephone lines to a computer that can construct the images onscreen. The graphics are of relatively low resolution, and a proprietary decoder is required.

video user interface See *VUI*.

videowall (n.) A rectangular configuration of monitors combined to form a large display. The monitors are generally controlled by a computer that distributes a single video image so that each tube contains one portion or quadrant of the complete image.

virtual (adj.) Describes the existence of an object, entity, or relationship in software or via networks, rather than in a tangible, physical condition. In computing, a virtual device could represent a hardware peripheral. The use of virtual devices helps programmers avoid hardware incompatibilities as actual configurations evolve. It is a commonly used term for any thing that exists but has no concrete manifestation. An ensemble of samplers playing a MIDI score is referred to as a virtual orchestra.

Virtual Address Extension/Virtual Memory System See *VAX/VMS*.

virtual disk (n.) A conceptual drive rather than a physical drive. The user is not concerned with how the data is physically written. A virtual drive may span multiple physical drives, but it appears to the user as only one drive.

virtual memory (n.) A combined software and hardware solution in response to demand for an increased amount of internal RAM. It makes use of hard disk space to simulate internal random access memory. It is not as fast as hardware RAM, but page memory management assists in placing the most frequently used information in buffers that are readily accessible.

virtual reality See *VR*.

Virtual Reality Modeling Language See *VRML*.

virus (n.) A self-replicating, destructive program.

VIS (n.) Video information system; a consumer multimedia player, introduced by Tandy Corporation in 1992, that is designed to plug into the home TV and provide playback of interactive titles and standard audio CDs.

Visual Basic See *VB*.

visualization (n.) In computer graphics, techniques that allow a computer to present graphic images or representations of phenomena that normally could not be viewed. Visualization is becoming an important tool in many fields of science and engineering.

VITC (n.) Vertical interval time code; SMPTE time code inserted in the vertical blanking interval between the two fields of a video frame. This method eliminates errors that may occur from tape stretch when using longitudinal time code.

VLSI (n.) Very-large-scale integration; an integrated circuit that generally incorporates thousands of command processes, or logic gates, on a single silicon chip.

voice-activated (adj.) Describes a program that is executed or controlled by the sound of a human voice.

voice coil (n.) An element present at both ends of a sound reinforcement system. In a microphone, the voice coil vibrates as sound waves strike it. In a loudspeaker, it is the wire coil connected to the cone that causes it to vibrate.

voice mail (n.) A system in which voice messages are recorded on a messaging system connected to a telephone PBX. The messages may be accessed later by the addressee.

voice recognition (n.) A system through which human speech is recognized by a computer and converted into binary code or text files.

volatile storage (n.) A type of storage device in which data is lost if operating power is interrupted, or battery backup is not provided.

volume (n.) A block of memory on a disk or a tape that may consume the entire medium or may represent just a partition.

volume label (n.) The name a user assigns to a disk or block of memory when it is formatted using MS-DOS.

volume-unit meter See *VU meter*.

voxel (n.) A volume element that is the three-dimensional equivalent of a pixel; the smallest region that may be defined discretely in a 3-D imaging system.

VR (n.) Virtual reality; a realistic, computer-generated world in which users may participate by using data gloves and head-mounted graphic display units.

VRAM (n.) Video random-access memory; special memory chips that are designed for video applications and usually have a port for video information while other data travels through another port.

VRML (n.) Virtual Reality Modeling Language; a programming environment for the World Wide Web, originally called "Markup," rather than "Modeling" language.

VTAM (n.) Virtual Telecommunications

Access Method; programs designed to control communications between nodes and applications in Systems Network Architecture (SNA).

VTR (n.) <u>V</u>ideo<u>t</u>ape <u>r</u>ecorder.

VUI (n.) <u>V</u>ideo <u>U</u>ser <u>I</u>nterface.

VU meter (n.) <u>V</u>olume-<u>u</u>nit <u>m</u>eter; a measuring device that is used in audio recording and broadcasting to indicate amplitude levels relative to a standard. A volume unit is a form of decibel reference. It is equal to the value of 1 milliwatt of power met with a 600-ohm load. VU meters are calibrated in order to indicate 0 dB (decibels) as the maximum undistorted signal level, with a red zone for levels that exceed that point.

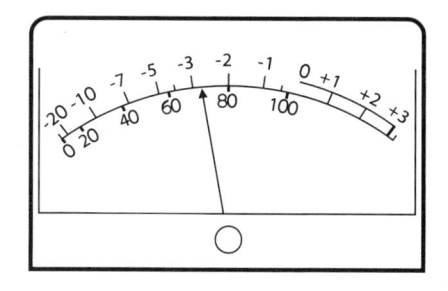

VU meter

V.x (n.) A series of CCITT standards for error correction, data compression, and testing for modem operations. Some of the later developments are listed below:

V.fast: The standard for modem communications at rates above 14.4 kilobits per second (Kbps).

V.54: This standard defines methods and devices for loop testing in modems.

V.42: The LAPM error correction scheme that incorporates MNP-4 fall-back.

V.42bis: A standard for data compression that exceeds MNP-5 in reliability.

V.34: The standard for modems that transmit at 28.8 kilobits per second (Kbps); it allows reception at the highest possible data transfer rate.

V.32: The standard for a 9600-bytes per second (Bps) modem with echo canceling; used for communication over common leased lines.

V.32bis: This standard applies to two-wire duplex modems that operate at up to 14.4 kilobits per second (Kbps) over common leased lines.

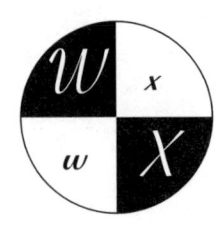

wafer (n.) A thin disk or slice of silicon on which separate chips can be fabricated and cut into individual die.

WAIS (n.) Wide area information server; an Internet utility that allows users to perform a full text search.

walk-through 1. (n.) A simulation that creates the effect of traveling through a computerized architectural model in which the viewer can interactively navigate a path. 2. (n.) In film and video production, a rehearsal without cameras.

WAN (n.) Wide area network; the integration of geographically distant or technologically incompatible LANs. Technologies that contribute to the existence of these networks include ATM, ISDN, CCITT X.25, and frame relay. See *LAN*.

warm boot (v.) To restart a computer without turning off the power. In the Macintosh OS this is accomplished by selecting Restart from the Special menu. On an IBM-compatible machine it is done by simultaneously pressing the key combination Ctrl-Alt-Delete, also known as a "three-fingered salute."

WATS (n.) Wide area telecommunications service; a long-distance toll service, inward or outward, offered at a discount by a telephone company.

WAV (n.) A Microsoft DOS and Windows file extension, or suffix, used to indicate a sound file made up of a set of digitized samples representing waveforms that can be realized by a sound card.

WAVE (n.) The preferred standard of multimedia sound for Microsoft and IBM. It is a RIFF (Resource Interchange File Format) file containing PCM waveform audio data and the .wav extension.

waveform monitor (n.) A test instrument that displays a video signal graphed over a selected interval of time, rather than a video picture itself. It measures video gain and sync pulses.

wavelength (adj.) Describes the distance between successive peaks of a regularly repeating waveform.

wavelet (n.) A complex mathematical algorithm applied to digital video compression.

wavetable synthesis (n.) Audio signals that are based on digital samples of recorded sounds rather than sounds that are synthesized artificially by a means such as frequency modulation.

Web site (n.) An address on the World Wide Web that contains one or more "pages," or HTML documents.

what you see is what you get See *WYSIWYG*.

white balance (n.) An adjustment made to a camera or other video source so that a white object will produce the proper signal. Most consumer camcorders have automatic white-balance circuits. It is imperative to calibrate a video camera when light conditions change. This is often accomplished by recording a white page of paper full screen at the depth of the background. The camera then automatically corrects color as needed.

White Book (n.) A standard specification, developed by Philips and JVC in 1993, for storing MPEG-1 video on a CD-ROM. It is an extension of the Red Book standard for digital audio, the Yellow book for CD-ROM, the Green Book for CD-I, and the Orange Book for CD-recordables. As with the other standards, the name describes the color of the cover of the standards document.

white flag (n.) In the transfer of film to videotape, a code that is used to mark a new full frame. It is also known as "full-frame ID."

white level (n.) The level of the brightest possible white value in a video signal. In most video formats it is equivalent to the minimum voltage.

wide area information server See *WAIS*.

wide area network See *WAN*.

wide area telecommunications service See *WATS*.

wideband (n.) A data transmission system with a large bandwidth and multiple channel access.

widescreen TV (n.) A proposed ratio for high-definition television (HDTV) broadcast of 16:9, or 1.78:1, rather than the normal 4:3 aspect ratio for the screen. It is a ratio more similar to film, since Cinemascope and Panavision exhibit aspect ratios in the range of 2.35:1. When the wider aspect ratio is shown on a standard screen, the result is called the "letter box" effect.

widow (n.) A single line of text that belongs with a paragraph but is separated and appears on the page following the paragraph.

wildcard (n.) In MS-DOS, a character such as "*" or "?" that permits a search for an unknown entity. It is also known as a global file specification.

Winchester disk (n.) The original development project for hard disk drives at IBM was called "Winchester." It is used to describe a drive that consists of a stack of platters.

window 1. (n.) A defined area on a monitor designated for video or other information. 2. (n.) The portion of a display in which a document or an application runs in a graphical user interface. An independent program will be displayed in its own window on the monitor, and several windows may be open at once in a multitasking environment.

Windows See *Microsoft Windows*.

Windows Metafile See *WMF*.

Windows 95 (n.) The version of Microsoft Windows delivered in 1995. It features a GUI interface, performs 32-bit addressing, and emulates MS-DOS rather than being predicated on it. Programs written in MS-DOS still run well in Windows 95, but the command line is gone. It has advanced memory management and plug-and-play capabilities.

Windows NT (n.) A 32-bit multitasking operating system developed by Microsoft in 1992. Two versions exist: the basic product, and the Advanced Server, which is designed for client-server networks. It is adaptable for powerful workstations and accommodates a wide range of platforms.

Windows Sockets See *WINSOCK*.

WinG (n.) A library of high-performance graphics routines that enhance the performance of Microsoft Windows. WinG adds halftone ability so that 24-bit color is effectively presented by a system with an 8-bit palette. The runtime library may be distributed without permission from Microsoft. It consists of the WING.DLL for 16-bit systems and WING32.DLL for 32-bit implementations.

WINSOCK (n.) Windows Sockets; the standard that specifies how to support Transmission Control Protocol/Internet Protocol (TCP/IP) with a dynamic link library (DDL) for Windows 95.

Win32 (n.) A 32-bit API that is supported by recent versions of Microsoft Windows and incorporates features such as multiple threads and remote control of networked computers.

WinToon (n.) An animation engine, developed by Microsoft, that runs in Windows 95. It layers a moving image in the foreground over a static background efficiently by minimizing the updates to redundant data from screen to screen.

wipe (v.) In video special effects, to erase an image as it replaces it with another one.

wireframe (n.) A three-dimensional object that is modeled with line segments prior to rendering.

wizard (n.) A help file with templates accessed through a dialog box and provided with Microsoft Windows applications.

WMF (n.) Windows Metafile; a format that stores an image as a series of Windows Graphic Device Interface (GDI) functions. The files, which are scalable drawings rather than bitmaps, require little storage space, display quickly on the screen, and are transportable among applications.

workstation (n.) A monitor and keyboard, with the possible connection of other devices, located on a network. It may take the form of a dumb terminal connected to a server, or it could be a powerful networked computer.

World Wide Web See *WWW*.

WORM (n.) Write-once-read-many; optical storage in which the laser physically alters the surface of the disk by burning pits in it, rendering it permanent. WORM drives are excellent for long-term storage of important data, but the medium can be used only once; the data cannot be erased and the space reclaimed. See *CD-R*.

writable optical media (n.) A catch-all phrase for all optical media to which data can be recorded by a user. Magneto optical cartridges used in WORM drives and CD-recordables, or "one-offs," both fit in this category.

write (v.) To move data from one physical place to another or from one medium to another.

write-once-read-many See *WORM*.

WWW (n.) World Wide Web; a virtual space accessible from the Internet that holds "pages" of text and graphics, all constructed in HTML, linked to one another and to individual files. Developed by the Swiss Research Center CERN, it is a rapidly growing resource for information and business. With high transfer rates, low-level multimedia communication may occur via the WWW.

WYSIWYG (n.) What you see is what you get; a graphic display mode in some desktop publishing applications in which the page on the screen shows exactly how the printed page will appear. (Pronounced **wizzywig**.)

XA (n.) Extended architecture; an evolution of the standard CD-ROM format that provides for ADPCM audio, multisession discs, Photo-CD, and CD-i compatibility. This CD format relies solely on Cross-Interleaved Reed-Solomon Code (CIRC) for error correction.

XAR (n.) Extended attribute record. Adhering to ISO 9660 standards, this is a record with attributes not listed in the Directory Record, including information regarding escape sequences, dates, permissions, and other private data.

XCMD (n.) External command. See *HyperCard*.

XFCN (n.) External function. See *Hypercard*.

X.500 (n.) The International Telephone and Telegraph Consultative Committee (CCITT) standard for directory services to be used with an X.400 message-handling system in a multivendor environment. X.500 may be used with proprietary message-handling systems.

X.400 (n.) The International Telephone and Telegraph Consultative Committee (CCITT) standard for a store-and-forward message-handling system in a multivendor environment.

XGA (n.) E̱xtended graphics a̱dapter; an IBM PS/2 graphics standard that provides a resolution of 1024 × 768 pixels with 8-bit color.

XLR connector (n.) An audio connector that is used for most low impedance microphones and for balanced lines between professional signal processing equipment. Three wires are soldered to pins inside the barrel of the connector. The ground wire or shield is typically connected to pin number one, and pins two and three carry the same signal in equal strength but opposite phase. This allows for the cancellation of unwanted noise and allows long cable lengths. Microphone lines that are used in most recording studios are 200-ohm balanced lines with the shield grounded at the preamp end only. This prevents ground loops, which produce 60-cycle hum if the shields are grounded at more than one point. *See illustration.*

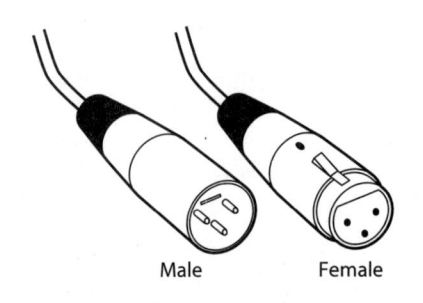

XLR connectors

XModem (n.) An error-correcting protocol for data transmission, developed by Ward Christensen in 1978, that is common in microcomputing applications. This protocol includes a system of adding check sums on transmission, and comparing the size of a block of data on reception. If an error is detected, the block of data is retransmitted.

X terminal (n.) A dedicated terminal that runs X-server software, a standard architecture for UNIX machines.

X.25 (n.) The CCITT standard for networks that employ packet switching protocol.

X Windows (n.) A standard windowing, multitasking distributed bitmapped graphics protocol developed at MIT. It is a graphical user interface used primarily with UNIX-based systems.

X-Y coordinates (n.) Points on a plane divided horizontally on the X axis and vertically on the Y axis, over a two-dimensional scale. X-Y coordinates are used to plot graphs and identify locations on a display. Another plane representing depth may be added, providing a Z axis for three-dimensional models.

X-Y zoom (n.) The capacity to reduce or enlarge the size of an image. Some digital systems give the user a zoom control.

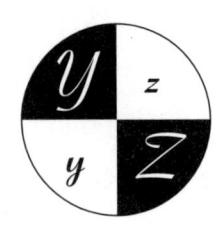

Yahoo (n.) Yet another hierarchically officious oracle; the name of a Web site that provides an index to other sites. It provides a mechanism for searching the World Wide Web for information or matching data strings.

YCC format See *color YCC*.

Y/C video See *S-video*.

Yellow Book (n.) The specification for standard CD-ROM data discs that is based on the Red Book audio standard that preceded it. This standard defines two new modes: Mode 1 and Mode 2, and it establishes a third layer of error correction.

yet another hierarchically officious oracle See *Yahoo*.

YMCK (n.) Yellow, magenta, cyan, and black. See *CMYK*.

YUV color system (n.) A method of defining video signals which separates the components of luminance and chrominance. Human vision is much more sensitive to variations in intensity than it is to variations in color. The YUV encoding process takes advantage of this phenomenon and provides a wider bandwidth for luminance (Y) information than for chrominance (UV) information. Individually, the letters YUV signify intensity, hue, and value.

z-buffer (n.) The memory allocated to holding the depth value of pixels.

zero-insertion force See *ZIF*.

ZIF (n.) Zero-insertion force; a type of socket used on a motherboard to allow manual replacement of one processor chip with another.

zig-zag sequence (n.) A reordering of quantized DCT coefficients designed to facilitate entropy coding by placing low-frequency coefficients before high-frequency coefficients.

ZIP (n.) An extension used for compressed files in the .zip format, commonly used on IBM-compatibles.

ZModem (n.) An upgraded version of the XModem file transfer protocol. It permits streaming and continues to send data until it receives a NAK signal from the receiver. It will then return to the failed block and begin re-transmitting from that point. The developer of this protocol was Chuck Forsberg.

zoom (v.) To enlarge or reduce the size of an image as it is displayed.

z-sorting (n.) In three-dimensional graphics, a method used to determine which pixels are shown by ordering polygons from front to back and displaying them in front. A more accurate method of sorting is z-buffering, in which the depth value of individual pixels is stored and the lowest value for each pixel is shown.

Copyright Issues

Ownership

The act of digitizing pictures, sounds, words, and other concrete forms of expression is commonplace. The proliferation of scanners and capture cards makes the acquisition of graphics and audio available to anyone with a computer. Yet multimedia producers must be especially careful about how the assets they digitize are used and distributed. A photograph is the property of the camera operator; each song belongs to its composer; text is owned by the writer; a graphic belongs to the artist; a sound is the property of the person who creates or samples it. Original work in any of these forms may not be copied and resold without express permission from the copyright holder, and it is the responsibility of the person who would digitize and use an asset to locate and secure permission from the owner.

A copyright provides ownership of intellectual property in which the author secures certain exclusive rights to an original work for a limited time. Copyright law is authorized by Article 1, Section 8 of the Constitution. The clause gives Congress the power "to promote science ... by securing for limited times to authors ... the exclusive right to their writings." Copyright protects the author's original expression only. It does not extend to ideas or facts presented in a copyrighted work. It does not include previously existing material that an author has incorporated into a new work.

Recognized Copyrights in the United States

Copyright should not be confused with personality rights, such as the right of privacy, which is used to protect the name, voice, or persona of an individual. Things that are created by people are referred to as intellectual property since they are products of the mind. A work must be original to be copyrighted, and this means that it was created by the author. The work need not be different from everything preceding it, but it must embody creativity and it must be the "expression of an author." Only nonutilitarian aspects of a work are protected by copyright. If something is both a work of authorship and a useful article, copyright will not protect the useful aspects. It must exist in a fixed, tangible medium of expression. An idea is not protectable, but the expression of an idea is. In the United States, copyright includes the following rights:

1. *Reproductive Right:* The right to make copies of a work.
2. *Adaptive Right:* The right to produce derivative works based on a copyrighted work.
3. *Distribution Right:* The right to distribute copies of a work. (This includes Importation right, the right to prevent unauthorized importation of a work.)
4. *Performance Right:* The right to perform a copyrighted work in public. (The performance right does not ordinarily apply to sound recordings, but a limited performance right prohibiting only digital performances of sound recordings was added in 1995.)
5. *Display Right:* The right to display a copyrighted work in public. (These rights apply to musical, dramatic, literary, choreographic, film and video programs only. They do not apply to audio recordings or architectural designs.)

In addition to the rights that are part of copyright, United States law also provides for an author's rights in certain works of visual art such as signed and numbered limited edition paintings, photographs, or sculptures. These rights are technically not part of copyright, because they belong only to the author of the work, do not survive the author, and cannot be bought or sold (although they may be waived by contract). The two rights of an author are the rights of attribution and integrity:

Attribution Rights: The right of the author to claim authorship of a work, and the right to prevent being incorrectly identified as the author of a work.

Integrity Rights: The right to prevent intentional distortion or destruction of a work, and to prevent others from attributing a distorted version of the work to the author.

Not all rights last for the same period of time. Typically, a copyright endures for the life of the author plus 50 years; an author's rights, on the other hand, endure only for the life of the author. A series of restrictions on rights are found in Sections 107 through 120 of the copyright law.

COPYRIGHT AND THE INTERNET

Usenet postings and e-mail messages are copyrighted. They are "original works fixed in a tangible medium of expression." Only a clear declaration by an author would place a work into public domain. The two doctrines that allow copying are fair use and implied license.

If the use was not commercial in nature, the posting was not an artistic or dramatic work, a short quotation was made for criticism and comment, and there was no impact on any market for the posting, it would probably qualify as fair use. Quoting of private e-mail messages that met such criteria would also qualify. However, disseminating some e-mail messages could lead to liability unrelated to copyright if the message were defamatory, an invasion of privacy, or a trade secret.

If a clearly visible limitation on the right to copy or quote is stated in the posting or message, it would be difficult to defend against infringement. On the other hand, implied license might be assumed for e-mail messages posted to a public mailing list without stated limitations.

Postings and e-mail messages are not usually registered with the Copyright Office. Registration is a requirement in order for a copyright owner to recover statutory damages and attorney fees. Therefore, if a copyright owner were to sue for infringement of an e-mail or posting, he or she would probably be limited to collecting actual damages caused by the infringement (i.e., an actual monetary loss or a profit to the infringer that resulted from the infringement). Because those damages are so negligible, it would be of little benefit to sue, even if the copying of an e-mail or posting is an infringement.

Fair Use

The "fair use" doctrine allows the courts to avoid rigid application of copyright statutes when this would inhibit creativity. Fair use originated "for criticism, comment, news reporting, teaching, ... scholarship, or research....the distinction between 'fair use' and infringement may be unclear and not easily defined. There is no specific number of words, lines, or notes that may be taken safely without permission. Acknowledging the source of the copyrighted material does not substitute for obtaining permission."

The 1961 Report of the Register of Copyrights on the General Revision of the United States Copyright Law provides the following examples of fair use:
1. Reproduction by a teacher or student of a part of a work to illustrate a lesson.
2. Summary of an address or article with short quotations in a news report.
3. Quotation of short passages in a scholarly or technical work for illustration or clarification of the author's observations.
4. Quotation of excerpts in a review or criticism for purposes of illustration or comment.
5. Reproduction by a library of a portion of a work to replace a missing or damaged section.
6. Incidental reproduction in a newsreel or broadcast of a work that appears imbedded in the scene of an event being reported.

Assuming that a piece of media (text, audio, graphic, or video) is the exclusive property of its creator, questions arise regarding conditions under which a portion of the media may be used legally without specific license from the author. Permission is not required to make "fair use" of a copyrighted work. Four factors are used to determine whether a proposed use of a copyrighted work is a fair use:

1. "The purpose and character of the use." A nonprofit educational use is more likely to be deemed a fair use than a commercial use.
2. "The nature of the copyrighted work." Copying of factual material is more likely to be considered a fair use than copying the same amount of artistic or fictional material.
3. "The amount and substantiality of the portion used in relation to the work as a whole." A small percentage or a limited amount is more likely to be allowable than a large part.
4. "The effect of the use upon the potential market or upon the value of a copyrighted work." No reduced earning capacity for the copyright holder should result from fair use.

The following guidelines are extracted from the 1996 Consortium of College and University Media Centers (CCUMC) Fair Access Working Committee draft addressing the extent to which multimedia content may be used by instructors and students in an educational setting:

1. Educators may use portions of lawfully acquired copyrighted works in producing and using their own multimedia programs as teaching tools in support of an identified curriculum in face-to-face instruction. Similar use is permitted for remote instruction over an institution's electronic network, provided there are technological limitations on access to the network programs (password or PIN), and on the total number of students enrolled
2. Related to motion media, up to 10% or three minutes, whichever is less, in the aggregate of a copyrighted motion media work may be reproduced or otherwise incorporated as part of a multimedia program produced by an educator or student for educational purposes.
3. Related to text material, up to 10% or 1000 words may be incorporated; less than 250 words in the case of a poem, but no more than one poem by a single poet or five poems from an anthology may be used.
4. Related to music, up to 10% of an individual composition, or up to 10% of a musical recording may be used for educational purposes. No more than 30 seconds of an individual copyrighted composition may be used in any case.
5. The reproduction of no more than five photographs and illustrations copyrighted by a single artist may be used in any one program. Not more than 10% or 15 images, whichever is less, may be used from a published collective work.

6. In any case where commercial reproduction and distribution will occur, licenses must be obtained.
7. Educators and students must obtain permission for all copyrighted works incorporated in programs that are distributed over uncontrolled electronic networks, for productions that are replicated beyond one copy, and in cases where institutions collaborate.
8. Citations and credit must be attributed to all sources of copyrighted works incorporated in multimedia programs, including those prepared under fair use. In the case of images used in remote instruction, the copyright notice, date, and name must appear onscreen with the image.

Replication of Audio Recordings

The Audio Home Recording Act (AHRA) was passed in October 1992. It added ten sections to the United States Copyright Act, one of which provided an alternative to the fair use analysis for musical recordings. The new section states:

"No action may be brought under this title alleging infringement of copyright based on the manufacture, importation, or distribution of a digital audio recording device, a digital audio recording medium, an analog recording device, or an analog recording medium, or based on the noncommercial use by a consumer of such a device or medium for making digital musical recordings or analog musical recordings."

This means consumers cannot be sued for making analog or digital audio copies for private noncommercial use. It applies to music only, not to recordings of spoken words. The AHRA provided that a royalty payment (the "DAT tax") be paid for each sale of digital audio tape to compensate composers for profits lost due to these copies.

The right to prevent the unauthorized fixation and trafficking in sound recordings and music videos was added to copyright law in 1994. "Rights in Unfixed Works," as they are called, resulted from the General Agreement on Tariffs and Trade (GATT).

Public Domain

A work in the public domain may be used by anyone for any purpose. Here are some of the ways in which a work may be deemed to be in the public domain:
1. The term of copyright has expired.
2. A work was created by the United States Government and cannot be copyrighted.
3. The work is a title, a name, or a short phrase or slogan, and although it could be considered a trademark, it may not be copyrighted.

4. The copyright is forfeited. The copyright is forfeited in works published without notice prior to a change in the law that eliminated the notice requirement. (March 1, 1988, the effective date of the Berne Convention Implementation Act.)
5. The copyright has been abandoned. A direct statement or overt act dedicating the work to public domain is required by the copyright holder (a statement that anyone may reproduce, perform, or display the work without restrictions). Posting a work on a computer network does not constitute abandonment.

If there are any restrictions declared by the author on the use of a work, it is not public domain. It is copyrighted, and restrictions are essentially limitations. For example, the restriction that a work may only be given away for free is a limitation using the distribution right. Once a work is in the public domain, whether by expiration or dedication by the copyright holder, it cannot be restored except under certain conditions provided by GATT in 1994.

Failure to assert copyright against an infringer does not place a work in the public domain. At most, it might prevent the copyright owner from recovering from that infringer, if, for example, a statute of limitations has expired, or if the infringer has relied on the copyright owner's failure to sue.

Securing Copyright on an Original Story or Song

In the United States and most other countries, a work is automatically copyrighted when it is created. The following statement is from Section 102 of the Copyright Act:

"Copyright protection subsists ... in original works of authorship fixed in any tangible medium of expression, now known or later developed, from which they can be perceived, reproduced, or otherwise communicated, either directly or with the aid of a machine or device."

"A work is fixed in a tangible medium of expression when its embodiment in a copy or phonorecord, by or under the authority of the author, is sufficiently permanent or stable to permit it to be perceived, reproduced, or otherwise communicated for a period of more than transitory duration."

It is not necessary to register a work with the Copyright Office or to provide a copyright notice on the work. However, it is wise to register a work and to include a copyright notice for purposes of defending it against infringement.

All Rights Reserved

According to the 1911 Buenos Aires Convention on Literary and Artistic Copyrights, once copyright is obtained for a work in one signatory country, the other signatories offered protection without requiring registration, if a notice reserving rights was stated. The notice that complies with Buenos Aires is "All Rights Reserved." The "All Rights Reserved" notice no longer serves a useful purpose since the Buenos Aires Convention is not relevant today, having been superseded by other copyright treaties, such as the Universal Copyright Convention and the Berne Convention.

An official copyright notice includes the letter "C" in a circle or the word "Copyright," the year of initial publication, and the name of the copyright owner. If a copyright notice is included on a work to which the defendant in an infringement suit had access, the offender may not plead "innocent infringement." It is wise to include a notice on all published copies of a work.

Duration of Copyright

The duration of a copyright depends on whether the work was created before or after January 1, 1978, the effective date of the Copyright Act of 1976. It lasts for 50 years beyond the life of the author for works created in 1978 or later, after which the work lapses into public domain. The copyright for a "joint work" lasts 50 years after the last surviving author dies. For works made for hire and anonymous works, copyright exists for 100 years from the date of creation, or 75 years from the date of first publication, whichever comes first. Copyrights are no longer renewable. Attribution and integrity rights endure only for the lifetime of the author.

For works created prior to 1978, copyright endures for 75 years from date of publication. In some cases, the term may be shorter because earlier law provided for a 28 year term, extendable to 56 years if the copyright was renewed. If the work was created but not published prior to 1978, the copyright lasts for 75 years from publication or 100 years from creation, or at until 2002 (2027, if published), whichever is longer.

How to Register a Copyright with the United States Copyright Office

Forms for registering are available from the Copyright Office at their online address: <http://lcweb.loc.gov/copyright/forms.html>. They are in the Adobe Acrobat (PDF) format. A copyright may be registered by filing the appropriate form with a $20 payment for registration and two copies of the work. A Copyright Office Information Package includes the appropriate forms and instructions for filing. For information, contact the United States Copyright Office at (202)-707-3000, or call (202)-707-6737 to order forms. Packages are available for the following types of media:

Computer programs: Form TX, Package 113
Photographs: Form VA, Package 107
Motion pictures and video recordings: Form PA, Package 110
Games: Form TX, Package 108
Drawings, prints, and visual artworks: Form VA, Package 115
Music (sheet or lyrics): Form PA, Package 105
Music (sound recording): Form SR, Package 121
Dramatic scripts, plays, and screenplays: Form PA, Package 119
Books, manuscripts and nondramatic literature: Form TX, Package 109

COPYRIGHT INFORMATION ON THE INTERNET

The Copyright Act is available on the World Wide Web at:
<www.law.cornell.edu/usc/17/overview.html>

The 1971 Paris Text of the Berne Convention is also at the Cornell site.
<www.law.cornell.edu/treaties/berne/overview.html>

The Multilaterals Project, which provides copies of both the Berne Convention and the Universal Copyright Convention, is available at Tufts.
<www.tufts.edu/fletcher/multilaterals.html>

The Coalition for Networked Information (CNI) sponsors CNI-Copyright, an Internet mailing list devoted to copyright issues. The FTP site is:
<ftp://ftp.cni.org/CNI/forums/cni-copyright>

Some Usenet newsgroups that address copyright issues are:
misc.legal, misc.legal.computing, misc.legal.moderated, and comp.software.licensing.

COPYRIGHT AND EMPLOYMENT

The company for which an employee works may own the copyrights to his or her work by applying either the assignment or the work-made-for-hire doctrine.

Assignment: Many companies automatically acquire a blanket assignment of copyright in any works created on the job at time of hiring.

Work made for hire: A work qualifies as a work made for hire if it was prepared by an employee within the scope of employment, or if it was specially commissioned and the parties agreed in writing that it was to be considered a work for hire.

DIFFERENCES BETWEEN COPYRIGHT AND PATENT

The primary differences between a copyright and a patent in the United States are as follows:
1. The subject matter protected: A copyright covers "works of authorship" (literary, dramatic, musical, pictorial, graphic, audio-video, sound recordings, and the like). A patent covers an invention or a useful new feature of a product or process.
2. The requirement for protection: To be copyrighted, a work must be original and fixed in a tangible medium of expression. A patented invention must be new and useful. A patent is not automatic; it must be issued by the United States Patent and Trademark Office.
3. When protection begins: Copyright protection currently begins when a work is created. Patent protection begins when a patent is issued.
4. Duration of protection: Copyright protection typically lasts for 50 years beyond the author's death. Patents filed after June 8, 1995 in the United State have a term of 20 years from the filing date. Patents in effect on that date have a term of 20 years, or 17 years from the date of issue, whichever is longer.
5. Infringement: If a person other than the copyright owner independently comes up with a similar work, there is no infringement. A patent confers a monopoly that prevents others from selling the patented invention, although a person may independently reinvent a patented invention.

Another significant difference is the cost. A copyright is free. A patent is costly and the patent application process is much more complex. A copyright protects an author's rights inherent in a work. A patent provides ownership to an inventor in exchange for publicly sharing the details and specifications of an invention.

INFRINGEMENT AND PENALTIES

Infringement is considered a civil matter (a tort). It may also be a federal crime in certain circumstances. If it is willful and committed for commercial advantage or financial gain, it is subject to criminal prosecution. In cases of offending reproduction or distribution rights of 10 or more copies with a value of more than $2,500 during any 180-day period, the offense is a felony. The statute of limitation for copyright infringement for both civil suits and criminal prosecutions is three years.

The United States government may be sued for copyright infringement. Whether a state may be sued is unclear. The Eleventh Amendment says that a state cannot be sued in federal court. The Copyright Act expressly states, however, that a state can be sued for copyright infringement. Until 1996, it was generally thought that the clause in the Copyright Act did indeed make a state liable for its infringements. However, a 1996 case involving an Indian tribe suing a state on an issue completely unrelated to copyright put some important restrictions on the ability of Congress to abrogate a state's immunity. As a result, there is considerable uncertainty today as to whether a state may be sued for copyright infringement.

Works of the United States government are generally considered to be in the public domain. For purposes of copyright law, the United States Postal Service, the District of Columbia, Puerto Rico, and organized territories of the United States are not considered to be part of the United States government.

If an independent contractor working for the government produces a work, it may be copyrighted, and nothing prevents that contractor from assigning the copyright to the government. Unlike federal government works, those credited to state governments are subject to copyright.

Protecting Rights with Specific Licenses

Creators of multimedia who have ownership in content may need to consider ways to protect their interests. A licensing contract is ambiguous if the rights granted are not specific. A licensee grants an implied negative covenant to the licensor not to use the ungranted portion of the copyright to the detriment of the licensee. There are four steps that parties may take to clarify contractual license agreements:
1. Specify the rights that are granted and those that are not. One right that many multimedia producers may wish to retain is the Right to Reuse Art, or to make a number of copies to show as portfolio samples. The wording in a contract might be as follows: ...Nothing in this Contract deprives the Licensor of the right to copy or display the Artwork otherwise exclusively licensed hereunder to the extent (1) the Artwork is not sold, (2) it is used solely for the purposes of promoting the Licensor's work in a portfolio, and (3) the Licensee shall have continuing nonexclusive rights to the Artwork.

2. The Reservation of Rights clause may be included in a license contract to avoid granting more rights than intended. It could be stated in the following terms: ...This Contract is a complete statement of the rights granted related to the Artwork that is licensed. All rights and licenses of any kind, including copyrights and rights that might otherwise be implied that are not expressly granted in this Contract are reserved exclusively by the Licensor.
3. Multimedia producers may wish to include a Merger clause in their licenses. Such a clause is intended to prevent a court from considering previous verbal agreements (or anything else) that may modify the terms of a contract. An example might read as follows: ...This contract sets forth the entire agreement of the parties relating to its subject matter and merges and supersedes all prior discussions or understandings of any kind, written or oral. The terms of this contract may not be changed, modified, canceled or terminated except by a written document signed by all parties to this contract that explicitly refers to this contract.
4. Producers and developers may choose to specify that the publisher of their work maintain accurate records related to royalties, and that an accountant be permitted to inspect the books on which royalties are based annually. This is a standard audit clause.

As they apply to interactive digital media, copyright laws are being defined and tested on a case-by-case basis. Precedents are being set at a time when new forms of art, and indeed the media and forms of communication by which they are fixed and transmitted, are evolving at an accelerated pace. Still, the age-old concepts of fairness and granting credit where it is due will guide decisions as they always have.

DOS Commands

Command	Usage	Description of Response or Effect
A:	A:	Switches the current drive to Drive A.
APPEND	APPEND [[drive:]path[;_] [/X:ON | /X:OFF] [/PATH:ON | /PATH:OFF] [/E]	Accesses files in other directories as if they existed in the current directory.
	APPEND ;	Undo all appended paths.
ASSIGN	ASSIGN [x[:]=y[:][...]]	Assigns disk drive *x* to disk drive *y*.
	ASSIGN /STATUS	Displays all current assignments.
	ASSIGN	Undo all current assignments.
ATTRIB	ATTRIB [ñA] [ñH] [ñR] [ñS] [drive:][path]filename [/S]	Displays or changes the attributes of a file. A plus sign (+) turns the attribute on. A minus sign (-) turns the attribute off.
	ñA	Turns on/off the archive attribute.
	ñH	Turns on/off the hidden file attribute.
	ñR	Turns on/off the read-only attribute.
	ñS	Turns on/off the system file attribute.
	/S	Processes all files in any subdirectory.
B:	B:	Switches the current drive to Drive B.
C:	C:	Switches the current drive to Drive C.
CALL	CALL [drive:][path]filename [batch-parameter]	Calls one batch program from another without causing the first batch program to stop.
CD	CD	Displays the current directory and path.
	CD [path]	Changes the current directory to path.

DOS Commands

CHDIR	CHDIR	Displays the current directory and path (same as CD).
	CHDIR [path]	Changes the current directory to *path*.
CHKDSK	CHKDSK [drive:] [[path]filename] [/F] [/V]	
		Examines and reports the status of specified drive or file.
	CHKDSK /F	Fixes any errors found.
	CHKDSK /V	Displays filenames as disk is checked.
CHOICE	CHOICE [/C[:]keys] [/N] [/S] [/T][:]c,nn] [text]	
		Prompts the user to make a choice in a batch file.
	CHOICE *your*	Will display *your* on the screen waiting for user input.
	CHOICE /C:ync	User will see [Y,N,C]?
	CHOICE /N	Will not display the prompt.
	CHOICE /S	Will be case-sensitive.
	CHOICE /T:n,5	If a key is not pressed in 5 seconds, "n" will be chosen. If a key is pressed before 5 seconds, user input is accepted.
CLS	CLS	Clears the screen.
COMMAND	COMMAND [[drive:]path] [device] [/E:nnnnn] [/P] [/C string] [/MSG]	
		Starts a new instance of COMMAND.COM.
	COMMAND A:\DOS /E:8192	Starts new COMMAND.COM from A:\DOS with an environment size of 8192 bytes.
COPY	COPY *source destination*	Copy from the source file to the *destination* file.
	COPY [d:][path]oldfile.ext [d:][path]newfile.ext	
		Copy from the *oldfile* to the *newfile*.
COPY CON	COPY CON *filename*	Copy all data entered into the keyboard to *filename* until a <Ctrl>+Z is entered.
DATE	DATE [mm-dd-yy]	Changes the current date setting. DATE without parameters displays the current date.

DOS Commands

DEFRAG	DEFRAG [*drive:*] [/F] [/S[:]*order*] [/B] [/SKIPHIGH] [/H]	
		Reorganizes files on a disk to optimize disk performance.
	DEFRAG [*drive:*] [/U] [/B] [/SKIPHIGH] [/H]	
	/F	Defrags files and ensures no empty space between files.
	/U	Defrags files and leaves empty space between files if necessary.
	/S	Provides sort order.
	n	by name (n- reverse order)
	e	by file extension (n- reverse order)
	d	by date/time earliest (d- reverse order)
	s	by size, smallest (s- reverse order)
	/B	Restarts computer after files are reorganzied.
	/SKIPHIGH	Loads DEFRAG in conventional memory. Default is upper memory.
	/H	Moves hidden files.
DEL	DEL [*drive:*][*path*]*filename* [/P]	Deletes the specified file.
	/P	Prompts the user for confirmation before deleting the file.
DELTREE	DELTREE [/Y] [*drive:*]*path* [[*drive:*]*path* [...]]	
		Deletes a directory and all files and subdirectories in it.
	DELTREE *path* /Y	Will not prompt for confirmation prior to deletion.
DIR	DIR [*drive:*][*path*][*filename*] [/P] [/W] [/A[[:]*attributes*]] [/O[[:]*sortorder*] [/S]	
	[/B] [/L] [/C]	Displays a list of a directory's files and subdirectories.
	/P	Pauses between screenfuls.
	/W	Displays filenames in a wide format.
	/A:H	Displays files ATTRIButed as hidden.
	/A:S	Displays system files.
	/A:D	Displays only names of directories.
	/A:A	Displays files ATTRIButed as archived.
	/A:R	Displays files ATTRIButed as read-only.
	/O:N	Displays alphabetically (A-Z) by filename.
	/O:E	Displays alphabetically (A-Z) by extension.

DOS Commands

	/O:D	Displays in date order, from oldest to newest.
	/O:S	Displays in size order, from smallest to largest.
	/O:G	Displays directories before files.
	/S	Searches through all subdirectories.
	/L	Displays in lowercase letters.
	/B	Displays only filenames and extension.
	/C	Displays compression ratio of compressed disks.
DISKCOMP	DISKCOMP [*drive1:*[*drive2:*]]	Compares the contents of two floppy disks.
DISKCOPY	DISKCOPY [*drive1:*[*drive2:*]]	Copies the contents of the floppy disk in *drive1* to the floppy disk in *drive2*.
DOSKEY	DOSKEY [/H] [/M]	Starts the DOSKEY program to recall commands, edit command lines, or create macros.
	/H	Displays list of all commands stored in memory.
	/M	Displays list of all DOSKEY macros.
DRVSPACE	DRVSPACE	Presents a menu that allows the user to compress a drive and manipulate the compressed drive. Key in HELP DRVSPACE for further details.
ECHO	ECHO [ON|OFF]	Displays (on) or hides (off) text in batch files.
	ECHO [*message*]	Will display user message on screen.
EDIT	EDIT [[*drive:*][*path*]*filename*]	Starts MS-DOS Editor.
EMM386	EMM386 [ON | OFF | AUTO]	Enables or disables expanded-memory support on 386 or higher systems. EMM386 without parameters displays current status.
ERASE	ERASE [*drive:*][*path*]*filename* [/P]	
		Erases the specified file.
	/P	Prompts the user for confirmation before erasing the file.
EXIT	EXIT	Quits the command processor and returns to the program that started the command processor.

DOS Commands

EXPAND	EXPAND [*drive:*][*path*]*filename* [[*drive:*][*path*]*filename*[...]]*destination*	Expands a compressed file to retrieve files from Set-up disks.
FASTHELP	FASTHELP [*command*]	Displays a list of all DOS commands with a brief explanation.
FASTOPEN	FASTOPEN *drive:*[[=]*N*] [*drive*]:[[*N*][...]] [/X]	Improves performance on computers with large directories. Decreases the time DOS takes to open frequently used files. Do not use with Windows.
	/N	Specifies number of files to track.
	/X	Creates name cache in extended memory.
FC	FC [/A] [/C] [/L] [/LBn] [/N] [/T] [/W] [/nnnn] [*drive1:*][*path1*]*filename1* [*drive2:*][*path2*]*filename2*	File compare; displays differences between two ASCII files.
	/C	Ignores upper vs. lowercase.
	/L	Compares files in ASCII mode.
	/W	Ignores white space in the files.
	/N	Displays line numbers.
	FC /B [*drive1:*][*path1*]*filename1* [*drive2:*][*path2*]*filename2*	Compares and displays differences between two binary files.
FDISK	FDISK	Formats and/or partitions a hard disk for use with MS-DOS.
FIND	FIND [/V] [/C] [/N] "*string*"[*filename*]	Searches for character strings within a file.
	/V	Locates every occurence of the string except the one selected.
	/C	Counts every occurence of the string.
	/N	Locates and displays line numbers of each occurrence of the string.
FOR	FOR %%*variable* IN (*set*) DO *command* [*command-parameter*]	Runs specified command for each file in set in batch file.

DOS Commands

FOR %variable IN (set) DO command [command-parameter]
: Runs specified command for each file in set on command line.

FORMAT FORMAT drive:[/V[:label]] [/Q] [/U] [/F:size] [/B | /S][/C]
FORMAT drive:[/V[:label]] [/Q] [/U] [/T:tracks /N:sectors] [/B | /S]
FORMAT drive:[/V[:label]] [/Q] [/U] [/1] [/4] [/B | /S]
FORMAT drive:[/Q] [/U] [/1] [/4] [/8] [/B | /S]
: Prepares a floppy disk for use with DOS.

/V:label
: Specifies a volume label.

/Q
: Deletes any previous file allocation table or root directory.

/U
: Unconditional format.

/F:size
: Specifies the disk size.

/B
: Reserves space for system files.

/S
: Copies system files onto formatted disk.

/T:tracks
: Specifies number of tracks on the disk.

/N:sectors
: Specifies number of sectors on the disk.

/1
: Formats one side of the disk only.

/4
: Formats a 5.25-inch double-density disk on a high-density disk drive.

/8
: Formats a 5.25-inch floppy disk to be compatible with MS-DOS version prior to 2.0.

/C
: Tests clusters that are curently marked bad.

GOTO GOTO label
: Directs DOS to line in batch file marked by a user-specified label.

GRAFTABL GRAFTABL[nnn]
: Displays extended characters for a specified graphics mode. Default is the U.S. character set.

IF IF [NOT] ERRORLEVEL number command
: Specifies true condition only if previous program run returned an exit code equal to or greater than number.

IF [NOT] string1=string2 command
: Specifies true condition if strings match.

IF [NOT] EXIST filename command
: Specified a true condition if *filename* exists.

NOT
: Command is carried out if condition is false.

253

DOS Commands

HELP	HELP [command]	Accesses online help about any MS-DOS command.
	command /?	Alternate shorthand.
JOIN	JOIN [drive1:[drive2:]path]	Joins a disk drive to a directory on another disk drive. JOIN without parameters displays all JOINs in effect.
	JOIN drive: /D	Cancels the JOIN for this drive.
LABEL	LABEL [drive:] [label]	Updates the volume label of any disk.
LOADHIGH	LOADHIGH [drive:][path]filename [parameters]	Loads a program into the upper memory area.
	LH [drive:][path]filename [parameters]	Alternate shorthand.
MD	MD [drive:]path	Creates a directory. Same as MKDIR.
MEM	MEM [/PROGRAM	/DEBUG	/CLASSIFY] [/FREE]	Displays current status of a system's used and free memory.
	/PROGRAM	Displays status of currently loaded programs. May also use /P.
	/DEBUG	Displays status of programs and drivers. May also use /D.
	/CLASSIFY	Displays status of programs loaded into conventional and upper memory areas. May also use /C.
	/FREE	Lists free areas of conventional and upper memory.
MEMMAKER	MEMMAKER	Starts memory optimization program. Key in HELPMEMMAKER for further details.
MIRROR	MIRROR [drive:[_]] [/1] [Tdrive]	Records information about one or more disks so that lost data may be recovered. Originally only available in PC Tools but now also available in DOS 5.0.
	/1	Records only the latest information.

DOS Commands

	/T*drive*	Loads a deletion-tracking program to be used by the UNDELETE command.
	MIRROR /U	Unloads deletion-tracking program.
	MIRROR /PARTN	Records hard disk partitioning information to be used by the UNFORMAT command.
MKDIR	MKDIR [*drive:*]*path*	Creates a directory. Same as MD.
MODE	MODE [*device*] [/STATUS]	Displays the status of all or any devices.
	MODE [*display*] [*shift*[,T]]	Sets the monitor characteristics. Values for *display* are:
	40	40 characters per row.
	80	80 characters per row.
	BW40	Black-and-white, 40 characters per row.
	BW80	Black-and-white, 80 characters per row.
	CO40	Color, 40 characters per row.
	CO80	Color, 80 characters per row.
	MONO	Monochrome, 80 characters per row.
	shift	L or R shifts display left or right.
	T	Aligns display with a test pattern.
	MODE CON[:] [COL=*c*] [LINES=*n*]	
		Sets other characteristics for the monitor (CON).
	COL=*c*	Number of columns.
	LINES=*n*	Number of lines.
	MODE LPT*n*[:] [COL=*c*] [LINES=*l*] [RETRY=*r*]	
		Sets characteristics for the printer (LPT*n*).
	COL=*c*	Characters per line (80 or 132 only).
	LINES=*l*	Lines per inch (6 or 8 only).
	RETRY=*r*	Specifies retry action if printer is busy.
	MODE CON[:] [RATE=*r* DELAY=*d*]	
		Sets the typematic rate for keyboards.
MORE	MORE < [*drive:*][*path*]*filename* *command* | MORE	Displays one screenful of output at a time.
MOVE	MOVE [/Y|-/Y] [*drive:*][*path*]*filename*[,[*drive:*][*path*]*filename*[...] *destination*	
		Moves one or more files to specified location or renames directories.
	/Y	Will not prompt user confirmation when replacing existing files.

DOS Commands

	-/Y	Will prompt for confirmation when replacing existing files. Default.
MSAV	MSAV [*drive:*]	Scans disk for known viruses. Key in HELP MSAV for further details.
MSBACKUP	MSBACKUP	Brings up a menu that allows the user to back up or restore files on a disk. Key in HELP MSBACKUP for details.
MSD	MSD	Provides detailed technical information about the user's computer.
PATH	PATH [[*drive:*][*path*[;_]]	Sets the path that DOS follows when searching for a file.
	PATH ;	Undoes all current paths.
	PATH	Displays all current paths.
PAUSE	PAUSE	Suspends operation of a batch file until user presses a key.
PRINT	PRINT [/D:*device*] [/B:*size*] [/U:*ticks1*] [/M:*ticks2*] [/S:*ticks3*] [/Q:*qsize*] [T] *filename*[_] [/C] [/P]	
	/D:*device*	Specifies a print device.
	/B:*size*	Sets the internal buffer size in bytes.
	/U:*ticks1*	Specifies the maximum number of clock ticks to wait for the printer to be available.
	/M:*ticks2*	Specifies the maximum number of clock ticks it takes to print a character.
	/S:*ticks3*	Specifies the number of clock ticks to allocate to the scheduler for background printing.
	/Q:*qsize*	Specifies the maximum number of files allowed in the print queue.
	/T	Terminates all print jobs waiting in the print queue.
	/C	Cancels printing of the preceding filename.
	/P	Adds the preceding filename to the print queue.
	PRINT	Displays the contents of the print queue.

DOS Commands

PROMPT	PROMPT [*text*]		Changes the current prompt display. Common values for text are:
	$p		Current drive and path.
	$v		Current version number.
	$t		Current time.
	$d		Current date.
	$g		> (greater-than sign).
QBASIC	QBASIC [/B] [/EDITOR] [/G] [/H] [[/RUN] [*drive:*][*path*]*filename*]		
			Starts the QBasic programming environment.
	/B		Displays QBasic in black-and-white.
	/EDITOR		Invokes the MS-DOS Editor.
	/G		Displays QBasic in graphics mode.
	/RUN		Runs program before displaying it.
RD	RD [*drive:*]*path*		Removes a subdirectory. A subdirectory may not be removed if it is the root, the default, or if there are still files in it. Same as RMDIR.
REM	REM		Allows use of comments in CONFIG.SYS or batch file. Useful for disabling commands. When REM is seen, DOS displays but does not execute what follows REM.
REN	REN [*drive:*][*path*] *oldname*[*.ext*] *newname*[*.ext*]		
			Changes a file's name from *oldname.ext* to *newname.ext*. Same as RENAME.
RENAME	RENAME [drive:][path] oldname[.ext] newname[.ext]		
			See REN.
REPLACE	REPLACE [*drive1:*][*path1*]*filename* [*drive2:*][*path2*] [/A] [/P] [/R] [/S] [/U] [/W]		
			Replaces files in the destination directory with identically named files in the source directory.
	/A		Adds new files to the destination directory. Cannot be used with /S or /U.
	/P		Prompts user for confirmation before each replace.
	/R		Replaces read-only files as well as unprotected files.

DOS Commands

	/S	Replaces files in all subdirectories of the destination directory. Cannot be used with /A.
	/U	Updates (replaces) only files that are older than source files. Cannot be used with /A.
	/W	Waits for the user to insert a disk.
RMDIR	RMDIR [*drive:*]*path*	See RD.
SCANDISK	SCANDISK [*drive:*[*drive...*] [/CHECKONLY]	Starts disk analysis and repair tool that checks drive for errors and corrects problems. Key in HELP SCANDISK for details.
	/CHECKONLY	Checks drive for errors but does not repair any damage.
SET	SET [*variable*=[*string*]]	Sets or updates variables in the DOS environment.
	SET	Displays current environment settings.
SETVER	SETVER [*drive:path*] *filename n.nn* [/D]	Sets the version number (*n.nn*) that DOS reports to *filename*. Used by older applications that require a specific version of DOS
SHARE	SHARE [/F:*space*] [/L:*locks*]	Installs file-sharing and locking capabilities on a hard disk.
SHELL	SHELL=[*drive:*][*path*]*filename* [*parameters*]	Specifies which command interpreter to use.
SHIFT	SHIFT	Changes position of replaceable parameters in batch files.
SMARTDRV	SMARTDRV /X	Starts or configures disk caching program. Do not use after Windows has started. For further details, key in HELPSMARTDRV
	/X	Disables write-behind caching. Usage is highly recommended.

DOS Commands

SORT	SORT [/R] [/+n] [<] *filename1* [> *filename2*]	Sorts the data in *filename1* in ASCII order, and optionally sends the output to *filename2*.
	[*command* |] SORT [/R] [/+n] [> *filename2*]	Sorts the output from command and sends it to *filename2*.
	/R	Reverses the sorting order.
	/+n	Sorts from the character in column *n*.
SUBST	SUBST [*drive1:*[*drive2:*]*path*]	Substitutes the single letter *drive1:* for [*drive2:*]path.
	SUBST *drive1:*/D	Undoes any substitutions for *drive1:*.
	SUBST	Displays all current substitutions.
SYS	SYS [*drive1:*][*path*] *drive2:*	Copies system files from *drive1:* to *drive2:*.
TIME	TIME [*hh:mm:ss*]	Sets or displays the current time.
TREE	TREE [*drive:*][*path*] [/F] [/A]	Displays the tree structure of a disk.
	/F	Displays filenames as well.
	/A	Displays text characters rather than graphics.
TRUENAME	TRUENAME	An undocumented command that displays the actual physical drive name of any assigned, substituted, or joined drives.
TYPE	TYPE [*drive:*][*path*]*filename*	Displays the contents of *filename*.
UNDELETE	UNDELETE	Recovers one or more deleted files. Available in DOS 5.0 and above. Key in HELP UNDELETE for details.
UNFORMAT	UNFORMAT *drive:*	Restores a disk erased by FORMAT. Available in DOS 5.0 or above. Key in HELP UNFORMAT for details.
VER	VER	Displays the current version of DOS.
VOL	VOL [*drive:*]	Displays the volume label of a disk.

DOS Commands

WIN	WIN		Begins Windows, the graphical user interface that works with DOS.
XCOPY	XCOPY *oldfile newfile* [/A |/M] [/D:*date*] [/P] [/S [/E]] [/V] [/W]		
			Copies files, subdirectories, and directories
	/A		Copies files ATTRIButed as archived without changing the archive attribute.
	/M		Copies files ATTRIButed as archived and turns off the archive attribute.
	/D:*date*		Copies files changed on or after the specified *date*.
	/P		Prompts user before creating each *newfile*.
	/S		Copies directories and subdirectories, except empty ones.
	/E		Copies directories and subdirectories, including empty ones.
	/V		Verifies each new file.
	/W		Prompts user to press a key before copying.
<	*command* < *command*		Redirection symbol; instructs DOS to get input from a place other than the standard input.
>	*command* > *command*		Redirection symbol; instructs DOS to redirect standard output of a command to a device or a file.
>>	*command* >> *command*		Redirection symbol; redirects standard output of a command to a device or a file and appends to that file instead of overwriting it.
|	*command* | *command*		Pipe symbol; the standard output of one command becomes the standard input of the next command.

Standards Organizations

As more individuals engage in creating and distributing multimedia products, the need for standardization regarding protocols, file types, compression techniques, and a host of other issues becomes increasingly critical. Much is at stake in the establishment and adoption of standards for hardware manufacturers, software developers, and multimedia producers, as well as for end-users. This appendix is an introduction to the organizations that make recommendations which ultimately determine how we create, deliver, and use digital media.

The International Organization for Standardization (ISO) in Geneva is the head of all national standardization bodies. "ISO" means "equal" in Greek. The name of the organization is a play on words rather than an acronym.

Along with the International Electrotechnical Commission (IEC), the ISO coordinates national standards activities worldwide. Results of their work are published as ISO standards. Among them are standards for electrical connectors, computer protocols, file formats, and programming languages. The ISO/IEC Joint Technical Committee 1 (JTC1) deals with information technology. The following is a list of ISO Technical Committees that address issues related to computing and multimedia:

ISO/IEC JTC 1	Information technology.
ISO/IEC JTC 1/WG 3	Open electronic data interchange.
ISO/IEC JTC 1/SC 1	Vocabulary.
ISO/IEC JTC 1/SC 6	Telecommunications, exchanges between systems.
ISO/IEC JTC 1/SC 7	Software engineering.
ISO/IEC JTC 1/SC 21	Information retrieval, transfer and management for OSI.
ISO/IEC JTC 1/SC 23	Optical disk cartridges for information interchange.
ISO/IEC JTC 1/SC 24	Computer graphics and image processing.
ISO/IEC JTC 1/SC 25	Interconnection of information technology equipment.
ISO/IEC JTC 1/SC 29	Coded representation of pictures, audio and multimedia.
ISO TC 42	Photography.
ISO TC 43	Acoustics.
ISO TC 130	Graphic technology.
ISO TC 171	Document and image recording methods, storage and use.

Standards Organizations

The accepted procedure for developing and approving International Standards is specified in the 1989 revision of the ISO/IEC Directives. It is an involved process with numerous activities and critical milestones. Procedures in which committees engage include five stages of development that lead to approval and publication.

1. The Proposal Stage: Members cast ballots on the creation of a new standards project.
2. The Preparatory Stage: Project Leader manages the development of a Working Draft.
3. The Committee Stage: Consensus is achieved on a Committee Draft (CD).
4. The Approval Stage: National bodies vote on a Draft International Standard (DIS).
5. The Publication Stage: ISO publishes the International Standard (IS).

ISO standard documents are copyrighted by ISO, and are not freely available as public domain documents. Other international standardization organizations (ITU and IETF) offer their documents on the Internet freely, or send out paper versions at no charge. By a liaison contribution from ISO/IEC JTC1/SC6 to the Internet Architecture Board (IAB), some of the OSI standards are available as PostScript files via ftp from <merit.edu> in the directory <pub/is>.

Standards documents may be obtained directly from ISO at:

ISO Sales
Case Postale 56
CH-1211 Geneve 20
Switzerland
e-mail: sales@isocs.iso.ch
hot line: +41 22 749-0222.

The *ISO Bulletin* contains information about current standardization activities and articles about various standards. It lists all the ISO standards published or withdrawn, the DISs circulated, and the CDs registered. An annual ISO Catalogue that lists all ISO standards in force and other ISO publications is also available.

The following is a selected, partial listing of a few of ISO standards documents that apply to computers, telecommunications, and multimedia.

ISO 646	7-bit ASCII with national variants [ECMA-6].
ISO 2022	ESC sequences for switching between various character sets [ECMA-35].
ISO 2382	Information technology—Vocabulary.
ISO 3166	Codes for the representation of names of countries. This standard defines a 2-letter, a 3-letter and a numeric code for each country. US/USA/840=United States, FR/FRA/250=France, DE/DEU/276=Germany. The 2-letter codes are Internet top-level domain names.
ISO 8632	Computer Graphics Metafile (CGM). This standard defines a file format for 2D vector graphics. Part 1 defines the elements (lines, filled polygons, text, colors) that appear in a CGM and the other parts define three different encodings for these graphic elements: character encoding, binary encoding, and clear text encoding. This standard format can store resolution-independent graphics. The main difference between CGM and Postscript is that Postscript is a full programming language while CGM is just a simple list of graphical elements which makes CGM suitable for re-editing.
ISO 8879	Standard Generalized Markup Language (SGML), a format for storing documents.
ISO 9127	User documentation and cover information for software packages.
ISO 9541	Font and Character Information Interchange.
ISO 9592	Programmer's Hierarchical Interactive Graphics Interface (PHIGS).
ISO 9593	PHIGS Language Bindings (Fortran, Pascal, Ada, C).
ISO 9636	Graphical device interfaces.
ISO 9660	CD-ROM volume and file structure [ECMA 119].
ISO 9899	The C programming language.
ISO 9945	UNIX style system calls and shell commands (POSIX).
ISO 10646	A 32-bit character set called UCS containing nearly all known characters.
ISO 10744	HyTime—A hypertext/multimedia extension to SGML.
ISO 10918	Still image data compression standard (JPEG).
ISO 11172	Digital video/audio compression and encoding (MPEG).
ISO 12083	Standardized SGML document type definitions for books, tables, and formulas.
IEC 824	Terminology related to microprocessors.

Another active organization whose work is becoming increasingly important as the need for global networks grows is the International Telecommunications Union (ITU), a United Nations agency that recommends standards for telecommunications.

One of its previous bodies was the International Telegraph and Telephone Consultative Committee (CCITT), which is now called ITU-T (Telecommunication Standardization Sector). A group from the CCITT/ITU-T meets every few years and compiles a list of 'questions' about possible improvements in international electronic communication. Experts from different countries meet in study groups to develop 'recommendations' which are adopted and published.

Relevant to computing are the ITU-T "V" series of recommendations on modems (V.32 and V.42) and the "X" series on data networks and OSI (X.25 and X.400). In telecommunications the "I" and "Q" series define ISDN. The "Z" series defines specification and programming languages (SDL and CHILL). The "T" series relates to text communication (facsimile and videotext), and the "H" series addresses digital sound and video encoding standards.

The names of committees have evolved in recent years. The former International Radio Consultative Committee (CCIR) and the International Frequency Registration Board (IFBR) are now together called ITU-R (Radiocommunication Sector). Previously known as the Telecommunications Development Bureau (BDT), this organization is now referred to as ITU-D.

ITU publishes many ISO computer and telecommunication-related standards under a different cover. Their recommendations and a free ITU List of Publications are available from:

International Telecommunication Union
General Secretariat—Sales Section
Place des Nations
CH-1211 Geneve 20
Switzerland
phone: +41 22 7305111
fax: +41 22 73051
e-mail: helpdesk@itu.ch

The following is a short list of ITU-T/CCITT recommendations that apply to multimedia and networked communications:

H.261	Video telephony standard.
V.21	Duplex 300 bps modem modulation.
V.22	Duplex 1200 bps modem modulation.
V.22bis	Duplex 2400 bps modem modulation.

V.32	Duplex modem modulation up to 9600 bps.
V.32bis	Duplex modem modulation up to 14 400 bps.
V.34	Duplex modem modulation up to 28 800 bps.
V.42	HDLC based error correction protocol for modems.
V.42bis	Lempel-Ziv-based data compression algorithm for HDLC protocols.
X.25	An interface to a public or private packet data network.
X.3/ X.28/ X.29	Specifies connection of asynchronous ASCII terminals to X.25 networks.

The European Computer Manufacturers Association, (ECMA), has been a forum for data processing experts since 1961. This group has prepared and submitted agreements for standardization to ISO, ITU, and other standards organizations. ECMA standards are free and may be ordered from:

European Computer Manufacturers Association
114 Rue du Rhone
CH–1204 Geneva
Switzerland
phone: +41 22 7353634
fax: +41 22 7865231
e-mail: helpdesk@ecma.ch

Internet standards have been developed to promote protocol-based interoperability. There are two primary areas of responsibility under which these standards are developed. The first is strategic concerns, which are handled by the Internet Society (ISOC) and the Internet Architecture Board (IAB). The second is technical development, which is handled by the Internet Engineering Task Force (IETF) and the Internet Research Task Force (IRTF).

The ISOC is a non-profit professional society with open membership. The Internet Architecture Board (IAB) is approved by the ISOC, as is the formal documentation of the Internet standards process. The IAB oversees the architecture and growth of the Internet and it approves members to the Internet Engineering Steering Group (IESG). Working groups belonging to the Internet Engineering Task Force (IETF) define specific Internet standards by consensus. Anyone may participate in the working groups, since much work is conducted by electronic mail. The IETF meets three times per year, and the documents they produce are freely available. Internet standards are published as the online Request for Comments (RFC) series.

Standards Organizations

The Institute of Electrical and Electronics Engineers (IEEE) also publishes standards. The URL for the IEEE Computer Society is <www.computer.org/>. Publications may be ordered by e-mail from the IEEE Computer Society Press at <cs.books@compmail.com>.

The European Telecommunication Standards Institute (ETSI), an organization that addresses European standards for telecommunications, may be contacted at:

ETSI
F–06921 Sophia Antipolis CEDEX
France
phone: +33 92 94 42 00
fax: +33 93 65 47 16

The Conference of European Posts and Telecommunications Administrations (CEPT), an agency that coordinates efforts in Europe, may be contacted at:

CEPT Liaison Office
Seilerstrasse 22
CH–3008 Bern
Switzerland
phone: +41 31 62 20 81
fax: +41 31 62 20 78

Two additional sources for standards in the United States are listed below:

Phillips Business Information
1201 Seven Locks Road
Potomac, MD 20854.
phone: +1 301 424 3338 or (800) 777 5006
fax: +1 301 309 3847

Document Center
1504 Industry Way, Unit 9
Belmont, CA USA 94002
phone: +1 415 591 7600
fax: +1 415 591 7617

Standards Organizations

Many standards documents are available on the Internet. The following table shows addresses where information may be accessed.

Address	Directory	Content
ftp.uu.net	networking/osi	ISODE
"	networking/x25	X.25 software
nic.ddn.mil	protocols	DoD and GOSIP related
"	rfc	RFC Repository
cs.ucl.ac.uk	src	ISODE, PP, OSIMIS, ...
"	osi-ds	Internet X.500 documents
"	ietf-osi-oda	Internet ODA documents
aun.uninett.no	ietf/mhs-ds	X.500 based routing drafts
ftp.ifi.uio.no	pub/SGML	SGML/HyTime related
dkuug.dk	i18n	internationalization standards
ftp.ripe.net	ripe/docs/iso3166-codes	ISO Country Codes
isode.com	*	ISODE Consortium documents
merit.edu	pub/iso	some ISO standards (CLNP, etc.)
osi.ncsl.nist.gov	*	GOSIP information
unicode.org	pub	Unicode/ISO 10646 material
sunsite.unc.edu	pub/Z39.50	ISO SR/Z39.50 drafts
ftp.cme.nist.gov	pub/step	ISO 10303/STEP archive
ftp.dstc.edu.au	pub/arch/RM-ODP	Open Distributed Processing

Standards Organizations

A few standards bodies located in individual countries are listed below with street address, telephone number, and facsimile number. There are approximately 100 individual national standards bodies. Contact information is listed on the following pages for the standards bodies identified by acronym as well as for other bodies.

AFNOR	Association francaise de normalisation	France
ANSI	American National Standards Institute	USA
BIS	Bureau of Indian Standards	India
BSI	British Standards Institution	United Kingdom
DIN	Deutsches Institut fur Normung	Germany
DS	Dansk Standard	Denmark
NNI	Nederlands Normalisatie-instituut	Netherlands
NSF	Norges Standardiseringsforbund	Norway
SAA	Standards Association of Australia	Australia
SANZ	Standards Association of New Zealand	New Zealand
SCC	Standards Council of Canada	Canada
UNI	Ente Nazionale Italiano di Unificazione	Italy

Australia
Standards Association
 of Australia
P.O. Box 1055
STRATHFIELD–N.S.W. 2135
phone: +61 2 746 47 00
fax: +61 2 746 84 30

Brazil
Associação Brasileira
 de Normas Técnicas
Av. 13 de Maio, nº 13–28º andar
Caixa Postal 1680
CEP: 20.003–RIO DE JANEIRO–RJ
phone: +55 21 210 31 22
fax: +55 21 532 21 43

Canada
Standards Council of Canada
45 O'Connor Street, Suite 1200
OTTAWA, ONTARIO
K1P 6N7
phone: +1 613 238 32 22
fax: +1 613 995 45 64

China
China State Bureau of
 Technical Supervision
4, Zhi Chun Road
Haidian District
P.O. Box 8010
BEIJING
phone: +86 1 202 58 35
fax: +86 1 203 10 10

Standards Organizations

Denmark
Dansk Standardiseringsraad
Baunegaardsvej 73
DK–2900 HELLERUP
phone: +45 39 77 01 01
fax: +45 39 77 02 02
e-mail: ds@itc.dk

France
Association française
 de normalisation
Tour Europe
Cedex 7
F–92049 PARIS LA DÉFENSE
phone: +331 42 91 55 55
fax: +331 42 91 56 56

Germany
DIN Deutsches Institut
 für Normung
Burggrafenstraße 6
D–10787 BERLIN
phone: +49 30 26 01 0
fax: +49 30 26 01 12 31

India
Bureau of Indian Standards
Manak Bhavan
9 Bahadur Shah Zafar Marg
NEW DEHLI 110002
phone: +91 11 331 79 91
fax: +91 11 331 40 62

Israel
Standards Institution of Israel
42 Chaim Levanon Street
TEL AVIV 69977
phone: +972 3 646 51 54
fax: +972 3 641 96 83

Italy
Ente Nazionale Italiano
 di Unificazione
Via Battistotti Sassi 11
I–20133 MILANO
phone: +39 2 70 02 41
fax: +39 2 70 10 61 06

Japan
Japanese Industrial
 Standards Committee
c/o Standards Department Agency
 of Industrial Science and Technology
Ministry of International Trade
 and Industry
1–3–1, Kasumigaseki, Chiyoda-ku
TOKYO 100
phone: +81 3 35 01 92 95/6
fax: +81 3 35 80 14 18

Mexico
Dirección General de Normas
Calle Puente de Tecamachalco N.º 6
Lomas de Tecamachalco
Sección Fuentes
Naucalpan de Juárez
53 950 MEXICO
phone: +52 5 520 84 94
fax: +52 5 540 51 53

Netherlands
Nederlands Normalisatie-Instituut
Kalfjeslaan 2
P.O. Box 5059
2600 GB DELFT
phone: +31 15 69 03 90
fax: +31 15 69 01 90

Standards Organizations

New Zealand
Standards Association
 of New Zealand
Private Bag
WELLINGTON
phone: +64 4 384 21 08
fax: +64 4 384 39 38

Norway
Norges Standardiseringsforbund
Postboks 7020 Homansbyen
N–0306 OSLO 3
phone: +47 2 46 60 94
fax: +47 2 46 44 57

Poland
Polish Committee for Standardization,
 Measures, and Quality Control
Ul. Elektoralna 2
00–139 WARSZAWA
phone: +48 22 20 54 34
fax: +48 22 20 83 78

Russian Federation
State Committee for Standardization,
 Metrology, and Certification
Leninsky Prospekt 9
MOSKVA 117049
phone: +7 095 236 40 44
fax: +7 095 236 82 09

Singapore
Singapore Institute of Standards
 and Industrial Research
1 Science Park Drive
SINGAPORE 0511
phone: +65 778 77 77
fax: +65 778 00 86

Spain
Asociación Española de
 Normalización y Certificación
Calle Fernández de la Hoz, 52
E–28010 MADRID
phone: +34 1 310 48 51
fax: +34 1 310 49 76

Sweden
SIS—Standardiseringskommissionen
 i Sverige
Box 3295
S–103 66 STOCKHOLM
phone: +46 8 613 52 00
fax: +46 8 11 70 35

Switzerland
Swiss Association for Standardization
Mülebachstr 54
CH–8008 ZÜRICH
phone: +41 1 254 54 54
fax: +41 1 254 54 74

United Kingdom
British Standards Institution
2 Park Street
GB–LONDON W1A 2BS
phone: +44 71 629 90 00
fax: +44 71 629 05 06

USA
American National Standards Institute
11 West 42nd Street, 13th floor
NEW YORK 10036
phone: +1 212 642 49 00
fax: +1 212 398 00 23

THE WORLD WIDE WEB

The explosive growth of interest and investment in the Internet has brought the World Wide Web to the attention of multimedia developers as a viable platform for delivery. As bandwidth increases, average computer users will be able to engage in interactive sessions with graphics, audio, and video in addition to text-based HTML documents. This reference explains how HTML documents are created.

The World Wide Web is a collection of interconnected HTML documents that qualify as interactive media because the user can control movement within and between documents by activating links. Documents can include graphics in the GIF and JPEG formats. Links may point to audio or video files that can be played in real time on a computer if the connection to the host server has adequate bandwidth and if the client computer has the necessary hardware and decoding programs, or plug-ins.

The two most widely used browsers are Netscape Navigator and Microsoft Internet Explorer. Although both are under rapid development and each has a few unique proprietary features, they are generally capable of reading standard HTML 2.0 files. The HTML version 3.2 proposal adds functionality to the 2.0 standard. The items included in this appendix are briefly described as follows:

1. Basic Tutorial on HTML. This section explains how each task is performed using HTML tags and identifies the conventions used in formatting.
2. HTML Tags and Attributes. An alphabetical list of tags that are recognized by most browsers. New features and capabilities are evolving rapidly, but they are not consistently implemented or standardized.
3. HTML 3.2 Elements. A structural classification of proposed tags.
4. HTML Color Table. A list of the hexadecimal codes and the RGB colors that are defined by their use. The table is organized by the color that will result when the code is specified in an HTML document.
5. HTML Coded Characters. This list shows the appropriate four-character code that is used to define special output characters in an HTML document.
6. CGI Scripts. This reference explains how Common Gateway Interface (CGI) scripts are used to facilitate feedback to users in response to their input. This extension to HTML makes it possible to structure response forms for users.

Basic Tutorial on HTML

This section is an introduction to the Hypertext Markup Language (HTML) used to create pages for the World Wide Web. Some of the features described were not initially defined in the version 2.0 specification, but they have been widely and consistently implemented in popular browsers. These features are included in HTML 3.2, which has been proposed by the World Wide Web Consortium. You will be able to create Web pages that are readable by almost all browsers if the procedures explained in this appendix are followed.

HTML Documents

HTML documents are plain-text (also known as ASCII) files that can be created using any text editor, such as Emacs or vi on a UNIX system, SimpleText on a Macintosh, or Notepad on an IBM-compatible machine. You can also use word-processing software if you save the document as "text only with line breaks." In order to make your HTML documents available to anyone with a Web browser on the Internet, you will need to have them posted on a server. A Webmaster at an educational institution, a corporation, or a commercial Internet Service Provider (ISP) will be able to assist you.

There are many WYSIWYG editors available to automate HTML development, such as HotMetal or Adobe PageMill. You may wish to try one of them after you learn some of the basics of HTML tagging. It is useful to know enough HTML to code a document before you become reliant on a WYSIWYG editor.

HTML Tags

An "element" is a fundamental component of the structure of a text document. Some examples of elements are heads, tables, paragraphs, and lists. HTML "tags" are used to mark the elements of a file for your browser. Elements may contain plain text, other elements, or both.

Tags identify the various elements in an HTML document. HTML tags consist of a left angle bracket (<), a tag name, and a right angle bracket (>). Tags are usually paired (e.g., <H1> and </H1>) to start and end the tag instruction. The end tag looks like the start tag except a slash (/) precedes the text within the brackets. Not all tags are supported by all Web browsers. A browser usually ignores a tag that it does not support.

Some elements may include an "attribute," which is additional information included inside the start tag. For example, you can specify the alignment of images (top, middle, or bottom) by including the appropriate attribute with the image source HTML code. Tags that have optional attributes are noted below.

Note: HTML is not case-sensitive. <title> is equivalent to <TITLE> or <TiTlE>. There are a few exceptions noted in Escape Sequences below.

A Minimal HTML Document

Every HTML document should contain certain standard HTML tags. Each document consists of head and body text. The head contains the title, and the body contains the actual text that is made up of paragraphs, lists, and other elements. Browsers expect specific information because they are programmed according to HTML and SGML specifications.

Required elements are shown in this sample document:

```
<html>
<head>
<TITLE>A Simple HTML Example</TITLE>
</head>
<body>
<H1>HTML is Easy To Learn</H1>
<P>Welcome to the world of HTML.
This is the first paragraph. While short it is
still a paragraph!</P>
<P>And this is the second paragraph.</P>
</body>
</html>
```

The required elements are the <html>, <head>, <title>, and <body> tags, along with their corresponding end tags. Because you should include these tags in each file, you might want to create a template file with them. Some browsers will format your HTML file correctly even if these tags are not included, while other browsers will not.

To view a copy of the file that your browser reads to generate the information in your current window, select View Source (or the equivalent) from the browser menu. The file contents, along with all the HTML tags, are displayed in a new window.

This is an excellent way to discover how HTML is used and to learn tips and constructs. Of course, the HTML that you find might not be technically correct. Once you become familiar with HTML and check the many online and hard-copy references on the subject, you will learn to distinguish between "good" and "bad" HTML. You can save a source file with the HTML codes and use it as a template for one of your Web pages, or you can modify the format to suit your purposes.

Markup Tags

HTML

This element tells your browser that the file contains HTML-coded information. The file extension .html also indicates that it is an HTML document. If you are restricted to 8.3 file names, use only .htm for your extension.

Head

The head element identifies the first part of your HTML-coded document that contains the title. The title is shown as part of your browser's window.

Title

The title element contains your document title and identifies its content in a global context. The title is displayed somewhere on the browser window (usually at the top), but not within the text area. The title is also displayed on someone's hot list or bookmark list, so choose something descriptive, unique, and relatively short. A title is also used during a WAIS search of a server.

For example, you might include a shortened title of a book with the chapter contents: NCSA Mosaic Guide (Windows): Installation. This tells the software name, the platform, and the chapter contents, which is more useful than calling the document Installation. Generally, titles should be restricted to 64 characters or fewer.

Body

The second—and largest—part of your HTML document is the body, which contains the content of your document (displayed within the text area of your browser window). The tags explained below are used in the body of your HTML document.

Headings

HTML has six levels of headings, numbered 1 through 6, with 1 being the most prominent. Headings are displayed in larger and/or bolder fonts than normal body text. The first heading in each document should be tagged <H1>.

The syntax of the heading element is: <Hy>Text of heading </Hy> where y is a number between one and six specifying the level of the heading.

Do not skip levels of headings in your document. For example, don't start with a level-one heading (<H1>) and then use a level-three (<H3>) heading.

Paragraphs

Unlike documents in most word processors, carriage returns in HTML files aren't significant. It doesn't matter how long your lines of text are, but it is best to restrict them to fewer than 72 characters in length. Word wrapping can occur at any point in your source file, and multiple spaces are collapsed into a single space by your browser.

In the example shown in the Minimal HTML Document section, the first paragraph is coded as

>   <P>Welcome to the world of HTML.
>   This is the first paragraph.
>   While short it is
>   still a paragraph!</P>

In the source file there is a line break between the sentences. A Web browser ignores this line break and starts a new paragraph only when it encounters another <P> tag.

Important: You must indicate paragraphs with <P> elements. A browser ignores any indentations or blank lines in the source text. Without <P> elements, the document becomes one large paragraph. (One exception is text tagged as "preformatted," which is explained below.) For example, the following would produce identical output as the Minimal HTML example:

>   <H1>Level-one heading</H1> <P>Welcome to the world of HTML. This is the first paragraph. While short it is still a paragraph! </P>

>   <P>And this is the second paragraph.</P>

To preserve readability in HTML files, put headings on separate lines, use a blank line or two where it helps identify the start of a new section, and separate paragraphs with blank lines in addition to the <P> tags. These extra spaces help you when you edit your files, but your browser will ignore the extra spaces because it has its own set of rules on spacing that do not depend on the spaces you put in your source file.

Note: The </P> closing tag can be omitted because browsers understand that when they encounter a <P> tag, it implies that there is an end to the previous paragraph.

Using the <P> and </P> as a paragraph container means that you can center a paragraph by including the ALIGN=alignment attribute in your source file.

> <P ALIGN=CENTER>
> This is a centered paragraph. [See the formatted version below.] </P>

> This is a centered paragraph.

LISTS

HTML supports unnumbered, numbered, and definition lists. You can nest lists, but use this feature sparingly because too many nested items can be difficult to follow.

UNNUMBERED LISTS

To make an unnumbered, bulleted list,

1. Start with an opening list <UL> (for unnumbered list) tag.
2. Enter the <LI> (list item) tag followed by the individual item; no closing </LI> tag is needed.
3. End the entire list with a closing list </UL> tag.

Below is a sample three-item list:

```
<UL>
<LI> apples
<LI> bananas
<LI> grapefruit
</UL>
```

The output is:

- apples
- bananas
- grapefruit

The <LI> items can contain multiple paragraphs. Indicate the paragraphs with the <P> paragraph tags.

NUMBERED LISTS

A numbered list (also called an ordered list, from which the tag name derives) is identical to an unnumbered list, except it uses <OL> instead of <UL>. The items are tagged using the same <LI> tag. The following HTML code:

```
<OL>
<LI> oranges
<LI> peaches
<LI> grapes
</OL>
```

produces this formatted output:

1. oranges
2. peaches
3. grapes

DEFINITION LISTS

A definition list (coded as <DL>) usually consists of alternating a definition term (coded as <DT>) and a definition (coded as <DD>). Web browsers generally format the definition on a new line.

The following is an example of a definition list:

```
<DL>
<DT> NCSA
<DD> NCSA, the National Center for Supercomputing Applications, is
located on the campus of the University of Illinois at Urbana-Champaign.
<DT> Cornell Theory Center
<DD> CTC is located on the campus of Cornell University in Ithaca, New
York.
</DL>
```

The output looks like:

NCSA
    NCSA, the National Center for Supercomputing Applications, is located on the campus of the University of Illinois at Urbana-Champaign.
Cornell Theory Center
    CTC is located on the campus of Cornell University in Ithaca, New York.

The <DT> and <DD> entries can contain multiple paragraphs (indicated by <P> paragraph tags), lists, or other definition information.

The COMPACT attribute can be used routinely in case your definition terms are short. If, for example, you are showing some computer options, the options may fit on the same line as the start of the definition.

```
<DL COMPACT>
<DT> -i
<DD>invokes NCSA Mosaic for Microsoft Windows using the initialization file
defined in the path
<DT> -k
<DD>invokes NCSA Mosaic for Microsoft Windows in kiosk mode
</DL>
```

The output looks like:

-i   invokes NCSA Mosaic for Microsoft Windows using the initialization file defined in the path.
-k   invokes NCSA Mosaic for Microsoft Windows in kiosk mode.

Nested Lists

Lists can be nested. You can also have a number of paragraphs, each containing a nested list, in a single list item.

Here is a sample nested list:

```
<UL>
<LI> A few New England states:
   <UL>
   <LI> Vermont
   <LI> New Hampshire
   <LI> Maine
   </UL>
<LI> Two Midwestern states:
   <UL>
   <LI> Michigan
   <LI> Indiana
   </UL>
</UL>
```

The nested list is displayed as:

- A few New England states:
  - Vermont
  - New Hampshire
  - Maine
- Two Midwestern states:
  - Michigan
  - Indiana

Preformatted Text

Use the <PRE> tag (which stands for preformatted) to generate text in a fixed-width font. This tag also makes spaces, new lines, and tabs significant (multiple spaces are displayed as multiple spaces, and lines break in the same locations as in the source HTML file). This is useful for program listings, among other things. For example, the following lines:

```
<PRE>
#!/bin/csh
cd $SCR
cfs get mysrc.f:mycfsdir/mysrc.f
cfs get myinfile:mycfsdir/myinfile
fc -02 -o mya.out mysrc.f
mya.out
cfs save myoutfile:mycfsdir/myoutfile
rm *
</PRE>
```

display as:

```
#!/bin/csh
cd $SCR
cfs get mysrc.f:mycfsdir/mysrc.f
cfs get myinfile:mycfsdir/myinfile
fc -02 -o mya.out mysrc.f
mya.out
cfs save myoutfile:mycfsdir/myoutfile
rm *
```

The <PRE> tag can be used with an optional WIDTH attribute that specifies the maximum number of characters for a line. WIDTH also signals your browser to choose an appropriate font and indentation for the text. Hyperlinks can be used within <PRE> sections. You should avoid using other HTML tags within <PRE> sections, however.

Note that because <, >, and & have special meanings in HTML, you must use their escape sequences (<, >, and &, respectively) to enter these characters. See the section on Escape Sequences for more information.

EXTENDED QUOTATIONS

Use the <BLOCKQUOTE> tag to include lengthy quotations in a separate block on the screen. Most browsers change the margins for the quotation to separate it from surrounding text.

In the example:

```
<BLOCKQUOTE>
<P>Omit needless words.</P>
<P>Vigorous writing is concise. A sentence should contain no unnecessary words, a paragraph no unnecessary sentences, for the same reason that a drawing should have no unnecessary lines and a machine no unnecessary parts.</P>
—William Strunk, Jr., 1918
</BLOCKQUOTE>
```

the result is:

> Omit needless words.
>
> Vigorous writing is concise. A sentence should contain no unnecessary words, a paragraph no unnecessary sentences, for the same reason that a drawing should have no unnecessary lines and a machine no unnecessary parts.
> —William Strunk, Jr., 1918

ADDRESSES

The <ADDRESS> tag is generally used to specify the author of a document, a way to contact the author (e.g., an e-mail address), and a revision date. It is usually the last item in a file.

For example, the last line of the online version of this guide is:

```
<ADDRESS>
A Beginner's Guide to HTML / NCSA / pubs@ncsa.uiuc.edu / revised April 96
</ADDRESS>
```

The result is:

A Beginner's Guide to HTML / NCSA / pubs@ncsa.uiuc.edu / revised April 96

Note: <ADDRESS> is not used for postal addresses. See "Forced Line Breaks" below to learn how to format postal addresses.

Forced Line Breaks/Postal Addresses

The <BR> tag forces a line break with no extra (white) space between lines. Using <P> elements for short lines of text such as postal addresses results in unwanted additional white space. For example, with <BR>:

National Center for Supercomputing Applications
605 East Springfield Avenue
Champaign, Illinois 61820-5518

The output is:

National Center for Supercomputing Applications
605 East Springfield Avenue
Champaign, Illinois 61820-5518

Horizontal Rules

The <HR> tag produces a horizontal line the width of the browser window. A horizontal rule is useful when you are separating sections of your document. For example, many people add a rule at the end of their text and before the <address> information.

You can vary a rule's size (thickness) and width (the percentage of the window covered by the rule). Experiment with the settings until you are satisfied with the presentation. For example, to create a centered line four pixels thick, which is half as wide as the window, use the tag <HR SIZE=4 WIDTH="50%">

Character Formatting

HTML has two types of styles for individual words or sentences—logical and physical. Logical styles tag text according to its meaning, while physical styles indicate the specific appearance of a section. For example, in the preceding sentence, the words "logical styles" might be tagged as a "definition." The same effect (formatting those words in italics) could be achieved with a different tag that tells your browser to "put these words in italics."

Note: Some browsers do not attach any style to the <DFN> tag, so you cannot be assured that all users would see the tagged phrase in italics.

Logical Versus Physical Styles

In the ideal SGML universe, content is divorced from presentation. Thus, SGML tags a level-one heading as a level-one heading, but it does not specify that the level-one heading should be, for instance, 24-point bold Times centered. The advantage of this approach (it's similar in concept to style sheets in many word processors) is that if you decide to change level-one headings to 20-point left-justified Helvetica, all you have to do is change the definition of the level-one heading in your Web browser. Indeed, many browsers today let you define how you want the various HTML tags rendered onscreen.

Another advantage of logical tags is that they help enforce consistency in your documents. It's easier to tag something as <H1> than to remember that level-one headings are 24-point bold Times centered, for example. Consider the <STRONG> tag. Most browsers render it in bold text. However, it is possible for a reader to prefer these sections to be displayed in red. Logical styles offer this flexibility.

Of course, if you want something to be displayed in italics, for example and do not want a browser's setting to display it differently, use physical styles. Physical styles, therefore, offer consistency because something you tag a certain way will always be displayed that way for readers of your document.

Try to be consistent about which type of style you use. If you tag with physical styles, do so throughout a document. If you use logical styles, stick with them within a document. Keep in mind that future releases of HTML might not support physical styles, which could mean that browsers will not display physical style coding.

Logical Styles

<DFN> for a word being defined. Typically displayed in italics.
(NCSA Mosaic is a World Wide Web browser.)

<EM> for emphasis. Typically displayed in italics.
(Consultants cannot reset your password unless you call the help line.)

<CITE> for titles of books, films, etc. Typically displayed in italics.
(For Whom the Bell Tolls)

<CODE> for computer code. Displayed in a fixed-width font.
(The <stdio.h> header file)

\<KBD\> for user keyboard entry. Typically displayed in plain fixed-width font. (Enter **passwd** to change your password.)

\<SAMP\> for a sequence of literal characters. Displayed in a fixed-width font. (Segmentation fault: **Core dumped.**)

\<STRONG\> for strong emphasis. Typically displayed in bold.
(Note: Always check your links to see how text is displayed.*)*

\<VAR\> for a variable, where you will replace the variable with specific information. Typically displayed in italics.
(rm *filename* deletes the file.)

Physical Styles

\<B\>   bold text
\<I\>   italic text
\<TT\> typewriter text, (fixed-width font)

Escape Sequences (a.k.a. Character Entities)

Character entities have two functions:

1. Escaping special characters.
2. Displaying other characters not available in the plain ASCII character set (primarily characters with diacritical marks).

Three ASCII characters—the left angle bracket (<), the right angle bracket (>), and the ampersand (&)—have special meanings in HTML and therefore cannot be used "as is" in text. (The angle brackets are used to indicate the beginning and end of HTML tags, and the ampersand is used to indicate the beginning of an escape sequence.) Double quote marks may be used as-is, but a character entity may also be used (").

To use one of the three characters in an HTML document, you must enter its escape sequence instead:

<   escape sequence for <
>   escape sequence for >
& escape sequence for &

Additional escape sequences support accented characters, such as:

ö   escape sequence for a lowercase o with an umlaut: ö

ñ   escape sequence for a lowercase n with a tilde: ñ

È escape sequence for an uppercase E with a grave accent: È

You can substitute other letters for the o, n, and E shown above. Refer to the HTML-Coded Characters section of the World Wide Web appendix for a complete list of special characters.

Note: Unlike the rest of HTML, the escape sequences are case sensitive. You cannot, for instance, use < instead of <.

LINKING

The chief power of HTML comes from its ability to link text and/or an image to another document or section of a document. A browser highlights the identified text or image with color and/or underlines to indicate that it is a hypertext link (often shortened to hyperlink or link).

HTML's single hypertext-related tag is <A>, which stands for anchor. To include an anchor in your document:

1. Start the anchor with <A (include a space after the A).
2. Specify the document you're linking to by entering the parameter HREF="filename" followed by a closing right angle bracket (>).
3. Enter the text that will serve as the hypertext link in the current document.
4. Enter the ending anchor tag </A>. (No space is needed before the end anchor tag.)

Here is a sample hypertext reference in a file called US.html:

    <A HREF="MaineStats.html">Maine</A>

This entry makes the word *Maine* the hyperlink to the document *MaineStats.html*, which is in the same directory as the first document.

Relative Path Names Versus Absolute Path Names

You can link to documents in other directories by specifying the relative path from the current document to the linked document. For example, a link to a file NYStats.html located in the subdirectory **AtlanticStates** would be:

<A HREF= "AtlanticStates/NYStats.html">New York</A>

These are called relative links because you specify the path to the linked file relative to the location of the current file. You can also use the absolute path name (the complete URL) of the file, but relative links are more efficient in accessing a server.

Path names use the standard UNIX syntax. The UNIX syntax for the parent directory (the directory that contains the current directory) is "..". (For more information consult a beginning UNIX reference text.)

If you were in the NYStats.html file and were referring to the original document US.html, your link would look like this:

<A HREF="../US.html">United States</A>

Generally, relative links should be used for the following reasons:

1. It is easier to move a group of documents to another location (because the relative path names will still be valid).
2. It is more efficient connecting to the server.
3. There is less to type.

However, use absolute path names when linking to documents that are not directly related. For example, consider a group of documents that comprise a user manual. Links within this group should be relative links. Links to other documents (perhaps a reference to related software) should use full path names. This way if you move the user manual to a different directory, none of the links would have to be updated.

URLs

The World Wide Web uses Uniform Resource Locators (URLs) to specify location the of files on other servers. A URL includes the type of resource being accessed (e.g., Web, Gopher, WAIS), the address of the server, and the location of the file. The syntax is *scheme://host.domain [:port]/path/ filename* where *scheme* is one of the following types:

file
  A file on your local system.
ftp
  A file on an anonymous FTP server.
http
  A file on a World Wide Web server.
gopher
  A file on a Gopher server.
WAIS
  A file on a WAIS server.
news
  A Usenet newsgroup.
telnet
  A connection to a Telnet-based service.

The *port* number can generally be omitted, unless it is specifically requested. For example, to include a link in your document to the NCSA primer (upon which this appendix is based), enter:

<A HREF="http://www.ncsa.uiuc.edu/General/Internet/WWW/HTMLPrimer.html">
NCSA's Beginner's Guide to HTML</A>

This entry makes the text *NCSA's Beginner's Guide to HTML* a hyperlink to your document.

LINKS TO SPECIFIC SECTIONS

Anchors can also be used to move a reader to a particular section in a document (either the same or a different document) rather than to the top, which is the default. This type of an anchor is commonly called a "named anchor" because to create the links, you insert HTML names within the document.

Internal hyperlinks are used to create a "table of contents" at the top of a long document. These hyperlinks move you from one location to another in the same document. You can also link to a specific section in another document.

LINKS BETWEEN SECTIONS OF DIFFERENT DOCUMENTS

Suppose you want to set a link from document A (documentA.html) to a specific section in another document (MaineStats.html).

The World Wide Web

Enter the HTML coding for a link to a named anchor:

documentA.html:

In addition to the many state parks, Maine is also home to
<a href="MaineStats.html#ANP">Acadia National Park</a>.

Think of the characters after the hash (#) mark as a tab within the MaineStats.html file. This tab tells your browser what should be displayed at the top of the window when the link is activated. In other words, the first line in your browser window should be the Acadia National Park heading.

Next, create the named anchor (in this example "ANP") in MaineStats.html:

<H2><A NAME="ANP">Acadia National Park</a></H2>

With both of these elements in place, you can bring a reader directly to the Acadia reference in MaineStats.html.

Note: You cannot make links to specific sections within a different document unless you have either permission to edit the coded source of that document, or that document already contains in-document named anchors. For example, you could include named anchors to the NCSA online HTML guide in a document you are writing because there are named anchors in this guide. But if this document did not have named anchors, you could not make a link to a specific section because you cannot edit the original file on NCSA's server.

LINKS TO SPECIFIC SECTIONS WITHIN THE CURRENT DOCUMENT

The technique is the same except the file name is omitted. For example, to link to the ANP anchor from within MaineStats, enter:

...More information about <A HREF="#ANP">Acadia National Park</a>
is available elsewhere in this document.

Be sure to include the <A NAME=> tag where you want the link to jump to (<H2><A NAME="ANP">Acadia National Park</a></H2>).

Named anchors are useful when you think readers will print an entire document or when you have a lot of short information you want to place online in one file.

Mailto

You can make it easy for a reader to send e-mail to a specific person or mail alias by including the mailto attribute in a hyperlink. The format is:

<A HREF="mailto:emailinfo@host">Name</a>

For example, enter:

<A HREF="mailto:mpegdisc@teleport.com">MPEG Benchmark Disc</a>

This creates a mail window configured to open a mail window for the MPEG Benchmark Disc alias. (You may put any valid Internet address in your mailto window.)

Inline Images

Most Web browsers can display inline images (images next to text) that are in X Bitmap (XBM), GIF, or JPEG format. Other image formats are being incorporated into Web browsers (e.g., the Portable Network Graphic (PNG) format). Each image takes time to process and slows down the initial display of a document. Carefully select your images and the number of images in a document.

To include an inline image, enter:

<IMG SRC=ImageName>

where *ImageName* is the URL of the image file.

The syntax for <IMG SRC> URLs is identical to that used in an anchor HREF. If the image file is a GIF file, then the file name part of *ImageName* must end with .gif. File names of X Bitmap images must end with .xbm; JPEG image files must end with .jpg or .jpeg; and Portable Network Graphic files must end with .png.

Image Size Attributes

Include two other attributes on <IMG> tags to tell your browser the size of the images it is downloading with the text. The HEIGHT and WIDTH attributes let the browser set aside the appropriate space (in pixels) for the images as it downloads the rest of the file. (Get the pixel size from your image-processing software, such as Adobe Photoshop.)

For example, to include a self-portrait image in a file along with the portrait's dimensions, enter:

<IMG SRC=SelfPortrait.gif HEIGHT=100 WIDTH=65>

Note: Some browsers use the HEIGHT and WIDTH attributes to stretch or shrink an image to fit into the allotted space when the image does not exactly match the attribute numbers. Not all browser developers think stretching/shrinking is a good idea. Do not assume your readers will have access to this feature. Check your dimensions and use the correct ones.

ALIGNING IMAGES

You have some flexibility when displaying images. You can have images separated from text and aligned to the left, right, or center, or you can have an image aligned with text. Try several possibilities to see how your information looks best.

ALIGNING TEXT WITH AN IMAGE

By default, the bottom of an image is aligned with the baseline of the text that follows it. You can align images to the top or center of a paragraph using the ALIGN= attributes TOP and CENTER.

To align text with the top of the image, use the tag:

(<IMG SRC = "MyImage.gif" ALIGN=TOP>)

Note that the browser aligns only one line and then jumps to the bottom of the image for the rest of the text.

For text that is centered on the image, use the tag:

(<IMG SRC = "MyImage.gif" ALIGN=CENTER>)

Only one line of text is centered; the rest is below the image.

IMAGES WITHOUT TEXT

To display an image without any associated text (e.g., your organization's logo), make it a separate paragraph. Use the paragraph ALIGN= attribute to center the image or adjust it to the right side of the window as shown on the following page:

```
<p ALIGN=CENTER>
<IMG SRC = "MyImage.gif">
</p>
```

The image is centered and the paragraph starts below it, left-justified.

ALTERNATE TEXT FOR IMAGES

Some World Wide Web browsers (primarily those that run on VT100 terminals) cannot display images. Some users turn off image loading if they have a slow connection, even if their software can display images. HTML provides a mechanism to tell readers what they are missing on your pages.

The ALT attribute lets you specify text to be displayed instead of an image. In the following example *UpArrow.gif* is the picture of an upward pointing arrow.

```
<IMG SRC="UpArrow.gif" ALT="Up">
```

With graphics-capable viewers that have image-loading turned on, the up arrow graphic is visible. With image-loading is turned off, or with a VT100 browser, the word *Up* is shown in your window. It's a good idea to include alternate text for each image you use in your document as courtesy for your readers.

BACKGROUND GRAPHICS

Newer versions of Web browsers can load an image and use it as a background when displaying a page. Some people like background images and some don't. In general, if you want to include a background, make sure your text can be read easily when displayed on top of the image. Background images can be a texture or an object, such as a logo. You create the background image as you do any image.

However, you only have to create a small piece of the image. Using a tiling feature, a browser takes the image and repeats it across and down to fill your browser window. Basically, you generate one image, and the browser replicates it enough times to fill your window. This action is automatic when you use the background tag.

Below is the tag to include a background image included in the <BODY> statement as an attribute:

<BODY BACKGROUND=*"filename.gif"*>

BACKGROUND COLOR

By default, browsers display text in black on a gray background. However, you can change both elements if you want. Some HTML authors select a background color and coordinate it with a change in the color of the text.

Always preview changes like this to make sure your pages are readable. (For example, many people find red text on a black background difficult to read.)

You change the color of text, links, visited links, and active links using attributes of the <BODY> tag. For example, enter:

<BODY BGCOLOR="#000000" TEXT="#FFFFFF" LINK="#9690CC">

This creates a window with a black background (BGCOLOR), white text (TEXT), and silvery hyperlinks (LINK).

The six-digit number and letter combinations represent colors by giving their RGB (red, green, blue) value. The six digits are three two-digit numbers in sequence, representing the amount of red, green, or blue as a hexadecimal value in the range 00-FF. For example, 000000 is black (no color at all), FF0000 is bright red, and FFFFFF is white (fully saturated with all three colors). These number and letter combinations are cryptic. The six-digit color codes that map specific colors in HTML 3.2 are provided in the HTML Color Tables section of the World Wide Web appendix.

EXTERNAL IMAGES, SOUNDS, AND ANIMATION

You may want to have an image open as a separate document when a user activates a link on either a word or a smaller inline version of the image included in your document. This is called an external image, and it is useful if you do not wish to slow down the loading of the main document with large inline images.

To include a reference to an external image, enter:

> <A HREF="MyImage.gif">link anchor</A>

You can also use a smaller image as a link to a larger image. Enter:

> <A HREF="LargerImage.gif"><IMG SRC="SmallImage.gif"></A>

The reader sees the SmallImage.gif image and clicks it to open the LargerImage.gif file. Use the same syntax for links to external animation and sounds. The only difference is the file extension of the linked file. For example, <A HREF="AdamsRib.mov">link anchor</A> specifies a link to a QuickTime movie. Some common file types and their extensions are:

File Type	Extension
plain text	.txt
HTML document	.htm (or .html)
GIF image	.gif
TIFF image	.tif (or .tiff)
X Bitmap image	.xbm
JPEG image	.jpg (or .jpeg)
PostScript file	.ps
AIFF sound file	.aif (or .aiff)
AU sound file	.au
WAV sound file	.wav
QuickTime movie	.mov
MPEG movie	.mpg (or .mpeg)

Keep in mind your intended audience's access to helper applications and plug-ins. For example, most UNIX workstations cannot view QuickTime movies.

TABLES

Before HTML tags for tables were finalized, authors had to format their tabular information carefully within <PRE> tags, counting spaces and previewing their output. Tables are useful for the presentation of tabular information as well as a boon to creative HTML authors who use the table tags to present their regular Web pages.

Think of your tabular information in light of the coding explained below. A table has heads where you explain what the columns/rows include, rows for information, and cells for each item. In the following table, the first column contains the header information, each row explains an HTML table tag, and each cell contains a paired tag or an explanation of the tag's function.

Table Elements

Element	Description
<TABLE>	Defines a table in HTML. If the BORDER attribute is present, your browser displays the table with a border.
<CAPTION>	Defines the caption for the title of the table. The default position of the title is centered at the top. The ALIGN=BOTTOM attribute can be used to position the caption below the table. *Note:* Any kind of markup tag can be used in the caption.
<TR>	Specifies a table row within a table. You may define default attributes for the entire row: ALIGN (LEFT, CENTER, RIGHT) and/or VALIGN (TOP, MIDDLE, BOTTOM). See Table Attributes at the end of this table for more information.
<TH>	Defines a table header cell. By default the text in this cell is bold and centered. Table header cells may contain other attributes to determine the characteristics of the cell and/or its contents. See Table Attributes at the end of this table for more information.
<TD>	Defines a table data cell. By default, the text in this cell is left-aligned and centered vertically. Table data cells may contain other attributes to determine the characteristics of the cell and/or its contents. See Table Attributes at the end of this table.

Table Attributes

Note: Attributes defined within <TH> ... </TH> or <TD> ... </TD> cells override the default alignment set in a <TR> ... </TR>. Attributes are listed below, along with their description.

ALIGN (LEFT, CENTER, RIGHT)
: Horizontal alignment of a cell.

VALIGN (TOP, MIDDLE, BOTTOM)
: Vertical alignment of a cell.

COLSPAN=n
: The number (n) of columns a cell spans.

ROWSPAN=n
> The number (n) of rows a cell spans.

NOWRAP
> Turn off word wrapping within a cell.

GENERAL TABLE FORMAT

The general format of a table looks like this:

`<TABLE`	`<==` start of table definition
`<CAPTION>` caption contents `</CAPTION>`	`<==` caption definition
`<TR>`	`<==` start of first row definition
`<TH>` cell contents `</TH>`	`<==` first cell in row 1 (a head)
`<TH>` cell contents `</TH>`	`<==` last cell in row 1 (a head)
`</TR>`	`<==` end of first row definition
`<TR`	`<==` start of second row definition
`<TD>` cell contents `</TD>`	`<==` first cell in row 2
`<TD>` cell contents `</TD>`	`<==` last cell in row 2
`</TR>`	`<==` end of second row definition
`<TR>`	`<==` start of last row definition
`<TD>` cell contents `</TD>`	`<==` first cell in last row
`<TD>` cell contents `</TD>`	`<==` last cell in last row
`</TR>`	`<==` end of last row definition
`</TABLE`	`<==` end of table definition

The `<TABLE>` and `</TABLE>` tags must surround the entire table definition. The first item inside the table, the CAPTION, is optional. Then you can have any number of rows defined by the `<TR>` and `</TR>` tags. Within a row you can have any number of cells defined by the `<TD>`...`</TD>` or `<TH>`...`</TH>` tags. Each row of a table is formatted independently of the rows above and below it. This lets you easily display tables like the one above with a single cell, such as Table Attributes, spanning columns of the table.

Tables for Nontabular Information

Some HTML authors use tables to present nontabular information. For example, because links can be included in table cells, some authors use a table with no borders to create "one" image from separate images. Browsers that can display tables properly show the various images seamlessly, making the created image seem like an image map (one image with hyperlinked quadrants). Using table borders with images can create an impressive display as well.

Fill-Out Forms

Web forms let you return information to a Web server for some action. For example, suppose you collect names and e-mail addresses so you can e-mail information to people who request it. For each person who enters his or her name and address, you need some information to be sent and the respondent's particulars added to a database. This processing of incoming data is usually handled by a script or program written in PERL or another language that manipulates text, files, and information.

The forms are not hard to code. They follow the same constructs as other HTML tags. What can be difficult is the program or script that takes the data submitted in a form and processes it. Because of the need for specialized scripts to handle the incoming form information, fill-out forms are not discussed in this primer. See the CGI Scripting section in the World Wide Web appendix for more information.

Troubleshooting

Avoid Overlapping Tags

Consider this example of HTML:

<B>This is an example of <DFN>overlapping</B> HTML tags.</DFN>

The word overlapping is in both the <B> and <DFN> tags. A browser might be confused by this coding and might not display it the way you intend. The only way to know is to check each popular browser (a time-consuming proposition).

In general, avoid overlapping tags. Look at your tags and try pairing them up. Tags (with the obvious exceptions of elements whose end tags may be omitted, such as paragraphs) should be paired without an intervening tag in between. Look again at the example above. You cannot pair the bold tags without another tag in the middle (the first definition tag). Try matching your coding up like this to see if you have any problem areas that should be fixed before you release your files to a server.

Embed Only Anchors and Character Tags

HTML protocol allows you to embed links within other HTML tags:

    `<H1><A HREF="Destination.html">My heading</A></H1>`

Do not embed HTML tags within an anchor:

    `<A HREF="Destination.html">`
    `<H1>My heading</H1>`
    `</A>`

Although most browsers currently handle this second example, the official HTML specifications do not support this construct, and your file may not work with future browsers. Remember that browsers can be forgiving when displaying improperly coded files. However, that forgiveness may not continue in the next version of the software! When in doubt, code your files according to the HTML specification.

Character tags modify the appearance of the text within other elements:

    `<UL>`
    `<LI><B>A bold list item</B>`
    `<LI><I>An italic list item</I>`
    `</UL>`

Avoid embedding other types of HTML element tags. For example, you might be tempted to embed a heading within a list in order to make the font size larger:

    `<UL>`
    `<LI><H1>A large heading</H1>`
    `<LI><H2>Something slightly smaller</H2>`
    `</UL>`

Although some browsers handle this well, formatting of such coding is unpredictable because it is undefined. For compatibility with all browsers, avoid these kinds of constructs. The Netscape <FONT> tag, which lets you specify how large individual characters will be displayed in your window, is not part of basic HTML 2.0.

What's the difference between embedding a <B> within a <LI> tag as opposed to embedding a <H1> within a <LI>? Within HTML the semantic meaning of <H1> is that it's the main heading of a document and that it should be followed by the content of the document. Therefore, it doesn't make sense to find a <H1> within a list.

Character formatting tags also are generally not additive. For example, you might expect that <B><I>some text</I></B> would produce bold-italic text. On some browsers it does; other browsers interpret only the innermost tag.

Final Steps

Validate your code. When you put a document on a Web server, check the formatting and each link (including named anchors). Ideally, you will have someone else read through and comment on your files before you consider a document finished.

You can run your coded files through an HTML validation service that will tell you if your code conforms to accepted HTML. If you are not sure your coding conforms to HTML specifications, this can be a useful teaching tool. Fortunately, the service lets you select the level of conformance you want for your files (i.e., strict, level 2, level 3). If you want to use some codes that are not officially part of the HTML specifications, this latitude is helpful.

Dummy Images

When an <IMG SRC> tag points to an image that does not exist, a dummy image is substituted by your browser software. When this happens during your final review of your files, make sure that the referenced image does in fact exist, that the hyperlink has the correct information in the URL, and that the file permission is set appropriately (world-readable). Then check online again.

Update Your Files

If the contents of a file are static (such as a biography of George Washington), no updating should be needed. Time-sensitive documents should be changed often.

Updating is important when the file contains information such as a weekly schedule or a deadline for a program funding announcement. Remove out-of-date files or note why something that seems dated is still on a server (e.g., the program requirements remain the same for the next cycle so the file is still available as an interim reference).

BROWSERS DIFFER

Web browsers display HTML elements differently. Remember that not all codes used in HTML files are interpreted by all browsers. Any code a browser does not understand is usually ignored.

You could spend a lot of time making your file look perfect using your current browser. If you check that file using another browser, it may display quite differently. Hence, these words of advice: code your files using correct HTML. Leave the interpreting to the browsers and hope for the best.

COMMENTING YOUR FILES

You might want to include comments in your HTML files. Comments in HTML are like comments in a computer program—the text you enter is not used by the browser in any formatting and is not directly viewable by the reader just as computer program comments are not used and are not viewable. The comments are accessible if a reader views the source file, however.

Comments such as the name of the person updating a file, the software and version used in creating a file, or the date that a minor edit was made are the norm.

To include a comment, enter:

    <!– your comments here –>

You must include the exclamation mark and the hyphens as shown.

This document was adapted from *A Beginner's Guide to HTML*, which was created by the National Center for Supercomputing. It was printed with permission from the Board of Trustees of the University of Illinois. Source URL: http://www.ncsa.uiuc.edu/General/Internet/WWW/HTMLPrimer.html revised April 96 edits: 7/96.

TABLE OF HTML TAGS WITH ATTRIBUTES

This table lists alphabetically the HTML tags that most browsers support. Attributes that may be defined within the delimiters of a tag are listed under each tag. A tag may have any number of attributes in any order, providing they do not conflict with one another. If a variable is followed by ",—" in the table, multiple values may be used as long as they are separated by a comma. Some of the attributes that accept standard variables are listed here.

URL: A Uniform Resource Locator. This may be a directory (http://www.teleport.com/mpegdisc), a file (http://www.teleport.com/mpegdisc/samples.htm), or a specific location within a file (http://www.teleport.com/mpegdisc/samples.htm#skiboat). The URL can refer to a local position within a current page without requiring a full path name.

Pixels: A measurement that defines the size of an area on the screen. It is expressed as a decimal number.

Color: A code that identifies the exact color to be used. It consists of the # symbol followed by a six-digit hexadecimal value. Each pair of digits specifies the amount of red, green, and blue respectively, that is used to make up the color. For example, magenta is #ff00ff, cyan is #00ffff, and gold is #d4a017.

Frame size: The size of a frame, which may be expressed in several ways. A measurement in pixels is represented by a number. A percentage is used to define a portion of the width of a page.

Alignment: Used to indicate the positioning of an image relative to surrounding text. It may also be used for positioning text on a page.

Table of HTML Tags with Attributes

HTML Tag/Attributes	Function
<!DOCTYPE>	Header info that defines the file format
HTML	Contents are an HTML document
PUBLIC	Contents are a readable document
"*standard*"	Specifies the version of HTML used
</*tag*>	Ends the effect of the tag shown, like a delimiter
<A HREF="*URL*">	Marks the beginning of a link to a document
METHODS="*method,—*"	Functions supported by the document (advanced)
REL="*value,—*"	Lists the relationship of a link (advanced)
REV="*value,—*"	Reverses the relationship of a link (advanced)
TITLE="*text*"	Provides a name for the page that is linked
URN="*URN*"	Resource Name of document (advanced)
<A NAME=*name*>	Names the location that becomes a target
<ADDRESS>	The text format for mailing addresses
<AREA>	Describes a single link on a mapped image
COORDS="*pixels,—*"	The left, top, right, and bottom of the link area
HREF="*URL*"	Location that is linked
NOHREF	This area is not a link
SHAPE="RECT"	Rectangular map area
<B>	Indicates that text is to be bold
<BASE>	Changes defaults for all URLs in a document
HREF="*URL*"	The new base for relative URLs
<BASEFONT>	Changes default for fonts in document
SIZE=*number*	Sets the default font size between 1 and 7
<BIG>	Increases text size
<BODY>	Indicates the beginning of page content
ALINK="*color*"	Sets active link color
BACKGROUND="*url*"	Sets an image as the backdrop for a page
BGCOLOR="*color*"	Sets a color for the background of a page
LINK="*color*"	Sets the color of an unvisited link

The World Wide Web

TEXT="*color*"	Sets the default text color
VLINK="*color*"	Sets the visited link color
 	Starts a new line of text
CLEAR=ALL	Starts the next line below an image
CLEAR=LEFT	Starts a new line below and left of image
CLEAR=RIGHT	Starts a new line below and right of image
<CAPTION>	Sets a caption for a table
ALIGN=BOTTOM	Places a caption below a table
ALIGN=TOP	Places a caption above a table (default)
<CENTER>	Centers text and images across a page
<CITE>	Text format for all citations
<CODE>	Text format for program code
<DIR>	A directory list
<DD>	Descriptor in definition list
<DL>	A definition list
<DT>	Defined term of a definition list
<EM>	Emphasizes text (italic)
<FONT>	Changes font attributes
COLOR=*color*	Changes the font color
SIZE=*number*	Changes the font to size (1-7)
SIZE=+*number*	Increases font size (up to +6)
SIZE=-*number*	Decreases font size (down to -6)
<FORM>	Structures a data input form
ACTION="*URL*"	Location to send data to
METHOD=*protocol*	Selects transfer protocol (GET or PUT)
ENCTYPE=*MIMEtype*	Format for data
<FRAME>	Sets the attributes for a frame

Table of HTML Tags with Attributes

MARGINHEIGHT=*pixels*	Sets the space above and below a frame
MARGINWIDTH=*pixels*	Sets the space at the edges of a frame
NAME=*frame*	Assigns a name to the frame
NORESIZE	Prevents the frame borders from being moved
SCROLLING=YES	Gives the frame scroll bars
SCROLLING=NO	Does not allow frame scroll bars
SCROLLING=AUTO	Makes scroll bars available as needed
SRC="*URL*"	Identifies a page to put into the frame
<FRAMESET>	Divides the screen into frames
COLS="*framesize,—*	Sets the width of the frame columns
ROWS="*framesize,—*	Sets the height of the frame rows
<H*number*>	Headline text format level (number 1-6)
ALIGN=CENTER	Centers the headline on the screen
<HEAD>	Indicates the page header
<HR>	Creates a horizontal rule line
ALIGN=*alignment*	Positions the rule line on the page
NOSHADE	Solid line, not shaded
SIZE=*pixels*	Sets thickness of the line in pixels
WIDTH=*number%*	Sets width of line as a percentage of space
WIDTH=*pixels*	Sets exact line width in pixels
<HTML>	Identifies an HTML formatted document
<i>	Italic font
<IMG>	Inserts a graphical image
ALIGN=*alignment*	Positions the image in relation to text
ALT="*text*"	Text replaces a graphic that cannot be displayed
BORDER=*pixels*	Identifies the thickness of a border around a graphic
HEIGHT=*pixels*	Sets the vertical size of an image on a page
HSPACE=*pixels*	Sets the horizontal space between an image and text
ISMAP	The image maps to more than one link
SRC="*URL*"	Source location of image to be displayed (required)
VSPACE=*pixels*	Vertical space between the image and text
WIDTH=*pixels*	Sets the width of an image horizontally
USEMAP="*URL*"	Points to a file defining links for the image

The World Wide Web

<INPUT>	A form field
ALIGN=*alignment*	Positions an image field in relation to text
CHECKED	A check box or an option button is selected
MAXLENGTH=*number*	Sets maximum number of characters user may enter
NAME="*name*"	Gives field a name
SIZE=*number*	Sets the size of a field in characters
SRC="*URL*"	Identifies an image file for a button on a form
TYPE=CHECKBOX	A basic checkbox (yes/no) in the field
TYPE=HIDDEN	Field is not visible to the user
TYPE=IMAGE	A graphical form submission button
TYPE=PASSWORD	Text entry field in which text is not displayed
TYPE=RADIO	An option select field (option button)
TYPE=RESET	A button that clears all fields
TYPE=SUBMIT	A form submission button
TYPE=TEXT	A text field with one line
TYPE=TEXTAREA	A text field with multiple lines
VALUE="*text*"	Default value for a field
<ISINDEX>	Indicates the page is a searchable index
PROMPT="*text*"	Text appears on search form
<KBD>	Text in keyboard format (monospaced)
<LI>	The start of a new item on a list
TYPE=1	Arabic numbers (1, 2, 3) (Default)
TYPE=a	Lowercase letters (a, b, c)
TYPE=A	Uppercase letters (A, B, C)
TYPE=i	Lowercase Roman numerals (i, ii, iii, iv)
TYPE=I	Uppercase Roman numerals (I, II, III, IV)
VALUE=*number*	Sets the entry counter for an ordered list
<LINK>	Shows a relationship to another document
METHODS="*method,—*"	Lists supported functions (advanced)
REL="*value,—*"	Lists relationship of the link (advanced)
REV="*value,—*"	Reverses relationship of the link (advanced)
TITLE="*text*"	Names the page which is linked
URN="*URN*"	Resource Name of the document (advanced)
<LISTING>	Indicates text format with a fixed spacing

Table of HTML Tags with Attributes

Tag/Attribute	Description
`<MAP>`	Defines the areas of an image that are links
NAME="*name*"	Names the map (required)
`<MENU>`	A menu list
`<META>`	Contains information defining a page
CONTENT="*text*"	The information contained (required)
HTTP-EQUIV="*text*"	Relates info with an HTTP response field
NAME="*text*"	The name of the information contained
`<NEXTID>`	An identifier selected by the computer for a document
N="*text*"	The named identifier for a document
`<NOBR>`	No line breaks are allowed in text
`<NOFRAMES>`	Instructs browsers not to create frames
`<OL>`	An ordered list by number or letter
START=*number*	The first value on the list
TYPE=1	Arabic numbers (1, 2, 3) (default)
TYPE=a	Lowercase letters (a, b, c)
TYPE=A	Uppercase letters (A, B, C)
TYPE=i	Lowercase Roman numerals (i, ii, iii, iv)
TYPE=I	Uppercase Roman numerals (I, II, III, IV)
`<OPTION>`	A menu choice on a form
DISABLED	This choice may not be selected
SELECTED	This is the default choice
VALUE="*text*"	This text is sent to the host if option is chosen
`<P>`	A text paragraph
ALIGN=*alignment*	Defines how text is aligned horizontally
`<PLAINTEXT>`	The rest of the document should be treated as text
`<PRE>`	Preformatted text
`<SAMP>`	Text format for text samples
`<SELECT>`	A menu field on a form

The World Wide Web

MULTIPLE	Allows more than one selection
NAME=*"text"*	The name of the field
SIZE=*number*	The number of items visible at once
<SMALL>	Instructs browser to use a smaller font
<STRIKE>	Display the text with a line through it
<STRONG>	Highlighted text (typically bold)
<SUB>	Subscript text
<SUP>	Superscript text
<TABLE>	Create a grid
ALIGN=*alignment*	Position text inside a grid cell
BORDER	Display a border around the table
BORDER=*pixels*	Defines thickness of a border
CELLPADDING=*pixels*	Distance between cell frame and contents
CELLSPACING=*pixels*	Distance between cells
HEIGHT=*number%*	The height of the table as percentage of space
HEIGHT=*pixels*	The height of the table in pixels
WIDTH=*number%*	The width of the table as percentage of space
WIDTH=*pixels*	The width of the table in pixels
<TD>	Definition of table cell contents
ALIGN=*alignment*	Horizontal positioning of text in cell
COLSPAN=*number*	The number of columns covered by a cell
HEIGHT=*number%*	Cell height as a percentage of table
HEIGHT=*pixels*	Cell height in pixels
NOWRAP	No line breaks allowed in the cell
ROWSPAN=*number*	Number of table rows covered by the cell
VALIGN=*alignment*	Vertical positioning of text inside a cell
WIDTH=*number%*	Cell width as a percentage of the table
WIDTH=*pixels*	Cell width in pixels
<TEXTAREA>	A text field with multiple lines in a form
COLS=*number*	The width of the field, in characters (required)
NAME=*"name"*	The name of the field (required)
ROWS=*number*	The height of the field, in characters (required)

Table of HTML Tags with Attributes

Tag	Description
`<TH>`	Table header cell (bold text by default)
ALIGN=*alignment*	Horizontal positioning of text in cell
COLSPAN=*number*	The number of columns covered by a cell
HEIGHT=*number%*	Cell height as a percentage of table
HEIGHT=*pixels*	Cell height in pixels
NOWRAP	No line breaks allowed in the cell
ROWSPAN=*number*	Number of table rows covered by the cell
VALIGN=*alignment*	Vertical positioning of text inside a cell
WIDTH=*number%*	Cell width as a percentage of the table
WIDTH=*pixels*	Cell width in pixels
`<TITLE>`	Defines the title of the page shown in the title bar
`<TR>`	Defines a table row
ALIGN=*alignment*	Horizontal positioning of text in cell
VALIGN=*alignment*	Vertical positioning of text inside a cell
`<TT>`	Teletype format with fixed-width font
`<UL>`	Unnumbered list
`<VAR>`	The text format to be used for program variables
`<WBR>`	Allows a break , overriding a `<NOBR>` instruction
`<XMP>`	An example of the text format to be used
`<!—text—>....`	The text is a comment, not an instruction

HTML 3.2 Elements

In May of 1996, the World Wide Web Consortium announced HTML 3.2. It confirmed that HTML 3.0 would not become a standard, nor would it be supported. The 3.2 proposal consists of the HTML 2.0 standard with selected enhancements from HTML+, HTML 3.0, and other proposals. While the TABLE markup and JAVA Applet Embedding are implemented in this version, the FRAMES and FIG features remain under development. Additional developments planned for 1997 include scripting, fill-out forms, math, link types, and more embedding objects.

An HTML 3.2 document begins with the prologue:

<!DOCTYPE HTML PUBLIC "-//W3C//DTD HTML 3.2//EN">

This declaration distinguishes it from other versions of HTML, and it is followed by HEAD, TITLE, and BODY elements. All other tags are optional.

The HEAD Element

This contains the document head. Both start and end tags may be omitted. Elements belonging to the document head are:

TITLE: Defines the document title, and is always needed.
ISINDEX: Used for simple keyword searches, see PROMPT attribute.
BASE: Defines absolute URL for resolving relative URLs.
STYLE: Reserved for future use with style sheets.
SCRIPT: Reserved for future use with scripting languages.
META: Used to supply meta info as name/value pairs.
LINK: Used to define relationships with other documents.

TITLE, STYLE, and SCRIPT are containers that require both start and end tags. The other elements are not containers and do not require end tags.

The BODY Element

This contains the document body. Start and end tags for BODY may be omitted. Key attributes are BACKGROUND, BGCOLOR, TEXT, LINK, VLINK and ALINK. A repeating background image and background and foreground colors for normal text and hypertext links may be set with these attributes. An RGB color may be specified by a hexadecimal number, such as "#FF0000" for red, or one of the 16 colors supported by the Windows VGA palette may be named (aqua, black, blue, fuchsia, gray, green, lime, maroon, navy, olive, purple, red, silver, teal, white, or yellow).

BLOCK- AND TEXT-LEVEL ELEMENTS

Most elements in the document body fall into one of two groups: block-level elements which cause paragraph breaks, and text-level elements which do not. Block-level elements include H1 through H6 (headers), P (paragraphs) LI (list items), and HR (horizontal rules). Text-level elements include EM, I, B and FONT (character emphasis), A (hypertext links), IMG and APPLET (embedded objects), and BR (line breaks). Block elements generally act as containers for text-level and other block-level elements (except headings and address elements), while text-level elements may contain other text-level elements only.

BLOCK-LEVEL ELEMENTS

P (paragraph): The paragraph element requires a start tag, but the end tag may be omitted. The ALIGN attribute sets the text alignment within a paragraph.

UL (unordered list): These require start and end tags, and contain one or more LI elements representing individual list items.

OL ordered (numbered list): These require start and end tags, and contain one or more LI elements representing individual list items.

DL (definition list): These require start and end tags and contain DT elements identifying terms, and DD elements with corresponding definitions.

PRE (preformatted text): Start and end tags are required. These elements are rendered with a monospaced font and preserve layout defined by whitespace and linebreak characters.

DIV (document division): Start and end tags are required. It groups related elements together and can be used with the ALIGN attribute: LEFT, CENTER, or RIGHT.

CENTER (text alignment): Requiring start and end tags, it centers text lines enclosed by the CENTER element.

BLOCKQUOTE (quoted passage): Start and end tags are required. It is used to enclose extended quotations and is typically rendered with indented margins.

FORM (fill-out form): This element requires start and end tags, and is used to define a fill-out form for processing by HTTP servers. The attributes are ACTION, METHOD, and ENCTYPE. Form elements cannot be nested.

ISINDEX (primitive HTML form): This is not a container, so no end tag is used. This predates FORM and is used for simple kinds of forms with a single text-input field.

HR (horizontal rule): This element is not a container, so no end tag is used. Attributes are ALIGN, NOSHADE, SIZE, and WIDTH.

TABLE (creates a table): Start and end tags are required. The attributes for TABLE are all optional. A table is rendered without a surrounding border by default. The table is generally sized automatically to fit the contents, but the WIDTH attribute may be used. BORDER, CELLSPACING and CELLPADDING control the table's appearance, along with the ALIGN attribute. The CAPTION element is used for captions rendered at the top or bottom of the table depending on the ALIGN attribute.

Each table row is contained in a TR element, although the end tag may be omitted. Table cells are defined by TD elements for data and TH elements for headers. Like TR, these are containers that do not require end tags. TH and TD support several attributes: ALIGN and VALIGN for aligning cell content, and ROWSPAN and COLSPAN for cells which span more than one row or column. A cell may contain other block- and text-level elements, including form fields and other tables.

HEADINGS

H1, H2, H3, H4, H5, and H6 are used for document headings. Both start and end tags are required. H1 elements define the most important level, and H6 elements are the least important. More important headings are rendered in a larger font than less important ones. The ALIGN attribute sets the text alignment within a heading.

TEXT-LEVEL ELEMENTS

These elements do not cause paragraph breaks. Text-level elements that define character styles may be nested. They may contain other text-level elements but not block level elements.

Font Style Elements

These elements require start and end tags:

TT: Defines teletype or monospaced text.
I: Defines italic text style.
B: Defines bold text style.
U: Defines underlined text style.
STRIKE: Defines strike-through text style.
BIG: Places text in a large font.
SMALL: Places text in a small font.
SUB: Places text in subscript style.
SUP: Places text in superscript style.

Phrase Elements

These also require start and end tags:

EM: Indicates basic emphasis, typically rendered in an italic font.
STRONG: Indicates strong emphasis, typically rendered in a bold font.
DFN: Used to define instance of the enclosed term.
CODE: Used for extracts from program code.
SAMP: Used for sample output from programs, scripts, etc.
KBD: Used for text to be typed by the user.
VAR: Used for variables or arguments to commands.
CITE: Used for citations or references to other sources.

Form Fields

The three form field elements are INPUT, SELECT, and TEXTAREA. INPUT elements are not containers and do not use end tags. INPUT, SELECT, and TEXTAREA are allowed only within FORM elements. INPUT can be used for a variety of form fields including single line text fields, password fields, checkboxes, radio buttons, submit and reset buttons, hidden fields, file upload, and image buttons. SELECT elements require start and end tags and contain one or more OPTION elements. SELECT elements are used for single or multi-selection menus. TEXTAREA elements require start and end tags, and are used to define multi-line text fields. The content of the element is used to initialize the field.

Special Text-Level Elements

The A (anchor) element: This element defines hypertext links and also identifies named locations for use as targets for hypertext links.

The attributes are NAME, HREF, REL, REV and TITLE. HREF is used to supply a URL identifying the linked document or image. NAME is used to associate a name with a section of a document for use with URLs that target a named section of a document. Anchors cannot be nested.

IMG: This element is used to insert an image. It is an empty element, so no end tag is used. Attributes are: SRC, ALT, ALIGN, WIDTH, HEIGHT, BORDER, HSPACE, VSPACE, USEMAP, and ISMAP. Images may be positioned vertically relative to the current text line or floated to the left or right.

APPLET: This element is supported by all Java-enabled browsers. Start and end tags are required. It allows a Java applet to be embedded into an HTML document. The contents of the element are substituted if the applet can't be loaded. Attributes are CODE, CODEBASE, NAME, ALT, ALIGN, WIDTH, HEIGHT, HSPACE, and VSPACE. APPLET uses associated PARAM elements to pass parameters to the applet.

FONT: This element allows you to change the font size and/or color for the enclosed text. Start and end tags are required. The attributes are SIZE and COLOR. Colors are given as RGB in hexadecimal notation or as one of 16 commonly used color names.

BR: This element is used to force a line break. It is an empty element and uses no end tag. The CLEAR attribute may be used to move past floating images on either margin.

MAP: This element defines client-side image maps. Start and end tags are required. MAP elements contain one or more AREA elements that specify hot zones on the associated image and bind these hot zones to URLs.

ADDRESS: This element requires start and end tags and identifies the address of the author of the document.

HTML 3.2 Color Tables

The following codes may be used to define the background color, text, and link colors in HTML 3.2 documents. They are hexadecimal triplets, with two digits for red, two for green, and two for blue. These functions are interpreted in Netscape Navigator 1.1 and later versions.

Colors may be designated as shown below:

<body bgcolor="#code"> for background color
<body text="#code"> for color of text (all non-hyperlinked items)
<body link="#code"> for color of unvisited links
<body vlink="#code"> for color of visited links
<body alink="#code"> for color of active links (while being selected)

An example in HTML: <body bgcolor="#FFFF33" text="#000000" link="#FF00FF" vlink="#7F0000" alink="#7E587E">

Color Name	Code
AliceBlue	eff7ff
AntiqueWhite	f9e8d2
AntiqueWhite1	feedd6
AntiqueWhite2	ebdbc5
AntiqueWhite3	c8b9a6
AntiqueWhite4	817468
Aquamarine	43b7ba
Aquamarine1	87fdce
Aquamarine2	7deabe
Aquamarine3	69c69f
Aquamarine4	417c64
Azure	efffff
Azure2	deecec
Azure3	bcc7c7

Color Name	Code
Azure4	7a7d7d
Beige	f5f3d7
Bisque	fde0bc
Bisque2	ead0ae
Bisque3	c7af92
Bisque4	816e59
Black	000000
BlanchedAlmond	fee8c6
Blue	0000ff
Blue1	1535ff
Blue2	1531ec
Blue3	1528c7
Blue4	151b7e
BlueViolet	7931df

The World Wide Web

Color Name	Code
Brown	980517
Brown1	f63526
Brown2	e42d17
Brown3	c22217
Burlywood1	fcce8e
Burlywood2	eabe83
Burlywood3	c6a06d
Burlywood4	806341
CadetBlue	578693
CadetBlue1	99f3ff
CadetBlue2	8ee2ec
CadetBlue3	77bfc7
CadetBlue4	4c787e
Chartreuse	8afb17
Chartreuse2	7fe817
Chartreuse3	6cc417
Chartreuse4	437c17
Chocolate	c85a17
Coral	f76541
Coral2	e55b3c
Coral3	c34a2c
Coral4	7e2817
CornflowerBlue	151b8d
Cornsilk	fff7d7
Cornsilk2	ece5c6
Cornsilk3	c8c2a7
Cornsilk4	817a68
Cyan	00ffff
Cyan1	57feff
Cyan2	50ebec
Cyan3	46c7c7
Cyan4	307d7e
DarkGoldenrod	af7817
DarkGoldenrod1	fbb117
DarkGoldenrod2	e8a317

Color Name	Code
DarkGoldenrod3	c58917
DarkGoldenrod4	7f5217
DarkGreen	254117
DarkKhaki	b7ad59
DarkOliveGreen	4a4117
DarkOliveGreen1	ccfb5d
DarkOliveGreen2	bce954
DarkOliveGreen3	a0c544
DarkOliveGreen4	667c26
DarkOrange	f88017
DarkOrange1	f87217
DarkOrange2	e56717
DarkOrange3	c35617
DarkOrange4	7e3117
DarkOrchid	7d1b7e
DarkOrchid1	b041ff
DarkOrchid2	a23bec
DarkOrchid3	8b31c7
DarkOrchid4	571b7e
DarkSalmon	e18b6b
DarkSeaGreen	8bb381
DarkSeaGreen1	c3fdb8
DarkSeaGreen2	b5eaaa
DarkSeaGreen3	99c68e
DarkSeaGreen4	617c58
DarkSlateBlue	2b3856
DarkSlateGray	25383c
DarkSlateGray1	9afeff
DarkSlateGray2	8eebec
DarkSlateGray3	78c7c7
DarkSlateGray4	4c7d7e
DarkTurquoise	3b9c9c
DarkViolet	842dce
DeepPink	f52887
DeepPink2	e4287c

HTML 3.2 Color Tables

Color Name	Code
DeepPink3	c12267
DeepPink4	7d053f
DeepSkyBlue	3bb9ff
DeepSkyBlue2	38acec
DeepSkyBlue3	3090c7
DeepSkyBlue4	25587e
DimGray	463e41
DodgerBlue	1589ff
DodgerBlue2	157dec
DodgerBlue3	1569c7
DodgerBlue4	153e7e
Firebrick	800517
Firebrick1	f62817
Firebrick2	e42217
Firebrick3	c11b17
FloralWhite	fff9ee
ForestGreen	4e9258
Gainsboro	d8d9d7
GhostWhite	f7f7ff
Gold	d4a017
Gold1	fdd017
Gold2	eac117
Gold3	c7a317
Gold4	806517
Goldenrod	edda74
Goldenrod1	fbb917
Goldenrod2	e9ab17
Goldenrod3	c68e17
Goldenrod4	805817
Gray	736f6e
Gray0	150517
Gray100	ffffff
Gray18	250517
Gray21	2b1b17
Gray23	302217

Color Name	Code
Gray24	302226
Gray25	342826
Gray26	34282c
Gray27	382d2c
Gray28	3b3131
Gray29	3e3535
Gray30	413839
Gray31	41383c
Gray32	463e3f
Gray34	4a4344
Gray35	4c4646
Gray36	4e4848
Gray37	504a4b
Gray38	544e4f
Gray39	565051
Gray40	595454
Gray41	5c5858
Gray42	5f5a59
Gray43	625d5d
Gray44	646060
Gray45	666362
Gray46	696565
Gray47	6d6968
Gray48	6e6a6b
Gray49	726e6d
Gray50	747170
Gray51	787473
Gray52	7a7777
Gray53	7c7979
Gray54	807d7c
Gray55	82807e
Gray56	858381
Gray57	878583
Gray58	8b8987
Gray59	8d8b89

The World Wide Web

Color Name	Code	Color Name	Code
Gray60	8f8e8d	Gray95	f0f1f0
Gray61	939190	Gray96	f4f4f3
Gray62	959492	Gray97	f6f6f5
Gray63	999795	Gray98	f9f9fa
Gray64	9a9998	Gray99	fbfbfb
Gray65	9e9c9b	Green	00ff00
Gray66	a09f9d	Green1	5ffb17
Gray67	a3a2a0	Green2	59e817
Gray68	a5a4a3	Green3	4cc417
Gray69	a9a8a6	Green4	347c17
Gray70	acaba9	GreenYellow	b1fb17
Gray71	aeadac	Honeydew	f0feee
Gray72	b1b1af	Honeydew2	deebdc
Gray73	b3b3b1	Honeydew3	bcc7b9
Gray74	b7b6b4	Honeydew4	7a7d74
Gray75	b9b8b6	HotPink	f660ab
Gray76	bcbbba	HotPink1	f665ab
Gray77	bebebc	HotPink2	e45e9d
Gray78	c1c1bf	HotPink3	c25283
Gray79	c3c4c2	HotPink4	7d2252
Gray80	c7c7c5	IndianRed	5e2217
Gray81	cacac9	IndianRed1	f75d59
Gray82	cccccb	IndianRed2	e55451
Gray83	d0cfcf	IndianRed3	c24641
Gray84	d2d2d1	IndianRed4	7e2217
Gray85	d5d5d4	Ivory	ffffee
Gray86	d7d7d7	Ivory2	ececdc
Gray87	dbdbd9	Ivory3	c9c7b9
Gray88	dddddc	Ivory4	817d74
Gray89	e0e0e0	Khaki	ada96e
Gray90	e2e3e1	Khaki1	fff380
Gray91	e5e6e4	Khaki2	ede275
Gray92	e8e9e8	Khaki3	c9be62
Gray93	ebebea	Khaki4	827839
Gray94	eeeeee	Lavender	e3e4fa

HTML 3.2 Color Tables

Color Name	Code
LavenderBlush	fdeef4
LavenderBlush2	ebdde2
LavenderBlush3	c8bbbe
LavenderBlush4	817679
LawnGreen	87f717
LemonChiffon	fff8c6
LemonChiffon2	ece5b6
LemonChiffon3	c9c299
LemonChiffon4	827b60
LightBlue	addfff
LightBlue1	bdedff
LightBlue2	afdcec
LightBlue3	95b9c7
LightBlue4	5e767e
LightCoral	e77471
LightCyan	e0ffff
LightCyan2	cfecec
LightCyan3	afc7c7
LightCyan4	717d7d
LightGoldenrod	ecd872
LightGoldenrod1	ffe87c
LightGoldenrod2	ecd672
LightGoldenrod3	c8b560
LightGoldenrod4	817339
LightGoldenrodYellow	faf8cc
LightPink	faafba
LightPink1	f9a7b0
LightPink2	e799a3
LightPink3	c48189
LightPink4	7f4e52
LightSalmon	f9966b
LightSalmon2	e78a61
LightSalmon3	c47451
LightSalmon4	7f462c
LightSeaGreen	3ea99f

Color Name	Code
LightSkyBlue	82cafa
LightSkyBlue2	a0cfec
LightSkyBlue3	87afc7
LightSkyBlue4	566d7e
LightSlateBlue	736aff
LightSlateGray	6d7b8d
LightSteelBlue	728fce
LightSteelBlue1	c6deff
LightSteelBlue2	b7ceec
LightSteelBlue3	9aadc7
LightSteelBlue4	646d7e
LightYellow	fffedc
LightYellow2	edebcb
LightYellow3	c9c7aa
LightYellow4	827d6b
LimeGreen	41a317
Linen	f9eee2
Magenta	ff00ff
Magenta1	f43eff
Magenta2	e238ec
Magenta3	c031c7
Maroon	810541
Maroon1	f535aa
Maroon2	e3319d
Maroon3	c12283
Maroon4	7d0552
MediumAquamarine	348781
MediumBlue	152dc6
MediumForestGreen	347235
MediumGoldenrod	ccb954
MediumOrchid	b048b5
MediumOrchid1	d462ff
MediumOrchid2	c45aec
MediumOrchid3	a74ac7
MediumOrchid4	6a287e

The World Wide Web

Color Name	Code
MediumPurple	8467d7
MediumPurple1	9e7bff
MediumPurple2	9172ec
MediumPurple3	7a5dc7
MediumPurple4	4e387e
MediumSeaGreen	306754
MediumSlateBlue	5e5a80
MediumSpringGreen	348017
MediumTurquoise	48cccd
MediumVioletRed	ca226b
MidnightBlue	151b54
MintCream	f5fff9
MistyRose	fde1dd
MistyRose2	ead0cc
MistyRose3	c6afac
MistyRose4	806f6c
Moccasin	fde0ac
NavajoWhite	fddaa3
NavajoWhite2	eac995
NavajoWhite3	c7aa7d
NavajoWhite4	806a4b
Navy	150567
OldLace	fcf3e2
OliveDrab	658017
OliveDrab1	c3fb17
OliveDrab2	b5e917
OliveDrab3	99c517
OliveDrab4	617c17
Orange	f87a17
Orange1	fa9b17
Orange2	e78e17
Orange3	c57717
Orange4	7f4817
OrangeRed	f63817
OrangeRed2	e43117

Color Name	Code
OrangeRed3	c22817
OrangeRed4	7e0517
Orchid	e57ded
Orchid1	f67dfa
Orchid2	e473e7
Orchid3	c160c3
Orchid4	7d387c
PaleGoldenrod	ede49e
PaleGreen	79d867
PaleGreen1	a0fc8d
PaleGreen2	94e981
PaleGreen3	7dc56c
PaleGreen4	4e7c41
PaleTurquoise	aeebec
PaleTurquoise1	bcfeff
PaleTurquoise2	adebec
PaleTurquoise3	92c7c7
PaleTurquoise4	5e7d7e
PaleVioletRed	d16587
PaleVioletRed1	f778a1
PaleVioletRed2	e56e94
PaleVioletRed3	c25a7c
PaleVioletRed4	7e354d
PapayaWhip	feeccf
PeachPuff	fcd5b0
PeachPuff2	eac5a3
PeachPuff3	c6a688
PeachPuff4	806752
Peru	c57726
Pink	faafbe
Pink2	e7a1b0
Pink3	c48793
Pink4	7f525d
Plum	b93b8f
Plum1	f9b7ff

HTML 3.2 Color Tables

Color Name	Code
Plum2	e6a9ec
Plum3	c38ec7
Plum4	7e587e
PowderBlue	addce3
Purple	8e35ef
Purple1	893bff
Purple2	7f38ec
Purple3	6c2dc7
Purple4	461b7e
Red	ff0000
Red1	f62217
Red2	e41b17
RosyBrown	b38481
RosyBrown1	fbbbb9
RosyBrown2	e8adaa
RosyBrown3	c5908e
RosyBrown4	7f5a58
RoyalBlue	2b60de
RoyalBlue1	306eff
RoyalBlue2	2b65ec
RoyalBlue3	2554c7
RoyalBlue4	15317e
Salmon1	f88158
Salmon2	e67451
Salmon3	c36241
Salmon4	7e3817
SandyBrown	ee9a4d
SeaGreen	4e8975
SeaGreen1	6afb92
SeaGreen2	64e986
SeaGreen3	54c571
SeaGreen4	387c44
Seashell	fef3eb
Seashell2	ebe2d9
Seashell3	c8bfb6

Color Name	Code
Seashell4	817873
Sienna	8a4117
Sienna1	f87431
Sienna2	e66c2c
Sienna3	c35817
Sienna4	7e3517
SkyBlue	6698ff
SkyBlue1	82caff
SkyBlue2	79baec
SkyBlue3	659ec7
SkyBlue4	41627e
SlateBlue	737ca1
SlateBlue1	7369ff
SlateBlue2	6960ec
SlateBlue3	574ec7
SlateBlue4	342d7e
SlateGray	657383
SlateGray1	c2dfff
SlateGray2	b4cfec
SlateGray3	98afc7
SlateGray4	616d7e
Snow	fff9fa
Snow2	ece7e6
Snow3	c8c4c2
Snow4	817c7b
SpringGreen	4aa02c
SpringGreen1	5efb6e
SpringGreen2	57e964
SpringGreen3	4cc552
SpringGreen4	347c2c
SteelBlue	4863a0
SteelBlue1	5cb3ff
SteelBlue2	56a5ec
SteelBlue3	488ac7
SteelBlue4	2b547e

The World Wide Web

Color Name	Code
Tan	d8af79
Tan1	fa9b3c
Tan2	e78e35
Thistle	d2b9d3
Thistle1	fcdfff
Thistle2	e9cfec
Thistle3	c6aec7
Thistle4	806d7e
Tomato	f75431
Tomato2	e54c2c
Tomato3	c23e17
Turquoise	43c6db
Turquoise1	52f3ff
Turquoise2	4ee2ec
Turquoise3	43bfc7

Color Name	Code
Turquoise4	30787e
Violet	8d38c9
VioletRed	e9358a
VioletRed1	f6358a
VioletRed2	e4317f
VioletRed3	c12869
VioletRed4	7d0541
Wheat	f3daa9
Wheat1	fee4b1
Wheat2	ebd3a3
Wheat3	c8b189
Wheat4	816f54
Yellow	ffff00
Yellow1	fffc17
YellowGreen	52d017

HTML CODED CHARACTERS

Code	Description
&#09;	Horizontal tab
&#10:	Line feed
&#13;	Carriage Return
&#32;	Space
&#33;	Exclamation mark
&#34;	Quotation mark
&#35;	Number sign
&#36;	Dollar sign
&#37;	Percent sign
&#38;	Ampersand
&#39;	Apostrophe
&#40;	Left parenthesis
&#41;	Right parenthesis
&#42;	Asterisk
&#43;	Plus sign
&#44;	Comma
&#45;	Hyphen
&#46;	Period (fullstop)
&#47;	Solidus (slash)
0 - 9	Digits 0–9
&#58;	Colon
&#59;	Semi-colon
&#60;	Less than
&#61;	Equals sign
&#62;	Greater than
&#63;	Question mark
&#64;	Commercial at
A - Z	Letters A–Z (upper case)
&#91;	Left square bracket
&#92;	Reverse solidus (backslash)
&#93;	Right square bracket
&#94;	Caret
&#95;	Horizontal bar (underscore)
&#96;	Acute accent
a–z	Letters a–z (lower case)
&#123;	Left curly brace

Code	Description
|	Vertical bar
&#125;	Right curly brace
&#126;	Tilde
	Non-breaking Space
&#161;	Inverted exclamation
&#162;	Cent sign
&#163;	Pound sterling
&#164;	General currency sign
&#165;	Yen sign
&#166;	Broken vertical bar
&#167;	Section sign
&#168;	Umlaut (diaeresis)
&#169;	Copyright
&#170;	Feminine ordinal
&#171;	Left angle quote, guillemet left
&#172;	Not sign
&#173;	Soft hyphen
&#174;	Registered trademark
&#175;	Macron accent
&#176;	Degree sign
&#177;	Plus or minus
&#178;	Superscript two
&#179;	Superscript three
&#180;	Acute accent
&#181;	Micro sign
&#182;	Paragraph sign
&#183;	Middle dot
&#184;	Cedilla
&#185;	Superscript one
&#186;	Masculine ordinal
&#187;	Right angle quote, guillemet right
&#188;	Fraction one-fourth
&#189;	Fraction one-half
&#190;	Fraction three-fourths
&#191;	Inverted question mark
&#192;	Capital A, grave accent
&#193;	Capital A, acute accent
&#194;	Capital A, circumflex accent
&#195;	Capital A, tilde

HTML Coded Characters

Code	Description
&#196;	Capital A, diaeresis or umlaut mark
&#197;	Capital A, ring
&#198;	Capital AE diphthong (ligature)
&#199;	Capital C, cedilla
&#200;	Capital E, grave accent
&#201;	Capital E, acute accent
&#202;	Capital E, circumflex accent
&#203;	Capital E, diaeresis or umlaut mark
&#204;	Capital I, grave accent
&#205;	Capital I, acute accent
&#206;	Capital I, circumflex accent
&#207;	Capital I, diaeresis or umlaut mark
&#208;	Capital Eth, Icelandic
&#209;	Capital N, tilde
&#210;	Capital O, grave accent
&#211;	Capital O, acute accent
&#212;	Capital O, circumflex accent
&#213;	Capital O, tilde
&#214;	Capital O, diaeresis or umlaut mark
&#215;	Multiply sign
&#216;	Capital O, slash
&#217;	Capital U, grave accent
&#218;	Capital U, acute accent
&#219;	Capital U, circumflex accent
&#220;	Capital U, diaeresis or umlaut mark
&#221;	Capital Y, acute accent
&#222;	Capital THORN, Icelandic
&#223;	Small sharp s, German (sz ligature)
&#224;	Small a, grave accent
&#225;	Small a, acute accent
&#226;	Small a, circumflex accent
&#227;	Small a, tilde
&#228;	Small a, diaeresis or umlaut mark
&#229;	Small a, ring
&#230;	Small ae diphthong (ligature)
&#231;	Small c, cedilla
&#232;	Small e, grave accent
&#233;	Small e, acute accent
&#234;	Small e, circumflex accent

Code	Description
&#235;	Small e, diaeresis or umlaut mark
&#236;	Small i, grave accent
&#237;	Small i, acute accent
&#238;	Small i, circumflex accent
&#239;	Small i, diaeresis or umlaut mark
&#240;	Small eth, Icelandic
&#241;	Small n, tilde
&#242;	Small o, grave accent
&#243;	Small o, acute accent
&#244;	Small o, circumflex accent
&#245;	Small o, tilde
&#246;	Small o, diaeresis or umlaut mark
&#247;	Division sign
&#248;	Small o, slash
&#249;	Small u, grave accent
&#250;	Small u, acute accent
&#251;	Small u, circumflex accent
&#252;	Small u, diaeresis or umlaut mark
&#253;	Small y, acute accent
&#254;	Small thorn, Icelandic
&#255;	Small y, diaeresis or umlaut mark

COMMON GATEWAY INTERFACE (CGI)

OVERVIEW

The Common Gateway Interface (CGI) is a standard for interfacing external applications with information servers, such as HTTP or Web servers. A plain HTML document that a Web browser retrieves is static, meaning it exists in a constant state—a text file that does not change. A CGI program, on the other hand, is executed in real-time so that it can output dynamic information. An obvious use for CGI is to connect a database to the World Wide Web, allowing users anywhere to query it. A CGI program may be created to send information to the database engine, receive the results back, and display them to the client. This is an example of a gateway, one of the original purposes for CGI.

The database example is a simple idea but often difficult to implement. There is no limit regarding what might be connected to the Web. Efficient CGI programs respond quickly and do not keep the user waiting too long for a response.

RECEIVING INFORMATION FROM THE SERVER

Each time a client requests the URL corresponding to your CGI program, the server will execute it in real-time. The output of your program will go to the client. A common misconception about CGI is that you can send command-line options and arguments to your program, such as:

command% myprog -qa blorf

CGI uses the command line for other purposes, so this procedure is not directly possible. Instead, CGI uses environment variables to send your program its parameters. The two major environment variables you will use for this purpose are QUERY_STRING and PATH_INFO.

QUERY_STRING

QUERY_STRING is defined as anything that follows the first ? in the URL. This information can be added by an ISINDEX document or by an HTML form (with the GET action). It can also be manually embedded into an HTML anchor that references your gateway. This string will usually be an information query (i.e., what the user wants to search for in the Archie databases), or the encoded results of your feedback GET form.

This string is encoded in the standard URL format of changing spaces to +, and encoding special characters with %xx hexadecimal encoding. You will need to decode it in order to use it.

If your gateway is not decoding results from a FORM, you will get the query string decoded for you onto the command line. This means that each word of the query string will be in a different section of ARGV. For example, the query string "forms rule" would be given to your program with argv[1]="forms" and argv[2]="rule". If you choose to use this, you don't need to do processing on the data before using it.

PATH_INFO

CGI allows for extra information to be embedded in the URL for your gateway which can be used to transmit extra context-specific information to the scripts. This information is usually made available as "extra" information after the path of your gateway in the URL. This information is not encoded by the server in any way.

The most useful example of **PATH_INFO** is transmitting file locations to the CGI program. To illustrate this, let's say I have a CGI program on my server called **/cgi-bin/foobar** that can process files residing in the DocumentRoot of the server. I need to be able to tell foobar which file to process. By including extra path information to the end of the URL, foobar will know the location of the document relative to the DocumentRoot via the **PATH_INFO** environment variable, or the actual path to the document via the **PATH_TRANSLATED** environment variable, which the server generates for you.

RETURNING A DOCUMENT TO THE CLIENT

Probably the most common error in CGI programs is failure to format the output properly so the server can understand it. CGI programs can return a myriad of document types. They can send back an image to the client, an HTML document, a plain text document, or an audio clip. They can also return references to other documents. The client must know what kind of document you're sending it so it can present it accordingly. In order for the client to know this, your CGI program must tell the server what type of document it is returning.

To tell the server what kind of document you are sending back (a full document or a reference to one), you must place a short header on your output. This header is

ASCII text, consisting of lines separated by either line feeds or carriage returns (or both) followed by a single blank line. The output body follows in the native format.

A Full Document with a Corresponding MIME Type

In this case, you must tell the server what kind of document you will be outputting via a MIME type. Common MIME types are things such as **text/html** for HTML, and **text/plain** for straight ASCII text.

For example, to send back HTML to the client, your output should read:

Content-type: text/html

<HTML><HEAD>
<TITLE>output of HTML from CGI script</TITLE>
</HEAD><BODY>
<H1>Sample output</H1>
What do you think of <STRONG>this?</STRONG>
</BODY></HTML>

A Reference to Another Document

Instead of outputting the document, you can tell the browser where to get the new one or have the server automatically output the new one for you.

You may wish to reference a file on your Gopher server. In this case, you should know the full URL of the item you want to reference and output these descriptors:

Content-type: text/html
Location: gopher://httprules.foobar.org/0

<HTML><HEAD>
<TITLE>Sorry...it moved</TITLE>
</HEAD><BODY>
<H1>Go to gopher instead</H1>
Now available at
<A HREF="gopher://httprules.foobar.org/0">a new location</A> on our gopher server.
</BODY></HTML>

The World Wide Web

Most current browsers are smart enough to automatically send you to the new document without ever seeing the above descriptor. If you choose not to output to the above HTML, NCSA HTTPd will output a default version for you that will support older browsers.

If you want to reference another file (not protected by access authentication) on your own server, you don't have to do nearly as much work. Just output a partial (virtual) URL, such as the following:

> Location: /dir1/dir2/myfile.html

The server will act as if the client had not requested your script, but instead requested http://yourserver/dir1/dir2/myfile.html. It will take care of the details, such as looking up the file type and sending the appropriate headers. Be sure to output the second blank line.

If you do want to reference a document that is protected by access authentication, you will need to have a full URL in the Location: since the client and the server need to retransact to establish that, you access the referenced document.

Advanced Usage

If you would like to output headers such as Expires or Content-encoding, you may do so if your server is compatible with CGI/1.1. Output them along with Location or Content-type and they will be sent back to the client.

Specifics

Since a CGI program is executable, it is basically the equivalent of letting the world run a program on your system, which is not safe. There are some security precautions to implement when using CGI programs. The one that will probably affect Web users most is the fact that CGI programs need to reside in a special directory so that the Web executes the program rather than just displaying it to the browser. This directory is often under direct control of the Webmaster, prohibiting the average user from creating CGI programs. There are other ways to allow access to CGI scripts, but it is up to your Webmaster to set these up for you. At this point, you may want to contact him or her about the feasibility of allowing CGI access.

If you have a version of the NCSA HTTPd server distribution, you will see a directory called /cgi-bin. This is the special directory mentioned above where all of your

Common Gateway Interface (CGI)

CGI programs currently reside. A CGI program can be written in any language that allows it to be executed on the system, such as C/C++, Fortran, PERL, TCL, any UNIX shell, Visual Basic, or AppleScript.

You may use any program that is available on your system. If you use a programming language like C or Fortran, you must compile the program before it will run. If you look in the /cgi-src directory that came with the server distribution, you will find the source code for some of the CGI programs in the /cgi-bin directory. If, however, you use one of the scripting languages instead, such as PERL, TCL, or a UNIX shell, the script itself only needs to reside in the /cgi-bin directory since no associated source code exists. Many people prefer to write CGI scripts instead of programs since they are easier to debug, modify, and maintain than a typical compiled program.

SECURITY ISSUES

Anytime a program is interacting with a networked client, there is the possibility of that client attacking the program to gain unauthorized access. Even the most innocent looking script can be dangerous to the integrity of your system. With that in mind, here are some guidelines to ensure that your program does not come under attack.

BEWARE OF THE "EVAL" STATEMENT

Languages like PERL and the Bourne shell provide an eval command that allows you to construct a string and have the interpreter execute that string. This can be dangerous. Observe the following statement in the Bourne shell:

```
eval 'echo $QUERY_STRING | awk 'BEGIN{RS="&"} {printf "QS_%s\n",$1}' '
```

This code takes the query string and converts it into a set of variable set commands. Unfortunately, this script can be attacked by sending it a query string which starts with a ;. This is a dangerous, yet innocent-looking script.

DO NOT TRUST THE CLIENT TO DO ANYTHING

A well-behaved client will escape any characters that have special meaning to the Bourne shell in a query string and thus avoid problems with your script misinterpreting the characters. A mischievous client may use special characters to confuse your script and gain unauthorized access.

Be Careful with Popen and System

If you use any data from the client to construct a command line for a call to popen() or system(), place backslashes before characters that have special meaning to the Bourne shell before calling the function. This can be achieved with a short C function.

Turn Off Server-Side Includes

If your server is unfortunate enough to support server-side includes, turn them off for your script directories. The server-side includes can be abused by clients that prey on scripts that directly output things they have sent.

CGI Environment Variables

In order to pass data about the information request from the server to the script, the server uses command line arguments as well as environment variables. These environment variables are set when the server executes the gateway program.

Specification

These environment variables are not request-specific and are set for all requests:

> SERVER_SOFTWARE
>> The name and version of the information server software answering the request (and running the gateway). Format: name/version.
>
> SERVER_NAME
>> The server's host name, DNS alias, or IP address as it would appear in self-referencing URLs.
>
> GATEWAY_INTERFACE
>> The revision of the CGI specification to which this server complies. Format: CGI/revision

The following environment variables are specific to the request being fulfilled by the gateway program:

> SERVER_PROTOCOL
>> The name and revision of the information protocol this request came in with. Format: protocol/revision.

SERVER_PORT
   The port number to which the request was sent.

REQUEST_METHOD
   The method with which the request was made. For HTTP, this is "GET", "HEAD", "POST", etc.

PATH_INFO
   The extra path data, as given by the client. Scripts can be accessed by their virtual path name, followed by extra data at the end of this path. The extra data is sent as **PATH_INFO**. This data should be decoded by the server if it comes from a URL before it is passed to the CGI script.

PATH_TRANSLATED
   The server provides a translated version of **PATH_INFO**, which takes the path and does any virtual-to-physical mapping to it.

SCRIPT_NAME
   A virtual path to the executed script, used for self-referencing URLs.

QUERY_STRING
   The information which follows the ? in the URL that referenced this script. This is the query information. It should not be decoded in any fashion. This variable should always be set when there is query information, regardless of command line decoding.

REMOTE_HOST
   The host name making the request. If the server does not have this information, it should set **REMOTE_ADDR** and leave this unset.

REMOTE_ADDR
   The IP address of the remote host making the request.

AUTH_TYPE
   If the server supports user authentication and the script is protected, this protocol-specific authentication method is used to validate a user.

REMOTE_USER
   If the server supports user authentication and the script is protected, this is the user authenticated name.

REMOTE_IDENT
> If the HTTP server supports RFC 931 identification, this variable will be set to the remote user name retrieved from the server. Usage of this variable should be limited to logging.

CONTENT_TYPE
> For queries which have attached information, such as **HTTP POST** and **PUT**, this is the content type of the data.

CONTENT_LENGTH
> The length of the said content as given by the client.

In addition to these, the header lines received from the client are placed into the environment with the prefix **HTTP_** followed by the header name. Any - characters in the header name are changed to _ characters. The server may exclude any headers it has processed, such as Authorization, Content-type, and Content-length, if including them would exceed any system environment limits. An example of this is the **HTTP_ACCEPT** variable defined in CGI/1.0. Another example is the header User-Agent.

HTTP_ACCEPT
> The MIME types, which the client will accept, as given by HTTP headers. Other protocols may need to get this information elsewhere. Each item in this list should be separated by commas as per the HTTP spec. Format: type/subtype, type/subtype

HTTP_USER_AGENT
> The browser the client is using to send the request. General format: software/version library/version

CGI COMMAND LINE OPTIONS

SPECIFICATION

The command line is used only in the case of an ISINDEX query, not in the case of an HTML form or any undefined query type. The server should search the query information (the **QUERY_STRING** environment variable) for a non-encoded = character to determine if the command line is to be used; if it finds one, the command line is not to be used. This trusts the clients to encode the = sign in ISINDEX queries, a practice considered safe at the time of the design of this specification.

For example, use the finger script and the ISINDEX interface to look up "httpd". You will see that the script will call itself with /cgi-bin/finger?httpd and will execute "finger httpd" on the command line and output the results to you.

If the server finds a "=" in the QUERY_STRING, the command line will not be used and no decoding will be performed. The query then remains intact for processing by an appropriate FORM submission decoder. Again, as an example, use this hyperlink to submit "httpd=name" to the finger script. Since this QUERY_STRING contained an unencoded "=", nothing was decoded, the script didn't know it was being submitted a valid query, and it gave you the default finger form.

If the server finds that it cannot send the string due to internal limitations, it should include NO command line information and provide the non-decoded query information in the environment variable QUERY_STRING.

Examples of command line use are better demonstrated than explained. For these examples, pay attention to the script output that explains what argc and argv are.

CGI Script Input

Specification

For requests that have information attached after the header, such as HTTP POST or PUT, the information will be sent to the script on stdin.

The server will send CONTENT_LENGTH bytes on this file descriptor. Remember that the server will give the CONTENT_TYPE of the data as well. The server is in no way obligated to send end-of-file after the script reads CONTENT_LENGTH bytes.

Let's take a form with METHOD="POST" as an example. Let's say the form results are 7 bytes encoded and look like a=b&b=c.

In this case, the server will set CONTENT_LENGTH to 7 and CONTENT_TYPE to application/x-www-form-urlencoded. The first byte on the script's standard input will be "a", followed by the rest of the encoded string.

CGI Script Output

The script sends its output to stdout. This output can be either a document generated by the script, or instructions to the server for retrieving the desired output.

Script Naming Conventions

Scripts produce output that is interpreted and sent back to the client. An advantage of this is that the scripts do not need to send a full HTTP/1.0 header for every request.

Some scripts may want to avoid the extra overhead of the server parsing their output and talk directly to the client. In order to distinguish these scripts from the other scripts, CGI requires that the script name begin with nph- if a script does not want the server to parse its header. In this case, it is the script's responsibility to return a valid HTTP/1.0 (or HTTP/0.9) response to the client.

Parsed Headers

The output of scripts begins with a small header. The header consists of text lines, in the same format as an HTTP header, terminated by a line with a linefeed or a CR/LF.

Any headers that are not server directives are sent directly back to the client. Currently, this specification defines three server directives:

> Content-type
> > This is the MIME type of the document you are returning.
>
> Location
> > This is used to specify to the server that you are returning a reference to a document rather than an actual document.

If the argument to this is a URL, the server will issue a redirect to the client. If the argument to this is a virtual path, the server will retrieve the document specified as if the client had requested that document originally. ? directives will work in here, but # directives must be redirected back to the client.

> Status
> > This is used to give the server an HTTP/1.0 status line to send to the client. The format is nnn xxxxx, where nnn is the 3-digit status code and xxxxx is the reason string, such as "Forbidden."

Examples

Let's say I have a fromgratz-to-HTML converter. When my converter is done, it will output the following on stdout. The lines that begin and end with three dashes (—) are for illustration and would not be output. Note the blank line after Content-type.

— start of output —
Content-type: text/html

— end of output —

Now, let's say I have a script which, in certain instances, wants to return the document /path/doc.txt from this server just as if the user had requested http://server:port/path/doc.txt to begin with. In this case, the script would output:

— start of output —
Location: /path/doc.txt

— end of output —

The server would then perform the request and send it to the client.

Let's say I have a script that wants to reference our Gopher server. In this case, if the script wanted to refer the user to **gopher://gopher.ncsa.uiuc.edu/**, it would output:

— start of output —
Location: gopher://gopher.ncsa.uiuc.edu/

— end of output —

I have a script that wants to talk to the client directly. Here, if the script is referenced with SERVER_PROTOCOL of HTTP/1.0, it would output this HTTP/1.0 response:

— start of output —
HTTP/1.0 200 OK
Server: NCSA/1.0a6
Content-type: text/plain

This is a plain text document generated on the fly for demonstration.

— end of output —

Decoding Forms with CGI

If you are unfamiliar with forms or how to write them, look at this guide to fill-out forms. They're plain HTML and not complicated, but decoding them is a different story.

Getting the Form Data

As you know, there are two methods that can be used to access your forms. These methods are GET and POST. Depending on which method you used, you will receive the encoded results of the form in a different way.

> The GET method
> If your form has METHOD="GET" in its FORM tag, your CGI program will receive the encoded form input in the environment variable QUERY_STRING.
>
> The POST method
> If your form has METHOD="POST" in its FORM tag, your CGI program will receive the encoded form input on stdin. The server will not send you an EOF on the end of the data. Instead, you should use the environment variable CONTENT_LENGTH to determine how much data you should read from stdin.

How to Decode the Form Data

When you write a form, each of your input items has a NAME tag. When the user places information in these items in the form, that information is encoded into the form data. The value that each of the input items is given by the user is called the value.

Form data is a stream of name=value pairs separated by the & character. Each name=value pair is URL encoded, so spaces are changed into plusses and some characters are encoded into hexadecimal. Because others have been presented with this problem as well, there are already a number of programs that will do this decoding for you. Some of these resources are listed below:

The Bourne Shell: The AA Archie gateway. Contains calls to sed and awk that convert a GET form data string into separate environment variables.

The default scripts for NCSA HTTP: These are C routines and example programs you can use to translate the query string into a group of structures.

PERL: The PERL CGI-lib. This package contains a group of useful PERL routines to decode forms.

PERL5: CGI.pm. A perl5 library for handling forms in CGI scripts. With a handful of calls, you can parse CGI queries, create forms, and maintain the state of the buttons on the form from invocation to invocation.

TCL: TCL argument processor. This is a set of TCL routines to retrieve form data and place it into TCL variables.

The basic procedure is to split the data by the ampersands. Then, for each name=value pair you get for this, you should URL decode the name, then the value, and then do what you like with them.

This document was adapted from *CGI—Common Gateway Interface*, which was created by the National Center for Supercomputing. It was printed with permission from the Board of Trustees of the University of Illinois. Source URL: http://hoohoo.ncsa.uiuc.edu/cgi/.

Recommended Reading

Books About Multimedia

Agnew, Palmer W. and Anne S. Kellerman. *Distributed Multimedia: Technologies, Applications, and Opportunities in the Digital Information Industry.* New York: ACM Press with Addison-Wesley, 1996.

Andleigh, Prabhat K. and Kiran Thakrar. *Multimedia Systems Design.* Upper Saddle River, NJ: Prentice-Hall, Inc., 1995.

Apple Computer. *Multimedia Demystified: A Guide to the World of Multimedia from Apple Computer, Inc.* New York: Random House, 1994.

Ball, Larry L. *Multimedia Network Integration and Management.* New York: McGraw-Hill, 1996.

Burger, Jeff. *The Desktop Multimedia Bible.* Reading, MA: Addison-Wesley, 1992.

Cotton, Bob and Richard Oliver. *Understanding Hypermedia: From Multimedia to Virtual Reality.* London: Phaidon Press, 1992.

D'Alleyrand, Marc. *Networks and Imaging Systems in a Windowed Environment.* New York: Bantam, 1993.

England, Elaine and Andrew Finney. *Managing Multimedia.* Reading, MA: Addison-Wesley, 1996.

Fluckiger, Francois. *Understanding Networked Multimedia.* New York and London: Prentice-Hall, 1995.

Frater, Harald and Dirk Paulissen. *Multimedia Mania.* Grand Rapids, MI: Abacus, 1992.

Goodwin, Michael. *Making Multimedia Work.* Foster City, CA: IDG Books Worldwide, 1995.

Harrel, William D. *The Multimedia Authoring Workshop.* San Francisco: Sybex, 1996.

Heath, Steve. *Multimedia and Communications Technology.* Oxford and Boston: Focal Press, 1996.

Hill, Margo and Cheryl Holzaepfel, eds. *Careers in Multimedia* (Vivid Media Series). Emeryville, CA: Ziff-Davis Press, 1995.

Holsinger, Erik. *How Multimedia Works.* Emeryville, CA: Ziff-Davis Press, 1994.

Jennings, Roger. *Discover Windows 3.1 Multimedia.* Carmel, IN: Que, 1992.

Jerram, Peter and Michael Gosney. *Multimedia Power Tools.* New York: Random House Electronic Publishing, 1993; 2nd edition, 1995.

Johnson, Scott. *Electronic Publishing Construction Kit: Creating Multimedia for Disk, CD-ROM, and the Internet.* New York: John Wiley and Sons, 1996.

Josephson, Hal and Trisha Gorman. *Careers in Multimedia: Roles and Resources.* Belmont, CA: Integrated Media Group, 1996.

Lopuck, Lisa. *Designing Multimedia: A Visual Guide to Multimedia and Online Graphic Design.* Berkeley, CA: Peachpit Press, 1996.

McCormick, John A. *Create Your Own Multimedia System.* New York and London: Windcrest/McGraw-Hill, 1994.

Microsoft Press. *Microsoft Windows Multimedia Authoring and Tools Guide.* Redmond, WA: Microsoft Press, 1991.

Rosch, Winn L. *The Winn L. Rosch Multimedia Bible.* Indianapolis: Sams Publishing, 1995.

Shaddock, Philip. *Multimedia Creations: Hands-On Workshop for Exploring Animation and Sound.* Corte Madera, CA: Waite Group Press, 1992.

Skibbe, L. J., Susan Hafemeister, and Angela M. Chesnut. *Optimizing Your Multimedia PC.* Foster City, CA: IDG Books Worldwide, 1995.

Stanek, William R., and Lee Purcell. *Electronic Publishing Unleashed.* Indianapolis: Sams Publishing, 1995.

Sumner, Daniel H. *Windows 95 Multimedia Programming*. New York: M&T Books, 1995.

Varchol, Douglas J. *The Multimedia Scriptwriting Workshop*. San Francisco: Sybex, 1996.

Vaughan, Tay. *Multimedia: Making It Work*. Berkeley, CA: Osborne McGraw-Hill, 1993; 3rd edition, 1996.

Wodaski, Ron. *Multimedia Madness*. Carmel, IN: Sams Publishing, 1992; 2nd edition, 1994.

Yager, Thomas. *Multimedia Production Handbook for the PC, Macintosh and Amiga*. Boston: Academic Press, 1993.

Yavelow, Christopher. *Macworld Music & Sound Bible*. San Mateo, CA: IDG Books, 1992.

DICTIONARIES OF COMPUTER-RELATED TERMS

Covington, Michael and Douglas Downing. *Dictionary of Computer Terms*. Woodbury, NY: Barron's, 1986; 5th edition, as *Dictionary of Computer and Internet Terms*. Hauppauge, NY: Barron's, 1996.

Freedman, Alan. *The Computer Glossary: The Complete Illustrated Dictionary*. 7th edition. New York: AMACOM, 1995.

Hordeski, Michael F. *The McGraw-Hill Illustrated Dictionary of Personal Computers*. 4th edition. New York: McGraw-Hill, 1995.

Latham, Roy. *The Dictionary of Computer Graphics Technology and Applications*. New York: Springer-Verlag, 1991.

Margolis, Philip E. *Random House Personal Computer Dictionary*. New York: Random House, 1991; 2nd edition, 1996.

McDaniel, George, ed. *IBM Dictionary of Computing*. New York: McGraw-Hill, 1994.

Microsoft Press. *Microsoft Press Computer Dictionary*. Redmond, WA and London: Microsoft Press, 1991; 3rd edition, Bellevue, WA: Microsoft Press, 1997.

Nader, Jonar C. *Prentice Hall's Illustrated Dictionary of Computing*. New York: Prentice-Hall, 1992; 2nd edition, New York and Sydney: Prentice-Hall, 1995.

Newton, Harry. *Newton's Telecom Dictionary*. 12th edition. New York: Flatiron, 1997.

Phelps, Martha F. and Ann Marie Menting. *Dictionary of Computer Words*. Boston: Houghton Mifflin, 1993; revised edition, 1995.

Princeton Language Institute. *21st Century Dictionary of Computer Terms*. New York: Laurel, 1994.

Sleurink, Hans. *The Multimedia Dictionary*. London: Academic Press, 1995.

South, David W., ed. *The Computer & Information Science & Technology Abbreviations & Acronyms Dictionary*. Boca Raton, FL: CRC Press, 1994.

DICTIONARIES PUBLISHED BY TECHNICAL STANDARDS COMMITTEES

American National Standards Institute. *American National Standard Dictionary for Information Systems*. New York: ANSI, 1992. (11 West 42nd St., New York, NY 10036)

Electronic Industries Association. *Fiber Optic Connector Terminology*. Washington, DC: EIA, 1995. (2001 Pennsylvania Avenue, N.W., Washington, DC 20006)

International Organization for Standardization/International Electrotechnical Commission, JTC1. *Information Technology Vocabulary* and the ISO/AFNOR *Dictionary of Computer Science* (ISO, Case Postale 56, CH-1211 Geneve 20, Switzerland)

DIRECTORIES

International Communications Industries Association. *Directory of Multimedia Equipment, Software & Services*. Fairfax, VA: ICIA, 1992; 3rd edition, 1994.

Nicholls, Paul T. *CD-ROM Buyer's Guide & Handbook: The Definitive Reference for CD-ROM Users*. 3rd edition. Wilton, CT: Eight Bit Books, 1993.

Rega, Regina and Matthew Finlay. *CD-ROMs in Print 1994: An International Guide to CD-ROM, Multimedia and Electronic Book Products.* Westport, CT: Mecklermedia, 1994.

Fort, Clancy, Jon Samsel, and Wendy Lewis, eds. *The Multimedia Directory.* 6th edition. San Francisco: Carronade Group, 1996. (Published twice yearly. CD-ROM version available.)

CD-ROM Production

Boden, Larry. *Mastering CD ROM Technology.* New York, John Wiley and Sons, 1995.

Caffarelli, Fabrizio and Deirdré Straughan. *Publish Yourself on CD-ROM: Mastering CDs for Multimedia.* New York: Random House Electronic Publishing, 1992.

Nadeau, Michael. *The Byte Guide to CD-ROM.* New York and Berkeley, CA: Osborne McGraw-Hill, 1994; 2nd edition, Berkeley: Osborne McGraw-Hill, 1995.

Sherman, Chris. *CD ROM Handbook.* New York: McGraw-Hill, 1988; 2nd edition, 1994.

Digital Video Production

Azarmsa, Reza. *Multimedia: Interactive Video Production.* Belmont, CA: Integrated Media Group, 1996.

Bunzel, Mark and Sandra Morris. *Multimedia Applications Development: Using DVI Technology.* New York: McGraw-Hill, 1992; 2nd edition, 1994.

Holsinger, Erik. *MacWEEK Guide to Desktop Video.* Emeryville, CA: Ziff-Davis Press, 1993.

Jack, Keith. *Video Demystified: A Handbook for the Digital Engineer.* Solano Beach, CA: HighText, 1993; 2nd edition, 1996.

Johnson, Nels, with Fred Gault and Mark Florence. *How to Digitize Video.* New York: John Wiley and Sons, 1994.

Ohanian, Thomas. *Digital Nonlinear Editing: New Approaches to Editing Film and Video.* Boston: Focal Press, 1993.

Ozer, Jan. *Publishing Digital Video*. 2nd edition, Boston: AP Professional Press, 1997.

Whitver, Kathryn Shaw. *The Digital Videomaker's Guide*. Studio City, CA: Michael Wiese Productions, 1995.

Wodaski, Ron. *PC Video Madness!* Carmel, IN: Sams Publishing, 1993.

QUICKTIME

Apple Computer. *Inside Macintosh: QuickTime Components*. Reading, MA: Addison-Wesley, 1993.

Borrell, Jerry. *Mastering the World of QuickTime*. New York: Random House Electronic Publishing, 1993.

STANDARDS

Cargill, Carl F. *Information Technology Standardization: Theory, Process, and Organizations*. Bedford, MA: Digital Press, 1989.

Cargill, Carl F., ed. *StandardView*. Mountain View, CA: Sun Microsystems. (An ACM publication about computer-related standardization issues.)

Taylor, Dave. *Global Software: Developing Applications for the International Market*. New York: Springer-Verlag, 1992.

LEGAL ISSUES

Dettig, Ronal. *Intellectual Property in the Information Age*. Boulder, CO: Westview, 1996.

Radcliffe, Mark F. and Dianne Brinson. *Multimedia Law and Business Handbook*. Menlo Park, CA: Ladera Press, 1996.

Smedinghoff, Thomas J. *The Software Publishers Association Legal Guide to Multimedia*. Reading, MA: Addison-Wesley, 1994.